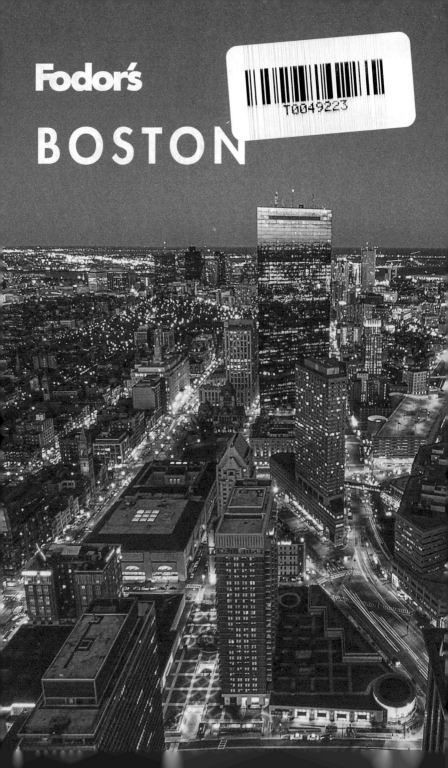

Fodor's

BOSTON

T0049223

Welcome to Boston

Bursting with Yankee pride, Boston attracts visitors for its rich past and vibrant present. From Boston Common to Faneuil Hall to Fenway Park, the city is a hub of American history and culture. Buzzing neighborhoods such as the North End, Beacon Hill, and the Back Bay mix venerable landmarks and lively street life. On the other side of the Charles River is bustling Cambridge, home of Harvard University and MIT. Wherever you choose to explore, Boston's locavore restaurants, chic galleries, and tempting shops are all easily accessible on satisfying strolls.

TOP REASONS TO GO

★ **Historic icons:** The Freedom Trail links sites from the American Revolution's start.

★ **The Charles:** The river's bridges and esplanade reward exploration by foot or boat.

★ **Great museums:** The Museum of Fine Arts and the New England Aquarium satisfy curious minds.

★ **Stylish shopping:** Newbury and Boylston Streets give shopaholics a boutique buzz.

★ **Cuisine:** Seafood restaurants and chef-led hot spots fuel a booming restaurant scene.

★ **Parks and squares:** Boston Public Garden and Copley Square have prime people-watching.

Contents

Fodor's Features

Follow the Redbrick Road:
Boston's Freedom Trail.............. 32

Chapter 1

EXPERIENCE BOSTON

20 ULTIMATE EXPERIENCES

Boston offers terrific experiences that should be on every traveler's list. Here are Fodor's top picks for a memorable trip.

1 Ride a Swan Boat in the Public Garden

No warm weather visit to Boston is complete without taking a spin on one of these emblematic foot-pedal–powered Swan Boats. Astonishingly, they've sailed this 4-acre pond in America's oldest botanical garden since 1877. *(Ch. 7)*

2 Visit Faneuil Hall

Dedicated to the creation of a new nation, Faneuil Hall has seen it all, from protesting colonists to World Series celebrations. *(Ch. 4)*

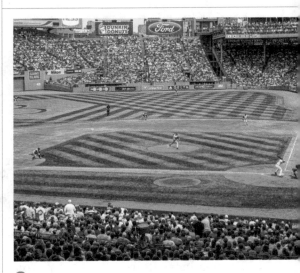

3 Catch a Game at Fenway

The nation's oldest Major League Baseball ballpark, home to the Red Sox since 1912 and where Babe Ruth swung for the fences, is hallowed ground for Bostonians. *(Ch. 8)*

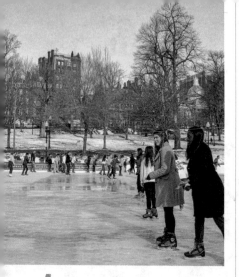

4 Ice-Skate on Frog Pond

Ice-skating on the Boston Common Frog Pond is an essential winter activity. With the golden dome of the State House as a backdrop, it is one for the memory books. *(Ch. 3)*

5 Visit the Isabella Stewart Gardner Museum

One of the city's most charming attractions is this small but lovely museum. It's a Venetian palazzo with an eclectic collection and gorgeous gardens. *(Ch. 8)*

6 Eat a Lobster Roll

Nothing says "New England" more than seafood, and nothing says it better—or tastier—than a lobster roll. Head to Boston's waterfront, where any number of restaurants beckon. *(Ch. 6, 12)*

7 Tour the USS *Constitution*

Better known as "Old Ironsides," the oldest commissioned warship in the U.S. fleet is docked at the Charlestown Navy Yard. Take a tour of the ship, and then head to the adjacent museum. *(Ch. 5)*

8 Spend the Day at the Museum of Fine Arts

With almost half a million carefully curated objects spanning the centuries, this massive museum is one of the most highly regarded in the world. *(Ch. 8)*

9 Get Out on the Charles River (Kayak, Canoe, Duck Boat)

The watery border between Boston and Cambridge offers a wealth of activities, from kayaking and canoeing to one of the city's ubiquitous duck boat tours. *(Ch. 3, 11)*

10 Visit the Institute of Contemporary Art

Filled with cutting-edge art, the gorgeous glass-walled cantilevered museum sits right on the edge of the Boston waterfront, offering breathtaking views both inside and out. *(Ch. 10)*

11 Walk Down Acorn Street in Beacon Hill

This charming one-lane cobblestone street, complete with 19th-century row houses and gas lamps, is said to be the city's most photographed street. *(Ch. 3)*

12 Revisit the Boston Tea Party

This hands-on, family-friendly, interactive museum includes 3-D holograms, talking portraits, actors clad in colonial-period costumes, and two ship replicas. *(Ch. 10)*

13 Visit Boston's Little Italy

The North End has an embarrassment of food riches, nearly all of them Italian-American in nature, from bakeries and markets to restaurants. *(Ch. 4)*

14 Walk the Freedom Trail

One of Boston's most famous (and free) attractions, this 2.5-mile line (painted red or paved in red brick) takes visitors to some of the city's most important sights. *(Ch. 3, 4, 5, 6)*

15 Walk Along the Emerald Necklace

This delightful string of six green spaces—the Back Bay Fens, the Riverway, Olmsted Park, Jamaica Pond, the Arnold Arboretum, and Franklin Park—runs from one end of the city to the other. *(Ch. 7, 9)*

16 Eat Oysters at the Union Oyster House

It gets a bad rap, but this National Historic Landmark—the National Park Service designated it the country's oldest continually run restaurant and oyster bar—is worth a visit. *(Ch. 4)*

17 Step Back in Time at the Mapparium

Located in the Mary Baker Eddy Library, this three-story, stained-glass globe is one of Boston's more unusual attractions. It depicts the world as it was in 1935, offering a glimpse into another era. *(Ch. 7)*

18 Head Out to the Boston Harbor Islands

Don't miss the chance to hop on a ferry to explore old forts, beaches, hiking trails, and even the nation's oldest continually used light station. *(Ch. 6)*

19 Stroll Down Newbury Street in the Back Bay

Boston's version of New York's 5th Avenue is an eight-block-long street jam-packed with upscale shops, trendy cafés, and quirky boutiques, all with great people-watching. *(Ch. 7)*

20 Take the Architecture Tour at Boston Public Library

The magnificent main branch of the city's library system is in an 1895 Renaissance Revival building that houses hidden treasures like murals by John Singer Sargent. *(Ch. 7)*

WHAT'S WHERE

1 **Beacon Hill, Boston Common, and the West End.** Beacon Hill's historic streets lined with Federal-style homes make this an atmospheric place to explore. Bordering the Hill, grassy Boston Common serves as the start of the Freedom Trail. The West End has the Museum of Science and the TD Garden, where the Bruins and Celtics play.

2 **Government Center and the North End.** Architecture buffs may admire Government Center's brutalist City Hall, but most scurry past en route to Faneuil Hall and Quincy Market. Across the Greenway, the North End attracts huge crowds to its Italian-American eateries, a vestige of the immigrants who settled here in the 19th century.

3 **Charlestown.** On the banks of Boston Harbor and the Mystic River, Charlestown's top sights—the towering Bunker Hill Monument and the USS *Constitution* at the Navy Yard— can't be missed.

4 **Downtown and the Waterfront.** Downtown has many Freedom Trail sights, including Old South

Meeting House and the Old State House, as well as a mishmash of shopping options. The Theater District is home to most of Boston's major stages (dance, opera, regional theater, and national Broadway tours). Chinatown—the country's third largest—offers a variety of authentic restaurants, while the lofty Leather District remains largely residential. The Financial District bustles with professionals during the day, and the Waterfront features wharves, walking paths, and Boston Harbor views.

5 The Back Bay and the South End. The Back Bay—so called because it was once a bay—features Boston's renowned brownstones, ritzy Newbury Street shopping, the city's tallest buildings, a fair amount of green space, and must-see destinations like the Boston Public Library and Trinity Church. More shopping awaits in the South End (a different experience as the boutiques are locally owned), which has the country's largest extant Victorian row house district. Today, it's become home to a thriving LGBTQ+ community.

WHAT'S WHERE

6 Fenway and Kenmore Square. Baseball fans, tourists, and intellectuals meet in the Fens, a meandering green space that serves as the first "jewel" in Frederick Law Olmsted's intentional Emerald Necklace park system. To the northwest, Fenway Park—Major League Baseball's oldest ballpark—is home to the Boston Red Sox. The Museum of Fine Arts and the Isabella Stewart Gardner Museum offer lessons in art history.

7 Brookline and Jamaica Plain. Locals refer to Jamaica Plain as "JP," and as one of the first-ever streetcar suburbs, it still feels like a community enhanced by Olmsted's 19th-century landscaped parks, including the Arnold Arboretum and Jamaica Pond. JP boasts a multicultural, though largely Latino, population, which is reflected in its main street restaurants and shops. Affluent Brookline features multimillion dollar homes and neighborhoods that just sound wealthy, like Chestnut Hill and Washington Square.

8 The Seaport, South Boston, and East Boston. Across from the Waterfront, the Seaport District is the poster child for revitalization, thanks to the continued development over the last 15 to 20 years, including the Boston Convention and Exhibition Center, the Institute of Contemporary Art, and swanky restaurants and hotels. Once a working-class Irish enclave, South Boston—very different from the South End—now mixes residential and commercial vibes for those who live there. Directly across Boston Harbor from Southie is busy international Logan Airport in East Boston.

9 Cambridge and Somerville. While Cambridge is often lumped in when people refer to (air quotes) Boston, it's actually a much artier, libertine city in its own right and has long been a haven for writers, academics, and iconoclasts. Harvard University plays a huge part in the personality of Harvard Square, while MIT asserts its tech and biotech leanings in Kendall and Central Squares. The adjacent city of Somerville feels like a cousin, with its collection of squares and indie airs.

Boston Today

Boston is the undisputed birthplace of American history. It's home to a number of firsts: first public park (Boston Common), first botanical garden (the Public Garden), and even the first phone call (made by Alexander Graham Bell in 1876). Much of the political ferment that spawned the nation happened here, and visitors are often awed by the dense concentration of landmarks. But this is a living city—not a museum—and, as such, its entrepreneurial spirit continues to evolve. Cambridge's Kendall Square, close to MIT, is a hotbed of technological progress, while Boston's Seaport District also boasts a number of start-ups.

NEIGHBORHOOD DEVELOPMENTS

In a city as old as Boston, there's always room for reinvention, so it's no surprise that a few different parts of town are currently making themselves over. The Seaport District, formerly commercial buildings, parking lots, and working fish piers, is now home to high-rise hotels and residences, upscale restaurants, and purposeful green space. Across the harbor, developers are polishing up East Boston's waterfront, albeit on a smaller scale.

THE HISTORIC HARBOR

This city has long been defined by its harbor: The first colonists were largely drawn here because of it, and local commerce has been inextricably bound to the water ever since. See the amazing views for yourself along the Boston Harborwalk, a 43-mile-long path that skirts the coastline and passes by piers, parks, working wharves, hotel lounges, and urban beaches. It's also the launching pad for loads of harbor cruises, whale watches, and tall ship sails.

LIGHTS! CAMERA! ACTION!

The Massachusetts film tax subsidy program that was implemented in 2006 has continued to draw more productions to the Bay State. As a result, playing "spot the star" is a popular pastime. Big-screen names like Chris Evans, Johnny Depp, Jennifer Lawrence, Ryan Reynolds, Rosamund Pike, and native sons Ben Affleck and Mark Wahlberg have all worked here.

FOOD SCENE SIZZLES

Boston lays claim to a long line of innovative chefs, such as Karen Akunowicz, Jody Adams, Jamie Bissonnette, Tiffani Faison, Barbara Lynch, Ken Oringer, Ana Sortun, Ming Tsai, and Tony Maws. But it all started circa the 1960s, when Julia Child launched a culinary revolution from her Cambridge kitchen. Today, the food scene is hopping, and there is no shortage of outstanding, fresh, top-quality meals. It is getting harder to try traditional Yankee dishes like baked beans, codfish cakes, and Indian pudding—although Union Oyster House is a holdout on all accounts, and other restaurants may offer a modernized version of one or two.

LASTING EFFECTS OF COVID-19

Boston has settled into a "new normal" since the COVID-19 pandemic of the last few years, and you may notice some changes during your visit. As of press time, most restaurants require dinner reservations, and time at your table may be limited. Likewise, most museums are open but are requiring advanced ticket purchase and timed reservation for entry. Some rideshare app drivers will not allow passengers in the front seat, and depending on the latest variant, a mask may be preferred at some businesses. Please go online or call ahead to make plans.

Frugal Fun in Boston

WHEN FREEDOM RINGS FREE

Walking the **Freedom Trail** is free, as is entrance to a few of its 16 attractions. For instance, the **Massachusetts State House** offers complimentary tours on weekdays, and its three historic burying grounds are free any day of the year. In season (usually Memorial Day through Columbus Day), **Boston National Historical Park** hosts guided tours of portions of the trail for free—but you do need to reserve a ticket.

WALK BOSTON'S OTHER TRAILS

The Freedom Trail's success has spawned other no-cost, less formal pedestrian routes, including the **Black Heritage Trail** and the **Norman B. Leventhal Walk to the Sea** (⊕ www.walktothesea. com), which traces four centuries of civic development from Beacon Hill to the tip of Long Wharf. More niche options include the **Irish Heritage Trail** (⊕ www. irishheritagetrail.com/boston), covering sites relating to Irish-American history in Boston, and the **Boston Women's Heritage Trail** (⊕ www.bwht.org), which pays tribute to ladies who gained fame as suffragettes and artists.

ARTSY ALTERNATIVES

Boston's cultural organizations consider the purse, especially for those who can be flexible. Most major museums waive admission during select time frames: the **Museum of Fine Arts, Boston,** four days per year and always for college students and members of the military; the **Institute of Contemporary Art/Boston** on Thursday after 5 pm, for ages 18 and under, and for families on the last Saturday of every month; the **Isabella Stewart Gardner Museum** for anyone named Isabella, college students, and active military, and also for ages 17 and under; the **Harvard Art Museums**

every Sunday, and always for ages 18 and under, students, and military families. As for performing arts, the **Boston Symphony Orchestra** offers limited $10 rush tickets to most performances; the **New England Conservatory** and **Berklee College of Music** both regularly offer free concerts and musical performances by rising stars. The **Boston Public Library,** filled with books, world-class art, and architecture, hosts free guided tours daily.

THE GREAT OUTDOORS

When you're ready for a rest, remember that the green in Boston's parks comes from Mother Nature herself. If you've already spent time exploring the **Public Garden** and **Boston Common,** you can check out the **Emerald Necklace,** a 7-mile string of pocket parks designed in 1878 by land-scape architect Frederick Law Olmsted that includes gems like **Jamaica Pond** and the **Arnold Arboretum.** Downtown, the **Rose Kennedy Greenway** features free diversions for the kids, including large-scale public art installations, interactive splash fountains, sitting areas, and a custom-made carousel. The **Boston Harbor-walk** offers visitors a bit of everything on its interconnected 43 miles of waterfront trails and pathways. Aside from scenic viewpoints (some with free binoculars), amenities range from interpretive panels to pocket museums.

HOLY GOOD MUSIC

In Copley Square, the architectural marvel that is **Trinity Church** hosts free, 30-minute Friday lunchtime organ recitals at 12:15 pm. Along the Freedom Trail, **King's Chapel** presents free weekly recitals on Tuesday at 12:15 pm, where the music ranges from jazz to folk to medieval and classical.

The Best Museums in Boston

MUSEUM OF FINE ARTS, BOSTON
Home to more than half a million objects spanning from ancient Egyptian artifacts to contemporary artwork, the Museum of Fine Arts, Boston is one of the most highly regarded museums in the world and a must-visit site. Daily free one-hour guided tours give a good overview.

INSTITUTE OF CONTEMPORARY ART/BOSTON
Inside the stunning glass-walled cantilevered building located on Boston's waterfront, you'll find cutting-edge art. The permanent collection includes works by Yayoi Kusama, Nick Cave, Mona Hatoum, and Nicholas Nixon, but there's always something new to see by today's emerging global artists.

ISABELLA STEWART GARDNER MUSEUM
This quirky museum, named for its owner, was built in the 19th century to mimic a Venetian palazzo. It's home to Gardner's impressive collection of art, with masterpieces like Titian's *Europa*. As specified in her will, nothing has been changed since her death.

JFK MUSEUM
This library and museum pays homage to the life and presidency of John F. Kennedy and his family, with re-creations of his desk in the Oval Office and the TV studio in which he debated Richard M. Nixon, plus exhibits ranging from the Cuban missile crisis to his assassination.

MUSEUM OF SCIENCE, BOSTON
With more than 700 exhibits covering astronomy, astrophysics, anthropology, medical progress, computers, earth sciences, and much more, this is the place to ignite your imagination and curiosity. Also, the Charles Hayden Planetarium offers exciting astronomical programs.

MUSEUM OF AFRICAN AMERICAN HISTORY
Established in 1964, this museum is composed of the Abiel Smith School, the first public school in the nation built specifically for Black children, and the African Meeting House, both on Boston's Black Heritage Trail, plus the African Meeting House on Nantucket.

BOSTON TEA PARTY SHIPS & MUSEUM

This hands-on interactive museum lets you toss (fake) tea overboard in a reenactment of the Boston Tea Party. Exhibits include 3-D holograms, talking portraits, and replicas of two of the three ships on hand that fateful night, the *Beaver* and the *Eleanor*.

HARVARD ART MUSEUM

Sculpture, photography, drawing: this art museum on the campus of Harvard University may not have the coffers of the MFA, but it certainly has plenty to offer art lovers in both its exhibitions and its permanent collections.

HARVARD MUSEUM OF NATURAL HISTORY

With more than 12,000 specimens, including dinosaurs, rare minerals, hundreds of mammals and birds, and Harvard's world-famous and gorgeous *Glass Flowers*, this museum offers both historic collections and new and changing exhibits.

MIT MUSEUM

Spanning more than 58,000 square feet, this museum's fascinating exhibits feature MIT projects and research from the past, present, and future, on topics like artificial intelligence, life sciences, and the intersection of art and engineering.

What to Eat and Drink in Boston

BAKED BEANS

A nod to Native American and Pilgrims times, as well as Boston's rum-producing role in the late-1700s "triangle trade," beans are slow-baked with molasses and salt pork and served with brown bread. Find them at Beantown Pub or Bostonia Public House.

BOSTON CREAM PIE

More cake than pie, this dessert is a true Boston original. It was first served in 1856 in the Parker House Hotel (also home to the Parker House Roll) and is made of sweet custard layered between yellow butter cake and topped with chocolate glaze. Find it at Parker's Restaurant at the Omni Parker House hotel and occasionally at any Flour Bakery.

LOBSTER ROLL

How do you like your lobster meat: cold and mixed with mayo or warm and drenched in melted butter? Whichever prep you decide on, one thing remains constant: a toasted hot dog bun is the only acceptable way to eat this Boston classic. Find one at James Hook & Co., Yankee Lobster, Alive & Kicking Lobsters, or B&G Oysters.

NEW ENGLAND CLAM CHOWDER

This New England soup-meets-stew is a rich, thick concoction of clams, potatoes, salt pork or bacon, and cream, topped with oyster crackers. A few local places also add mussels or fish chunks. Find it anywhere, really, but it's best at Neptune Oyster and famous at Legal Sea Foods.

CANNOLI

Boston loves these masterpieces, as evidenced by the lines at North End Italian pastry shops like Mike's Pastry and Modern Pastry (there's an ever-lasting feud on who has the better ones). These crunchy tubes are stuffed with delicate ricotta or cream, sometimes dipped and covered in chocolate chips. Also try them at Bova's Bakery.

CLAMBAKE

The traditional clambake is a coastal and casual meal of lobster, clams, corn, and red potatoes steamed over a seaweed fire. You can still find these around in season and often catered, but at local restaurants, find them no-frills (at The Barking Crab) and fancier (at Neptune Oyster).

YANKEE POT ROAST

An homage to the patience and frugality of yesteryear's working-class New Englanders, the dish is made from tough cuts of beef roasted for hours and served with onions, carrots, potatoes, and parsnips or turnips. The *best* place to find it is at Henrietta's Table.

FRAPPE

In Massachusetts, a milkshake is just milk and syrup that's been whipped up. Add a couple of scoops of ice cream before mixing and you've got a creamy, dreamy frappe (rhymes with "slap"). As if the drink isn't filling on its own, locals often pair it with a burger and fries. Get one at South Street Diner or at Mr. Bartley's.

OYSTERS

Eating raw oysters in Boston is like eating crayfish in New Orleans. You just must. The majority served in restaurants are caught "locally" along the coast from Duxbury and Wellfleet, Massachusetts, to Point Judith, Rhode Island. Try them at Row 34 and The Hourly.

FLUFFERNUTTER

With the early 20th-century invention of Marshmallow Fluff, a creamy marshmallow spread, in the nearby town of Lynn, it wasn't long before the Fluffernutter came to be. Spread Fluff and peanut butter on the most basic white bread you can find, and there you have it! Get a fried version at Local 149.

Boston's Historical Sites: Revolutionary and Beyond

MASSACHUSETTS STATE HOUSE

Famous for its golden dome, the Charles Bulfinch–designed State House has been the Commonwealth's seat of government since 1798. Today, visitors can tour the building while learning about the quirks of its political past.

BLACK HERITAGE TRAIL

During the late 18th and early 19th centuries, the abolition movement launched in Beacon Hill. This cultural trail explores sites relevant to the cause. Visit the 1806 African Meeting House where Frederick Douglass spoke, and walk past numerous private homes that served the Underground Railroad.

USS *CONSTITUTION*

The trip to Charlestown is worth it to see the still-commissioned USS *Constitution*, America's Ship of State. She's been in service since the War of 1812, but has never gone down in battle. Also, in the Navy Yard, the USS *Constitution* Museum features artifacts and interactive exhibits.

FREEDOM TRAIL

A conversation about history in Boston is never complete without mention of the American Revolution. At its heart: the Freedom Trail, a self-guided walking path a little more than 2 miles long that winds through Downtown, the North End, and Charlestown, stopping at 16 historically significant sites, like Faneuil Hall and the Paul Revere House, along the way.

OLD NORTH CHURCH HISTORIC SITE

Here stands the pivotal steeple where Robert Newman signaled to Paul Revere with two lanterns and launched him on his midnight ride to Concord and Lexington. At the time, the congregation was, ironically, loyal to the British government, and still today it remains Episcopal. Highlights include crypt and bell tower tours, the colonial-era Clough House, and five gardens.

BOSTON PUBLIC LIBRARY

One of the architectural marvels of Copley Square, Boston Public Library opened its McKim building in 1895. A century and a quarter later, visitors continue to gape at John Singer Sargent's triumphant murals, artwork by Pierre Puvis de Chavannes, an open-air courtyard, and rare books including early Shakespeare folios and original writings by Copernicus and Newton.

HARVARD YARD
The campus of America's oldest university—at nearly 400 years old—has a lot of stories to tell. It's been a grazing ground for livestock, a place partly built by slavery, a protesting site, and a home to thousands of the world's brightest minds.

THE KENNEDYS ON COLUMBIA POINT
Boston's most storied political family holds court at the JFK Presidential Library and Museum, as well as at the Edward M. Kennedy Institute for the United States Senate.

MASS GENERAL HOSPITAL AND PAUL S. RUSSELL MUSEUM
Inside the world-renowned hospital's most historic building, the Ether Dome marks the site of the first public demonstration of the use of anesthesia. Around the corner, the Russell Museum delves into Mass General's medical legacy and its ongoing work, from targeted cancer therapies to deep brain stimulation.

THE EMERALD NECKLACE
Less known outside the city's history annals is the work of Frederick Law Olmsted, the visionary landscape architect who designed major green spaces from New York City's Central Park to the U.S. Capitol grounds. But before all that, Olmsted spent 20 years here in his hometown, building and linking six gorgeous parks that Bostonians know as the Emerald Necklace.

BOSTON TEA PARTY SHIPS & MUSEUM
Near the original site of the infamous "Tea Party," this museum honors the 18th-century protest with 21st-century holographic exhibits, a mock town meeting, and historic replicas of the actual ships.

Boston with Kids

FOLLOW THE REDBRICK ROAD

Travel back to the Revolutionary era and take the kids along while walking the Freedom Trail. Sign kids up for the free National Park Service Junior Ranger program (⊕ www.nps.gov/bost/learn/kidsyouth/beajuniorranger.htm), which uses fun and games to help them digest the history lesson. Most people follow the trail south to north, but reverse order actually works best for families; it allows you to start with the **USS *Constitution*** and the **Bunker Hill Monument** (star attractions in young eyes) in Charlestown and then end in Boston Common (an ideal place to unwind after a long trek).

MAKE A FOWL PLAY

In season (April through August), the **Swan Boats** take up residency in the **Public Garden** lagoon, and you can take a slow, peddle-powered ride for less than $5. Once you get your sea legs back, waddle over to the nearby *Make Way for Ducklings* bronze sculpture for a photo op with Mrs. Mallard and her quacking offspring, introduced by Robert McCloskey in his 1941 book, *Make Way for Ducklings*.

KID AROUND

The multistory climbing structure that dominates the lobby of the **Boston Children's Museum** could be a tough act to follow, but the museum manages it with some seriously cool exhibits, including an interactive dinosaur exploration, an authentic merchant's home from Japan, and a playing space that's just for kids under three.

YELL "EUREKA"

No place does gizmos and gadgets like the **Museum of Science,** where almost everything is meant to be pushed, pulled, or otherwise maneuvered.

FIND NEMO

The **New England Aquarium** features endless exhibits, including its central Giant Ocean Tank and the live shark and ray touch tank. There are in-the-water animal encounters and behind-the-scenes tours for visitors willing to pay over and above admission—they're worth every penny. The aquarium also organizes whale-watching trips to Stellwagen Bank, late March to November.

EMBRACE ISLAND LIFE

Boston Harbor conceals 34 idyllic islands, and while most of them are open to the public, they manage to fly under the radar. It's perfect for a fun family day of exploring nature, coastline, and abandoned military forts—especially at **Georges Island.** Find free resources at the Islands website (⊕ www.bostonharborislands.org/kids-and-families).

HAVE A BALL

Major League Baseball's oldest ballpark, small but mighty **Fenway Park** has become a pilgrimage site for baseball fans of all ages and team preferences. Daily one-hour tours—and, even better for families with tiny tots, 15-minute tours—provide the ultimate insider's view of the Red Sox's home field, with a look at the press box, the Green Monster (schedule permitting), and more.

TOUR THE TOWN

Boston by Foot (☎ 617/367–2345) features specialized "Boston by Little Feet" tours for 6- to 12-year-olds, June through October. **Boston Duck Tours** (☎ 617/267–3825) operates amphibious vehicles for a land and water journey around Boston—lucky kids get to captain the ship. And **Old Town Trolley** (☎ 855/396–7433) offers hop-on, hop-off tours for anyone who would rather ride than walk.

What to Read and Watch

THE HEAT (2013)
Melissa McCarthy and Sandra Bullock show off their comedic chops in this hilarious film set in and around a blue-collar Boston neighborhood. As polished FBI agent Sarah Ashburn, Bullock butts heads with McCarthy's rough-around-the-edges Boston Police Department detective Shannon Mullins on their joint quest to take down a local drug lord.

THE GIVEN DAY BY DENNIS LEHANE
Boston-born, mega-talented writer Dennis Lehane has famously set many of his novels in and around Boston. But this one takes a look at the city just after World War I through the lens of two families—one white and one black. It wades through an accurate depiction of the era's political and societal atmosphere, where fictitious members of a fractious community have varying allegiances and motivations. It's a Boston you won't recognize.

THE DEPARTED (2006)
Martin Scorsese's Academy Award–winning film tells the story of a South Boston mob boss and his protégé who infiltrates the Boston Police Department's special forces.

MONDAY MORNING PODCAST
Boston-raised comedian Bill Burr has been doling out acerbic observations about the state of things in Hollywood, gender roles, sports, and other topics in his popular, opinionated podcast-slash-rant for more than a decade now.

JOHN ADAMS BY DAVID MCCULLOUGH
In his Pulitzer Prize–winning biography of the United States' second president, historian David McCullough shares personal and political details of the brilliant lawyer, patriot, and founding father. Readers will get a sense of what Boston was like during Revolutionary times, what drove its people, and how America was built.

I SHIMMER SOMETIMES, TOO BY PORSHA OLAYIWOLA
Poignant words written by the city's current poet laureate and self-proclaimed hip-hop feminist-futurist croon from the pages of her 2019 release. In this book of verse, Olayiwola considers some of the challenges of living while Black, female, and queer in Boston.

LAST SEEN, SEASON 1
The first season of this true-crime podcast, presented by WBUR with the Boston Globe, takes a deep dive into what happened at the Isabella Stewart Gardner Museum in what has become Boston's most famous, yet-to-be-solved whodunnit. In 1991, 13 priceless works of art were stolen without a trace.

CHEERS (1982–93)
These days you'll have to stream it to see it. Gen Xers and Boomers wax nostalgic over this beloved sitcom that centers around a beer-loving cast of commiserating regulars in a Boston bar where "everybody knows your name." The cast includes some of acting's greats: Ted Danson, Shelley Long, Rhea Perlman, George Wendt, Woody Harrelson, Bebe Neuwirth, and Kelsey Grammer. The real bar that inspired the location of Cheers is still open on Beacon Hill today.

GOOD WILL HUNTING (1997)
This is the movie that launched Matt Damon and Ben Affleck into Hollywood's stratosphere. With scenes taking place across town, predominantly in South Boston and Cambridge, Good Will Hunting follows a young, working-class MIT janitor—and quiet genius—trying to navigate his way from a messy past to a promising future. Featured in the film, L Street Tavern is still a popular place for a pint.

Boston Sports: Where and How to See Them

Everything you've heard about the zeal of Boston sports fanatics is true. Here, you root for the home team; you cheer, and you pray, and you root some more. How else can you explain how the Red Sox reversed the curse in 2004 for the team's first World Series victory since 1918?

BASEBALL

The Boston Red Sox may be New England's most storied professional sports team of all time. For 86 years, the club suffered a World Series drought, a streak of bad luck that fans attributed to the "Curse of the Bambino," spelled in 1920 when the Sox sold Babe Ruth to the New York Yankees. All that changed in 2004, when a maverick squad broke the curse in a thrilling seven-game semifinals series against the Yankees, followed by a four-game sweep of St. Louis in the finals. Repeat World Series wins in 2007, 2013, and 2018 have cemented Bostonians' sense that the universe is back in order.

Ticket-holding Sox fans can browse display cases mounted inside Fenway Park before and during a ball game; these shed light on and show off memorabilia from particular players and eras over the course of the team's history. Speaking of Fenway, it is Major League Baseball's oldest ballpark and has seen some stuff since its 1912 opening, including such events of this millennia as Curt Schilling's bloody sock in 2004, the 19–3 massacre of the Yankees during the 2019 season, and, well, the entire legacy of Big Papi, home run by home run.

The Red Sox play home games at Fenway Park from April to October, accessible from all parts of Boston by foot or the T's Green Line. It's typically not too difficult to get single tickets to a game (buy them online at ⊕ www.mlb.com/redsox/tickets/single-game-tickets), and some sell for as little as $15. Although the team is officially tied to Boston, it has earned time-honored fans from across the country and all economic strata. There's nothing quite like sitting in the stands as "Sweet Caroline" plays during the eighth inning. For a most unique viewing experience, try to get tickets for the Monster Seats, aptly perched on top of the Green Monster in left field. Do splurge for food inside the park—if you're gonna do it somewhere, it might as well be here. Order a Sam Adams beer, a Fenway Frank with all the fixings, a slice of Sal's pizza, and—you know it's coming—some Cracker Jacks. But, for modern palates, the ballpark has taken its menu up a notch, featuring food by local kitchens, as well as gluten-free, vegetarian, and kosher options.

BASKETBALL

The Boston Celtics franchise ties with rival Los Angeles Lakers for most championship titles in the NBA, with 17 banners, which is at least 10 more than any other team. It's a mind-blowing stat, yes, but today's fans will note that 11 of those wins were earned between 1957 and 1969 (thanks, Bill Russell), with the most recent coming in 2008 after a sweet victory over the Lakers. It's been a mixed journey, for sure.

So, what to expect at a Celtics game from today's squad? An all-around fun experience, a charged atmosphere and devotion, from the fans to the team and the team to the fans. You'll hear "Let's Go, Cel-tics" no matter the score. For a truly unique day, die-hard sports fans should take advantage of a Celtics–Bruins doubleheader, which means both pro teams play at the TD Garden on the same day, just hours apart. There's at least one per season, and it usually happens in November, on Black Friday.

From anywhere in Boston, it's easy to get to the Garden, since North Station (servicing Commuter Rail trains and the MBTA's Orange and Green Lines) is located within the complex. For pre- and postgame nourishment, The Hub on Causeway, also at North Station, opened in the fall of 2019, featuring a number of restaurants and bars. Or, take a walk down Canal, Friend, and Portland Streets to find a bar that's to your liking.

FOOTBALL

St. Patrick's Day 2020 was miserable for New England football fans, who learned of the eminent departure of the Patriots' greatest-of-all-time quarterback, Tom Brady, after a historic 20-year run—and six Super Bowl wins—with this home-town team.

Over its entire history since 1959, the Pats have been successful and less-so. In fact, the franchise was one of the American Football League's eight original teams. They first played at Boston University Field, and intermittently at Harvard Stadium and Fenway Park, until building the team's first official arena, Schaefer Stadium, 20 miles outside the city in Foxboro, Massachusetts.

Today, the New England Patriots take the field at Robert Kraft's massive, 2002-built Gillette Stadium, also in Foxboro, from August through January. It is a challenge to get single game tickets through the Patriots' box office, so resellers like Ticketmaster and StubHub are your best bet. Regardless of your point of purchase, tickets are expensive.

The MBTA Commuter Rail services trains to Gillette Stadium from both Boston and Providence before and after every home game; round-trip tickets are $20 (buy them in person at South Station or Back Bay, or via the mTicket app; find more information online at ⊕ *www.mbta.com/ destinations/gillette-stadium*). To take full advantage of the Patriots' pregame experience, drive to Gillette and bring some food and a grill (no open flames); parking lots ($30–$60) open four hours before kickoff.

HOCKEY

In 1924, the Boston Bruins became the first U.S. ice hockey team to enter the NHL. Fun fact: In looking for a name, team owner Charles Adams sought out something that would represent an "untamed animal embodied with size, strength, agility, ferocity, and cunning."

The Bruins have been playing at the Garden since 1928 (although the original Boston Garden was rebuilt in 1995) and have won six Stanley Cup titles over that time. Great players to skate for the Big Bad Bruins have included Bobby Orr and Phil Esposito in the early 1970s, Ray Bourque in the 1980s and 1990s, and current players feisty left wing Brad Marchand and right wing David Pastrnak. Spectators can see the championship banners hanging in the rafters above the ice and the stands, which are packed for every home game, despite high ticket prices.

Fans are loud, vocal, and extremely loyal, so ticket holders with delicate personalities may not feel comfortable. However, Saturday afternoon games are a win for the family. Single tickets are available at the TD Garden Box Office or through Ticketmaster. For a real pre-game experience, stop by a real dive, Sullivan's Tap on Canal Street, for a few beers.

FOLLOW THE REDBRICK ROAD

BOSTON'S FREEDOM TRAIL

by Mike Nalepa

Paul Revere

Benjamin Franklin

Samuel Adams

John Hancock

Paul Revere's ride

The Freedom Trail is more than a collection of historic sites related to the American Revolution or a suggested itinerary connecting Boston's unique neighborhoods. It's a chance to walk in the footsteps of our forefathers—literally, by following a crimson path on public sidewalks—and pay tribute to the figures all schoolkids know, like Paul Revere, John Hancock, and Benjamin Franklin. In history-proud Boston, past and present intersect before your eyes, not as a re-creation, but as living history accessible to all.

Boston played a key role in the dramatic events leading up to the American Revolution. Many of the Founding Fathers called the city home, and many of the initial meetings and actions that sparked the fight against the British took place here. In one day, you can visit Faneuil Hall—the "Cradle of Liberty"—where outraged colonial radicals met to oppose British authority; the site of the incendiary Boston Massacre; and Old North Church, where lanterns hung to signal Paul Revere on his thrilling midnight ride. Colonists may have originally landed in Jamestown and Plymouth, but if you really want to see where America began, come to Boston.

Boston Common, Founder's Statue

⊕ www.nps.gov/bost
⊕ www.thefreedomtrail.org

☎ 617/242–5642

🎟 Admission to the Freedom Trail itself is free. Several museum sites charge for admission. However, most attractions are free monuments, parks, and landmarks.

(Left) The Old South Meeting House, built in 1729, where many protesters gathered during the American Revolution

PLANNING YOUR TRAIL TRIP

USS *Constitution*

THE ROUTE

The 2½-mile Freedom Trail begins at Boston Common, winds through Downtown, Government Center, and the North End, and ends in Charlestown at the Bunker Hill Monument. The entire Freedom Trail is marked by a red line on the sidewalk; it's made of paint or brick at various points on the Trail. ⇨ *For more information on Freedom Trail sites, see listings in Neighborhood chapters.*

GETTING HERE AND BACK

The route starts near the Park Street T stop. When you've completed the Freedom Trail, head for the nearby Charlestown water shuttle, which goes directly to the downtown area. For schedules and maps, visit ⊕ *www.mbta.com.*

TIMING

If you're stopping at a few (or all) of the 16 sites, it takes a full day to complete the route comfortably. ■TIP➔ **If you have children in tow, you may want to split the trail into two or more days.**

VISITOR CENTERS

There are Freedom Trail information centers in Boston Common (Tremont Street), outside of Faneuil Hall (near the Old State House), and at the Charlestown Navy Yard Visitor Center (in Building 5).

TOURS

The National Park Service's free 90-minute Freedom Trail walking tours begin at the Boston National Historical Park Visitor Center outside of Faneuil Hall and cover sites from Old South Meeting House to Old North Church. Check online for times; it's a good idea to show up at least 30 minutes early, as the popular tours are limited to 30 people.

Half-hour tours of the USS *Constitution* are offered Tuesday through Sunday. Note that visitors to the ship must go through security screening.

FUEL UP

The trail winds through the heart of Downtown Boston, so finding a quick bite or a nice sit-down meal isn't difficult. Quincy Market, near Faneuil Hall, is packed with cafés and eateries. Another good lunch choice is one of the North End's wonderful Italian restaurants.

WHAT'S NEARBY

For a short break from revolutionary history, be sure to check out the major attractions nearby, including the Boston Public Garden, New England Aquarium, and Union Oyster House.

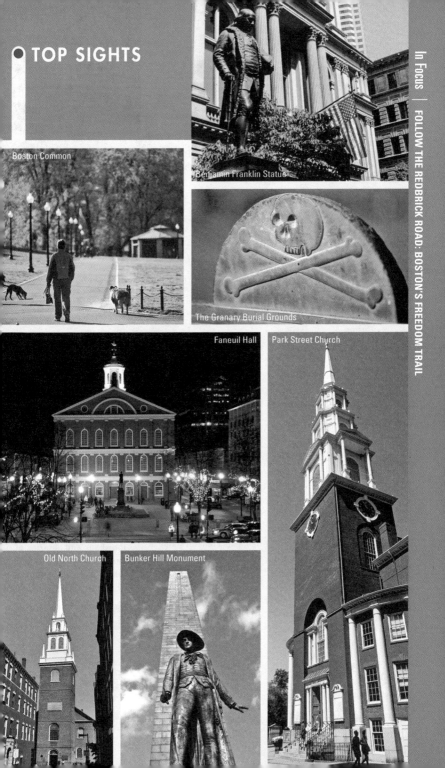

● TOP SIGHTS

Boston Common

Benjamin Franklin Statue

The Granary Burial Grounds

Faneuil Hall

Park Street Church

Old North Church

Bunker Hill Monument

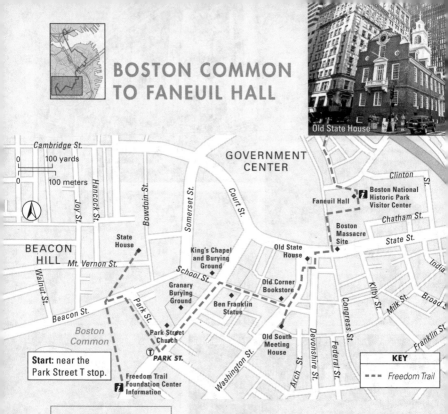

BOSTON COMMON TO FANEUIL HALL

Old State House

Cambridge St.

0   100 yards

0   100 meters

GOVERNMENT CENTER

Clinton St.

Faneuil Hall

Boston National Historic Park Visitor Center

Chatham St.

Hancock St.

Joy St.

Bowdoin St.

Somerset St.

Court St.

State House

BEACON HILL

Mt. Vernon St.

King's Chapel and Burying Ground

School St.

Old State House

Boston Massacre Site

State St.

Kilby St.

Milk St.

Broad S

India

Walnut St.

Beacon St.

Park St.

Granary Burying Ground

Ben Franklin Statue

Old Corner Bookstore

Congress St.

Devonshire St.

Federal St.

Franklin St

Boston Common

Park Street Church

T PARK ST.

Old South Meeting House

Washington St.

Arch St.

Start: near the Park Street T stop.

Freedom Trail Foundation Center Information

KEY

--- Freedom Trail

Many of the Freedom Trail sites between Boston Common and the North End are close together. Walking this 1-mile segment of the trail makes for a pleasant morning.

THE ROUTE

Begin at ★ **Boston Common**, then head for the **State House**, Boston's finest example of Federal architecture. Several blocks away is the **Park Street Church**, whose 217-foot steeple is considered to be the most beautiful in New England. The church was actually founded in 1809, and it played a key role in the movement to abolish slavery.

Reposing in the church's shadows is the ★ **Granary Burying Ground,** final resting place of Samuel Adams, John Hancock, and Paul Revere. A short stroll to Downtown brings you to **King's Chapel**, founded in 1686 by King James II for the Church of England.

Follow the trail past the **Benjamin Franklin statue** to the **Old Corner Bookstore** site, where Hawthorne, Emerson, and Longfellow were published. Nearby is **Old South Meeting House**, where arguments in 1773 led to the Boston Tea Party. Overlooking the site of the Boston Massacre is the city's oldest public building, the **Old State House**, a Georgian beauty. In 1770 the Boston Massacre

occurred directly in front of here—look for the commemorative stone circle.

Cross the plaza to ★ **Faneuil Hall** and explore where Samuel Adams railed against "taxation without representation." ■TIP→ A good mid-trail break is the shops and eateries of **Faneuil Hall Marketplace,** which includes **Quincy Market.**

Old Corner Bookstore Site

★ = Fodor's Choice   ★ = Highly Recommended   ☾ = Family Friendly

NORTH END TO CHARLESTOWN

Freedom Trail sites between Faneuil Hall and Charlestown are more spread out along 1½ miles. The sites here, though more difficult to reach, are certainly worth the walk.

THE ROUTE

When you depart Faneuil Hall, follow the red stripe to the North End, Boston's Little Italy.

The ♺ **Paul Revere House** takes you back 200 years—here are the hero's own saddlebags, a toddy warmer, and a pine cradle made from a molasses cask. It's also air-conditioned in the summer, so try to stop here in mid-afternoon to escape the heat. Next to the Paul Revere House is one of the city's oldest brick buildings, the **Pierce-Hichborn House**.

Next, peek inside a place guaranteed to trigger a wave of patriotism: ★ **Old North Church** of "One if by land, two if by sea" fame. Then head toward **Copp's Hill Burying Ground**, where you can view graves from the late 17th century through the early 19th

century. Afterward, cross the bridge over the Charles and check out that revered icon, the ♺ **USS Constitution**, "Old Ironsides." You'll need about an hour for a visit, so plan accordingly.

The perfect ending to the trail? A walk to the top of the ♺ **Bunker Hill Monument** for the incomparable vistas. The hill was the site one of the first battles of the Revolutionary War. Though the colonial rebels actually lost, they inflicted large casualties on the better-trained British, proving themselves against the empire.

USS *Constitution*

Bunker Hill Monument

USS Constitution

Water Shuttle Dock

Boston National Historic Park Visitor Center

End: In Charlestown head for the nearby water shuttle, which takes you downtown

1st Ave.

CHARLESTOWN

Charlestown Bridge

0   100 yards
0   100 meters

NORTH END

Commercial St.

Copp's Hill Burying Ground

Hull St.
Snow St.
Charter St.

Salem St.
Tileston St.

Old North Church

Prince St.

Endicott St.

Margin St.

Pierce-Hichborn House

Paul Revere House

Hanover St.

North St.

Richmond St.

John F. Fitzgerald Surface Rd.

Cross St.

GOVERNMENT CENTER

Clinton St.

Faneuil Hall

State St.

Paul Revere House

Did You Know?

If the Freedom Trail leaves you eager to see more Revolutionary War sites, drive about 30 minutes to Lexington and Concord, where the "shot heard 'round the world" launched the first battles in 1775.

Chapter 2

TRAVEL SMART

Updated by
Cheryl Fenton

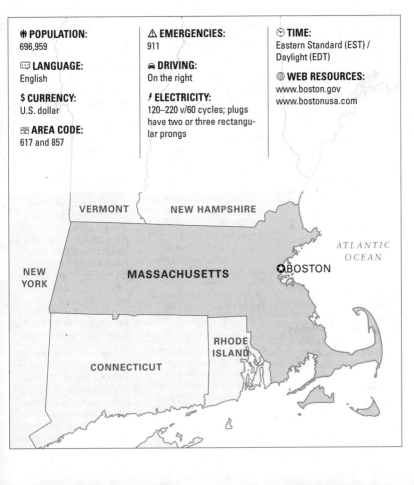

POPULATION:
696,959

LANGUAGE:
English

$ CURRENCY:
U.S. dollar

AREA CODE:
617 and 857

⚠ EMERGENCIES:
911

🚗 DRIVING:
On the right

⚡ ELECTRICITY:
120–220 v/60 cycles; plugs have two or three rectangular prongs

🕐 TIME:
Eastern Standard (EST) /
Daylight (EDT)

🌐 WEB RESOURCES:
www.boston.gov
www.bostonusa.com

VERMONT   NEW HAMPSHIRE

ATLANTIC
OCEAN

NEW
YORK

MASSACHUSETTS   ✪BOSTON

RHODE
ISLAND

CONNECTICUT

Know Before You Go

Are tips expected? What's the best way to see the city? When's the best time to visit? What should I wear? Is weed legal? Are sports really that important to the city? We've got answers and a few tips to help you make the most of your visit.

WHAT TO PACK

As the old joke goes: If you don't like the weather in New England, wait five minutes—it'll change. A chilly, overcast morning can become a sunny, warm afternoon—and vice versa. Try to layer your clothing so that you can remove or add garments as needed for comfort. Rain may appear with little warning, so pack a raincoat or an umbrella if you have the room. Boston is a great walking city—despite picturesque but bumpy cobblestone streets, brick walkways, and uneven asphalt—so be sure to bring comfortable shoes. In all seasons, it's often breezier (and colder) along the coast; so bring a warm layer when touring the beach or harbor areas.

BE A SPORT

Boston is known for the zeal of its sports fans. Locals mark off seasons by checking the sports lineup. When the team plays at home, "Red Sox Nation" is out braving Jersey Street outside legendary Fenway Park (the country's oldest ball park), munching on Fenway Franks or sausage subs from The Sausage Guy, and bellowing "Sweet Caroline" in the middle of the eighth inning. Sox aside, this city is also home to six-time Stanley Cup winners in the Bruins, six-time Super Bowl champion New England Patriots, and 17-time NBA champion Celtics.

If you can't score tickets to watch Bruins hockey or Celtics basketball, you can still visit The Sports Museum at the TD Garden. Come early on game day and you might see players warming up. Football fans get a kick out of Gillette Stadium in Foxborough, the Pats' home turf, and sprawling Patriot Place, with its restaurants, entertainment complex, and high-tech Hall of Fame. The city is also home to the Boston Marathon, New England's largest sporting event and the world's oldest annual marathon.

Bostonians' long-standing fervor for sports is equally evident in their leisure-time activities. Once harsh winters give way, Boston's extensive parks, paths, woods, and waterways teem with sun seekers and weekend warriors—until November's bitter winds bite again, and that energy is redirected toward white slopes and frozen rinks.

BOSTON WAS MADE FOR WALKING

"America's Walking City," with all its historic nooks and crannies, is best explored on foot. The most popular way to see all the city's notable sites is the Freedom Trail, an important page out of the city's history book. Follow the redbrick road, a 3-mile trail connecting most of Boston's National Historical Park sites, including the Granary Burial Ground, King's Chapel Burying Ground, the Old State House, and the Boston Massacre Site. There's also the Black Heritage Trail, a 1.6-mile path winding through important African American history sights, and the Boston Women's Heritage Trail, which highlights the city's influential women.

BOOK IT TO THE LIBRARY

Boston has always been home to noted authors (John Updike, Junot Diaz, Robert Parker) and poets (Robert Pinsky, Sylvia Plath, Mary Oliver), and the city remains a haven for readers (tributes are seen throughout, including the Edgar Allan Poe and adorable *Make Way for Ducklings* bronze statues).

Bookworms adore the Boston Public Library, just as Ralph Waldo Emerson and his literary buddies did in the 1800s. The building stands proudly as America's first municipal library and was originally proclaimed "the palace of the people." Translation: anyone can browse its vast collection, reading halls, and courtyard. A newly expanded children's section is worth a visit with tots.

Among its books, the Mary Baker Eddy Library houses a Mapparium (a mammoth walk-in glass globe spanned by a 30-foot bridge) and a virtual fountain spewing famous quotes.

The John F. Kennedy Presidential Library and Museum at Dorchester's Columbia Point feels like hallowed ground for Boston's lost son, with memorabilia and multimedia on display.

JOIN THE FESTIVITIES

While the Brits who founded Boston get a lot of attention, they were only the first of many immigrant groups who helped shape this city. Locals applaud the others' colorful legacy through equally colorful celebrations. In America's third-largest Chinatown, dragon parades and firecrackers mark Chinese New Year, while the August Moon Festival features dancing lions, lanterns, and moon cakes around the Gateway. And Irish eyes are always smiling on the Sunday closest to March 17, when the famous St. Patrick's Day Parade passes through Southie, the city's infamous Irish neighborhood.

The North End hosts summer weekend street festivals, honoring Italy's patron saints on their name days with processions, brass bands, and Italian delicacies like zeppole (a stuffed fried dough pastry), pizza, and pasta. St. Anthony of Padua's is the biggie, going three days in late August.

DON'T WORRY, BE HAPPY.

Since 1984, Boston has banned the term "happy hour," but that doesn't mean restaurants and bars haven't found a way to keep you happy. Most places have discounted food items between 4 and 6 pm.

THIS CITY DOES SLEEP

While most big cities enjoy their nightlife way into the wee hours, most of Boston's bars close at 2 am. After the public transporation's last call (the last T is around 1 am, depending on the line and service), it's Uber/Lyft, taxi, or foot to get home.

WEED IS LEGAL

Don't be alarmed if you walk by a marijuana dispensary; recreational pot became legal in Massachusetts in mid-2017. Be sure to check into local purchasing and usage laws/guidelines.

BOSTON ACTUALLY LOVES TEA

Despite its tea-stained past, Boston actually loves a good tea party. Several of the local high-end hotels, like Mandarin Oriental, the Ritz-Carlton, and Boston Harbor Hotel (with Rowes Wharf harbor views), host afternoon teas, complete with finger sandwiches, scones, champagne toasts, and steaming pots. The Boston Public Library is also known for its Courtyard Tea Room settings Wednesday through Sunday.

THE CITY OF FIRSTS

Boston is a special city. Just ask any of its residents. They're proud of its place as many of America's firsts and oldests—first public park, oldest restaurant, first public school, first subway system, oldest MLB park, first marathon, first post office, and first restaurant, to name a few.

TAKE TO THE SEAS

This city embraces its waterfront location. There are plenty of harbor cruises, whale-watching tours, and water taxi experiences available throughout the spring, summer, and fall.

DINE ON TRADITION

With a rich colonial history, international influences, and a seaside locale, Boston certainly has a seat at the table as a culinary influencer. Take a page out of history's cookbook with Boston Baked Beans or Yankee Pot Roast, and don't forget to visit the original home of the Boston Cream Pie—Parker's Restaurant at the Omni Parker House hotel.

BRIDGING TWO COMMUNITIES

While residents of Cambridge and Boston joke that they are firmly against traveling across the great divide (aka the Charles River) between the two cities, it's easy (and worth it) to make the journey across any of the several stately bridges. Both areas offer an abundance of things to see and do.

Getting Here and Around

Boston's maze of old and new fuses together remarkably well with a little patience. Follow its endless array of narrow, twisting one-way streets radiating from Boston Harbor in the east, and you'll reach the bustle of the Italian-flavored North End. Go west and hit Faneuil Hall, the quaintly named streets of Downtown, and the bricky expanse of Government Center; head southwest toward the West End, the Garden—home of the Celtics and Bruins—and historic Beacon Hill. The Back Bay's orderly (and alphabetical) grid of streets runs southwest from the base of Beacon Hill, where you'll discover the retail wonderland near patrician Copley Square, the Prudential Center, and high-end boutique- and gallery-filled Newbury Street (known as the Rodeo Drive of the East). Beyond that, Fenway opens onto many art museums, the Emerald Necklace's skein of parkland and ponds, and Fenway Park, baseball field of the much-loved yet oft-reviled Red Sox. To the south spreads the eclectic, trendy South End with its streets lined with shops, eateries, and mimosa brunches.

The Charles River serves as a natural division between Boston and its northern neighborhoods and suburbs, including Charlestown and the cities of Cambridge and Somerville. The Fort Point Channel and its picturesque waterside Harborwalk beneath the spectacularly suspended Zakim Bridge links Downtown with the lively Seaport and Fan Pier districts and South Boston.

Walking is by far the best way to explore, and in good weather, biking is also an option (see the Bicycle section), as are pedicabs. But the next-best transport within Boston or its near environs is the MBTA system, aka "the T," which you can ride to nearly all the city's major points of interest.

✈ Air

More than 40 airlines operate at Logan International Airport (BOS), offering nonstop flights to 120 cities. Flying times to Boston from New York average 1 hour; it's 1½ hours from Washington, D.C., 2¼ hours from Chicago, 3 hours from Miami, 3½ hours from Dallas, 5½ hours from Los Angeles, 6½ hours from London, 13 hours from Tokyo, and 20 hours from Sydney. Delta, American Airlines, and Jet-Blue run daily shuttle flights from New York and Washington, D.C.

The Greater Boston Convention & Visitors Bureau's website (⊕ www.bostonusa. com ☎ 888/733–2678) has direct links to worldwide airlines and national bus lines that service the city. You can book flights here, too.

AIRPORTS

Boston's major airport, Logan International (BOS), is across the harbor, barely 2 miles from Downtown, and can be easily reached by taxi, water taxi, or bus/subway via MBTA's Silver or Blue Line. Logan's four passenger terminals are identified by the letters A, B, C, and E. Some airlines use different terminals for international and domestic flights; most international flights arrive at Terminal E. There's a visitor center in Terminal C.

Worcester Regional Airport (ORH), T. F. Green International Airport (PVD) in Providence, Rhode Island, and Manchester–Boston Regional Airport (MHT) in New Hampshire are about an hour's drive from Boston.

GROUND TRANSPORTATION
BUSES OR SHUTTLE VANS

Free airport shuttles run between the terminals and airport hotels; most companies provide door-to-door service to Back Bay and Downtown hotels. Reservations are not required because vans swing by all the terminals every 15 minutes. One-way fares hover around $17 (less for additional people). The best deal is Logan Express, with buses from the airport to the suburbs of Braintree, Framingham, Peabody, Woburn, and the Back Bay. One-way fares are $12 to the suburbs and free from Logan Airport to Boston or $3 (by credit/debit card) to Logan; accompanied children under 10 ride free.

CAR

For recorded information about traveling to and from Logan Airport, as well as details about parking, contact the airport's ground-transportation hotline (☎ 800/235–6426). Traffic in the city can be maddening; it's a good idea to take public transportation on the Silver and Blue T Lines (Airport Station).

When driving from Logan to Downtown Boston, the most direct route is the Sumner Tunnel ($2.05). On weekends, holidays, and after 10 pm weekdays, you can get around Sumner Tunnel backups by using the Ted Williams Tunnel ($2.05), which will steer you onto the Southeast Expressway south of Downtown Boston. Follow the signs to I-93 northbound to head back into the Downtown area.

🚲 Bicycle

The city has a growing number of stands for locking your bike, and they can be hitched to racks on the front of most buses or carried onto subway cars (with the exception of the Green Line) during nonpeak hours ("peak" is 7–10 am and 4–7 pm). "Pedal and Park" bike cages are available to cyclists at major transit hubs like Alewife and Forest Hills Stations.

■TIP→ **Helmets are required for anyone 16 or younger.**

BIKE RENTAL

The typical fee for a hybrid bike (with helmet and lock) is $40 per eight-hour day. Centrally located bike rental and repair shops include Papa Wheelies, Landry's Bicycles, and Urban AdvenTours; some bike shops offer guided tours. Helmets are available to rent.

BLUEBIKES

Boston's short-term bike rental program is primarily commuter-oriented, but it can also be a handy and fun way for travelers to cover relatively short distances. Members are able to unlock a bike from a dock, ride it for up to two hours at a time (45 minutes a trip if you choose a monthly membership), and then return it to any other dock. There's no additional charge for any ride that lasts less than 30 minutes, and the docks are in dozens of metro area locations.

The short-term Adventure Pass membership is available for 24 hours ($10), and there is a monthly pass for $26.75. You must be 18 or over to join. Sign up online or via one of the kiosks at each dock. Note that the prices don't include a helmet or a lock.

Before taking a bike out, plan your route to the next dock—Bluebikes' website and the free app show dock locations and how many bikes and empty spaces are available at each. If you don't manage to return a bike within the alloted time, an overtime fee will be charged to your credit card. Such fees can be stiff, especially if you've kept the bike longer than an hour.

🚤 Boat

Several boat companies make runs between the airport and Downtown destinations. Take the free Shuttle Bus 66 from any terminal to the airport's ferry dock to catch Boston's water taxis.

Getting Here and Around

Rowes Wharf Water Taxi goes from Logan Airport to Rowes Wharf, Downtown, or other stops, for $15 per person ($40 round-trip with luggage storage). It operates daily year-round.

MBTA Harbor Express water taxis take passengers from Logan Airport to Long Wharf, Downtown, and to Hingham and Hull on the South Shore (one-way fares range from $3.70 to $9.75). Boats leave approximately every 40–45 minutes from 6:20 am to 10:30 pm on weekdays, and from 8:20 am to 10:30 pm on weekends.

Boston Harbor Cruises has an on-call boat service between the airport and several Downtown locations that operates year-round from 6:30 am to 10 pm Monday through Saturday and 6:30 am to 8 pm on Sunday. One-way fares to or from the airport are $15, and round-trip tickets are $20. One-way service to Charlestown or North Station is $20 and $18 to the Black Falcon Cruise Ship Terminal.

GETTING AROUND BY BOAT

MBTA commuter boat service operates weekdays between several Downtown harbor destinations, Charlestown, and quite a few locations on the South Shore. One-way fares range from $3.70 to $9.75 depending on destination; seniors and students ride half-price, and children under 11 are free. Schedules change seasonally, so call ahead.

🚌 Bus

Greyhound has buses to Boston from all major cities in North America. Besides its main location at South Station, there are also suburban terminals in Newton and Framingham. Peter Pan Bus Lines connects Boston with cities elsewhere in southern New England, New Jersey, New York, and Maryland.

Concord Coach runs buses between Boston and several cities in New Hampshire and Maine. C&J sends buses up the New Hampshire coast to Newburyport, Massachusetts; Dover, New Hampshire; Durham, New Hampshire; and Portsmouth, New Hampshire. Concord and C&J both leave from South Station (which is connected to the Amtrak station) and Logan Airport. BoltBus offers cheap fares on well-kept buses between Boston, New York City, Philadelphia, and Washington, D.C. (express service between Boston and New York City is also available). Megabus also offers low fares and serves New York City and points south along the East Coast. Both companies leave from South Station.

GETTING AROUND BY BUS

Massachusetts Bay Transportation Authority (MBTA) buses crisscross the metropolitan area and travel farther into suburbia than the subway and trolley lines. Most bus routes run from 5:30 am to 12:30 am.

One-way fares within the city are $1.70 whether paying with cash or a prepurchased CharlieCard (*see the Public Transit section*); fares are higher for longer suburban lines. Fare machines accept paper currency but do not return change.

🚗 Car

In a place where roads evolved from cow paths and colonial lanes, driving is not for the faint of heart. One-way streets, inconsistent signage, lack of parking, rotaries (traffic circles), and aggressive local drivers add to the confusion.

■ TIP→ **When entering a rotary, the law states that cars entering traffic circles must yield to cars already in the circle, but don't expect all drivers to obey this rule.**

PARKING

Parking on Boston streets is tricky. Some neighborhoods have strictly enforced commercial plate or residents-only rules, with just a handful of two-hour visitors' spaces; others have meters, which cost 25¢ for 12 minutes, with a two-hour limit. On-street parking is free before 8 am and after 8 pm, and all day Sunday and most major holidays. Keep $5 in quarters handy, as some city meters take nothing else. Newer meters accept credit cards and issue receipts that you leave on your dashboard, on the street side. You may also be able to pay with the ParkBoston app on your smartphone.

The parking police are watchful and ruthless—it's not unusual to find a ticket on your windshield five minutes after your meter expires. Repeat offenders who don't pay fines may find the "boot" (an immovable steel clamp) secured to a wheel.

Major public lots are at Government Center, Quincy Market, beneath Boston Common (entrance on Charles Street), beneath Post Office Square, at Prudential Center, at Copley Place, and off Clarendon Street near the John Hancock Tower. Smaller lots and garages are scattered throughout Downtown, especially around the Theater District and off Atlantic Avenue in the North End. Most are expensive; expect to pay up to $12 an hour. The few city garages are a comparative bargain, such as the large one beneath Boston Common. Theaters, restaurants, stores, and tourist attractions often provide patrons with discounted parking; ask your establishment to validate your receipt. Most Downtown restaurants offer valet parking.

RENTAL CARS

Rates in Boston begin at about $50 a day on a weekly rate for an economy car with unlimited mileage. This doesn't include gas, insurance, or the 6.25% tax and $10 surcharge. All major agencies have branches at Logan International Airport, even Zipcar.

🚲 Pedicab

Pedicabs, human-powered three-wheeled bicycle rickshaws that hold two adults easily and three with difficulty, are popular in spring and summer around Boston and Cambridge. You can hail one on the street, or phone ☎ 617/266–2005 for one, with an average wait of 15–20 minutes. They are usually used to get from point A to a not-too-distant point B; on Red Sox game days, pedicabs swarm towards Fenway Park, usually arriving ahead of auto traffic.

There are no fixed fares, since the bikers work for tips; pay your biker (cash only) what you think the ride was worth, though be ready for a sour look if you pay much less than $10 a mile or so. Try to agree on a fee ahead of time. Most pedicabs also offer tours, with minimum fixed fees.

Ⓜ Public Transit

The "T," as the subway system is affectionately nicknamed, is the cornerstone of a far-reaching public transit network that also includes aboveground trains, buses, and ferries. Its five color-coded lines will put you within a block of virtually anywhere. Subways operate from 5 am to 1 am (schedules vary by line). The same goes for buses, which crisscross the city and suburbia.

FARES AND THE CHARLIECARD

Retro music fans recall the 1959 Kingston Trio hit about a fellow named Charlie, who, unable to pay his fare,

Getting Here and Around

"never returned" from Boston's subway system. Charlie lives on as the mascot of the MBTA's ticketing scheme. There are two stored-value options: a plastic CharlieCard or paper CharlieTicket, both of which are reusable and reloadable with cash or credit or debit cards. Getting a CharlieCard makes it easier to transfer between the subway and the bus because such transfers are free and you don't need to keep track of individual tickets. At a station, obtain a CharlieCard from an attendant or a CharlieTicket from a machine. CharlieCards can't yet be used on commuter rail, commuter boats, or Inner Harbor ferries. A standard adult subway fare is $2.40 with cash or a CharlieCard (children ages 11 and under ride free, while senior citizens and students with proper ID are discounted). For buses it's $1.70 with cash or a CharlieCard (more for an Inner or Outer Express bus). Commuter rail and ferry fares depend on the route. For details on schedules, routes, and rates, visit the MBTA (Massachusetts Bay Transportation Authority) website. For most visitors, the best deal will be the unlimited one-day ($12.75) or one-week ($22.50) pass.

GETTING AROUND ON THE "T"

"Inbound" trains head into the city center (Park Street Station) and "outbound" trains head away from it. If you get on the Red Line at South Station, the train heading toward Alewife (Cambridge) is inbound. But once you reach Park Street, the train becomes outbound. Similarly, the Green Line to Fenway Park would be the Boston College or Cleveland Circle train. Large maps prominently posted at each station show the line(s) that serve it, with each stop marked; small maps are overhead in each car. Free 24-hour shuttle buses connect Airport Blue Line Station with all airline

terminals. Shuttle Bus 22 runs between the subway and Terminals A and B, and Shuttle Bus 33 runs between the subway and Terminals C and E.

The Red Line originates at Braintree and Quincy Center to the south; the routes join near South Boston at the JFK/UMass stop and continue to Alewife, the northwest corner of Cambridge by suburban Arlington. (The Mattapan high-speed line, or M-line, is considered part of the overall Red Line. Originating in Ashmont Station, it transports passengers via vintage yellow trolleys to Mattapan Square.)

The Orange Line is bookended by Forest Hills to the south near the Arnold Arboretum in Jamaica Plain and end-of-the-line Oak Grove in the north suburban Malden. The line takes you through such neighborhoods as Chinatown, Downtown Crossing, State Street, Haymarket, and the new Assembly Row station in Somerville.

The Green Line operates elevated trolleys that dip underground in the city center. The line originates at the newly added Union Square stop, heads south, and divides into four westward routes: B ends at Boston College (Commonwealth Avenue); C ends at Cleveland Circle (Beacon Street, in Brighton); D ends at Riverside (Newton at Route 128); and E ends at Heath Street (Huntington Avenue in Jamaica Plain).

The Blue Line runs weekdays from Bowdoin Square (and weeknights and weekends from Government Center) to the Wonderland Racetrack in Revere, north of Boston. The Blue Line is best if you're heading to North Station, Faneuil Hall, the North End/Waterfront, or the Back Bay (the Hynes Convention Center, Prudential Center area).

The Silver Line (a bus line with its own dedicated lanes) has four routes. SL1 connects South Station to Logan Airport; SL2 runs between South Station and the Design Center; SL4 connects Dudley Square and South Station; and SL5 runs between Downtown Crossing and Dudley Square, also stopping in Boylston.

🚕 Taxi

Cabs are available around the clock. You can find them outside most hotels and at designated cabstands around the city. Taxis generally line up around South Station, near Faneuil Hall Marketplace, at Long Wharf, near Massachusetts General Hospital, in the Theater District, and in Harvard Square. You can also call or use smartphone apps, such as Lyft or Uber, to get a taxi or other hired car.

A taxi ride within the city of Boston costs $2.60 at entry for the first 1/7 mile, and 40¢ for each 1/7 mile thereafter. Licensed cabs have meters and provide receipts. If you're going to or from the airport or to the suburbs, ask about flat rates. Cab drivers may charge extra for multiple stops. One-way streets and major traffic jams make circuitous routes necessary but also add to the fare.

Avoid "rogue taxis." These sleek black town cars (legitimate Boston taxis are white) aggressively offer rides on the street and at airports; their drivers often charge more than the agreed-upon rate and may even be dangerous. Always check for a valid taxi medallion plate and a posted photo ID of the driver.

Taxis can be hired outside each terminal at Logan Airport. Fares to and from Downtown should be about $20, including tip. Taxis must pay an extra toll

of $5.25 and a $2.75 airport fee when leaving the airport, which will be tacked onto your bill at the end of the trip. On the way back to the airport, you'll pay the $2.75 fee again, but not the $5.25 toll.

🚆 Train

Boston is served by Amtrak at North Station, South Station, and Back Bay Station. North Station is the terminus for Amtrak's *Downeaster* service from Boston to New Hampshire and Maine. South Station and Back Bay Station, nearby, accommodate frequent Northeast Corridor departures to and arrivals from New York, Philadelphia, and Washington, D.C. Amtrak's Acela train cuts the travel time between Boston and New York to 3½ hours. South Station and Back Bay Station are the two stops in Boston for Amtrak's *Lake Shore Limited*, which travels daily between Boston and Chicago by way of Albany, Buffalo, and Cleveland.

The MBTA runs commuter trains to nearby points south, west, and north. Trains bound for Worcester, Needham, Forge Park, Providence (Rhode Island), and Stoughton leave from South Station and Back Bay Station; those to Fitchburg, Lowell, Haverhill, Newburyport, and Rockport operate out of North Station; those to Middleboro/Lakeville, Kingston/Route 3, Plymouth, and Greenbush depart from South Station.

MBTA commuter-rail stations generally accept only cash. Buy your ticket in advance, or be ready to pay a $1–$2 surcharge in cash when you're on board.

Essentials

Activities

Whether it's taking advantage of being by the water with harbor strolls, riverfront Frisbee games, or logging in picturesque miles of jogging, active Bostonians love their extensive parks, paths, and waterways. Winter winds redirect that energy to white slopes, frozen rinks, and, for those who don't want to don down coats, sheltered gyms and pools.

BEACHES

After more than 20 years of massive cleanup efforts, the water in Boston Harbor is safe for swimming, though many locals and visitors still prefer to head to more traditional beaches that are a short drive or train ride away. The rocky North Shore—about an hour away—is studded with New England beach towns, each with its favorite swimming spot. Alternatively, if the traffic isn't too awful (and during the summer, that's a big if), you can reach the southern base of Cape Cod in a little over an hour.

Dining

In a city synonymous with tradition, Boston chefs have spent recent years rewriting culinary history. The stuffy, wood-paneled formality is gone; the endless renditions of chowder, lobster, and cod have retired; and the assumption that true foodies better hop the next Amtrak to New York is also—thankfully—a thing of the past. Small, upscale neighborhood spots that use local New England ingredients—fresh fish and shellfish, locally grown fruits and vegetables, handmade cheeses, and humanely raised heritage game and meats—to delicious effect have taken their place. Traditional eats can still be found (Beantown Pub remains the best place for baked beans),

but many diners now gravitate toward innovative food in understated environs. Whether you're looking for casual French, down-home Southern cooking, some of the country's best sushi, or Vietnamese banh mi sandwiches, Boston restaurants are ready to deliver.

RESERVATIONS

Reservations generally need to be made at least a few nights in advance, but this is easily done by your concierge, online at ⊕ opentable.com and ⊕ resy.com, or by calling the restaurant directly. Tables can be hard to come by if you want to dine between 7 and 9 pm, or on Friday or Saturday night. But most restaurants will get you in if you show up and are willing to wait.

Price per person for a median main course or equivalent combination of smaller dishes.

WHAT IT COSTS in U.S. Dollars			
$	$$	$$$	$$$$
RESTAURANTS			
under $18	$18–$24	$25–$35	over $35

Lodging

Because of its status as a major college town, Boston students dictate the flow of hotel traffic. Commencement weekends in May and June book months in advance; prices can be triple the off-season rate, with minimum stays of two to four nights. Those returning students invade their city again for the move-in months of August and September. Leaf-peepers arrive in early October, and fall conventions bring waves of business travelers, especially in the Seaport

Where Should I Stay?

NEIGHBORHOOD	VIBE	PROS	CONS
Beacon Hill and Boston Common	Old brick and stone buildings host luxe boutique hotels and B&Bs in Beacon Hill; Boston Common has some skyscraper luxury lodging.	Safe, quaint area with lamp-lighted streets; chain-free upscale shopping and dining; outdoor fun abounds in the park; good T access.	Street parking is extremely hard to come by; not budget-friendly; close to noisy hospital; Boston Common can be sketchy at night.
Downtown Boston	The Financial District hums with busy hotels during the week; new boutique lodging competes with big-box chains.	Great for business travelers; frequent low weekend rates; T and bus access; theaters and some museums walkable.	All but dead at night; expensive garage parking during the day; Downtown Crossing is mobbed at lunchtime and on weekends.
The Back Bay	High-priced hotels in the city's poshest neighborhood; Comm. Ave. is lined with historic brownstones.	Easy, central location; safe, beautiful area to walk around at night; ample T access; excellent people-watching.	Rooms, shopping, and eating can be ridiculously expensive; Newbury Street is overcrowded with tourists on weekends.
The South End	Small, funky lodgings in a hip and LGBTQ-friendly area; awesome independent restaurants and shops.	Great dining scene; easy T and bus access; easy walking to the Back Bay and Downtown; main avenues safe at night with foot traffic.	Some bordering blocks turn seedy after dusk; difficult street parking (and few garages); only a handful of hotel options.
Fenway and Kenmore Square	A sampling of large and small hotels and inns; a mix of students, young professionals, and diehard Sox fans.	Close to Fenway Park (home of the Red Sox); up-and-coming dining scene; less expensive than most 'hoods; accessible by the T.	No street parking on game days (and pricey garages); crowds for concerts and sporting events; some bars are loud and tacky.
The Seaport	Modern and massive; tons of dining and entertainment; excellent water views.	Lots of bustling restaurants; waterfront location; younger crowds.	Opposite of Boston's historical charm; parking is expensive; traffic congested.
Brookline and Jamaica Plain	Midsize chain hotels in student neighborhoods; coffee shops, convenience stores, and rowdy college bars; Brookline has lovely inns.	Cheap rates on rooms in Brighton and parts of Brookline; easier driving than in Downtown.	No overnight street parking in Brookline; far from city center; some areas get dicey at night; T ride into city can be an hour.
Cambridge	A mix of hotels pepper the hip, multiuniversity neighborhood; young freethinkers and efficient (if laid-back) service.	Hallowed academia; verdant squares; good variety of eating and lodging; few chain anythings.	Spotty T access; less of a city feel; a few areas can be slightly dodgy at night; difficult driving and parking.

Essentials

District. Events such as the Boston Marathon in April and the Head of the Charles in October are busy times for large hotels and small inns alike.

PRICES

The hotel tax (combined with other energy, service, or occupancy surcharges) in Boston can add 14.95% to your bill. Though it's not an absolute necessity, many visitors prefer to bring a car, but then parking is another expense to consider. Almost all lodgings have parking, and most charge for the privilege—anywhere from $15 per day for self-garaging to as high as $63 for valet. When looking for a hotel, don't write off the pricier establishments immediately. Price categories are determined by "rack rates"—the list price of a hotel room, which is usually discounted. Specials abound, particularly in Downtown on weekends. With so many new rooms in Boston, pricing is very competitive, so always check out the hotel website in advance for current special offers.

Prices are for two people in a standard double room in high season, excluding 14.95% tax and service charges.

WHAT IT COSTS in U.S. Dollars			
$	$$	$$$	$$$$
HOTELS			
under $200	$200–$299	$300–$399	over $399

Ⓢ Money

Prices are generally higher in Beacon Hill, the Back Bay, and Harvard Square than other parts of town. You're more likely to find bargains in the North End, Kenmore Square, Downtown Crossing, and Cambridge's Central Square. Many museums offer free admission on one weekday evening, and reduced admissions at all times for children, students, and senior citizens.

Ⓨ Nightlife

Whether it's cheering on local sports at a watering hole, rocking out at an underground club, applauding a symphonic performance, or chilling with cocktails in an elegant lounge, Boston has a nightlife vibe to suit all types and moods. Consider it a Cinderella city, set aglow with energy that for some ends all too soon. With the T (subway and bus) making its final runs between midnight and 1 am, most nightspots follow accordingly, closing their doors typically by 2 am. Though night owls may be disappointed by the meager late-night options, except in Chinatown, visitors find plenty of possibilities for stepping out on the early side. The martini set may stroll Newbury and Boylston streets in the Back Bay or Downtown, selecting from swank restaurants, lounges, and clubs. Coffee and tea drinkers can find numerous cafés in Cambridge and Somerville, particularly Harvard and Davis squares.

Microbrew enthusiasts find viable options at sports bars, pop-up beer gardens, and craft breweries, especially on the Rose Kennedy Greenway, along the water in the thriving Seaport, and near campuses and sports arenas. The thriving "lounge" scene in Downtown's cooler hybrid bar-restaurant-clubs provides a mellower, more mature alternative to the collegiate indie spots, and DJs spin the late-night dance parties into a frenzy with house music at crowded clubs like The Grand in the Seaport and Allston's new Roadrunner Boston, billed as the largest indoor general admission venue in New England, with space for 3,500 concertgoers. Tourists crowd Faneuil Hall for its pubs, comedy spots, and dance scenes. The South and North Ends cater to the "dinner-and-drinks" set. Several casual indie rock and music clubs abound with plenty of local bands on stage and cold beer behind the bar in Allston, Somerville, and Cambridge.

GETTING INFORMED

The best source of arts and nightlife information is the *Boston Globe*'s "Arts & Entertainment" section (⊕ *www. bostonglobe.com*). Also worth checking out are the Thursday "Calendar" section of the *Boston Globe*; the Friday "Scene" section of the *Boston Herald*; and the calendar listings on *DigBoston* (⊕ *digboston.com*). The *Globe*, *Dig*, and specialized sites as diverse as the thoroughly classical Boston Musical Intelligencer (⊕ *www. classical-scene.com*) and the scruffy indie-rock broadside Boston Hassle (⊕ *bostonhassle.com*), provide up-to-the-minute information online. Other reliable websites include "The ARTery" newsletter from ⊕ *wbur.org*, the radio station of Boston University.

◉ Performing Arts

MUSEUMS

Boston's compilation of art museums is a bracing mix of old-world aesthetics and new-world experimentation. At the classical end of the spectrum, revered institutions like the Museum of Fine Arts (MFA) and the Isabella Stewart Gardner Museum offer refined experiences, while the edgy Institute of Contemporary Art (ICA) features electronic concerts, graffiti and multimedia exhibitions, and a less reverential attitude toward the arts. All these institutions have one thing in common—they also host special shows, events, and festivals in strikingly handsome performance spaces.

See the Sights section of each chapter for more information on Boston's museums.

MUSIC

For its size, Boston has a great diversity and variety of live music choices. Supplementing appearances by nationally known artists are performers from the area's many colleges and conservatories, which also provide music series, performing spaces, and audiences. Berklee College of Music has made itself especially visible, with student (and/or faculty) ensembles popping up at formal and informal venues far and wide, especially in summer months, playing mainly jazz, blues, rock, indie, pop, and world music. Other college-owned concert halls, such as Harvard University's Sanders Theatre, the New England Conservatory's Jordan Hall, MIT's Kresge Auditorium, and Agganis Arena at Boston University, regularly host homegrown and visiting ensembles.

For live shows, head to the compact Theater District to see traveling Broadway revues, national comedy, opera companies, rock bands, and premiere previews headed to New York.

Classical music aficionados love the Boston Symphony Orchestra, which performs at Symphony Hall October through early May and at Tanglewood Music Center in Lenox, Massachusetts, from late June through August, as well as the Handel and Haydn Society performing Baroque and Classical. A favorite of TV audiences, the Boston Pops presents concerts of "lighter music" from May to July (their outdoor July 4 concert at the Hatch Shell is legendary) and during December. Throughout the year choose from an active roster of orchestral, chamber, and choral ensembles that enrich Boston's musical ambience.

Essentials

THEATER

In the 1930s Boston had no fewer than 50 performing-arts theaters; by the 1980s the city's Downtown Theater District had all but vanished. Happily, since the 1990s several historic theaters, extensively restored, have reopened to host pre-Broadway shows, visiting artists, comedy, jazz, and local troupes. The glorious renovation of the Opera House in 2004 added new light to the district. Established companies, such as the Huntington Theatre Company and the American Repertory Theater in Cambridge, stage classic and modern repertory, premiere works by major writers like David Mamet, August Wilson, Tom Stoppard, and Don DeLillo, and pieces by new talents like Lydia Diamond and Diane Paulus. ArtsEmerson provides the city with contemporary world theater in the Emerson Cutler Majestic Theatre and the Emerson Paramount Center.

🛍 Shopping

Shopping in Boston in many ways mirrors the city itself: a mix of classic and cutting-edge, the high-end and the handmade, and international and local sensibilities. There is a strong network of idiosyncratic gift stores, handicrafts shops, galleries, and a growing number of savvy, independent fashion boutiques. Boston's shops and department stores lie concentrated in the area bounded by Quincy Market, the Back Bay, and Downtown, with plenty of bargains in the Downtown Crossing area. The South End's gentrification creates its own kind of consumerist milieus, from housewares shops to avant-garde art galleries. In Cambridge you can find many shops around Harvard and Central Squares, with independent boutiques migrating west along Massachusetts Avenue ("Mass. Ave.") toward Porter Square and beyond. There's no state sales tax on clothing. However, there's a 6.25% sales tax on clothes priced higher than $175 per item; the tax is levied on the amount in excess of $175.

Most major shopping neighborhoods are easily accessible on the T: Boston's Charles Street and Downtown Crossing and Cambridge's Harvard, Central, and Porter Squares are on the Red Line; Copley Place, Faneuil Hall, and Newbury Street are on the Green Line; the South End is an easy trip on the Orange Line.

📍 Visitor Information

Contact the city and state tourism offices for general information, details about seasonal events, discount passes, trip planning, and attraction information. The National Park Service office screens an entertaining and informative eight-minute slide show on Boston's historic sites and supplies you with maps and directions. The Welcome Center, Boston Common Visitor Information Center, and the Cambridge Tourism Office offer general information.

ONLINE RESOURCES

Boston.com, home of the *Boston Globe* online, has news and feature articles, ample travel information, and links to towns throughout Massachusetts. Revolutionary Spaces (formerly the Bostonian Society) answers frequently asked questions about Boston history on its website. The iBoston page posts wonderful photographs of buildings of architectural and historical importance. Wicked Local provides a more relaxed (and somewhat irreverent) take on Boston and suburban news and information.

Contacts

✈ Air

AIRPORT INFORMATION
Logan International Airport (Boston). ✉ *I–90 East to Ted Williams Tunnel, Boston* ☎ *800/235–6426* ⊕ *www.massport.com/logan-airport* Ⓜ *Airport.*
Manchester Boston Regional Airport. ✉ *Off I–293N/Rte. 101W, Exit 13, Manchester* ☎ *603/624–6539* ⊕ *www.flymanchester.com.* **T. F. Green Airport.** ✉ *2000 Post Rd., off I–95, Exit 13, Warwick* ☎ *401/691–2000* ⊕ *www.pvdairport.com.*

GROUND TRANSPORTA-TION Easy Transportation. ☎ *617/869–7760.* **Logan Express.** ☎ *800/235–6426* ⊕ *www.massport.com/logan-airport.*

🚲 Bicycle

BICYCLE INFORMATION
Papa Wheelies. ✉ *362 Commonwealth Ave., Back Bay* ☎ *617/247–2336* ⊕ *papa-wheelies.com.* **Bluebikes.** ☎ *855/948–2929* ⊕ *www.bluebikes.com.* **Landry's Bicycles.** ✉ *1048 Commonwealth Ave., Allston* ☎ *617/232–0446* ⊕ *www.landrys.com.* **MassBike (Massachusetts Bicycle Coalition).** ✉ *50 Milk St., 16th fl., Downtown* ☎ *617/542–2453* ⊕ *massbike.org.*

⛴ Boat

BOAT INFORMATION
Boston Harbor Cruises. ☎ *617/227–4321* ⊕ *www.bostonharborcruises.com.* **MBTA Harbor Express.** ☎ *617/222–6999, 617/222–3200* ⊕ *www.mbta.com/schedules/ferry.* **Boston Water Taxi.** ☎ *617/406–8584 pickup line, 617/261–6620 questions* ⊕ *www.bostonwatertaxi.com.*

🚌 Bus

BUS CONTACTS C&J. ☎ *800/258–7111* ⊕ *www.ridecj.com.* **Concord Coach.** ☎ *800/639–3317* ⊕ *www.concordcoachlines.com.* **Megabus.** ☎ *877/462–6342* ⊕ *www.megabus.com.* **Peter Pan Bus Lines.** ☎ *800/343–9999* ⊕ *www.peterpanbus.com.*

STATION INFORMATION
South Station. ✉ *2 South Station, Atlantic Ave. and Summer St., Downtown* Ⓜ *South Station.*

🎭 Performing Arts

CONTACTS BosTix. ⊕ *www.bostix.org.* **Broadway Across America-Broadway in Boston.** ☎ *866/523–7469* ⊕ *boston.broadway.com.*

🚊 Public Transportation

CONTACT MBTA. ☎ *800/392–6100, 617/222–3200, 617/222–5146* ⊕ *www.mbta.com.*

📍 Visitor Information

CONTACTS Boston Common Visitor Information Center. ☎ *617/536–4100* ⊕ *www.bostonusa.com/visit/planyourtrip/resources/vic.* **Cambridge Office for Tourism Information Booth.** ✉ *Outside main T entrance, Harvard Square* ☎ *617/497–1630* ⊕ *www.cambridgeusa.org.* **Cambridge Office for Tourism.** ✉ *4 Brattle St., Harvard Square* ☎ *800/862–5678 hotline* ⊕ *www.cambridgeusa.org.* **Greater Boston Convention & Visitors Bureau.** ✉ *2 Copley Pl. Suite 105, Back Bay* ☎ *888/733–2678, 617/536–4100* ⊕ *www.bostonusa.com.* **iBoston.** ⊕ *www.iboston.org.* **National Parks Service Visitor Center.** ✉ *Faneuil Hall, Downtown* ☎ *617/242–5601* ⊕ *www.nps.gov/bost.* **Revolutionary Spaces.** ✉ *310 Washington St., Boston* ⊕ *www.revolutionaryspaces.org.*

Great Itineraries

Boston in 4 Days

Clearly every traveler moves at a different pace. One might be content to snap a pic of the Bunker Hill Monument and push on; another might insist on climbing the obelisk's 294 spiraling steps and studying the adjacent museum's military dioramas. Nevertheless, in four days you should be able to see the city highlights without feeling rushed. With more time, explore nearby communities.

DAY 1: HIT THE TRAIL

About 3 million visitors walk the Freedom Trail every year—and there's a good reason why: taken together, the route's 16 designated sites offer a crash course in colonial history. That makes the trail a must, so tackle it sooner rather than later. Linger wherever you like, leaving ample time to lunch amid magicians and mimes in Faneuil Hall Marketplace. Next, cross into the North End via the Rose Kennedy Greenway. Though hemmed in by water on three sides, this bustling neighborhood is crammed full of history and Italian heritage. Don't miss Old North Church and Paul Revere's former home (Boston's oldest house, constructed almost 100 years prior to his arrival); then, after wandering the narrow Italianate streets, fortify yourself with espresso or gelato and cross the Charlestown Bridge. See the currently drydocked USS *Constitution* and visit the grounds of the famed Bunker Hill Monument (reopening to climbers soon after a huge renovation) before catching the MBTA water shuttle back to Downtown.

DAY 2: HEAD FOR THE HILL

Named for the signal light that topped it in the 1800s, Beacon Hill originally stood a bit taller until locals dug earth off its summit and used it as landfill nearby. Now its shady, gas-lighted streets, brick sidewalks, tidy mews, and stately Brahmin brownstones evoke a bygone Boston. (Lovely Mt. Vernon Street opens onto leafy Louisburg Square, where Louisa May Alcott once lived.) Be sure to snap a photo on Acorn Street, the most photographed street in the nation. When soaking up the ambience, take in some of Beacon Hill's major sites from Boston's various theme trails: the gold-domed Massachusetts State House, the Boston Athenaeum, the Granary Burying Ground, and the African Meeting House. Afterward, stroll to the Common and the Public Garden. Both promise greenery and great people-watching. If shopping's your bag, cruise for antiques along Charles Street, the thoroughfare that separates them. In the evening, feast on dumplings or dim sum in pan-Asian Chinatown or hit an ubertrendy restaurant (the W Hotel lounge is a sexy hot spot for cocktails and light bites, while Nash Bar & Stage is a bustling locale for live music and down-home cookin') in the Theater District, where restorations in recent years have been, well, dramatic.

DAY 3: TAKE IT ALL IN

From the Back Bay you can cover a lot of Boston's attractions in a single day. Plot a route based on your interests. Architecture aficionados can hit the ground running at the neoclassical Public Library (the nation's first) and Romanesque Trinity Church. Shoppers can opt for stores along Newbury Street and in Copley Place, a high-end mall anchored by Neiman Marcus. Farther west in the Fens, other choices await. Art connoisseurs might view the collections at the Museum of Fine Arts or Isabella Stewart Gardner Museum. Carnival-like Fenway Park beckons baseball fans to the other side of the Fens. Depending on your taste—and ticket availability—cap the day with a Symphony Hall concert or a Red Sox game.

DAY 4: ON THE WATERFRONT

A spate of openings and reopenings in recent years has transformed the Seaport District into a magnet for museum hoppers. Begin your day artfully at the Institute of Contemporary Art (ICA) on Fan Pier. The mod museum's bold cantilevered design makes the most of its waterside location. It makes the most of its art collection, too, by offering programs and exhibits that appeal to little tykes and hard-to-please teens. Keep tiny tots engaged with a run to the Children's Museum and its innovative exhibits; then relive a turning point in American history at the Boston Tea Party Ships & Museum's authentic-looking vessels and interpretive center. From there, continue on to that waterfront favorite, the New England Aquarium, where you can watch the sea lions and penguins frolic. On the wharf, sign up for a harbor cruise, a whale-watch, or a ferry ride to the beckoning Boston Harbor Islands.

Beyond Boston Proper

DAY 1: EXPLORE CAMBRIDGE

From pre-Revolutionary times, Boston was the region's commercial center and Cambridge was the burbs: a retreat more residential than mercantile, with plenty of room to build the nation's first English-style, redbrick university. The heart of the community—geographically and practically—is still Harvard Square. It's easy enough to while away a day here browsing the shops and lounging at a café, then wandering to the riverbank to watch crew teams practice. But Harvard Square is also the starting point for free student-led campus tours, as well as for strolls along Brattle Street's "Tory Row" (No. 105 was occupied by both Washington and Longfellow!). Fine museums include the family-friendly Harvard Museum of Natural History, loaded with dinosaur bones, gemstones, and 21 million stuffed critters. The newly remodeled Harvard Art Museums is another must. End your day in true Cantabrigian style by taking in a concert or lecture at Harvard's Sanders Theatre or with a show at the American Repertory Theater, helmed by noted artistic director Diane Paulus.

DAY 2: STEP BACK IN TIME

You only have to travel a short distance to visit historic places you read about in grade school. For a side trip to the 17th century, head 35 miles south to Plymouth. The famed rock doesn't live up to its hype in terms of its size, but Plimoth Patuxet Museums (an open-air museum re-creating life among Pilgrims) and the *Mayflower II* are well worth the trip. A second option is to veer northwest to explore Revolutionary-era sites in handsome, suburban Lexington. Start at the National Heritage Museum for a recap of the events that kicked off the whole shebang; then proceed to the Battle Green, where "the shot heard round the world" was fired. After stopping by Minute Man National Historical Park, continue to Concord to tour the homes of literary luminaries like Ralph Waldo Emerson, Louisa May Alcott, and Nathaniel Hawthorne. Conclude your novel excursion with a walk around Walden Pond, where transcendentalist Henry David Thoreau wrote one of the founding documents of the environmental movement, *Walden*.

DAY 3: A SHORE THING

Anyone eager to taste the salt air or feel the surge of the sea should take a day trip to the North Shore towns of Salem and Gloucester. The former has a Maritime National Historic Site—complete with vintage wharves and warehouses—that proves there is more to the notorious town than just witchcraft. Or, hop on the 90-minute ferry ride to Provincetown for a taste of Cape Cod.

Back Bay Art and Architecture Walk

In the folklore of American neighborhoods, Boston's Back Bay stands alongside New York's Park Avenue as a symbol of chic. In the 1850s, Boston's power brokers built Victorian mansions amid lush green spaces, and by the time the Great Depression hit, the Back Bay was the city's poshest address.

COPLEY SQUARE

The Back Bay's hub embraces a range of architectural styles from Romanesque Revival to Bauhaus-inspired skyscrapers. The Fairmont Copley Plaza hotel's OAK Long Bar + Kitchen, with its catbird seats, offers a perfect place to begin your walk. Designed in 1912 by Henry Hardenbergh five years after his famed Plaza Hotel in Manhattan, the hotel underwent a $20-million centenary renovation. The Boston Public Library, housing 9 million books, was conceived by architectural firm McKim, Mead and White, who opted for an Italian Renaissance palazzo. Modern architect Philip Johnson's 1972 wing respectfully reflects the original.

THE PRU AND COMMONWEALTH AVENUE

Heading up Boylston Street with the library on your left, you'll find the 52-story Prudential Tower. Built in the 1960s, today it is a retail mecca affectionately dubbed "The Pru." With the Pru behind you, take Gloucester Street across Newbury to Commonwealth Avenue, where if you look to the right, you will see the Mall—a linear park that stretches all the way to the edge of the Public Garden. The Mall's 32 acres were designed in the French boulevard style by Arthur Gilman in 1856. Turn left, and cross Massachusetts Avenue to 395 Commonwealth, where you'll see Louis Comfort Tiffany's famous Ayer Mansion.

HIGHLIGHTS
Copley Square's handsome ensemble of church, park, library, and skyscraper; Boston Public Garden

WHERE TO START
OAK Long Bar in Fairmont Copley Plaza

LENGTH
1.6 miles or about 1½ hours with brief stops

WHERE TO END
Back where you started, people-watching from an OAK Long Bar settee or a bench facing the Boston Public Library or Trinity Church

BEST TIME TO GO
Any time when you can see all the sights in daylight

WORST TIME TO GO
Rush hour or when it's raining or very cold

EDITOR'S CHOICE
Strolling the Comm. Ave. Mall in the snow, tiny cloister garden behind Trinity Church, George Washington with his attendant pigeons

BOSTON PUBLIC GARDEN

At the bronze statue of George Washington at the foot of Commonwealth Avenue, enter Boston Public Garden, America's oldest botanical garden, sheltering 24 acres of weeping willow, elm, spruce, and dawn redwood. The garden pond is spanned by a faux-suspension bridge, while the garden itself abuts Boston Common. Exit with Washington behind you, walk one block to Newbury Street, turn right and head toward the Gothic Revival Church of the Covenant, on Newbury Street at Berkeley, built in 1867.

TRINITY CHURCH AND 200 CLARENDON

Take Berkeley one block to Boylston Street, then head back up Boylston to Copley Square to visit its crowning centerpiece, Trinity Church. This 1877 Romanesque Revival masterpiece conceived by Henry Hobson Richardson exhibits sumptuously carved interior woodwork, ornamented ceilings, and intricate stained glass. Another architectural award winner is 200 Clarendon Street (previously the John Hancock Tower), behind Trinity Church at St. James Avenue. Architect Henry Cobb managed to construct this modernist 58-story building without disrupting the square's scale and proportion in part by having the glass panels mirror Trinity Church.

Best Tours

🚲 Bike Tours

★ Urban AdvenTours

BIKING | A variety of themed excursions run throughout Boston and Cambridge, with most covering about 10 to 12 miles. They leave from Urban AdvenTours's Atlantic Avenue headquarters and are offered almost every day; in winter, the tours depend on the weather—call to confirm. The main tours start at $60 per person, and tickets are available for purchase through the website; bike, helmet, and water are all included. A variety of rental bikes are also available, including the new e-bikes. ⊠ *103 Atlantic Ave., Downtown* ☎ *617/670–0637 for rentals and tours* ⊕ *www.urbanadventours.com* Ⓜ *Aquarium.*

⭕ Boat Tours

Boston Duck Tours

BOAT TOURS | FAMILY | Paul Revere would have trouble calling this one, since this city tour is by land and by sea. Hop aboard and discover Boston as your "conDUCKtor" weaves through streets and harbor waterways on one of its famed WWII-style amphibious landing vehicles. There are three departure locations: the Museum of Science, the Prudential Center, and the New England Aquarium. You'll enjoy a fully narrated, historic tour of Boston, as you cruise by all the places that highlight Boston's prominent place in the country's history, from the golden-domed State House to Boston Common, the historic North End to fashionable Newbury Street. Then it's time for a Big Splash as you head straight into the Charles River for breathtaking views of the Boston and Cambridge skylines. ⊠ *4 Copley Pl., Suite 4155, Boston* ☎ *617/267–3825* ⊕ *bostonducktours.com* ⊠ *$48.99.*

Boston Harbor Cruises

CRUISES | Take to the seas to see the city from a new vantage point with Boston Harbor Cruises. They offer ferries to Georges or Spectacle Islands (two of the more popular Harbor Islands) from Long Wharf in Downtown. The boat touring company also offers leisurely sunset and brunch harbor cruises, as well as narrated historical sightseeing ventures, such as whale-watching. Thrill seekers love a get-wet trip on their Codzilla, a turbo-charged craft. Check the website for ticket prices and schedules. ⊠ *Long Wharf, Waterfront* ☎ *617/227–4321* ⊕ *www.cityexperiences.com/boston/city-cruises/harbor-islands* Ⓜ *Aquarium.*

🍴 Food Tours

Bites of Boston Food Tours

FOOD AND DRINK TOURS | Boston's most mouth-watering neighborhoods, including the South End, Chinatown, and Downtown/Beacon Hill, are explored on foot during a three-hour walking tour with Bites of Boston. You'll visit five to six spots and leave full. ⊠ *Boston* ☎ *617/702-2483* ⊕ *bitesofbostonfoodtours.com* ⊠ *$82 per person* ☞ *Tickets must be purchased in advance.*

🧭 Specialty Tours

Boston Women's Heritage Trail

GUIDED TOURS | Boston Women's Heritage Trail has several self-guided walks that highlight more than 200 remarkable women who have played an integral role in shaping the history of Boston and the nation as patriots, intellectuals, abolitionists, suffragists, artists, and writers. In addition, there are various trails through different Boston neighborhoods and themed trails, such as a women artist trail in the Back Bay. View maps on the organization's website. Guided tours available upon request. ⊠ *Back Bay* ⊕ *www.bwht.org.*

On Location Tours

GUIDED TOURS | On Location Tours takes you to Boston's TV and movie hot spots like the South Boston of *The Departed,* the *Ally McBeal* building, the L Street tavern from *Good Will Hunting, American Hustle*'s big deal site, *The Town*'s chase scene locale, the *Cheers* bar, and Red Sox home base Fenway Park, which served as filming location for movies like *Field of Dreams* and *Fever Pitch.* Guides share filming secrets and trivia from movies like *Legally Blonde* and *Mystic River* along with the best celeb spots in town. The "theater-on-wheels" bus tour takes two to three hours, depending on traffic ($61 ticket fee), and you can get out and explore at some sites. Exact pickup location is sent once you purchase tickets. ⊠ *Downtown* ☎ *617/379–6770 to purchase tickets* ⊕ *onlocationtours.com/ tour/boston-tv-movie* ⌑ *$61* ⊙ *Tours run daily at 10 am and 2 pm* Ⓜ *Park.*

Samuel Adams Boston Brewery

BREWERY | Tour the Boston beer company's Jamaica Plain facility, where it conducts research and develops new products. There are a few different tours (21+ only) at different price points, all including samples and a souvenir glass. Smell and taste the components of brewing (hops, malt, and barley), look at the flavoring process, and hear about—perhaps even see—new beers in development. Tours run Thursday through Monday and you must book online. Whether you take a tour or not, you can enjoy a beer in the Boston Tap Room, which is open daily, or the Beer Garden, in nice weather.

■TIP→ **Parking is limited, so consider taking the T to Stony Brook.** ⊠ *30 Germania St., Jamaica Plain* ☎ *617/368–5080* ⊕ *www.samueladams.com* ⊙ *No tours Tues. and Wed.* Ⓜ *Stony Brook.*

Fenway Park Tours

SPECIAL-INTEREST TOURS | Baseball fans who can't catch a Red Sox game can still see the Green Monster up close by going on a tour of the park. The one-hour Fenway walking tour runs year-round, and if you go on the last tour on a home-game day, you can watch batting practice. Tours run hourly from 9 am (10 am November through March) to 5 pm (or three hours before game time). Check the site for info on premium tours. ⊠ *Boston* ☎ *617/226–6666* ⊕ *mlb.com/ redsox/ballpark/tours* ⌑ *$21.*

🧭 Trolley Tours

Old Town Trolley Tours

GUIDED TOURS | FAMILY | Talk about flexible. With these state-of-the-art stadium trolleys, you have unlimited hop-on and hop-off options as often as you like all day long. Live guides ride along with you, as passengers learn as much (or as little) as they want about Boston. Enjoy double-decker height views while protected from the elements. There are 18 trolley stops, including Faneuil Hall, the historic North End, the Charles Street Meeting House, the *Cheers* bar, the Prudential Center, and the USS *Constitution* and Museum. They also host a Ghosts & Gravestones Frightseeing tour. ⊠ *Boston* ☎ *855/396–7433* ⊕ *www.trolleytours. com/boston* ⌑ *From $50.*

On the Calendar

January

Boston Wine Festival. The country's longest running food and wine festival features an all-star lineup of hosted dinners, seminars, and receptions January through March at Boston Harbor Hotel with chef David Daniels at the helm. ⊕ *www.bostonwinefestival.net*

February

Beanpot Hockey Tournament. Boston College, Boston University, Harvard, and Northeastern face off in this annual, fiercely contested tournament. ⊕ *www.beanpothockey.com*.

March

St. Patrick's Day Parade. Bands, floats, and veterans groups all walk proudly along the main streets of Boston's robust Irish Southie neighborhood, lined with rowdy revelers. ⊕ *southbostonparade.org*.

April

Boston Marathon. Every Patriots' Day (the third Monday in April), fans gather along the Hopkinton-to-Boston route of the Boston Marathon to cheer on more than 25,000 runners from all over the world. ⊕ *www.baa.org*.

Esplanade Summer Events. From April through September, the art deco Hatch Shell on the Esplanade is abuzz with free concerts, movie showings, and more. ⊕ *www.mass.gov*.

Paul Revere's Ride. This live reenactment on Patriot's Day follows the horseback route of this famed activist, beginning in the North End and culminating at the Battle Green in Lexington.

May

Lilac Sunday. This day-long celebration includes tours of the lilacs and family activities, and is the only day picnicking is permitted at the Arnold Arboretum. ⊕ *www.arboretum.harvard.edu*.

Duckling Day. A Mother's Day tradition, more than 1,000 costume-clad children and their parents follow the Harvard marching band through Boston Common, celebrating the classic children's book *Make Way for Ducklings*. ⊕ *www.friendsofthepublicgarden.org*.

June

Jimmy Fund Scooper Bowl. The nation's largest all-you-can-eat ice cream festival, located at Patriot's Place in Foxborough, includes a 21+ Scoop at Night with Harpoon beer, local wines, music, and entertainment. ⊕ *www.jimmyfund.org*.

July

Boston Pops Fireworks Spectacular. Independence Day is capped off with world-renowned pyrotechnics, celebrity musical guests, and live performances from the Boston Pops along the Charles River. ⊕ *bostonpopsjuly4th.org*.

Harborfest. Boston's four-day July 4 celebration sponsors more than 200 events, including Revolutionary War reenactments, curated art festivals, pet parades, craft markets, classic car shows, and free concerts. ⊕ *www.bostonharborfest.com*.

Shakespeare on the Common. On July and August evenings, the Commonwealth Shakespeare Company produces free performances of Shakespeare on Boston Common, such as *Much Ado About Nothing* (2022). ⊕ *commshakes.org*.

Summer in the City at Boston Harbor Hotel. Each weeknight of summer, dazzling things happen at Rowes Wharf—soul-bros and-sisters enjoy Motown on Tuesday, Rat-Packers salute Frankie and Sammy on Wednesday, blues lovers get on that Blue Barge on Thursday, and cine-philes catch starry silver-screen classics on Friday. Boston Harbor Hotel hosts these events along the Harborwalk from 6 to 10 pm. ⊕ *www.bhh.com.*

September

Boston Film Festival. Get "reel" at this week-long fall forum for evolving film-makers to express their artistic visions. This is where top independent films premiere, many with Massachusetts ties. There will be both live and virtual programs. The festival offers audiences first-hand access to the filmmakers and filmmaking process during the Q&A sessions with the director and talent following every screening. ⊕ *www.bostonfilmfestival.org.*

October

Salem Haunted Happenings. Salem hosts harvest-time events including a Grand Parade, the Haunted Biz Baz Street Fair, Family Film Nights, costume balls, ghost tours, haunted houses, live music, and chilling theatrical presentations. ⊕ *www.hauntedhappenings.org.*

Head of the Charles Regatta. In October, sculling crew teams compete in the world-famous Head of the Charles Regatta, a tradition for more than 50 years. The world's largest two-day rowing event draws athletes from their teens to their 80s, collegians and clubbers, from England, Australia, and worldwide. Food, beer, and clothing vendors set up tents, and hordes gather atop the Charles River's many bridges to watch the races. ⊕ *www.hocr.org.*

November

Nutcracker Ballet. Under the artis-tic direction of Mikko Nissinen, this Christmas-time classic is performed in the historic Boston Opera House by the world-renowned Boston Ballet. Show times are scheduled annually, beginning the Friday after Thanksgiving through December 31. ⊕ *www.bostonballet.org.*

December

Boston Holiday Pops. These seasonal performances find beloved conductor Keith Lockhart and the Boston Pops celebrating with holiday music favorites, sing-alongs, and Santa's visit in historic Symphony Hall. ⊕ *www.bso.org.*

First Night Boston. This New Year's Eve celebration schedules events through-out the city to help ring in the new year. ⊕ *www.firstnightboston.org.*

How to Speak Bostonian

Boston vocab can be interesting to follow if you're visiting for the first time. Frappes are milkshakes (with ice cream). Grinders are sandwiches (on sub rolls). And wicked? Well, that's how you describe almost everything to the extreme (usually good things).

There's also a strong accent to be aware of. Many Bostonians drop the final "r" in a word, as in the pronunciation of the famous sports arena, "the Gahden." Bostonians also lengthen their vowels, so chowder sounds like "chowdah." Town names in Massachusetts are often spoken very differently than they are spelled; Gloucester, for example, becomes "Glawstuh." Bostonians also rush their speech, so "Hi, how are you?" is "hihawaya?" and "Did you eat?" sounds like "Jeet?"

VOCABULARY AND PRONUNCIATIONS

- **Bang a U-ey.** Make a U turn.

- **Beantown.** Announces that you're a visitor; don't use it.

- **Bubbler.** Water fountain.

- **The Cape.** Short for Cape Cod; if you're visiting, you're "going down the Cape."

- **Chowder ("chowdah").** Always New England–style, never Manhattan-style.

- **Coffee regular.** Coffee with with cream and sugar, not black

- **Comm. Ave.** Commonwealth Avenue in Boston.

- **Dot.** Dorchester.

- **Dunks.** Locals run on coffee from Dunkin' Donuts (aka Dunkies or Dunks). Order like a native by asking for a coffee regular—that's cream and sugar (two of each for a small, three for a medium, and so on).

- **Eastie.** East Boston.

- **Fens.** Fenway, the neighborhood, not the ball park.

- **Frappes.** Milkshakes, but with a scoop of ice cream blended in.

- **Grinder ("grindah").** Also known as heros, hoagies, or subs in other parts of the country, these are sandwich fillings served on a sub roll.

- **The Hub.** Boston's nickname.

- **Jimmies.** Chocolate sprinkles on ice cream.

- **Mass. Ave.** Massachusetts Avenue in Boston.

- **Nor'easter ("Nor'eastah").** Strong winter storm on the East Coast.

- **Packie/Package store.** Liquor store.

- **The Pats.** Nickname for the New England Patriots, the most revered NFL team.

- **The Pike.** Nickname for the Massachusetts Turnpike.

- **The Pru.** The Prudential Center.

- **Rotary.** Traffic circle or roundabout.

- **Southie.** South Boston, refers to the neighborhood south of Boston. Not to be confused with the South End.

- **Statie.** State trooper.

- **The T.** The only accepted term used to refer to the MBTA transit system.

- **Wicked.** A synonym for "very" or "extremely" when describing something (usually something good), for example, a wicked good time, a wicked tasty burger, and so on.

BEACON HILL, BOSTON COMMON, AND THE WEST END

3

Updated by
Leigh Harrington

⊙ Sights	🍴 Restaurants	🛏 Hotels	🛍 Shopping	🍸 Nightlife
★★★★☆	★★★☆☆	★★★☆☆	★★★★☆	★★★☆☆

NEIGHBORHOOD SNAPSHOT

TOP EXPERIENCES

■ **Start the Freedom Trail:** From Boston Common, follow the red-painted and-brick path to knock off four of its 16 stops.

■ **Discover the Black Heritage Trail:** At sanctuaries, schools, and Underground Railroad sites, this self-guided historical walk visits early Boston's African American community.

■ **Window shop:** Shop Charles Street for clothing, specialty products, and contemporary gifts.

■ **Embrace your inner science nerd:** Explore space, the human body, electricity, and more at the Museum of Science.

■ **See picturesque history:** One of Boston's most photographed locales, Acorn Street features elements from the Colonial era through the Victorian period.

■ **Gear up for game day:** Visit the TD Garden to root for the Boston Celtics or Boston Bruins, or take a spin around The Sports Museum.

QUICK BITES

■ **Anna's Taqueria.** Locals love this Mexicali take-out chain. ⊠ *242 Cambridge St., Beacon Hill* ⊕ *www.annastaqueria.com* Ⓣ *Charles/MGH, Bowdoin.*

■ **The Paramount.** There's usually a line at this cafeteria-style standout, but it moves quickly. ⊠ *44 Charles St., Beacon Hill* ⊕ *www.paramountboston.com* Ⓣ *Charles/MGH.*

■ **Tatte.** Incredible tea cakes, coffee, tarts, and Israeli-inspired lunch fare. ⊠ *70 Charles St., Beacon Hill* ⊕ *www. tattebakery.com/ boston* Ⓣ *Charles/MGH.*

GETTING HERE

Beacon Hill is best experienced on foot. Bounded by Cambridge Street, Beacon Street, and Bowdoin Street, the neighborhood is an array of short, tight, winding roads, and street parking (free on Sunday) is at a minimum. To reach Beacon Hill via the T, take the Green Line to Park Street and walk through the Common toward Beacon Street; or take the Red Line to Charles/MGH for access to Charles Street. The Blue Line's Bowdoin stop offers access to both Beacon Hill and the West End.

Across Cambridge Street, the West End is home to Massachusetts General Hospital, the TD Garden, the Museum of Science, and residential high-rises. There's plenty of garage parking; street parking is limited. To access by T, take the Red Line to Charles/ MGH for the hospital and Charlesbank Park; the Green Line to Science Park for the Museum of Science, or to North Station for the TD Garden.

PLANNING YOUR TIME

■ From top to bottom, historic Beacon Hill can easily be explored in half a day. Shoppers will want to visit Charles Street after noon, when shops are more likely to be open. Add an extra few hours if you wish to linger on Boston Common or visit the State House or other historical sites. The West End is larger in area, so you'll walk more between attractions. The Museum of Science is worth a full day; smaller museums about an hour each.

Beacon Hill is Boston at its most Bostonian. Redbrick row houses dressed with black shutters and the occasional violet-hued windowpane filter into view, and narrow streets return you to the 19th century just as surely as if you had stumbled into a time machine. Across Beacon Street from Beacon Hill, the wide expanse of Boston Common has provided green space for locals since 1634.

Its history dates to the Colonial Era; in ensuing years, Beacon Hill achieved a narrative that includes the abolitionist movement, politics, and, even, prostitution. Blue-blood Brahmins, with surnames like Cabot and Shaw, are perpetual residents, but the Hill gets a consistent influx of the contemporary at pricey boutiques on its main thoroughfare, Charles Street.

Boston Common had its start as a place for cattle to graze, then as an encampment for British regulars during the Revolutionary War, as a place for public assembly, and today, as a wonderful recreation area.

Beacon Hill and Boston Common

Once the seat of the Commonwealth's government, Beacon Hill was called "Trimountain" and later "Tremont" by early colonists because of its three summits: Pemberton, Mt. Vernon Hill, and Beacon

Hill (named for the warning light set on its peak in 1634). In 1799, settlers leveled out the ground for residences, using it to create what is now Charles Street. By the early 19th century, the crests of the other two hills had also been lowered.

When the Hill's fashionable families decamped for the new development of the Back Bay starting in the 1850s, enough residents remained to ensure that the south slope of the Hill never lost its wealthy Brahmin character. By the mid-20th century, most of the multistory single-family dwellings on Beacon Hill had been converted to condominiums and apartments, which are today among the most expensive in the city.

A good place to begin an exploration of Beacon Hill is at the Boston Common Visitor Information Center, where you can buy a map or a complete guide to the Freedom Trail.

Beacon Hill and Boston Common

Quick Bites ▼	5 Tatte Bakery & Café **D3**	**Hotels** ▼
1 Anna's Taqueria **F1**	6 The Upper Crust	1 The Whitney Hotel
2 The Paramount **D4**	Pizzeria **D4**	Boston **D2**
3 Savenor's Market **D2**		2 XV Beacon **H3**
4 The Sevens		
Ale House **D3**		

28

◉ Sights

★ Acorn Street

STREET | Often called the city's most photographed passageway, Acorn Street offers its visitors an iconic image of "historic Boston." Short, steep, and narrow, the cobblestone street may be Boston's roughest ride, so leave your car behind. Brick row houses—once the homes of 19th-century artisans and tradespeople—line one side, and on the other, doors lead to Mt. Vernon's hidden gardens. Find American flags, creative door knockers, window boxes, and gas lights aplenty. ⊠ *Between W. Cedar and Willow Sts., Beacon Hill* Ⓜ *Park, Charles MGH.*

Beacon Street

STREET | Some New Englanders believe that wealth is a burden to be borne with a minimum of display. Happily, the early residents of Beacon Street were not among them. They erected many fine architectural statements, from the magnificent State House to grand patrician mansions. Here are some of the most important buildings of Charles Bulfinch, the ultimate designer of the Federal style in America: dozens of bowfront row houses, the Somerset Club, and the glorious Harrison Gray Otis House. ⊠ *Beacon Hill* Ⓜ *Park.*

Boston Athenæum

LIBRARY | One of the oldest libraries in the country, the Athenæum was founded in 1807 from the seeds sown by the Anthology Club (headed by Ralph Waldo Emerson's father). It moved to its imposing, present-day quarters—modeled after Palladio's Palazzo da Porta Festa in Vicenza, Italy—in 1849. Membership in this cathedral of scholarship has been passed down for generations, but the Athenæum is open in part to the public. The first floor houses an art gallery with rotating exhibits, marble busts, porcelain vases, lush oil paintings, and books. The children's room features secluded nooks overlooking the Granary Burying Ground.

To see one of the most marvelous sights in Boston academe, take a guided tour, which visits the fifth-floor Reading Room. Among the Athenæum's holdings are most of George Washington's private library, as well as King's Chapel Library, sent from England by William III in 1698. With a nod to the Information Age, an online catalog contains records for more than 600,000 volumes. ⊠ *10½ Beacon St., Beacon Hill* ☎ *617/227–0270* ⊕ *www.bostonathenaeum.org* ☜ *From $10* ◷ *Closed Sun. and Mon.* Ⓜ *Park.*

★ Boston Common

CITY PARK | **FAMILY** | Nothing is more central to the city than Boston Common, the oldest public park in the United States. Dating from 1634, the Common started as 50 acres where freemen could graze their cattle. (Cows were banned in 1830.) Don't confuse the Common with its sister park, the Public Garden, where the Swan Boats glide. Around the park, visit-worthy sites include Brewer Fountain Plaza, the start of the Freedom Trail, the Boston Common Visitor Information Center, the Soldiers and Sailors Monument, the Frog Pond, the Central Burying Ground, and the newly restored Robert Gould Shaw 54th Regiment Memorial. ■ **TIP→ This is Freedom Trail stop 1.** ⊠ *Bounded by Beacon, Charles, Tremont, and Park Sts., Beacon Hill* ⊕ *www.boston.gov/parks/boston-common* Ⓜ *Park, Boylston.*

Boston Common Frog Pond

ICE SKATING | **FAMILY** | The Boston Common Frog Pond is a hot spot, no matter the season. In winter (November to March), city dwellers and visitors alike can skate around the man-made pool (skate rentals available), which vibes an atmosphere reminiscent of a Currier & Ives painting. In warm weather, the Frog Pond transforms into a shallow spray pool, free to all. Nearby, a carousel opens for most of the year, and a large playground is open year-round. ⊠ *Boston*

Touring Beacon Street

After the **Boston Athenæum**, Beacon Street highlights begin at No. 34, originally the Cabot family residence and, until 1996, the headquarters of Little, Brown and Company, once a mainstay of Boston's publishing trade. At 33 Beacon, the **George Parkman House** shows off a gracious facade hiding more than a few secrets. One of the first sensational "trials of the century" involved the murder of Dr. George Parkman, a wealthy landlord and Harvard benefactor. He was bludgeoned to death in 1849 by Dr. John Webster, a Harvard medical professor and neighborhood acquaintance who allegedly became enraged by Parkman's demands that he repay a personal loan. At the conclusion of the trial, the professor was hanged; he's buried in an unmarked grave on Copp's Hill in the North End. Parkman's son lived in seclusion in this house overlooking the Common until he died in 1908. The building is now used for civic functions.

Notice the windows of the twin **Appleton-Parker Houses**, built by the pioneering textile merchant Nathan Appleton and a partner at Nos. 39 and 40. These are the celebrated purple panes of Beacon Hill; only a few buildings have them, and they are incredibly valuable. Their amethystine color was the result of the action of the sun's ultraviolet light on imperfections in a shipment of glass sent to Boston circa 1820. The mansions aren't open to the public.

The quintessential snob has always been a Bostonian—and the **Somerset Club**, at 42 Beacon, has always been the inner sanctum of blue-blood Cabots, Lowells, and Lodges. The mansion is a rare intrusion of the granite Greek Revival style into Beacon Hill. The older of its two buildings was erected in 1819 by David Sears and designed by Alexander Parris, the architect of Quincy Market.

A few doors down at No. 45 resides the grandest of the three homes that Harrison Gray Otis, a U.S. senator and Boston's third mayor, built for himself. They are also the city's most splendidly ostentatious Federal-era houses, all designed by Charles Bulfinch and all still standing. Otis moved in circa 1805 and stayed until his death in 1848. The **Otis House** was once freestanding and surrounded by English-style gardens; today, it's the headquarters of the American Meteorological Society.

Common, Beacon Hill ☎ 617/635–2120 ⊕ www.bostonfrogpond.com Ⓜ Park.

Boston Common Visitor Information Center
VISITOR CENTER | FAMILY | Run by the Greater Boston Convention & Visitors Bureau, this visitor information center not only serves as a well-staffed source of things to see and do, it is a frequent meeting spot for walking tours around town and is the first stop on Boston's historic Freedom Trail. ■ TIP➔ **Find it on the Tremont Street side of Boston Common, equidistant** between the Green Line's Boylston and Park Street T stops. ✉ 139 Tremont St., Beacon Hill ☎ 617/536–4100 ⊕ www.bostonusa.com/plan/visitor-centers-and-guides Ⓜ Park, Boylston.

Central Burying Ground
CEMETERY | The Central Burying Ground may seem an odd feature for a public park, but remember that in 1756, when the land was set aside, this was a lonely corner of Boston Common. It's the final resting place of Tories and Patriots alike,

Several Founding Fathers rest at the Granary Burial Ground, a picturesque Freedom Trail stop.

as well as many British casualties of the Battle of Bunker Hill. The most famous person buried here is Gilbert Stuart, the portraitist best known for his likenesses of George and Martha Washington. ⊠ *Boston Common, along Boylston St., Downtown* ⊕ *www.boston.gov/cemeteries/central-burying-ground* Ⓜ *Boylston.*

★ Charles Street

STREET | You won't see any glaring neon signs, in keeping with the historic character of the area, but Charles Street more than makes up for the general lack of commercial development on Beacon Hill with a plethora of clothing, antiques, and gift boutiques, plus cafés. Once the home of Oliver Wendell Holmes and the publisher James T. Fields (of the famed Bostonian firm of Ticknor and Fields), Charles Street sparkles at dusk from gas-fueled lamps, making it a romantic place for an evening stroll. ⊠ *Between Beacon and Cambridge Sts., Beacon Hill* Ⓜ *Charles/MGH.*

Granary Burying Ground

CEMETERY | Boston's cemeteries are among the most historic in America, and the Granary, established in 1660, is no exception. Headstones are elaborately ornamented with skeletons and winged skulls among other carved Colonial folk art. Samuel Adams, John Hancock, Paul Revere, and Benjamin Franklin's parents are among the impressive list of the estimated 5,000 folks interred here; there hasn't been a new burial since 1880. Note the winged hourglasses carved into the stone gateway of the burial ground; they are a 19th-century addition. ■ **TIP→ This is Freedom Trail stop 4.** ⊠ *95 Tremont St., Beacon Hill* ⊕ *www.thefreedomtrail.org/trail-sites/granary-burying-ground* Ⓜ *Park.*

Louisburg Square

PLAZA/SQUARE | Charming Louisburg Square (don't drop the "s") was an 1840s model for a town-house development that was never built on the Hill because of space restrictions. Today, it features a central grassy square enclosed by a wrought-iron fence and a history of famous tenants, including former U.S. secretary of state John Kerry. ⊠ *Between Mt. Vernon and Pickney Sts., Beacon Hill* Ⓜ *Charles/MGH, Park.*

Massachusetts State House

GOVERNMENT BUILDING | FAMILY | On July 4, 1795, the surviving fathers of the Revolution were on hand to enshrine the ideals of their new Commonwealth in a graceful seat of government designed by Charles Bulfinch. Governor Samuel Adams and Paul Revere laid the cornerstone; Revere would later roll the copper sheathing for the dome. Inside the building, visitors can check out Doric Hall, with its statuary and portraits; the Hall of Flags, where an exhibit shows the battle flags from all the wars in which Massachusetts regiments have participated; the Great Hall, an open space used for state functions that houses 351 flags from the cities and towns of Massachusetts; the governor's office; and the chambers of the House and Senate. Free guided tours are available; call for reservations. ∎**TIP➜ This is Freedom Trail stop 2.** ⊠ *24 Beacon St., Beacon Hill* ☎ *617/727–3676* ∰ *www.sec.state. ma.us/trs/trsidx.htm* ☉ *Closed weekends* Ⓜ *Park.*

Mt. Vernon Street

STREET | Mt. Vernon Street runs from the flat of the Hill, past Louisburg Square, and all the way up to the Massachusetts State House. Along with Chestnut Street, it has some of Beacon Hill's most distinguished addresses, but Mt. Vernon is the grander of the two, with houses set back farther and rising taller. Henry James once wrote that Mt. Vernon Street was "the only respectable street in America," and he must have known, as he lived with his brother William at No. 131 in the 1860s. James was just one of many literary luminaries who resided here, including Julia Ward Howe, who composed "The Battle Hymn of the Republic" and lived at No. 32, and the

poet Robert Frost, who lived at No. 88. ⊠ *Mt. Vernon St., Beacon Hill* Ⓜ *Park.*

Museum of African American History

HISTORY MUSEUM | FAMILY | The Museum of African American History was established in 1964 to recognize Boston's African American community, from slavery through the abolitionist movement. The Abiel Smith School, the first public school in the nation built specifically for Black children, now serves as the museum's main building, filled with exhibits. Just around the corner, the African Meeting House was built in 1806 entirely by Black labor; in 1832, William Lloyd Garrison formed the New England Anti-Slavery Society here, and in 2011 the building completed a $9.5 million restoration. ⊠ *46 Joy St., Beacon Hill* ☎ *617/725– 0022* ∰ *maah.org* ⬟ *$10* ☉ *Closed to walk-in visitors.* ⬟ *Must reserve a ticket online to visit.* Ⓜ *Park.*

Nichols House Museum

HISTORIC HOME | The only Mt. Vernon Street home open to the public, the Nichols House was built in 1804 and is attributed to Charles Bulfinch. It became the lifelong home of Rose Standish Nichols (1872–1960), Beacon Hill eccentric, philanthropist, peace advocate, and one of the first female landscape designers. Nichols inherited the Victorian furnishings, but she added a number of Colonial-style pieces to the mix, and the result is a delightful mélange of styles. To see the house, you must take a guided tour. ⊠ *55 Mt. Vernon St., Beacon Hill* ☎ *617/227–6993* ∰ *www.nicholshouse- museum.org* ⬟ *$12* ☉ *Closed Sun.–Wed.* Ⓜ *Park.*

Park Street Church

HISTORIC SIGHT | If this Congregationalist church at the corner of Tremont and Park Streets could sing, you'd hear Samuel Smith's iconic hymn "America," which was first sung here in 1831. But that's only one fun fact about this historic site. It was designed by Peter Banner and erected in 1810. The Handel & Haydn

The Black Heritage Trail

Until the end of the 19th century, a vibrant, free, Black community—more than 8,000 at its peak—settled on the north slope of Beacon Hill. Here, Black-owned businesses lined the streets, and the community built houses, schools, and churches that stand to this day. For example, you can visit the African Meeting House, once called the Black Faneuil Hall, where orators rallied against slavery. Visitors can rediscover this 19th-century legacy on the Black Heritage Trail.

Established in the late 1960s, the self-guiding trail stitches together 14 sites along a 1½-mile walk. To tour on your own, pick up brochures from the **Museum of African American History** (✉ 46 Joy St.) or download one online at ⊕ www.maah.org. National Park rangers give guided tours Wed.– Sun. Memorial Day through Columbus Day (⊕ www.nps.gov/boaf/planyour-visit/hours.htm).

Start at the stirring **Robert Gould Shaw 54th Regiment Memorial** in Boston Common. Shaw, a young white officer from a prominent Boston abolitionist family, led the first Black regiment to be recruited in the North during the Civil War. From here, walk up Joy Street to 5–7 Pinckney Street to see the 1797 **George Middleton House**, Beacon Hill's oldest existing home built by Black Americans. Nearby, the **Phillips School** at Anderson and Pinckney Streets was one of Boston's first integrated schools. The **John J. Smith House**, at 86 Pinckney, was a rendezvous point for abolitionists and escaping enslaved people, and the **Charles Street Meeting House**, at Mt. Vernon and Charles Streets,

was once a Baptist church and later a community center. In 1876 the building became the site of the **African Methodist Episcopal Church**, which was the last Black institution to leave Beacon Hill, in 1939. The **Lewis and Harriet Hayden House** at 66 Phillips Street, the home of freed enslaved people turned abolitionists, was a stop on the Underground Railroad. Harriet Beecher Stowe, author of *Uncle Tom's Cabin*, visited here in 1853 for her first glimpse of fugitive enslaved people. The Haydens reportedly kept a barrel of gunpowder under the front step, saying they'd blow up the house before they'd surrender a single person. At **2 Phillips Street**, John Coburn, cofounder of a Black military company, ran a gaming house, described as a "private place for gentlemen."

The five residences on **Smith Court** are typical of African American Bostonian homes of the 1800s, including No. 3, the 1799 clapboard house where William C. Nell, America's first published Black historian and a crusader for school integration, boarded from 1851 to 1865. At the corner of Joy Street and Smith Court is the **Abiel Smith School**, the city's first public school for Black children. The school's exhibits interpret the ongoing struggle started in the 1830s for equal school rights. Next door is the venerable **African Meeting House**, which was the community's center of social, educational, and political activity. The ground level houses a gallery; in the airy upstairs, you can imagine the fiery sermons that once rattled the upper pews.

Society was founded here in 1815. William Lloyd Garrison began his long public campaign for the abolition of slavery here in 1829. Just outside the church is Brimstone Corner, and whether the name refers to the fervent thunder of the church's preachers, the gunpowder that was once stored in the church's crypt, or the burning sulfur that preachers once scattered on the pavement to attract potential churchgoers, we'll never know—historians simply can't agree. This Freedom Trail site is not open for tours, only services. ■ TIP→ **This is Freedom Trail stop 3.** ⊠ *1 Park St., Beacon Hill* ☎ *617/523–3383* ⊕ *www.parkstreet. org* ⊘ *Closed as a historic site. Open for services.* Ⓜ *Park.*

Park Street Station

TRAIN/TRAIN STATION | FAMILY | One of the first four stops on the first subway in America, Park Street Station opened for service in 1897, against the warnings of those convinced it would make buildings along Tremont Street collapse. The copper-roof kiosks are National Historic Landmarks—outside them cluster vendors, street musicians, and partisans of causes and beliefs ranging from Irish nationalism to Krishna Consciousness. The station is the heart of Boston's subway system; "inbound" trains are always traveling toward Park Street. ⊠ *Park St. at Tremont St., Beacon Hill* ⊕ *www.mbta. com* Ⓜ *Park.*

William Hickling Prescott House

HISTORIC HOME | Now a modest but engaging house museum, this 1808 Federal-style structure was designed by Asher Benjamin. From 1845 to 1859, it was the home of noted historian William Hickling Prescott, and today it's the headquarters for the National Society of the Colonial Dames of America in the Commonwealth of Massachusetts. Guided tours venture through rooms furnished with period furniture, including Prescott's former study with his desk and "noctograph," which helped the nearly blind scholar write. Fun fact: Prescott's secret staircase allowed him to escape into his study when bored by guests in the parlor. ⊠ *55 Beacon St., Beacon Hill* ☎ *617/742–3190* ⊕ *nscda. org* ⊠ *$10* ⊘ *Closed Oct.–May for guided tours, unless by appointment.* Ⓜ *Park, Arlington.*

🍴 Restaurants

Eminently walkable, this is one of Boston's smallest and most historic neighborhoods, filled with brick sidewalks, shimmering gas lamps, and 19th-century row houses. On the food front you'll find an appealing blend of fancy and casual restaurants, as well as cafés, along the main pedestrian path of Charles Street. There are also a few standouts near the State House. In general, expect somewhat higher prices in Beacon Hill than you will find elsewhere in Boston.

Harvard Gardens

$ | AMERICAN | A Beacon Hill legend, this was the first bar in the city to get its liquor license after the repeal of Prohibition. It opened in 1930, and was owned by the same family until the 1990s. **Known for:** a Reuben sandwich stuffed with corned beef that's made in-house; casual, comfortable vibe that's a little bit different from a typical Beacon Hill experience; a killer, house-made Bloody Mary mixed with the bar's own peppercorn vodka. ⑤ *Average main: $17* ⊠ *316 Cambridge St., Beacon Hill* ☎ *617/523–2727* ⊕ *www. harvardgardens.com* Ⓜ *Charles/MGH.*

Mooo....

$$$$ | STEAKHOUSE | Do dress nicely for a visit to Mooo...., a luxurious, refined steak house inside the swanky XV Beacon hotel that remains civilized despite the restaurant's somewhat whimsical name. Prime, dry-aged steaks are served à la carte, and, although the Japanese A5 Wagyu sirloin will set you back $190, portions are as exaggerated as the prices. **Known for:** delightful, attentive service; hefty prices; unbelievably delicious steaks served in a dining room with "cow" art. ⑤ *Average main: $75* ✉ *XV Beacon Hotel, 15 Beacon St., Beacon Hill* ☎ *617/670–2515* ⊕ *www.mooorestaurant.com* Ⓜ *Park.*

1928 Beacon Hill

$$$$ | AMERICAN | Just off bustling Charles Street, this cozy neighborhood gem is filled to the brim with New England charm in the form of antique-chic decor that celebrates Boston's history. The menu of elevated American classics, from wedge salad to lobster rolls and filet mignon, is well curated, and the cocktails shine. **Known for:** collection of bourbon and whiskey; oysters and lobster; brunch and after-work drink scene. ⑤ *Average main: $36* ✉ *97 Mt. Vernon St., Beacon Hill* ☎ *857/233–5662* ⊕ *www.1928beaconhill.com* Ⓜ *Charles/MGH.*

★ No. 9 Park

$$$$ | EUROPEAN | Welcome to the first and now flagship restaurant in acclaimed chef Barbara Lynch's empire. Even after 25 years, No. 9 Park continues to win rave reviews for Lynch's stellar, unique interpretation of fine French and Italian cuisine. **Known for:** polished service; Lynch's memorably rich, prune-stuffed gnocchi; a chef's six-course, wine-paired tasting menu. ⑤ *Average main: $48* ✉ *9 Park St., Beacon Hill* ☎ *617/742–9991* ⊕ *www.no9park.com* Ⓜ *Park.*

Peregrine

$$$ | MEDITERRANEAN | Owner and chef Josh Lewin serves up a sophisticated take on rustic, coastal Mediterranean food, and diners are meant to rest, order slowly, and enjoy a meal in multiple stages. Everything is made from scratch in the kitchen, and although the preparations are Italian-based, there's a nod to New England ingredients and seasonality. **Known for:** curated wine selection from small vineyards; all-day dining; signature family-style Sunday suppers. ⑤ *Average main: $35* ✉ *The Whitney Hotel, 170 Charles St., Beacon Hill* ☎ *617/826–1762* ⊕ *www.peregrineboston.com* Ⓜ *Charles/MGH.*

The Tip Tap Room

$$ | AMERICAN | FAMILY | Befitting its name, chef Brian Poe's casual Beacon Hill restaurant focuses on two main things: meat and interesting beers on tap. But, Poe's menu of meat goes beyond steak and chicken staples, and depending on the season and what's readily available from purveyors, dinner entrées may feature bison, camel, ostrich, emu, kangaroo, snake, yak, elk, or antelope. **Known for:** exotic meat specials, like kangaroo and ostrich; amazing local beer menu; a half-dozen-plus styles of meat tips, from steak to swordfish, and even tofu. ⑤ *Average main: $24* ✉ *138 Cambridge St., Beacon Hill* ☎ *857/350–3344* ⊕ *www.thetiptaproom.com* Ⓜ *Bowdoin, Charles/MGH.*

☕ Coffee and Quick Bites

Anna's Taqueria

$ | MEXICAN | FAMILY | Inspired by the authentic Mexican takeout readily available in West Coast cities, Anna's owner moved to Boston and opened shop more than 25 years ago. This small, local chain has been a hit ever since for its burritos, tacos, and quesadillas. **Known for:** fat, flavorful burritos; bringing the heat with really spicy sauces you can add on; tacos al pastor—marinated, rotisserie cooked pork with pineapples and onions. ⑤ *Average main: $8* ✉ *242 Cambridge St., Beacon Hill* ☎ *617/227–8822* ⊕ *www.annastaqueria.com* Ⓜ *Charles/MGH.*

★ The Paramount

$ | AMERICAN | FAMILY | Don't be surprised to see a queue at this neighborhood hot spot, no matter the time of day. Regulars happily line up for waffles topped with fresh fruit, caramel and banana french toast, huge salads, and hefty sandwiches, all made to order as you do from the counter. **Known for:** decadent, all-day breakfast items; Old Bay–seasoned home fries; long, but quick-moving, lines. ⑤ *Average main: $12* ✉ *44 Charles St.,*

Beacon Hill ☎ *617/720–1152* ⊕ *www.
paramountboston.com* Ⓜ *Charles/MGH.*

Savenor's Market

$ | **SANDWICHES** | In need of snacks for a
cocktail party or something for the grill,
Beacon Hill residents pop over to this
market famous for being Julia Child's
favorite butcher and known for procur-
ing exotic game meats. Tamer choices
include sandwiches, prepared salads,
outstanding cheeses, breads, tinned fish,
hummus, dips and more—this place is
a foodie's nirvana. **Known for:** delicious
sandwiches to-go; exotic meat and game
selections at its butcher counter; supply-
ing established and emerging chefs with
inspiration. Ⓢ *Average main: $10* ✉ *160
Charles St., Beacon Hill* ☎ *617/723–6328*
⊕ *www.savenorsmarket.com* 🕑 *Closed
Sun.* Ⓜ *Charles/MGH.*

The Sevens Ale House

$ | **AMERICAN** | This classic dive bar has
been serving beer and wine (no liquor)
since 1933. Today, it's pleasantly untrendy
and an easygoing alternative to Beacon
Hill's tony stuffiness, with its battered
dark wood bar and booths, simple
setup, dartboard, perfectly poured pints,
and great pub food. **Known for:** a tasty
French dip; a no-frills environment; great
selection of small producer craft beers in
addition to the usual suspects. Ⓢ *Average main: $11* ✉ *77 Charles St., Beacon
Hill* ☎ *617/523–9074* Ⓜ *Charles/MGH.*

★ Tatte Bakery & Café

$ | **ISRAELI** | This upscale bakery and café
with several locations in Boston takes
pastries to the next level. From tea cakes
to the Jerusalem bagel, expect hearty
baked goods with an air of elegance and
influenced by the owner's Israeli heritage. **Known for:** signature nut tarts that
are as pretty as they are tasty; convivial
atmosphere; traditional North African
shakshuka. Ⓢ *Average main: $12* ✉ *70
Charles St., Beacon Hill* ☎ *617/723–5555*
⊕ *www.tattebakery.com* Ⓜ *Charles/MGH.*

The Upper Crust Pizzeria

$$ | **PIZZA** | Walk into the Upper Crust's
first location, and you'll see the staff
pulling scratch-made dough in the open
kitchen. The Neapolitan-style pizza—you
can order by the slice (they're huge) or
by the pie—is really tasty, and toppings
go creatively beyond a classic cheese or
pepperoni. **Known for:** creative topping
combinations; limited seating options;
deliciously thin, Neapolitan-style pizza
crust. Ⓢ *Average main: $20* ✉ *20 Charles
St., Beacon Hill* ☎ *617/723–9600* ⊕ *www.
theuppercrustpizzeria.com* Ⓜ *Charles/
MGH.*

🛏 Hotels

If you want calm, serenity, and class,
then stay on Beacon Hill, one of the
poshest neighborhoods in Boston. Its
streets are lined with elegant brick
buildings holding unique shops and
restaurants, within close proximity to
many other neighborhoods, including the
Back Bay, Downtown, and Government
Center.

★ The Whitney Hotel Boston

$$$$ | **HOTEL** | This luxury boutique hotel
fits right in with its Beacon Hill surroundings, views of which you can enjoy
while you relax in-room in a plush Frette
bathrobe with a cup of Nespresso coffee.
Pros: excellent location within walking
distance of the Back Bay, the West End,
and Downtown; excellent restaurant
on-site, Peregrine; complimentary bicycles. **Cons:** high noise levels from traffic
in Storrow Drive–facing rooms; long wait
for the valet; high valet fee. Ⓢ *Rooms
from: $600* ✉ *170 Charles St., Beacon
Hill* ☎ *617/367–1866* ⊕ *www.whitneyho-
telboston.com* ⇆ *65 rooms* 🍽 *No Meals*
Ⓜ *Charles/MGH.*

★ XV Beacon

$$$$ | **HOTEL** | The 1903 Beau-Arts exterior
of this intimate, luxury boutique hotel is
a study in sophistication and elegance.
Pros: rooftop deck with amazing city

views; complimentary Lexus car service; dogs of any size welcome for no fee. **Cons:** can be expensive on weekends during peak months; no view from classic rooms; some rooms are small. $ *Rooms from: $900* ✉ *15 Beacon St., Beacon Hill* ☎ *617/670–1500* ⊕ *www.xvbeacon.com* ⌁ *63 rooms* ⦿ *No Meals* Ⓜ *Park.*

♈ Nightlife

There are no dance clubs in this leafy, patrician enclave. In fact, nightlife options are scarce, but not altogether missing, and most live up by the State House.

BARS

Carrie Nation

BARS | Right around the corner from the Massachusetts State House, this bar channels speakeasy vibes with jazzy tunes, tasty food, and fantastic cocktails. On Sunday, check out the buffet brunch and drag show; you'll need to reserve a ticket. ✉ *11 Beacon St., Beacon Hill* ☎ *617/227–3100* ⊕ *www.carrienation-cocktailclub.com* Ⓜ *Park Street.*

Cheers

BARS | This pub—dismantled in England, shipped to Boston, and reassembled—formerly known as The Bull & Finch, later became the inspiration for the now-classic TV series *Cheers.* Enjoy a burger at the model bar of the Hollywood set and imagine Sam and Diane walking in the door and calling your name. The crowd tends to be heavily tourists, so locals stay away. No children after 10 pm. ✉ *84 Beacon St., Beacon Hill* ☎ *617/227–9605* ⊕ *www.cheersboston.com* Ⓜ *Park, Arlington.*

Roxanne's

BARS | With a wall lined in tropical wallpaper and a neon purple sign, this cocktail bar offers a rare nightlife outpost in the Beacon Hill neighborhood, and a trendy one at that. On the menu, the ingredients that make up the drink offerings are just as creative as their names and include such things as butterfly pea

flower–infused gin and Aztec chocolate bitters. This place is popular, so reservations are strongly recommended. ✉ *6B Beacon St., Beacon Hill* ☎ *857/338–1113* ⊕ *www.roxannesboston.com* Ⓜ *Park Street.*

The 21st Amendment

BARS | Named for the amendment that ended Prohibition, this longstanding convivial pub, right across the street from the State House, draws legislators, lobbyists, and neighborhood regulars who trade gossip and insider info over notched wooden tables and beers. The food is surprisingly good. ✉ *150 Bowdoin St., Beacon Hill* ☎ *617/227–7100* ⊕ *www.21stboston.com* Ⓜ *Park.*

⬤ Shopping

Most of the commerce that happens in Beacon Hill today happens on its main thoroughfare, Charles Street. Until recently, Charles Street was a premier destination for antiques shopping, but over the last few decades, posh, independently owned gift, jewelry, and women's clothing boutiques have moved in and taken over the expensive commercial real estate of this upper class neighborhood.

ANTIQUES

Boston Antiques and Lamp Shades

ANTIQUES & COLLECTIBLES | This flea market–style collection of dealers has been in business since 1981. The shop focuses on lamp shades (as its name indicates), plus vintage items, china, silver, home decor pieces, pillows, and jewelry. ✉ *119 Charles St., Beacon Hill* ☎ *617/367–9000* ⊕ *www.bostonantiquesandlampshades. com* Ⓜ *Charles/MGH.*

Upstairs Downstairs Home

ANTIQUES & COLLECTIBLES | This Beacon Hill standout features furniture and home decor in a variety of styles. While much of it is antiques or vintage pieces from Federal and Asian to art deco and mid-century modern, some items are new and/or reproduction pieces. Artwork by local artists and antique prints rounds out the selection. ✉ *69 Charles St, Beacon Hill* ☎ *617/367-1950* ⊕ *www.upstairs-downstairsboston.com* Ⓜ *Charles/MGH.*

CLOTHING
Crush Boutique
WOMEN'S CLOTHING | Find weekend casual outfits, jeans, silky shifts, and even party attire at this feminine boutique. Accessories are not overlooked, as Crush offers jewelry and handbags that will dress up any ensemble. ✉ *138 Charles St., Beacon Hill* ☎ *617/720-0010* ⊕ *www.shopcrushboutique.com* Ⓜ *Charles/MGH.*

December Thieves
WOMEN'S CLOTHING | The edgiest clothing boutique on the Hill, December Thieves stocks fashion-forward, contemporary, emerging designers and brands from Europe, Asia, Latin America, and other places across the globe. Find a curated and wildly fun array of apparel, scarves, handbags, jewelry, beauty products, and home decor. ✉ *51 Charles St., Beacon Hill* ☎ *857/239-9149* ⊕ *decemberthieves.com* Ⓜ *Charles/MGH.*

Dress
WOMEN'S CLOTHING | True to its name, this locally owned specialty store curates designer party dresses, but the selection doesn't end there. Women will also find tops and pants, shoes, accessories, handbags, and even a few home goods items. ✉ *70 Charles St., Beacon Hill* ☎ *617/248-9910* ⊕ *www.dressboston.com* Ⓜ *Charles/MGH.*

East Coast Ivy
WOMEN'S CLOTHING | This ultra-tiny space makes on-trend clothing at a mid-range price point its business. From tops and dresses to swimwear, these are apparel items designed for going out of the house. ✉ *88 Charles St., Beacon Hill* ☎ *717/364-6842* ⊕ *east-coast-ivy.myshopify.com* Ⓜ *Charles/MGH.*

French + Italian
WOMEN'S CLOTHING | Exquisite European fabric and design comes to this upscale neighborhood boutique that spotlights emerging designers from Paris, Milan, and New York. Pieces can be expensive, but they're meant to be versatile wardrobe staples. ✉ *119 Charles St., Beacon Hill* ☎ *857/990-3141* ⊕ *www.frenchitalian.com* Ⓜ *Charles/MGH.*

Helen's Leather
SHOES | Channel your inner Western spirit at this family-owned shop specializing in cowboy wear, including hand-tooled boots embroidered, dyed, and crafted from leather and exotic skins. Browse leather sandals, jackets, briefcases, luggage, and other accessories from top quality brands, including Lucchese, Dan Post, Frye, and Old Gringo. ✉ *110 Charles St., Beacon Hill* ☎ *617/742-2077* ⊕ *www.helensleather.com* Ⓜ *Charles/MGH.*

Whitney + Winston
MIXED CLOTHING | This too cute—and a bit bohemian—mom and kid clothing store features looks from fairly expensive, small brands, and there's no question as to its place in Beacon Hill society. This is where the neighborhood women come to buy frocks that aren't made to be worn to the office. There's also a nice selection of toys and kid gift items, including stuffed animals and sensory jars. ✉ *113 Charles St., Beacon Hill* ☎ *617/720-2600* ⊕ *shopcrushboutique.com/collections/whitney-winston* Ⓜ *Charles / MGH.*

GIFTS
★ Beacon Hill Chocolates
CANDY | Let this store's aroma entice you to enter before it wows you with stunning display cases lined with local and European artisan chocolates that you can buy by the piece. You can also shop a vast array of gourmet chocolate bars, some bagged candy, and a few flavors of gelato. Yum! ✉ *91 Charles St., Beacon Hill* ☎ *617/725-1900* ⊕ *beaconhillchocolates.com* Ⓜ *Charles/MGH.*

Blackstones

SOUVENIRS | If you've shopped Charles Street in the last 45 years, you'll recognize this long-standing shop, now in a much larger location. Many of the gifts, books, and greeting cards on display are made in the United States and locally focused. The back room boasts an awesome selection of spices, Swedish dish cloths, and small kitchen utensils. ⊠ *40 Charles St., Beacon Hill* ☎ *617/227–4646* ⊕ *www.blackstonesbeaconhill.com* Ⓜ *Charles/MGH.*

Flat of the Hill

SOUVENIRS | Look for the lifelike golden retriever that guards the entrance to this shop named for its location at the base— or, flat—of Beacon Hill. The semi-preppy selection includes loads of candles, unique jewelry, hand-woven totes from Mexico, and a well-curated range of fancy souvenirs like Boston University winter hats and embroidered canvas Massachusetts travel bags. ⊠ *60 Charles St., Beacon Hill* ☎ *617/619–9977* ⊕ *www.flatofthehill.com* Ⓜ *Charles/MGH.*

★ Gus & Ruby

STATIONERY | Sure, we love our technology, but we still also really love paper products and that's the majority of what this cool gift store stocks. First, explore the entire section devoted to wares by Rifle Paper Co., and then pick up something for the cherished infant in your life from the edited selection of precious and expensive baby clothing. There are also artful gift items focused on the cities of Boston and Portland, Maine. ⊠ *99 Charles St., Beacon Hill* ☎ *617/651–5151* ⊕ *gusandruby.com* Ⓜ *Charles/MGH.*

The Happy Journey

TOYS | Need a unique gift for a tot under the age of three years old? This small store stocks books and toys you definitely won't find at big chain stores. If you've got kids with you, there's a nice back room where they can play while you shop. ⊠ *73 Charles St., Beacon Hill* ☎ *617/936–3917* Ⓜ *Charles/MGH.*

Paws on Charles

PET STORES | If there is one constant in Beacon Hill, it's the number of dogs that live with residents of the neighborhood and are always walking along Charles Street or in the Common. This makes it only more fitting that there's a pet shop nearby, filled with dog food and treats, leashes, collars, and chew toys. Want to dress up the pooch? This place has you covered. ⊠ *123 Charles St., Beacon Hill* ☎ *617/936–4163* ⊕ *www.pawsoncharles.com* Ⓜ *Charles/MGH.*

Rugg Road Paper Company

STATIONERY | This longtime Charles Street destination attracts patrons who like to put pen to paper. Elegant greeting cards from Crane and The British Museum pair up with notebooks from Moleskin, and a healthy selection of pens. ⊠ *105 Charles St., Beacon Hill* ☎ *617/742–0002* ⊕ *www.ruggroadpaper.com* Ⓜ *Charles/MGH.*

JEWELRY

Persona Jewelry

JEWELRY & WATCHES | Using precious metals and a variety of gemstones, Gary Shteyman crafts gorgeous, unique pieces from his in-store workshop for Persona's own line of fine jewelry. Elsewhere in the store, necklaces, earrings, bangles, and bold cocktail rings by a few local designers fill the cases. ⊠ *62 Charles St., Beacon Hill* ☎ *617/266–3003* ⊕ *www.personastyle.com* Ⓜ *Charles/MGH.*

BEAUTY

Follain

COSMETICS | If you're focused on eco-friendly choices as much as you are personal beauty, stop into this boutique that got its start right here in Boston. Follain carries all manner of skin care, face and hand wash, makeup, and more by clean beauty brands both local and national. Not sure what's right for you? Try it out—there's even an in-store sink to wash off what you don't like. ⊠ *65 Charles St., Beacon Hill* ☎ *857/233–5211* ⊕ *follain.com* Ⓜ *Charles/MGH.*

Overlooking the Charles River, the Museum of Science—sitting half in Cambridge and half in Boston—focuses on science, technology, and hands-on learning.

The West End

One of Boston's less-traveled neighborhoods, the West End features primarily recent construction—the brick tenements housing myriad ethnic groups and the tangled web of streets of the old West End were razed in the 1960s in the name of urban renewal. A few structures survived, namely Massachusetts General Hospital and the former Suffolk County Jail, which now houses The Liberty, a luxury hotel.

Today, the West End remains largely residential, except for Causeway Street and its offshoots. This is where the TD Garden holds court, hosting Bruins and Celtics games. In recent years, a number of hotels and restaurants have moved in.

Where the Charles River separates the West End in Boston from the city of Cambridge, the Museum of Science puts a cool spin on technology, earth sciences, and more. And, on the skyline one can spy the Leonard P. Zakim Bunker Hill Memorial Bridge, a majestic and modern piece of transportation architecture.

◉ Sights

The Ether Dome at Mass General Hospital

HISTORIC SIGHT | FAMILY | Tiny, but well worth the 15 minutes you'll spend here if you're already in the neighborhood, this operating theater is open to the public because of its historical significance. In fact, it served as Mass General Hospital's first operating room, in use from 1821 to 1867, and it was here where the world witnessed the first public demonstration of surgical anesthesia, in 1846. Today, the room contains two 19th-century operating chairs complete with red velvet to mask patients' blood, a teaching skeleton, and, interestingly, an authentic Egyptian mummy. ⊠ *Mass General's Bulfinch Bldg., 55 Fruit St., West End* ✛ *Enter historic gray Bulfinch Bldg. at its main door, Ether Dome is on 4th floor* ☎ *617/724–8009* ⊕ *www.massgeneral.org/museum/*

exhibits/ether-dome ⏱ *Closed Sat.–Sun.* Ⓜ *Charles/MGH.*

Leonard P. Zakim Bunker Hill Memorial Bridge

BRIDGE | Dedicated in 2002, the Zakim Bridge is the crown jewel of Boston's legendary Big Dig construction project. The Zakim rings in at 1,432 feet, is one of the widest cable-stayed hybrid bridges ever built, and is the first to use an asymmetrical design. At night, the illuminated bridge glows different colors. ✉ *Old West End.*

★ Museum of Science

SCIENCE MUSEUM | **FAMILY** | From its perch above the Charles River, the Museum of Science sits half in Cambridge and half in Boston. This unique trait is the first of many at this 70-plus-year-old institution that's focused on science, technology, and hands-on learning. Diverse permanent exhibits explore dinosaurs, the electromagnetic spectrum, modern conservation, math, motion, nanotechnology, the natural world, space travel, and more. The Theater of Electricity hosts explosive daily lightening shows. Add-ons to admission include: the multisensory 4-D Theater, the Charles Hayden Planetarium, and the newly renovated Mugar Omni Theater with IMAX programming. ✉ *Science Park, 1 Museum of Science Driveway, Old West End* ☏ *617/723–2500* ⊕ *www.mos.org* 🎟 *$29* ♿ *Timed tickets required; reserve in advance.* Ⓜ *Science Park.*

Otis House

HISTORIC HOME | The stately Federal-style manor on Cambridge Street was designed by Charles Bulfinch for former Boston mayor and lawyer Harrison Gray Otis. Today, the National Historic Landmark serves as the headquarters for the heritage organization Historic New England, and visitors can stop in for guided tours that offer insight into wealthy domestic life during the early 1800s. ✉ *141 Cambridge St., Old West End* ☏ *617/994–5920* ⊕ *www.*

> ## Duck Boats ◉
>
> Have you noticed the unusual looking, boat-like vehicles touring around Boston's streets? While carrying more than half a million people every year, these **Boston Duck Tours** (☏ 617/267–3825) are amphibious journeys that venture into the Greenway and the Back Bay, Downtown, and the West End, to explore the city's many points of interest before coasting into the Charles River. You might even get to captain for awhile; 80-minute tours (🎟 $49) depart from the Prudential Center, the Museum of Science, and, seasonally, the New England Aquarium.

historicnewengland.org/property/otis-house 🎟 *$15* ⏱ *Closed Mon.–Thurs.* Ⓜ *Charles/MGH, Bowdoin.*

Paul S. Russell, MD Museum of Medical History and Innovation

SCIENCE MUSEUM | The campus of Mass General Hospital is a fitting site for this small museum dedicated to the hallowed medical institution's past, present, and future discoveries. Shiny copper and glass walls enfold interesting exhibits on topics like patient care, fMRI development, depression and dementia, and targeted cancer therapy. Interactive displays ask visitors to try out mirror therapy and train for laproscopic surgery like a doctor would. Historical artifacts—some quite terrifying—are peppered around the space for an eye-opening lesson in our forefathers' medical techniques. A few temporary exhibits and films rotate in and out. ✉ *2 N. Grove St., Old West End* ☏ *617/724–8009* ⊕ *www.massgeneral. org/museum* ⏱ *Closed Sun.* Ⓜ *Charles/ MGH.*

The West End

KEY

- ① Sights
- ① Restaurants
- ① Quick Bites
- ① Hotels
- Ⓣ Subway station
- ‒ ‒ ‒ Black Heritage Trail

The Sports Museum

SPORTS VENUE | FAMILY | The fifth and sixth levels of the TD Garden house The Sports Museum, where displays of memorabilia and photographs showcase New England–based amateur and pro sports history and legends. Test your sports knowledge with interactive games, see how you stand up to life-size statues of heroes Carl Yastrzemski and Larry Bird, and take an hour-long tour of the museum. ⊠ *100 Legends Way, West End* ⊹ *Use TD Garden's The Hub on Causeway grand entrance for access* ☎ *617/212–6814* ⊕ *www.sportsmuseum. org* ✉ *$20* ⊘ *Closed during games and TD Garden events; check up-to-date calendar on website.* Ⓜ *North Station.*

TD Garden

SPORTS VENUE | FAMILY | This mammoth, modern facility opened in 1995 to the chagrin of diehard local sports fans who occasionally still grieve the crusty, old Boston Garden. Today, the home arena of the Boston Celtics (basketball) and Boston Bruins (hockey) seats nearly 20,000 patrons and also hosts headlining musical acts, Disney on Ice, wrestling events, and Boston's famed Beanpot tourney. ⊠ *100 Legends Way, Old West End* ⊹ *Use The Hub on Causeway grand entrance for access to TD Garden* ☎ *617/624–1000* ⊕ *www.tdgarden.com* ⊘ *Closed during ticketed events* Ⓜ *North Station.*

🍴 Restaurants

A&B Kitchen & Bar

$ | AMERICAN | FAMILY | Sourcing ingredients from small, family farms is the main goal of this local, casual restaurant where hungry diners clamor for salads, burgers, and a few entrées. With its proximity to the TD Garden, it can and does get busy on game days, and service tends to slow down. **Known for:** hot spot before Bruins and Celtics games; delicious burgers;

nice patio in fair weather. Ⓢ *Average main: $15* ⊠ *115 Beverly St., Old West End* ☎ *857/449–2251* ⊕ *www.anbkitchen. com* ⊘ *Closed Mon.* Ⓜ *North Station.*

Alcove

$$$ | CONTEMPORARY | A mix of New England seafood dishes, European-style charcuterie, and an international flair to most everything else describes what you'll see on the menu at this West End restaurant with a view; you're meant to share plates with your guests, but you can also order solo if that's your preference. Meals here are comfortable, with coastal vibes and spectacular views of the Zakim Bridge. **Known for:** fantastic, small-producer wine program, with hands-on customer approach; fantastic views; tasty weekend brunch. Ⓢ *Average main: $28* ⊠ *50 Lovejoy Wharf, West End* ☎ *617/248–0050* ⊕ *www.alcoveboston. com* Ⓜ *North Station.*

Momosan Ramen Boston by Morimoto

$$ | JAPANESE FUSION | Iron Chef Masaharu Morimoto brings his signature Japanese fusion to this casual ramen spot next door to the TD Garden. Of course, ramen (six styles, and a dozen toppings) is only one portion of the menu, which also features sushi, small plates, and grilled fish, meat, and seafood. **Known for:** A5 Waygu steak seared tableside; extra busy during TD Garden events; extensive sake menu. Ⓢ *Average main: $20* ⊠ *80 Causeway St., Old West End* ☎ *617/263–8800* ⊕ *www. hubhallboston.com* Ⓜ *North Station.*

★ Scampo

$$$$ | ITALIAN | The Italian word "scampo" translates to "escape" in English, and that's what this restaurant at The Liberty hotel—the former site of the Charles Street Jail—is: an escape into chef-owner Lydia Shire's delectable, buttery take on Italian-American cuisine. Everything is made from scratch, down to the bread, and including a dozen different exceptional pastas and nearly as many crusty pizzas. **Known for:** tandoori-oven–cooked, crusty pizzas (the lamb is a classic) and breads; eclectic vibe; unique meal specials on the weekends. ⑤ *Average main: $41 ⊠ The Liberty Hotel, 215 Charles St., Old West End ☎ 617/536–2100 ⊕ www. scampoboston.com ⓜ Charles/MGH.*

☕ Coffee and Quick Bites

Hub Hall

$ | **INTERNATIONAL** | **FAMILY** | Situated in the TD Garden, this unique food hall serves up more than a dozen different food and drink options, many of which are little sister outposts for chefs and restaurants local to the Boston and New England area. Try barbecue at The Smoke Shop or Italian desserts at Mike's Pastry. **Known for:** packed during Celtics and Bruins games; lots of Boston favorites under one roof; quick service. ⑤ *Average main: $14 ⊠ 80 Causeway St., Old West End ☎ 617/263–8900 ⊕ www.hubhallboston. com ⓜ North Station.*

Night Shift Brewing Tap Room

$ | **AMERICAN** | More than just a tap room, this place satisfies a variety of different needs, although beer is at the forefront; there are more than two dozen beers on tap—as well as a couple hard seltzers and some nonalcoholic varieties. The lunch and dinner menu has items made from scratch like salads, sandwiches, flatbreads, and main dishes. **Known for:** roasts its own coffee beans; tasty food; brews its own beers. ⑤ *Average main: $17 ⊠ 1 Lovejoy Wharf, Old West End ☎ 617/294–4233 ⊕ www.nightshiftbrew- ing.com ⓜ North Station.*

Hotels

The Boxer Boston

$$$$ | **HOTEL** | This lovely boutique hotel in one of Boston's only flatiron buildings features a contemporary, "industrial chic" look. **Pros:** always free Wi-Fi;

Peloton machines in fitness center; close to popular areas. **Cons:** far from Back Bay shopping; area can be rowdy at night by the TD Garden; small rooms. ⑤ *Rooms from: $400 ⊠ 107 Merrimac St., Old West End ☎ 617/624–0202 ⊕ www. theboxerboston.com ⌁ 80 rooms ⦾ No Meals ⓜ North Station.*

citizenM Boston

$$$ | **HOTEL** | Boston's citizenM hotel is one of only a few of its kind in the United States; the brand keeps the jet-setting traveler in mind, but not necessarily one who is overly wealthy, just one who appreciates the finer things in life. **Pros:** bold, contemporary, and colorful aesthetic; attached to North Station; open kitchen filled with snacks and drinks, 24/7. **Cons:** strictly no more than two people per room; no pets; small rooms. ⑤ *Rooms from: $300 ⊠ 70 Causeway St., Old West End ☎ 617/861–4360 ⊕ www. citizenm.com ⌁ 272 rooms ⦾ No Meals ⓜ North Station.*

Courtyard by Marriott Downtown Boston/ North Station

$$$ | **HOTEL** | **FAMILY** | Guest rooms at this Marriott property are clean and comfortable, and the views are pretty good, too, from 14 stories up. **Pros:** free Wi-Fi; close to popular tourist destinations like Faneuil Hall; check-out time at 12 pm. **Cons:** no extra flourishes; far from Newbury Street shopping and universities; no pets allowed. ⑤ *Rooms from: $340 ⊠ 107 Beverly St., Old West End ☎ 617/725– 0003 ⊕ www.marriott.com ⌁ 220 rooms ⦾ No Meals ⓜ North Station.*

Hotel Indigo Boston Garden

$$$ | **HOTEL** | Fresh off a renovation, Hotel Indigo takes up a small plot in the West End with just under 100 hotel rooms. **Pros:** rooms have a cool design where the past meets the present; pets allowed for $75 per stay; proximity to TD Garden and popular tourist attractions like Faneuil Hall. **Cons:** small fitness center; can be loud because of TD Garden events; pricey per night parking. **$** *Rooms from: $300* ✉ *280 Friend St., Old West End* ☎ *617/720–5544* ⊕ *www.ihg.com* ⇆ *88 rooms* 🍽 *No Meals* Ⓜ *North Station.*

★ The Liberty

$$$$ | **HOTEL** | Few places in town can rival the soaring lobby—ringed by several layers of revamped metal catwalks—of the chic Liberty, formerly Boston's Charles Street Jail. **Pros:** Lydia Shire's popular restaurant Scampo; exclusive daily events, including art exhibits, live music, and yoga sessions; proximity to the Esplanade and Beacon Hill. **Cons:** very small fitness center; parking is expensive; loud in-house nightlife. **$** *Rooms from: $450* ✉ *215 Charles St., Old West End* ☎ *617/224–4000* ⊕ *www.liberty-hotel.com* ⇆ *298 rooms* 🍽 *No Meals* Ⓜ *Charles/MGH.*

Nightlife

Banners Kitchen & Tap

BARS | The name of this bar pays tribute to the championship banners for the Boston Bruins and Boston Celtics that are hanging next door from the ceiling of the TD Garden. This is a sports bar to the max, featuring beers, burgers, and other bar classics, plus the biggest indoor LED TV screen on the East Coast and the second-level Topgolf Swing Suite, which hosts a variety of sports simulation games. ✉ *82 Causeway St., Old West End* ☎ *617/263–8200* ⊕ *www.patina-group.com/banners* Ⓜ *North Station.*

Activities

SPORTS

Boston Bruins

SPORTS VENUE | **FAMILY** | In 1924, the Boston Bruins became the first U.S. ice hockey team to enter the NHL. The Bruins have been playing at the Garden since 1928 (although the original Boston Garden was rebuilt in 1995) and have won six Stanley Cup titles over that time. Spectators can see the championship banners hanging in the rafters above the ice and the stands, which are packed for every home game, despite high ticket prices. Fans are loud, vocal, and extremely loyal, so spectators with delicate personalities won't feel comfortable. Saturday afternoon games are a win for the family. Seasons run from October until April; playoffs last through early June. ✉ *TD Garden, 100 Legends Way, West End* ☎ *617/624–2327* ⊕ *www.nhl.com/bruins* Ⓜ *North Station.*

Boston Celtics

SPORTS VENUE | **FAMILY** | The Boston Celtics franchise is tied with the L.A. Lakers for the most championship titles in the NBA, with 17 banners, which is at least 10 more than any other team. So, what to expect at a Celtics game from today's squad? An all-around fun experience, a charged atmosphere and devotion, from the fans to the team and the team to the fans. You'll hear "Let's Go, Cel-tics" no matter the score. The season runs from late October to April, and playoffs last until mid-June. ✉ *TD Garden, 100 Legends Way, Old West End* ☎ *866/423–5849* ⊕ *www.nba.com/celtics* Ⓜ *North Station.*

GOVERNMENT CENTER AND THE NORTH END

4

Updated by
Cheryl Fenton

◉ Sights	🍴 Restaurants	🛏 Hotels	🛍 Shopping	🍸 Nightlife
★★★★☆	★★★★★	★★★☆☆	★★★★☆	★★★★★

NEIGHBORHOOD SNAPSHOT

TOP EXPERIENCES

■ **Shop the market:** Visit the countless shops and kiosks of Quincy Market, the country's oldest pushcart market.

■ **Take a history lesson:** Imagine the debates of old during a tour of historic Faneuil Hall, spot Old North Church, or dine across from Paul Revere's house.

■ **Smell the roses:** Stroll the Rose Kennedy Rose Garden, dedicated to the matriarch of the beloved local family.

■ **Grab a pint:** Raise a glass at pubs, including the Union Oyster House and the Sam Adams Boston Taproom.

■ **Come hungry, leave happy:** Visit the North End, Boston's Little Italy, for pasta and cannoli.

GETTING HERE

While Government Center is best explored on foot, nearby Green Line stops include Park Street and Haymarket. On the Blue Line, the nearest stations are State and Bowdoin. These stations are all within a five-minute walk of Government Center Station. The T is your best bet for accessing the North End. Get off the Orange Line at Haymarket and walk southeast to Hanover Street; take a left there to enter the North End. Alternatively, exit the Blue Line at Aquarium and walk northeast on Atlantic Avenue, past Christopher Columbus Park, to access the North End.

PLANNING YOUR TIME

Plan to spend several hours hitting the eateries, boutiques, and historic sites of the Faneuil Hall and Quincy Market complex. On Friday and Saturday, join crowds at the Haymarket farmers' market; wear good walking shoes, as the cobblestones get slippery with trampled produce.

Allow two hours for a walk through the North End, longer if you plan on stopping in a café. This part of town is made for strolling, day or night. Many people like to spend part of a day at Quincy Market, then head over to the North End for dinner.

QUICK BITES

■ **Mike's Pastry.** Expect crowds at this bustling North End café for cappuccino and worth-the-wait cannoli. ✉ *300 Hanover St., North End* ⊕ *www.mikespastry.com.*

■ **Quincy Market.** Filled with stalls of every imaginable food—lobster rolls to Indian to ice cream—grab your grub and enjoy it outside on the benches between the North and South Markets. ✉ *Bordered by Clinton, Commercial, and Chatham Sts, Government Center* ⊕ *www.quincy-market.com* Ⓣ *Government Center, Aquarium, State.*

■ **Saus.** Grab a beer-brined pork brat and choose from 15 homemade sauces to douse it with. ✉ *33 Union St.* ⊕ *www.sausboston.com* Ⓣ *Government Center, State.*

FREEDOM TRAIL SIGHTS

■ The Freedom Trail snakes through the city; within Government Center and the North End, you'll find the Boston Massacre Site, the Copp's Hill Burying Ground, Faneuil Hall, Old North Church, the Old State House, and the Paul Revere House.

Government Center is a section of town Bostonians love to hate. While it's not Boston's prettiest locale (it's home to some of the city's bleakest architecture), it does have plenty of feathers in its tricorn cap, including City Hall Plaza (the site of political rallies, summer concerts, and festivals), the country's oldest pushcart market (cobblestoned Quincy Market), and the site of many speeches encouraging independence from Great Britain (18th-century Faneuil Hall).

Just a short stroll across the Rose Kennedy Greenway sits the charming, crowded North End, Boston's proud Italian community and oldest neighborhood. It can be summed up in one word—*mangia*. This is where you find a good meal, along with a little city history, including Paul Revere's house.

Government Center

The seat of Boston's city hall and financial center, Government Center is, at least for tourists, usually just a way station to get to Faneuil Hall, Quincy Market, and other downtown attractions, unless there happens to be a festival or outdoor concert, which turns it into a bustling, jubilant spot.

The area overlooks those historic brick beehives of activity, the Old State House and Faneuil Hall, and the haunting, transparent New England Holocaust Memorial. The Rose F. Kennedy Greenway, a mile-long parkland built over the depressed central artery, links the North End (the warren of small streets on the northeast side of Government Center) to Chinatown with gardens and trees, and parallels the hotel-rich stretch of the Harborwalk.

The curving six-story Center Plaza building, across from the glass entrance of the Government Center T stop and City Hall Plaza, echoes the much older Sears Crescent, a curved commercial block next to the Government Center T stop. The Center Plaza building separates Tremont Street from Pemberton Square and the old and "new" courthouses to the west.

 Sights

Blackstone Block

PLAZA/SQUARE | Between North and Hanover Streets, near the Haymarket, lies the

Government Center

KEY
- ➊ Sights
- ➊ Restaurants
- ➊ Quick Bites
- ➊ Hotels
- Ⓣ Subway station
- --- Freedom Trail

0 — 400 ft
0 — 100 m

Sights ▶

1 Blackstone Block..........**D1**
2 Boston National Historical Park— Faneuil Hall..........**E3**
3 Boston Public Market....**D2**
4 City Hall Plaza..............**C3**
5 Faneuil Hall Marketplace................**F3**
6 Haymarket.....................**D2**
7 The New England Holocaust Memorial......**D2**
8 Quincy Market................**F3**

Restaurants ▶

1 Bar Cicchetti..............**D3**
2 Ned Devine's Irish Pub... **F3**
3 Union Oyster House **E2**

Quick Bites ▶

1 Saus................**E2**

Hotels ▶

1 The Bostonian...........**E2**
1 Hyatt Centric Faneuil Hall Boston.... **D3**

Blackstone Block, now visited mostly for its culinary landmark, the Union Oyster House. Named for one of Boston's first settlers, William Blaxton, or Blackstone, it's the city's oldest commercial block, for decades dominated by the butcher trade. As a tiny remnant of Old Boston, the Blackstone Block remains the city's "family attic"—to use the winning metaphor of critic Donlyn Lyndon: more than three centuries of architecture are on view, ranging from the 18th-century Capen House to the modern Bostonian hotel. A colonial-period warren of winding lanes surrounds the block.

Facing the Blackstone Block, in tiny Union Park, framed by Congress Street and Dock Square, are two bronze figures, one seated on a bench and the other standing eye-to-eye with passersby. Both represent James Michael Curley, the quintessential Boston pol and a questionable role model for urban bosses. It's just as well that he has no pedestal. Also known as "the Rascal King" or "the Mayor of the Poor," and dramatized by Spencer Tracy in *The Last Hurrah* (1958), the charismatic Curley was beloved by the city's dominant working-class Irish for bringing them libraries, hospitals, bathhouses, and other public-works projects. His career got off to a promising start in 1903, when he ran—and won—a campaign for alderman from the Charles Street Jail, where he was serving time for taking someone else's civil-service exam.

Over the next 50 years he dominated Boston politics, serving four nonconsecutive terms as mayor, one term as governor, and four terms as congressman. No one seemed to mind the slight glitch created when his office moved, in 1946, to the federal penitentiary, where he served five months of a 6- to 18-month sentence for mail fraud: he was pardoned by President Truman and returned to his people a hero. ⊠ *Blackstone St., Government Center* Ⓜ *Haymarket.*

Boston National Historical Park at Faneuil Hall

VISITOR CENTER | FAMILY | A 7,400-square-foot National Park Service visitor center at Faneuil Hall features history exhibits, a film-screening area, and a bookstore. It's the starting point for NPS rangers' two different 60-minute Freedom Trail tours and other talks; there's a sister site at Charlestown's Navy Yard. It's open daily from 9 to 4. Other Boston NPS sights include the Boston African American National Historic Site on Beacon Hill, home to guided tours of the Black Heritage Trail, and the Boston Harbor Islands National Recreation Area, with trails, forts, wildlife, and camping on 34 islands. ⊠ *Faneuil Hall Visitor Center, Government Center* ☎ *617/242–5642* ⊕ *www.nps.gov/bost.*

Boston Public Market

MARKET | FAMILY | Open year-round, the indoor Boston Public Market offers a great place to grab a sandwich, sample local foods, and even pick up a souvenir. The New England–centric marketplace has 30 vendors, selling everything from fresh herbs and fruit to meat and seafood. Everything sold at the market is produced or originates in New England. There's also a food demonstration kitchen, where visitors might be able to catch a live cooking class (with samples). The Kids' Nook is a designated area to gather and play, and there are kids activities throughout the week. ⊠ *100 Hanover St., Government Center* ☎ *617/973–4909* ⊕ *www.bostonpublicmarket.org* Ⓜ *Haymarket.*

City Hall Plaza

GOVERNMENT BUILDING | Over the years, various plans—involving gardens, restaurants, music, and hotels—have been floated to make this a more people-friendly site. Possibly the only thing that would ameliorate Bostonians' collective distaste for the chilly Government Center is tearing it down. Locals are getting their wish, as the entire City

In 1772 Samuel Adams stood on the steps of Quincy Market and stoked the fires of revolution; today it's the center of Boston's Faneuil Hall Marketplace.

Hall Plaza area (one of the largest civil spaces in Boston) is now in the middle of a several-stage, multiyear makeover. City Hall itself is an upside-down ziggurat design on a brutalist redbrick plaza that is being torn up and revamped to create a more aesthetically pleasing array of tree canopies, terraces, and improved public spaces. Once this is complete, the plaza will return as the site of many of the city's famed festivals, rallies, and outdoor concerts. ⊠ *1 City Hall Sq., Government Center* Ⓜ *Government Center.*

★ Faneuil Hall Marketplace

HISTORIC SIGHT | FAMILY | Faneuil Hall (pronounced *Fan*-yoo'uhl or *Fan*-yuhl) was erected in 1742, the gift of wealthy merchant Peter Faneuil, who wanted the hall to serve as both a place for town meetings and a public market. It burned in 1761 and was immediately reconstructed according to the original plan of its designer, the Scottish portrait painter John Smibert (who lies in the Granary Burying Ground). In 1763 the political leader James Otis helped inaugurate the

era that culminated in American independence when he dedicated the rebuilt hall to the cause of liberty.

In 1772 Samuel Adams stood here and first suggested that Massachusetts and the other colonies organize a Committee of Correspondence to maintain semiclandestine lines of communication in the face of hardening British repression. In later years the hall again lived up to Otis's dedication when the abolitionists Wendell Phillips and Charles Sumner pleaded for support from its podium. The tradition continues to this day: in presidential-election years the hall is the site of debates between contenders in the Massachusetts primary.

Faneuil Hall was substantially enlarged and remodeled in 1805 according to a Greek Revival design of the noted architect Charles Bulfinch; this is the building you see today. Its purposes remain the same: the balconied Great Hall is available to citizens' groups on presentation of a request signed by a required number of responsible parties; it also plays host to regular concerts.

Inside Faneuil Hall are dozens of paintings of famous Americans, including the mural *Webster's Reply to Hayne* and Gilbert Stuart's portrait of Washington at Dorchester Heights. Park rangers give informational talks about the history and importance of Faneuil Hall every half hour. There are interactive displays about Boston sights, and National Park Service rangers at the visitor center on the first floor can provide maps and other information.

On the building's top floors are the headquarters and museum and library of the Ancient and Honorable Artillery Company of Massachusetts, which is free to visit (but a donation is welcome). Founded in 1638, it's the oldest militia in the Western Hemisphere, and the third oldest in the world, after the Swiss Guard and the Honourable Artillery Company of London. The museum is open Wednesday through Friday from 11 am to 3 pm.

When such men as Andrew Jackson and Daniel Webster debated the future of the Republic here, the fragrances of bacon and snuff—sold by merchants in Quincy Market across the road—greeted their noses. Today the aroma of coffee wafts through the hall from a snack bar. The shops at ground level sell New England bric-a-brac. ■ TIP➜ **This is Freedom Trail stop 11.** ⊠ *Faneuil Hall Sq., Government Center* ☎ *617/523–1300* ⊕ *www.nps.gov/bost/learn/historyculture/fh.htm* ⊠ *Free* Ⓜ *Government Center, Aquarium, State.*

Haymarket

MARKET | Loud, self-promoting vendors pack this exuberant maze of a marketplace at Marshall and Blackstone Streets on Friday and Saturday from dawn to dusk (most vendors are usually gone by 5). As they have since 1829, pushcart vendors hawk fruits and vegetables against a backdrop of fish, meat, and cheese shops. The accumulation of debris left every evening has been celebrated in a whimsical 1976 public-arts project—Mags Harries's *Asaroton,* a Greek word meaning "unswept floors," a term used for Roman floor mosaics depicting banquet debris—consisting of bronze fruit peels and other detritus smashed into pavement. Another Harries piece, a bronze depiction of a gathering of stray gloves, tumbles down between the escalators in the Porter Square T station in Cambridge. At Creek Square, near the Haymarket, is the Boston Stone. Set into a brick wall, this was allegedly a marker used as milepost zero in measuring distances from Boston. ⊠ *Blackstone St., between Hanover St. and North St., Government Center* ⊕ *www.haymarketboston.org* ☉ *Closed Sun.–Thurs.* Ⓜ *Government Center.*

The New England Holocaust Memorial

MONUMENT | Located at the north end of Union Park, the Holocaust Memorial is the work of Stanley Saitowitz, whose design was selected through an international competition; the finished memorial was dedicated in 1995. During the day the six 50-foot-high glass-and-steel towers seem at odds with the 18th-century streetscape of Blackstone Square behind it; at night, they glow like ghosts while manufactured steam from grates in the granite base makes for a particularly haunting scene. Recollections by Holocaust survivors are set into the glass-and-granite walls; the upper levels of the towers are etched with 6 million numbers in random sequence, symbolizing the Jewish victims of the Nazi horror. ⊠ *Union St. near Hanover St., Government Center* ☎ *617/457–8750* ⊕ *www.nehm.org* Ⓜ *Haymarket, Government Center, State.*

★ Quincy Market

MARKET | FAMILY | Quincy Market was designed in 1826 to alleviate the cramped conditions of Faneuil Hall and clean up the refuse that collected in Town Dock, the pond behind it. The structure

The haunting New England Holocaust Memorial sits at the north end of Union Park; at night, the six 50-foot-high glass-and-steel towers glow.

has kept its traditional market-stall layout, but the stalls now purvey international and specialty foods: sushi, frozen yogurt, bagels, calzones, sausage-on-a-stick, Chinese noodles, barbecue, and baklava, plus all the boutique chocolate-chip cookies your heart desires. Along the arcades on either side of the building are vendors selling sweatshirts, photographs of Boston, and arts and crafts—some schlocky, some not—alongside a couple of patioed bars and restaurants. ⊠ *Bordered by Clinton, Commercial, and Chatham Sts., Government Center* ☎ *617/523–1300* ⊕ *www.quincy-market.com* Ⓜ *Government Center, Aquarium, State.*

🍴 Restaurants

Government Center is home to touristy Faneuil Hall Marketplace and Quincy Market, both packed with grab-and-go concessions as well as some more serious sit-down alternatives.

Bar Cicchetti

$$$ | **ITALIAN** | Fuel up after your Faneuil Hall trip with dinner in this small yet mighty spot, just steps from the famed marketplace. A gorgeous marble bar wraps around the center, with high- and low-top tables that invite you to share the personal Roman-style pizzas thick and piled high. **Known for:** Brussels and brie pizza; wine by the glass; chianti-braised lamb shank. Ⓢ *Average main: $32* ⊠ *54 Devonshire St., Government Center* ⊕ *www.barcicchettiboston.com* Ⓜ *Government Center.*

Ned Devine's Irish Pub

$$$ | **IRISH** | A trifecta of Celtic celebration, this Quincy Market hot spot is part Irish pub, part lounge, and part live music hall. A destination for tourists and townies alike, the menu is a mix of classic Irish dishes, like chicken curry, warm Jameson bread pudding, and beef stew, alongside New England favorites, such as chowder fries, Samuel Adams chicken tenders, and clam chowder. **Known for:** live music; great location; Irish eats. Ⓢ *Average*

main: $26 ⊠ 1 Fanueil Hall Marketplace, Government Center ☎ 617/248–8800 ⊕ www.neddevinesboston.com Ⓜ Government Center, Aquarium.

Union Oyster House

$$$ | **SEAFOOD** | Opening its door in 1826 and earning a place on the National Historic Landmark list, the Union Oyster House is Boston's oldest restaurant. Dine like Daniel Webster (alongside his nightly hangover-heavy tumbler of brandy and water) and order oysters on the half shell at the ground-floor raw bar in the oldest part of the restaurant. **Known for:** long waits on weekends; oysters; oldest Boston restaurant. $ *Average main: $34* ⊠ 41 Union St., Government Center ☎ 617/227–2750 ⊕ www.unionoysterhouse.com Ⓜ Haymarket.

☕ Coffee and Quick Bites

Saus

$ | **CAFÉ** | With 15 unique sauces on the menu, including homemade hot beer mustard, truffle ketchup, cheddar ale, smoky chipotle mayo, and gravy, Saus believes in the power of condiments, which accompany its made-from-scratch sandwiches. The hand-cut fries are house-aged and twice fried, and they're known for their hand-rolled beer-brined pork bratwurst. **Known for:** large variety of dipping sauces; tiny space; beer-brined sausages. $ *Average main: $9* ⊠ 33 Union St., Government Center ☎ 617/248–8835 ⊕ www.sausboston.com Ⓜ Government Center.

🛏 Hotels

The Bostonian

$$$ | **HOTEL** | **FAMILY** | Near historic Faneuil Hall, The Bostonian has guest rooms featuring Frette linens, pillow-top mattresses, and 40-inch TVs—many also have French doors with step-out balconies showcasing city views and the popular North End. Warmed up with red wall coverings, the lobby provides sofas and arm chairs, perfect for relaxing with a book chosen from one of the floor-to-ceiling bookshelves. **Pros:** updated fitness center; great location for sightseeing; on-site restaurant. **Cons:** Faneuil Hall can get clogged with tourists; self parking is expensive; some rooms get street noise. $ *Rooms from: $320* ⊠ Faneuil Hall Marketplace, 26 North St., Downtown ☎ 617/523–3600, 866/866–8086 ⊕ www.millenniumhotels.com ⤴ 204 rooms ‖◌‖ No Meals Ⓜ Haymarket, Aquarium.

Hyatt Centric Faneuil Hall Boston

$$$ | **HOTEL** | Across the street from Faneuil Hall, this coveted spot from the trusted brand is literally steps away from dozens upon dozens of Boston landmarks, parks, and restaurants. **Pros:** city views; unbeatable location; outstanding on-site restaurant. **Cons:** noise from street can be heard at lower floors; parking is expensive; small rooms. $ *Rooms from: $399* ⊠ 54–68 Devonshire St, Government Center ☎ 617/720–1234 ⊕ www.hyatt.com ⤴ 163 rooms ⌇ Pet friendly Ⓜ Government Center.

🍸 Nightlife

BARS

The Bell in Hand Tavern

PUBS | America's oldest continuously operating pub (founded 1795) is named after its original owner, town crier Jimmy Wilson, whose bell-ringing wooden sign still hangs on the wall. On the edge of the Freedom Trail, this glassed-in flatiron pub serves fried haddock sandwiches, burgers, and New England's favorite entrées, against a background of live music. Bands (and the occasional comedian) play each night downstairs, and DJs spin Top 40 for dancers Thursday through Saturday upstairs; there's karaoke every Tuesday. ■ **TIP→ Expect long lines of twentysomethings on the weekends.** ⊠ 45–55 Union St., Government Center ☎ 617/227–2098 ⊕ www.bellinhand.com Ⓜ Haymarket.

The Black Rose

PUBS | Hung with 20 bright county banners, decorated with pictures of Ireland and portraits of Samuel Beckett, Lady Gregory, and James Joyce, The Rose draws as many tourists as Irish-loving locals. Friendly Irish bartenders serve up pints, blarney, and far more Irish whiskeys (28) than Scotches (12). Nightly shows by traditional Irish and contemporary musicians confirm its abiding Gaelic good cheer, or *craic*. Dine on Guinness beef stew and fish-and-chips—all served by staffers with authentic brogues. ✉ *160 State St., Government Center* ☎ *617/742–2286* ⊕ *www.blackroseboston.com* Ⓜ *Aquarium, State.*

The Green Dragon Tavern

PUBS | Less rowdy than its Faneuil Hall neighbors, this now-Irish bar claims to have housed the "Headquarters of the Revolution" and was the inn where silversmith Paul Revere overheard plans for a British assault on Lexington and Concord, prompting his famous ride. While yesteryear found John Hancock (whose brother lived next door) strolling past its doors, today The Green Dragon is known for a great Guinness pour and Irish music—soloists play in the evenings from 5 to 9 Wednesday through Friday, and bands bring it on nightly beginning at 9. There's comedy night every Monday and a selection of Top 40 cover bands playing Tuesday through Sunday. ■TIP→ **College students and young professionals tend to crowd the bar in the evenings.** ✉ *11 Marshall St., Government Center* ☎ *617/367–0055* ⊕ *www.somerspubs.com* Ⓜ *Haymarket, Government Center.*

Hennessy's Bar

PUBS | Grab a seat by the windows overlooking Faneuil Hall on hot summer days, or cozy up to a coal fireplace in winter, and enjoy your pint (or a pick from one of the largest selections of single malt whiskies in Boston). There's live music at Hennessy's most nights of the week, as well as plenty of rowdy crowds that overrun the yellow-and-black confines for Top 40 cover bands mixed with DJs on weekends from 9 pm to 1 am at Upstairs at Hennessy's. ✉ *25 Union St., Government Center* ☎ *617/742–2121* ⊕ *www.somerspubs.com* Ⓜ *Haymarket, Government Center.*

Sam Adams Boston Taproom

BREWPUBS | Aptly overlooking its namesake's statue, the 15,000-square-feet Sam Adams Boston Taproom boasts three floors, including a rooftop terrace with views over Faneuil Hall. Drink like a local, by choosing a flight of innovative styles and rotating experimental beers from the nano-brewery as well as fan favorites such as Boston Lager and seasonal brews like Summer Ale. Suds occasionally sit secondary to fun events like yoga, drag shows, and comedy nights. Thursday translates to newly introduced drafts on the menu. ✉ *60 State St., Government Center* ☎ *617/466–6418* ⊕ *samueladams.com* Ⓜ *State Street, Government Center.*

🛍 Shopping

The heart of Government Center is the Shops at Faneuil Hall Marketplace, where approximately 18 million people come each year to stroll through the pushcarts, farm stands, and kiosk shops, which first appeared in 1742. There are also plenty of indoor storefronts along the promenades on either side of the marketplace.

FOOD

★ Boston Public Market

MARKET | Open year-round, the indoor Boston Public Market offers a great place to grab a sandwich, sample local foods, and even pick up a tasty souvenir. The New England–centric marketplace has 30 vendors, selling everything from fresh herbs and fruit to meat and seafood, as well as plenty of food stalls. Everything sold at the market is produced or originated in New England, including onperishables like wool and carved wooden bowls. There's also a food demonstration kitchen, where visitors might be able to catch a live cooking class (with samples). Since it's all about staying with the season, the exciting thing about visiting the BPM is that no two days are the same. The Kids' Nook is a designated area for kids to gather and play, with activities throughout the week. ✉ *100 Hanover St., Government Center* ⊕ *bostonpublicmarket.org* Ⓜ *Haymarket/ Government Center.*

SHOPPING CENTERS

Faneuil Hall Marketplace

MARKET | This complex is both huge and hugely popular (drawing 18 million people a year), but not necessarily unique—most of its independent shops have given way to Banana Republic, Uniqlo, Urban Outfitters, and other chains. Founded in 1742 as a market for crops and livestock, the place has plenty of history and offers one of the area's great à la carte casual dining experiences (Quincy Market). Pushcarts sell everything from apparel to jewelry to candy to Boston souvenirs. Live bands set up gigs throughout the weekend days, while buskers perform crowd-pleasing feats such as break dancing and juggling routines. Have your dollar bills ready for when the hat gets passed around. ✉ *Bounded by Congress St., Atlantic Ave., the Waterfront, and Government Center* ☎ *617/523–1300* ⊕ *www.faneuilhallmarketplace.com* Ⓜ *Government Center.*

The North End

On the northeast side of Government Center is the North End, Boston's Little Italy. In the 17th century the North End was Boston, as much of the rest of the peninsula was still under water or had yet to be cleared. Here the town bustled and grew rich for a century and a half before the birth of American independence. Now visitors can get a glimpse into

The Rose Kennedy Greenway 👁

The one linear mile of winding parks known as the Rose Fitzgerald Kennedy Greenway starts in the North End and goes thru Chinatown and Government Center. ⇨ *For more information about the Greenway, see the complete listing in the Downtown and the Waterfront chapter.*

Revolutionary times while filling up on some of the most scrumptious pastries and pastas to be found in modern Boston.

Today's North End is almost entirely a creation of the late 19th century, when brick tenements began to fill up with European immigrants—first the Irish, then Central European Jews, then the Portuguese, and finally the Italians. For more than 60 years, the North End attracted an Italian population base, filling the area with Mediterranean verve, volubility, and Roman Catholicism. This is Boston's haven not only for Italian restaurants but also for Italian groceries, bakeries, bocce courts, churches, social clubs, cafés, and street-corner debates over home-team soccer games.

■ **TIP→ July and August are highlighted by a series of street festivals, or** *feste,* **honoring various saints, and by local community events that draw people from all over the city. A statue of St. Agrippina di Mineo—which is covered with money when it's paraded through the streets—is a crowd favorite.**

Though small, only 0.36 square miles, the neighborhood has nearly 100 businesses and a variety of tourist attractions. Although hordes of visitors follow the redbrick ribbon of the Freedom Trail through the North End, the jumbled streets retain a neighborhood feeling, from the grandmothers gossiping on fire escapes to the laundry strung on back porches. Gentrification has diluted the quarter's ethnic character some, but linger for a moment along Salem or Hanover Street and you can still hear people speaking with Abruzzese accents. If you wish to study up on this fascinating district, head for the North End branch of the Boston Public Library on Parmenter Street, where a bust of Dante acknowledges local cultural pride.

◉ Sights

Clough House at Old North

HISTORIC HOME | FAMILY | Built in 1712, this house (whose name rhymes with "fluff") is now the only local survivor of its era aside from Old North Church, which stands nearby. Picture the streets lined with houses such as this, with an occasional grander Georgian mansion and some modest wooden-frame survivors of old Boston's many fires—this is what the North End looked like when Paul Revere was young. Today, Clough House is home to two new attractions: The Printing Office of Edes & Gill, which offers visitors live colonial-printing demonstrations, and Heritage Goods + Gifts, a shop dedicated to New England artisans and small businesses with a special focus on locally made products from BIPOC- and women-owned businesses. ⊠ *21 Unity St., North End* ☎ *617/523–4848* ⊕ *www. oldnorth.com/clough-house.*

Copp's Hill Burying Ground

CEMETERY | An ancient and melancholy air hovers like a fine mist over this colonial-era burial ground. The North End graveyard incorporates four cemeteries established between 1660 and 1819. Near the Charter Street gate is the tomb of the Mather family, the dynasty of church divines (Cotton and Increase were the most famous sons) who held sway in Boston during the heyday of the old theocracy. Also buried here is Robert Newman, who crept into the steeple of Old North Church to hang the lanterns warning of the British attack the night of Paul Revere's ride. Look for the tombstone of Captain Daniel Malcolm; it's pockmarked with musket-ball fire from British soldiers, who used the stones for target practice. Across the street is 44 Hull (Boston's historic Skinny House), the city's narrowest house, measuring at just a mere 10 feet wide, which recently fetched a selling price of $1.5 million.
■ TIP→ **This is Freedom Trail stop 14.**
⊠ *Intersection of Hull St. and Snowhill Rd., North End* ☎ *617/635–7361* ⊕ *www. cityofboston.gov/parks/hbgi/CoppsHill. asp* Ⓜ *North Station.*

Hanover Street

STREET | FAMILY | This is the North End's main thoroughfare, along with the smaller and narrower Salem Street. It was named for the ruling dynasty of 18th- and 19th-century England; the label was retained after the Revolution, despite a flurry of patriotic renaming (King Street became State Street, for example). Hanover's business center is thick with restaurants, pastry shops, and cafés, all celebrating the cuisine of the Old Country and most offering valet parking to combat the lack of parking. Hanover is one of Boston's oldest public roads, once the site of the residences of the Rev. Cotton Mather and the colonial-era patriot Dr. Joseph Warren, as well as a small dry-goods store run by Eben D. Jordan—who went on to launch the now defunct Jordan Marsh department stores. ⊠ *Between Commercial and Congress Sts., North End* Ⓜ *Haymarket, North Station.*

★ Old North Church

HISTORIC SIGHT | At one end of the Paul Revere Mall is a church famous not only for being the oldest standing church building in Boston (built in 1723) but also for housing the two lanterns that glimmered from its steeple on the night of April 18, 1775. This is Christ, or Old

North, Church, where Paul Revere and the young sexton Robert Newman managed that night to signal the departure by water of the British regulars to Lexington and Concord. Newman, carrying the lanterns, ascended the steeple, while Revere began his clandestine trip by boat across the Charles.

Although William Price designed the structure after studying Christopher Wren's London churches, Old North—which still has an active Episcopal congregation (including descendants of the Reveres)—is an impressive building in its own right. Inside, note the gallery and the graceful arrangement of pews; the bust of George Washington, pronounced by the Marquis de Lafayette to be the truest likeness of the general he ever saw; the brass chandeliers, made in Amsterdam in 1700 and installed here in 1724; and the clock, the oldest still running in an American public building. Try to visit when changes are rung on the bells, after the 11 am Sunday service; they bear the inscription, "We are the first ring of bells cast for the British Empire in North America." The steeple itself is not the original—the tower was destroyed in a hurricane in 1804 and was replaced in 1954. On the Sunday closest to April 18, descendants of the patriots reenact the raising of the lanterns in the church belfry during a special ticketed evening service, which also includes readings of Longfellow's renowned poem, "Paul Revere's Ride," and Revere's first-person account of that fateful night. Visitors are welcome to drop in for a self-guided tour or a 15-minute guided crypt tour.

Behind Old North is the Washington Memorial Garden, where volunteers cultivate a plot devoted to plants and flowers favored in the 18th century. ■TIP➔ **This is Freedom Trail stop 13.** ✉ 193 Salem St., North End ☎ 617/858–8231 ⊕ www.old-north.com ✍ $5, additional $5 for crypt tour Ⓜ Haymarket, North Station.

A Sticky Subject

Boston has had its share of grim historic events, from massacres to stranglers, but on the sheer weirdness scale, nothing beats the Great Molasses Flood. In 1919 a steel container of molasses exploded on the Boston Harbor waterfront, killing 21 people and 20 horses and injuring 150 people. More than 2.3 million gallons of goo oozed onto unsuspecting citizenry, a veritable tsunami of sweet stuff that reached speeds up to 35 mph. The smell of the molasses lasted for decades, and its memory lives on.

Paul Revere House

HISTORIC HOME | FAMILY | Originally on the site was the parsonage of the Second Church of Boston, home to the Rev. Increase Mather, the Second Church's minister. Mather's house burned in the great fire of 1676, and the house that Revere was to occupy was built on its location about four years later, nearly 100 years before Revere's 1775 midnight ride through Middlesex County. Revere owned it from 1770 until 1800, although he lived there for only 10 years and rented it out for the next two decades. Pre-1900 photographs show it as a shabby warren of storefronts and apartments. The clapboard sheathing is a replacement, but 90% of the framework is original; note the Elizabethan-style overhang and leaded windowpanes. A few Revere furnishings are on display here, and just gazing at his silverwork—much more of which is displayed at the Museum of Fine Arts—brings the man alive. Special events are scheduled throughout the year, many designed with children in mind, such as role play by characters dressed in period costume

The statue of Paul Revere outside Old North Church commemorates his famous ride.

serving apple-cider cake and other colonial-era goodies, a silversmith practicing his trade, a dulcimer player entertaining a crowd, or a military-reenactment group in full period regalia.

The immediate neighborhood also has Revere associations. The little cobblestone park in North Square is named after Rachel Revere, his second wife, and the adjacent brick Pierce-Hichborn House once belonged to relatives of Revere. The garden connecting the Revere House and the Pierce-Hichborn House is planted with flowers and medicinal herbs favored in Revere's day, but is sadly closed for tours. ■TIP→ This is Freedom Trail stop 12. ⊠ *19 North Sq., North End* ☎ *617/523–2338* ⊕ *www.paulreverehouse.org* ⊠ *$6* ⊗ *Closed Mon. Jan.–Mar.* Ⓜ *Haymarket, Aquarium, Government Center.*

Paul Revere Mall (*The Prado*)
PLAZA/SQUARE | FAMILY | Known to many locals as The Prado, this makes a perfect time-out spot from the Freedom Trail. Bookended by two landmark churches—Old North and St. Stephen's—the mall is flanked by brick walls lined with bronze plaques bearing the stories of famous North Enders. An appropriate centerpiece for this enchanting cityscape is Cyrus Dallin's equestrian statue of Paul Revere. Despite his depictions in such statues as this, the gentle Revere was stocky and of medium height—whatever manly dash he possessed must have been in his eyes rather than his physique. That physique served him well enough, however, for he lived to be 83 and saw nearly all his Revolutionary comrades buried. ■TIP→ Take a seat at one of the benches and enjoy your to-go treat from any of the North End Italian trattorias and bakeries. ⊠ *Bordered by Tileston, Hanover, and Unity Sts., North End* Ⓜ *Haymarket, Aquarium, Government Center.*

St. Stephen's
CHURCH | Rose Kennedy, matriarch of the Kennedy clan, was christened here; 104 years later, St. Stephen's held mourners at her 1995 funeral. This is the only Charles Bulfinch church still standing in Boston, and a stunning example of the

Paul Revere's Ride

👁

Test: Paul Revere was (1) a patriot whose midnight ride helped ignite the American Revolution; (2) a part-time dentist; (3) a silversmith who crafted tea services; (4) a printer who engraved the first Massachusetts state currency; (5) a talented metallurgist who cast cannons and bells; or (6) all of the above. The correct response is (6). But there's much more to this outsize Revolutionary hero—bell ringer for Old North Church, founder of the copper mills that still bear his name, and father of 16 children.

Although his life spanned eight decades (1734–1818), Revere is most famous for that one night, April 18, 1775, when he became America's most celebrated Pony Express rider. "Listen, my children, and you shall hear / Of the midnight ride of Paul Revere" are the opening lines of Henry Wadsworth Longfellow's poem, which placed the event at the center of American folklore. Longfellow may have been an effective evangelist for Revere, but he was an indifferent historian.

Revere wasn't the only midnight rider. As part of the system set in motion by Revere and William Dawes Jr., also dispatched from Boston, there were at least several dozen riders, so that the capture of any one of them wouldn't keep the alarm from being sounded. It's also known that Revere never looked for the lantern signal from Charlestown. He told Robert Newman to hang two lanterns from Old North's belfry since the redcoats were on the move by water, but by that time Revere was already being rowed across the Charles River to begin his famous ride.

Revere and Dawes set out on separate routes, but had the same mission: to warn patriot leaders Samuel Adams and John Hancock that British regular troops were marching to arrest them and alarm the countryside along the way. The riders didn't risk capture by shouting the news through the streets—and they never uttered the famous cry "The British are coming!," since Bostonians still considered themselves British. When Revere arrived in Lexington a few minutes past midnight and approached the house where Adams and Hancock were lodged, a sentry challenged him, requesting that he not make so much noise. "Noise!" Revere replied. "You'll have noise enough before long."

Despite Longfellow's assertion, Revere never raised the alarm in Concord because he was captured en route. He was held and questioned by the British patrol, and eventually released, without his horse, to walk back to Lexington in time to witness part of the battle on Lexington Green.

Poetic license aside, this tale has become part of the collective American spirit. Americans dote on hearing that Revere forgot his spurs, only to retrieve them by tying a note to his dog's collar, then awaiting its return with the spurs attached. The resourcefulness he showed in using a lady's petticoat to muffle the sounds of his oars while crossing the Charles is greatly appreciated. Little wonder that these tales resonate in the hearts and imagination of America's citizenry, as well as in Boston's streets on the third Monday of every April, Patriots' Day, when Revere's ride is reenacted—in daylight—to the cheers of thousands of onlookers.

Federal style to boot. Built in 1804, it was first used as a Unitarian Church; since 1862 it has served a Roman Catholic parish. When the belfry was stripped during a major 1960s renovation, the original dome was found beneath a false cap; it was covered with sheet copper and held together with hand-wrought nails, and later authenticated as being the work of Paul Revere. ⊠ *401 Hanover St., North End* ☎ *617/523–1230* Ⓜ *Haymarket, Aquarium, Government Center.*

Salem Street

STREET | This ancient and constricted thoroughfare, one of the two main North End streets, cuts through the heart of the neighborhood and runs parallel to and one block west of Hanover. Between Cross and Prince Streets, Salem Street contains numerous restaurants and shops. One of the best is Shake the Tree, one of the North End's trendiest boutiques, selling stylish clothing, gifts, and jewelry. The rest of Salem Street is mostly residential, but makes a nice walk to the Copp's Hill Burying Ground. ⊠ *Between Cross and Prince Sts., North End* Ⓜ *Haymarket.*

🍴 Restaurants

Third-generation Italians may have decamped to the suburbs, yet today's North End still echoes with brass parades in summer street fairs honoring saints. The friendly neighborhood attracts resident young professionals with convenient and safe housing, and entices all by wafting aromas of bitter espresso, pastries, fish specialties, red-sauce pasta, and pizza. Most, if not all, restaurants have a populated bar scene; while even the smaller locales serve beer and wine and let you linger over your casual counter-service meal to enjoy a drink.

★ Antico Forno

$$$ | ITALIAN | Many of the menu choices here come from the eponymous wood-burning brick oven, which turns out surprisingly delicate thin-crust pizzas simply topped with tomato and buffalo mozzarella or complicated combos like pistachio pesto, fresh mozzarella, and sausage. While the name, which translates to "old oven," gives the pizzas top billing, Antico excels at a variety of Italian country dishes that harken back to the Old Country, like veal parmigiana, *osso buco* with pork shank, chicken saltimbocca, and handmade pastas; the specialty, gnocchi, is rich and creamy but light. **Known for:** Italian country classics; casual, jovial atmosphere; wood-fired, brick-oven pizza. Ⓢ *Average main: $28* ⊠ *93 Salem St., North End* ☎ *617/723–6733* ⊕ *www.anticofornoboston.com* Ⓜ *Haymarket.*

Bricco

$$$$ | ITALIAN | A sophisticated but unpretentious enclave of nouveau Italian, Bricco has carved out quite a following, which is no wonder because the handmade pastas alone are reasons for reservations, not to mention the buzz-worthy stuffed zucchini flowers just like nonna used to make. Simple but well-balanced main courses, such as veal osso buco, roast chicken marinated in seven spices, and a brimming *brodetto* (fish stew) with half a lobster and a pile of seafood, may linger in your memory. **Known for:** dark, elegant atmosphere; pillowy homemade pastas; sophisticated Italian classics. Ⓢ *Average main: $45* ⊠ *241 Hanover St., North End* ☎ *617/248–6800* ⊕ *bricco.com* 🕙 *No lunch* Ⓜ *Haymarket.*

Ciao Roma

$$$ | ITALIAN | Located on the Freedom Trail and overlooking the country's oldest public square, the vintage-looking facade of Ciao Roma is an elevated alternative to dining old-school in the North End. Classics are simple in nature but complex in taste, with dishes such as squid ink linguini, chicken parm, and Sunday ragù vying for your attention. **Known for:** Italian classics; white tablecloths; beautifully displayed crudo. Ⓢ *Average main: $30* ⊠ *5 North Sq., North End*

☎ 617/829–4975 ⊕ www.ciaoromanorth-end.com Ⓜ Haymarket.

★ The Daily Catch

$$ | **SEAFOOD** | You've just got to love this newly renovated shoebox-size place—for the noise, the intimacy, the complete absence of pretense, and, above all, the Sicilian-style seafood, which proved so popular, it spawned two other locations (one in Brookline and another in Boston's Seaport area). With garlic and olive oil forming the foundation for almost every dish, this cheerful, bustling spot specializes in calamari, black squid-ink pastas, and linguine with clam sauce, all served in the skillets in which they were cooked, hot from the stove. **Known for:** luscious seafood skillet pastas; intimate, elbow-to-elbow dining; garlic-rich preparations. ⑤ Average main: $24 ⊠ 323 Hanover St., North End ☎ 617/523–8567 ⊕ thedailycatch.com ⊟ No credit cards Ⓜ Haymarket.

Lucia Ristorante

$$$ | **ITALIAN** | The Frattaroli Family, who opened Lucia shortly after emigrating to Boston from the Abruzzo region of Italy, pack the kitchen with classic dishes that showcase flavors from their beloved home, which is why weekend evenings get packed. The long menu includes apps, such as fresh caprese salad and crispy calamari, and entrée favorites, including a buttery-smooth *sogliola pescarese* (filet of sole dipped in egg and fried with limoncello), *pollo marsala*, and *ammazzafame*, a house specialty of penne *rigate*, porcini mushrooms, sausage, broccoli, sun-dried tomatoes, and capers. **Known for:** lines on weekends; outdoor patio; Ammazzafame penne specialty. ⑤ Average main: $27 ⊠ 415 Hanover St., North End ☎ 617/367–2353 ⊕ luciab.st ⊗ Closed Mon.

Mamma Maria

$$$ | **ITALIAN** | Don't let the clichéd name fool you: Mamma Maria is far from a typical red-sauce joint. From the handmade pappardelle layered with braised rabbit to the authentic sauces and entrées to some of the best desserts in the North End, you can't go wrong here. **Known for:** charming setting with outdoor patio; good service; white-cloth Italian cuisine. ⑤ Average main: $30 ⊠ 3 North Sq., North End ☎ 617/523–0077 ⊕ www.mammamaria.com ⊗ No lunch Ⓜ Haymarket.

Mare Oyster Bar

$$$$ | **MODERN ITALIAN** | When a restaurant's very name conjures up images of the ocean waters, its menu choices should follow suit. Mare does exactly that, focusing on a locally sourced oyster program, fresh and innovative crudo dishes, and simple yet elegant entrées highlighting the natural flavors of its fresh, sustainable seafood. **Known for:** dark intimate setting; whole grilled fish; fresh crudo and oysters. ⑤ Average main: $45 ⊠ 3 Mechanic St., North End ☎ 617/723–6273 ⊕ www.mareoysterbar.com Ⓜ Haymarket.

★ Neptune Oyster

$$$ | **SEAFOOD** | This *piccolo* oyster bar, the first of its kind in the neighborhood, has only 22 chairs, but the long marble bar adorned with mirrors has extra seating for 15 more patrons, who can watch the oyster shuckers deftly undo handfuls of more than a dozen different kinds of bivalves to savor as an appetizer or on a Neptune plateau, a gleaming tower of oysters and other raw-bar items piled over ice that you can order from the slip of paper they pass out listing each day's crustacean options. Daily specials run the gamut, from lobster spaghetti to scarlet prawns to sea urchin bucatini. **Known for:** Italian-style seafood; generously packed lobster roll; casual setting. ⑤ Average main: $34 ⊠ 63 Salem St., North End ☎ 617/742–3474 ⊕ www.neptuneoyster.com Ⓜ Haymarket.

Prezza

$$$$ | **MODERN ITALIAN** | Chef Anthony Caturano pays homage to his Italian grandmother at this warm, convivial

The North End

Sights

1 Clough House at Old North **F3**
2 Copp's Hill Burying Ground **E2**
3 Hanover Street........... **F4**
4 Old North Church **F3**
5 Paul Revere House **F5**
6 Paul Revere Mall **F3**
7 St. Stephen's **G4**
8 Salem Street **E4**

Restaurants

1 Antico Forno............. **E5**
2 Bricco.................... **E5**
3 Ciao Roma **F5**
4 The Daily Catch **F5**
5 Lucia Ristorante **G3**
6 Mamma Maria **F4**
7 Mare Oyster Bar........ **E6**
8 Neptune Oyster **E5**
9 Prezza.................... **G4**
10 Quattro.................. **E5**
11 Regina Pizzeria.......... **D3**
12 Tresca................... **E5**

F G H I J

Fiskes Wharf

Coast Guard Station

Constitution Wharf

Commercial St.

Battery Wharf

1

Old North Church

NORTH END

Battery Wharf

Battery St.

Sumner Tunnel (Toll)

Callahan Tunnel

Hanover Ave.

6   5

7   Harris St.

Tileston St.

Hanover St.

N. Bennet St.

Clark St.

Union Wharf

3   3

9   Fleet St.

5   3

North St.

Sargents Wharf

4

6   Moon St.

Lewis St.

5

North Square

Garden St.

Atlantic Ave.

Lewis Wharf

Fulton St.

Commercial St.

Richmond St.

North St.

Cross St.

Rose Kennedy Greenway

Christopher Columbus Park

Commercial Wharf

Long Wharf

0   500 ft

0   150 m

KEY

- ❶ Sights
- ❶ Restaurants
- ❶ Quick Bites
- ❶ Hotels
- Ⓣ Subway station
- - - - Freedom Trail

eatery by naming it after the tiny Abruzzese village where she was born and then putting a modern twist on the rustic dishes she would have cooked. An emphasis on garden-fresh ingredients means appetizers like baby gem salad with soppressata and roasted red peppers and wood-grilled squid and octopus with white beans, while "Gravy Sunday" specials translate to heaping plates of traditional dishes like homemade meatballs and gnocchi bolognese. **Known for:** generous portions; impressive Italian wine list; scrumptious country-style Italian. $ *Average main: $37* ✉ *24 Fleet St., North End* ☎ *617/227–1577* ⊕ *www. prezza.com* ⊟ *No credit cards.*

Quattro

$$$ | ITALIAN | When the *pizzaiolo* (certified pizza maker noted by the Napoli Pizza Council) is from Naples and he works on a hand-built brick Marra Forni pizza oven, chances are he's churning out some authentic Neapolitan pizza. Toppings stay simple, with four-cheese, margarita, or prosciutto, while creative combos also keep the customers coming back. **Known for:** piping hot pies; authentic Neapolitan pizza; shrimp limoncello. $ *Average main: $26* ✉ *264 Hanover St., North End* ☎ *617/720–0444* ⊕ *quattro-boston.com.*

Regina Pizzeria

$$ | ITALIAN | This North End institution has been doing what it does best since the Polcari family took over in 1956—creating thin-crusted, brick-oven-charred pizzas with fresh toppings, excellent sauce, and just the right amount of cheese. With 13 locations, they only offer what they excel in: incredibly well-made pies, like the Margherita, which contains fresh basil leaves baked into the cheese so they don't burn; try a combo from their Old Time Favorites menu, such as the Old World Style Anchovy or the St. Anthony's, a white pizza with sausage, cheese, and peppers. **Known for:** good prices; no-frills atmosphere; excellent thin-crust pizzas. $ *Average main: $24* ✉ *11½*

Thatcher St., North End ☎ *617/227–0765* ⊕ *www.pizzeriaregina.com.*

Tresca

$$$ | ITALIAN | An intrigue in both meaning and sentiment, this captivating North End trattoria on historic Hanover Street serves up multiregional Italian cuisine through fresh and fine ingredients that fuse together the sights, scents, and tastes of the Old Country. Styled after a Tuscan villa, the dark woods, candles, dim lighting, and marble accents build the perfect surroundings for sipping fine Italian wines from one of the area's most extensive wine lists. **Known for:** owned by Bruins hockey legend Ray Bourque; balcony seating for two; old-school Italian dishes. $ *Average main: $35* ✉ *233 Hanover St., North End* ⊕ *www.trescanorthend.com* ☞ *Validate parking at the Haymarket Garage ($3 for 3 hours).*

☕ Coffee and Quick Bites

Bova's Bakery

$ | ITALIAN | FAMILY | The allure of Bova's Bakery, a neighborhood institution since 1926, lies not only in its takeaway Italian breads, calzones, and pastries, but also in its hours: 24 a day (the deli closes at 1 am, however). Family owned and operated, this is where you can not only satisfy a hunger with their homemade Italian breads, oversized subs, and Sicilian pizza and calzones, but also a sweet tooth with their famed Sicilian chocolate-dipped cannoli, Florentine cannoli, award-winning tiramisu, and raspberry and blueberry turnovers. **Known for:** tiramisu; fresh baked bread; open 24/7. $ *Average main: $10* ✉ *134 Salem St., North End* ☎ *617/523–5601* ⊕ *bovabakeryboston.net* Ⓜ *Haymarket.*

★ Bricco Salumeria

$ | ITALIAN | Frank DePasquale's sandwich and pasta shop is easy to miss, but just follow the steady stream of savvy locals down the alley adjacent to his award-winning restaurant to find the tiny spot packed with imported Italian meats and cheeses, vinegars, tomatoes, olive oils, and more. The monumental Italian sandwich is a heaping pile of mortadella, Genoa salami, soppressata, provolone, and all the fixings, while the packed Chicken Parmagiano is a shareable feast. **Known for:** huge, made-to-order Italian sandwiches; house-made breads; local favorite. $ *Average main: $13* ⊠ *11 Board Alley, North End* ☎ *617/248-9629* ⊕ *www.briccosalumeria.com.*

Caffè dello Sport

$ | **ITALIAN** | An Italianate version of a sports bar, Caffè dello Sport has two wide screens transmitting live soccer. The buzz is from not only the world games excitement but also the espressos, pastries, beer, wine, cordials, and gelato. **Known for:** full espresso bar; gelato; soccer games. $ *Average main: $10* ⊠ *308 Hanover St., North End* ☎ *617/523–5063* ⊕ *www.caffedellosport.net.*

★ Caffé Vittoria

$ | **ITALIAN** | **FAMILY** | Established in 1929, Caffé Vittoria—Boston's oldest Italian café—is rightfully known as Boston's most traditional Italian café, which is one of the reasons the place is packed with locals. With gleaming brass, marble tabletops, four levels of seating, three bars that serve aperitifs, one of the city's best selections of grappa, and one massive, ancient espresso maker, this old-fashioned café will make you want to lose yourself in these surroundings. **Known for:** grapa; gelato; specialty coffee drinks. $ *Average main: $10* ⊠ *290–296 Hanover St., North End* ☎ *617/227–7606* ⊕ *www.caffevittoria. com* ▭ *No credit cards.*

Mike's Pastry

$ | **BAKERY** | Every local knows the white box with the blue and white string as a to-go treasure chest of Italian delicacies. Known for their cannoli (they're the self-proclaimed "home of" the tubular treat), Mike's has been bringing the best in pastries and cookies to the North End (and presidential patrons like Bill Clinton)

Mike's vs. Modern

Welcome to Boston's long-standing cannoli war. Mike's Pastry and Modern Pastry are widely considered the North End's two best cannoli spots, but locals can't seem to agree on which is better, splitting their strong allegiance right down the center. Modern's cannoli are smaller and more delicate than Mike's, while Mike's are crunchier, sweeter, and boast more flavors (18 to be exact). Which will you choose?

since 1946. **Known for:** long lines; cases of Italian cookies; cannoli. $ *Average main: $9* ⊠ *300 Hanover St., North End* ☎ *617/742–3050* ⊕ *www.mikespastry. com.*

Modern Pastry

$ | **ITALIAN** | The North End's other favorite cannoli king, Modern is a hit with the locals. Using Old World recipes that were relied on for more than 150 years, their crusts are flaky, their fillings rich, and they have a selection of torrone nougat confections, cookies, French horns, and Napoleons. **Known for:** deliciously moist cakes; handmade Italian candies; dainty cannoli. $ *Average main: $8* ⊠ *257 Hanover St., North End* ☎ *617/523–3783* ⊕ *www.modernpastry.com* ▭ *No credit cards.*

Pauli's North End

$ | **CAFÉ** | In this North End nook, the lobster roll—in 7 ounces, 14 ounces, and at 28 ounces, the "U.S.S. Lobstitution," the biggest lobster roll in Boston—reigns supreme. **Known for:** fresh sandwich fixings; pasta entrées to go; Boston's largest lobster roll. $ *Average main: $13* ⊠ *65 Salem St., North End* ☎ *857/284–7064* ⊕ *www.paulisnorthend. com* Ⓜ *Haymarket.*

Hotels

Battery Wharf Hotel
$$$$ | HOTEL | FAMILY | One of the growing number of lodgings clustered along Boston's ever-expanding Harborwalk—a pretty pedestrian path that runs from Charlestown to Dorchester—the Battery Wharf Hotel looks more like a gated community than a chain hotel. **Pros:** walking distance to more than 80 world-class restaurants; on-site Exhale Spa has discounted spa services and fitness classes for hotel guests; pet-friendly; water taxi stand on-site. **Cons:** 15- to 20-minute walk to nearest T stations; hotel is in two separate buildings; far from Newbury Street and South End shopping. $ *Rooms from: $400* ⊠ *3 Battery Wharf, North End* ☎ *617/657–1834* ⊕ *www.batterywharfhotelboston.com* ↵ *150 rooms* Ⓜ *Haymarket, North Station.*

Nightlife

BARS

Farmacia
COCKTAIL LOUNGES | Open in a part of the Ciao Roma space, this apothecary-inspired cocktail bar boasts only nine seats and hundreds of cocktail potentials. During one of his ticketed progressive journeys, creator Phillip Rolfe (of Wink & Nod fame) creates individually tailored concoctions made from high-end spirits, homemade syrups, infusions and tinctures, and freshly cold-pressed juices. House-made pickles, dips, roasted nuts, and gelato pair nicely but aren't meant to fill you up. Because it's so small, Farmacia is booked months out, so plan accordingly. ⊠ *5 North Sq., North End* ⊕ *www.farmacianorthend.com* ↵ *Reservations are required.*

Shopping

BOOKS

I AM Books
BOOKS | Once you've eaten your fill of pasta and cannoli, nourish your noggin at this independent, Italian American bookstore, where you'll find more than 1,200 titles in English and Italian. In addition to books written in Italian, including many children's books like Dr. Seuss, you'll find books devoted to Italian cooking, art, history, language, literature, and more, along with Italian comic books, card games, magazines, ceramics, and fragrances. ⊠ *124 Salem St., North End* ☎ *617/530–1106* ⊕ *www.iambooksboston.com.*

CLOTHING

★ Shake the Tree
OTHER SPECIALTY STORE | Irresistible defines this one-stop shop, brimming with an eclectic array of floral dresses and tops, wide-legged pants, letterpress greeting cards, small brand apothecary, craft cocktail supplies, global cookbooks, woven baskets, and mixed media jewelry that you never knew you needed. Owner Marian Klausner creates an inspiring award-winning selection from her global travels. ⊠ *67 Salem St., North End* ☎ *617/742–0484* ⊕ *www.shakethetree-boston.com* Ⓜ *Haymarket.*

FOOD

Polcari's Coffee
FOOD | If you're not able to kill a whole afternoon sipping cappuccino, this circa 1932 spot sells dried goods by the pound—coffees, teas, herbs, and spices (their secret dipping oil mix is well-known) displayed in antique brass bins—as well as a variety of nuts and Italian delicacies and candies. ⊠ *105 Salem St., North End* ☎ *617/227–0786* ⊕ *www.polcariscoffee.com.*

Chapter 5

CHARLESTOWN

Updated by
Cheryl Fenton

◉ Sights	🍽 Restaurants	🛏 Hotels	🛍 Shopping	🍸 Nightlife
★★★☆☆	★★★☆☆	★☆☆☆☆	★☆☆☆☆	★★☆☆☆

NEIGHBORHOOD SNAPSHOT

TOP EXPERIENCES

■ **Get vertical:** Climb 294 steps to the Bunker Hill Monument top and enjoy city views while imagining battles of the past.

■ **Step aboard a 1700s naval vessel:** Tour the USS *Constitution,* and discover why the world's oldest commissioned warship still afloat is nicknamed "Old Ironsides."

■ **Raise a glass to the patriots:** Grab a pint at Warren Tavern, the same pub frequented by George Washington and Paul Revere.

■ **Cityscape views:** The Harborwalk is a raised section along the water that affords miles of peaceful Boston views.

■ **Stroll through a park with purpose:** Visit the Charlestown Navy Yard, a National Park Service site complete with a gift shop and museum.

GETTING HERE

The closest subway stop to the Charlestown Navy Yard is North Station (on the Green and Orange Lines), about a 15-minute walk. Take Causeway Street northeast and make a left to walk over the Charlestown Bridge. Take a right on Chelsea Street and right again on Warren Street. Constitution Road will be your next left. From here you can enter the Navy Yard. From Downtown Crossing, take the 93 Bus, which drops you at the Navy Yard. If you're coming from Downtown, try the water shuttle from Long Wharf near the Aquarium. Boats run on the hour and half hour for the 10-minute ride.

QUICK BITES

■ **Emack & Bolio's.** This funky ice cream and smoothie shop boasts crazy flavors and a rock 'n' roll vibe. ✉ *100 City Sq., Charlestown* ⊕ *www.emackandbolios.com.*

■ **Sorelle Bakery & Cafe.** This neighborhood spot is known for delicious sandwiches and refreshing iced coffees. ✉ *100 City Sq., Charlestown* ⊕ *www.sorellecafe.com.*

■ **Zume's Coffee House.** A cheerful vibe and friendly service accompany great coffee and housemade burritos at this local spot. ✉ *221 Main St., Charlestown* ⊕ *www.zumescoffeehouse.com.*

PLANNING YOUR TIME

■ This little tight-knit community (Boston's oldest neighborhood) is only one square mile. Give yourself two to three hours for a Charlestown walk. A daytime visit affords the best harbor views. You may want to save Charlestown's stretch of the Freedom Trail, which adds considerably to its length, for a second-day outing. If you drive yourself, be mindful of weekday resident-only parking spots.

This is Boston's beginning. Charlestown was a thriving settlement a year before colonials headed across the Charles River at William Blaxton's invitation to found the city proper. Today the district's attractions include two of the most visible—and vertical—monuments in Boston: the Bunker Hill Monument, which commemorates the grisly battle that became a symbol of patriotic resistance against the British, and the USS *Constitution*, whose masts continue to tower over the waterfront where it was built more than 200 years ago.

The blocks around the Bunker Hill Monument are a good illustration of how gentrification has changed the neighborhoods. Along streets lined with gas lamps are impeccably restored Federal and mid-19th-century town houses; cheek by jowl are working-class quarters of similar vintage but more modest recent pasts. Near the Navy Yard along Main Street is City Square, the beginning of Charlestown's main commercial district, which includes City Square Park, with brick paths and bronze fish sculptures. On Phipps Street is the grave marker of John Harvard, a minister who in 1638 bequeathed his small library to the fledgling Cambridge College, thereafter renamed in his honor. The precise location of the grave is uncertain, but a monument from 1828 marks its approximate site.

◉ Sights

★ Bunker Hill Monument

MONUMENT | Two misunderstandings surround this famous monument. First, the Battle of Bunker Hill was actually fought on Breed's Hill, which is where the monument sits today. (The real Bunker Hill is about ½ mile to the north of the monument.) In truth, Bunker was the originally planned locale for the battle, and for that reason its name stuck. Second, although the battle is generally considered a colonial success, the Americans lost. It was a Pyrrhic victory for the British Redcoats, who sacrificed nearly half of their 2,200 men; American casualties numbered 400 to 600. One thing is true: the Battle of Bunker Hill put the British on notice that they were up against a formidable opponent. According to history books, this is also the location of the famous war cry, "Don't fire until you see the whites of their eyes," uttered by American colonel William Prescott or General Israel Putnam (there's still debate on who gave the actual command). This was a shout out to an 18th-century Prussian warning to soldiers that lack of ammunition and notorious musket inaccuracy meant every shot needed to count. The Americans did employ a deadly delayed-action strategy on June 17, 1775, and conclusively proved themselves capable of defeating the forces of the British Empire.

Among the dead were the brilliant young American doctor and political activist Joseph Warren, recently commissioned as a major general but fighting as a private, and the British major John Pitcairn, who two months prior had led the Redcoats into Lexington. Pitcairn is believed to be buried in the crypt of Old North Church.

In 1823 the committee formed to construct a monument on the site of the battle chose the form of an Egyptian obelisk. Architect Solomon Willard designed a 221-foot-tall granite obelisk, a tremendous feat of engineering for its day. The Marquis de Lafayette laid the cornerstone of the monument in 1825, but because of a lack of funds, it wasn't dedicated until 1843. Daniel Webster's stirring words at the ceremony commemorating the laying of its cornerstone have gone down in history: "Let it rise! Let it rise, till it meets the sun in his coming. Let the earliest light of the morning gild it, and parting day linger and play upon its summit."

The monument's zenith is reached by a flight of 294 tightly spiraled steps, a space that's unfortunately still undergoing renovation and is closed to climbers. With an opening day on the horizon, take note: there's no elevator, but the views from the observatory are worth the effort of the arduous climb. Due to high numbers, all visitors who wish to climb

A Good Walk ⦿

If you choose to hoof it to Charlestown, follow Hull Street from Copp's Hill Burying Ground to Commercial Street; turn left on Commercial and, two blocks later, right onto the bridge. The entrance to the **Charlestown Navy Yard** is on your right after crossing the bridge. Just ahead is the Charlestown Navy Yard Visitors Center; inside the park gate are the **USS *Constitution*** and the associated **USS *Constitution* Museum.** From here, the Red Line of the Freedom Trail takes you to the **Bunker Hill Monument.**

must first obtain a pass from the Bunker Hill Museum at 43 Monument Square. Climbing passes are free, but limited in number and can be either reserved up to two weeks in advance or on a first-come, first-served basis. The museum's artifacts and exhibits tell the story of the battle, while a detailed diorama shows the action in miniature. ■ TIP→ This is Freedom Trail stop 16. ⊠ *Monument Sq., Charlestown* ☎ *617/242–5641* ⊕ *www. nps.gov/bost/historyculture/bhm.htm* 🎟 *Free* Ⓜ *Community College.*

Charlestown Navy Yard

MILITARY SIGHT | FAMILY | A National Park Service site since it was decommissioned in 1974, the Charlestown Navy Yard was one of six established to build warships. For 174 years, as wooden hulls and muzzle-loading cannons gave way to steel ships and sophisticated electronics, the yard evolved to meet the Navy's changing needs. Here are early-19th-century barracks, workshops, and officers' quarters; a ropewalk (an elongated building for making rope, not open to the public), designed in 1834 by the Greek Revival architect Alexander Parris and used by the Navy to turn out cordage

Charlestown

KEY
- 1 Sights
- 1 Restaurants
- 1 Quick Bites
- Subway station
- - - - Freedom Trail

Sights ▶
1 Bunker Hill Monument ... **D2**
2 Charlestown Navy Yard ... **E2**
3 USS Cassin Young ... **F3**
4 USS Constitution ... **E3**
5 USS Constitution Museum ... **E2**

Restaurants ▶
1 Brewer's Fork ... **E2**
2 Dovetail ... **E2**
3 Monument Restaurant & Tavern ... **C1**
4 Pier 6 ... **G3**
5 Sullivan's Public House ... **D2**
6 Warren Tavern ... **C2**

Quick Bites ▶
1 Emack & Bolio's ... **D3**
2 Sorelle Bakery & Cafe ... **D3**
3 The Shop at Dovetail ... **F2**
4 Tradesman Coffee Shop & Lounge ... **A1**
5 Zume's Coffee House ... **C2**

EAST BOSTON

Mystic River

CHARLESTOWN NAVY YARD

Boston Inner Harbor

Charlestown Bridge

0   1/4 mi
0   1/4 km

for more than 125 years; and one of the oldest operational naval dry docks in the United States. The USS *Constitution* was the first to use this dry dock in 1833. In addition to the ship itself, check out the *Constitution* Museum, the collections of the Boston Marine Society, and the USS *Cassin Young*. The Charlestown Navy Yard Visitors Center has exhibits on ships and a fun souvenir shop. A 10-minute movie about the Navy Yard runs every 15 minutes in a small theater. ⊠ *55 Constitution Rd., Charlestown* ☎ *617/242–5601* ⊕ *www.nps.gov/bost/historyculture/cny. htm* 🖾 *Free* Ⓜ *North Station; MBTA Bus 92 to Charlestown City Sq. or Bus 93 to Chelsea St. from Haymarket; or Boston Harbor Cruise water shuttle from Long Wharf to Pier 4.*

USS *Cassin Young*

MILITARY SIGHT | Built in 1943, this Fletcher-class U.S. Navy destroyer survived action in Asian waters during World War II (including seven Pacific battles and two kamikaze hits). She served the Navy until 1960. Walk beside her and take in her size, explore her top deck, or go below deck for a guided tour offered by the National Park Service. She is the namesake of Captain Cassin Young, who was awarded the Medal of Honor for his heroism at the Japanese attack on Pearl Harbor; he was killed in the Naval Battle of Guadalcanal in the fall of 1942. Check the website for special opening hours. ⊠ *Charlestown Navy Yard, 55 Constitution Rd., Charlestown* ☎ *617/242–5601* ⊕ *www.nps.gov/bost/historyculture/ usscassinyoung.htm* 🖾 *Free* ☉ *Closed Nov.–May* Ⓜ *North Station; MBTA Bus 92 to Charlestown City Sq. or Bus 93 to Chelsea St. from Haymarket; or Boston Harbor Cruise water shuttle from Long Wharf to Pier 4.*

★ USS *Constitution*

MILITARY SIGHT | **FAMILY** | Affectionately known as "Old Ironsides," the USS *Constitution* rides proudly at anchor in her berth at the Charlestown Navy Yard.

The oldest commissioned ship in the U.S. fleet is a battlewagon of the old school, of the days of "wooden ships and iron men"—when she and her crew of 200 succeeded at the perilous task of asserting the sovereignty of an improbable new nation. Every July 4, she's towed out for a celebratory turnabout in Boston Harbor, where her keel was laid in 1797.

The venerable craft has narrowly escaped the scrap heap several times in her long history. She was launched on October 21, 1797, as part of the nation's fledgling navy. Her hull was made of live oak, the toughest wood grown in North America; her bottom was sheathed in copper, provided by Paul Revere at a nominal cost. Her principal service was during Thomas Jefferson's campaign against the Barbary pirates, off the coast of North Africa, and in the War of 1812. In 42 engagements her record was 42–0.

The nickname "Old Ironsides" was acquired during the War of 1812, when shots from the British warship *Guerrière* appeared to bounce off her hull. Talk of scrapping the ship began as early as 1830, but she was saved by a public campaign sparked by Oliver Wendell Holmes's poem "Old Ironsides." She underwent a major restoration in the early 1990s. Today she continues, the oldest commissioned warship afloat in the world, to be a part of the U.S. Navy. In 2015, she was dry docked for a 26-month restoration that included replacement of select hull planks, the 1995 copper sheathing, and deck beams, returning to the water in 2017.

The navy personnel who look after the *Constitution* maintain a 24-hour watch. Instead of taking the T, you can get closer to the ship by taking MBTA Bus 93 to Chelsea Street from Haymarket. Or you can take the Boston Harbor Cruise water shuttle from Long Wharf to Pier 4. ■ **TIP→ This is Freedom Trail stop 15.** ⊠ *Charlestown Navy Yard, 55 Constitution Rd., Charlestown* ☎ *617/242–7511*

⊕ *ussconstitutionmuseum.org* ✉ *Free* Ⓜ *North Station.*

★ USS *Constitution* Museum

HISTORY MUSEUM | **FAMILY** | With nearly 2,000 artifacts and more than 10,000 archival records pertaining to the USS *Constitution* on display, exhibits spark excitement about maritime culture and naval service. All ages enjoy "All Hands on Deck: A Sailor's Life in 1812," complete with opportunities to scrub decks, scramble aloft to furl a sail, eat a meal of salted meat and ship's biscuit, and crawl into a hammock. History buffs get a stem-to-stern look at the ship's history, from its creation to battles. ✉ *Charlestown* ✛ *Adjacent to USS Constitution, Charlestown Navy Yard* ☎ *617/426–1812* ⊕ *www.ussconstitutionmuseum. org* ✉ *Suggested donation from $5* Ⓜ *North Station; MBTA Bus 93 from the Haymarket or Sullivan Square Station to Charlestown Navy Yard stop; or Boston Harbor Cruise water shuttle from Long Wharf (near the New England Aquarium) to Pier 4.*

🍴 Restaurants

Known for its brick town houses and war-time history, this neighborhood also contains a vibrant mix of affordable eateries and taverns, mainly along Main Street and in City Square, that cater to the area artists, working families, and young couples.

Brewer's Fork

$$ | **AMERICAN** | With the Bunker Hill Monument in your sights, relax with a wood-fired pizza and a pint. Brewer's Fork's list of 30 draft cider and craft beers is impressive (yet approachable) and its wine list massive. **Known for:** lively brunch; beer program; creative pizzas. ⑤ *Average main: $18* ✉ *7 Moulton St., Charlestown* ☎ *617/337–5703* ⊕ *www. brewersfork.com.*

Dovetail

$$$ | **AMERICAN** | With the dainty twinkle lights sitting against exposed brick elements, this neighborhood spot creates an intimate atmosphere with a lively energy. Chilled seafood starters along with smaller plates like mushroom toast and mussels Mozambique are perfect for lighter snacks, while housemade pastas and entrées, including pork Milanese, bean cassoulet, and Ora King salmon, are hearty additions to the table. **Known for:** sangria; brunch dishes; gorgeous patio with twinkle lights. ⑤ *Average main: $25* ✉ *1 Sixth Street, Charlestown* ☎ *617/337-5230* ⊕ *www.dovetailcharlestown.com.*

Monument Restaurant & Tavern

$$ | **AMERICAN** | **FAMILY** | A "gastropub meets bistro," Monument Restaurant & Tavern is quintessential Charlestown with a brownstone vibe of brick and weathered woods, 16-foot ceilings, and a 40-foot bar. Pizza is the menu's superstar, coming out piping and bubbly from the open kitchen's 900-degree oven, which is also used for wings, crab-artichoke dip, and roasted brick chicken. **Known for:** brunch prosecco pails; wood-fired pizza; piled-high sandwiches. ⑤ *Average main: $22* ✉ *251 Main St., Charlestown* ☎ *617/337–5191* ⊕ *www.monumentcharlestown.com.*

Pier 6

$$$ | **SEAFOOD** | For a meal on the waterfront, try Pier 6 in the Charlestown Navy Yard just steps from the USS *Constitution*, where you'll be treated to New England seafood coupled with outstanding harbor views. Plates are piled high with fried calamari, seared octopus, and lobster rolls, and the giant shellfish platter of local oysters, clams, shrimp, and lobster will draw all eyes to your table. **Known for:** lively cocktail scene; fresh shellfish dishes; waterfront location. ⑤ *Average main: $30* ✉ *1 8th St., Pier 6, Charlestown* ☎ *617/337–0054* ⊕ *pier6boston.com.*

Sullivan's Public House

$ | IRISH | This authentic Irish addition to Charlestown focuses on food, offering Scotch eggs wrapped in housemade sausage, pulled pork nachos, loaded potato soup, soda bread, wings, potato boxty, grilled cheese, curry brick chicken, sirloin steak, and more. But don't worry: there will still be plenty of drinking, as the restaurant also offers a big selection of beer, wine, cider, and cocktails (including chilled Irish coffee) for settling into the dark and cozy atmosphere for the night. **Known for:** traditional Irish vibe; newly expanded menu; Scotch eggs. $ Average main: $15 ⊠ 85 Main St., Charlestown ⊕ www.sullivansph.com.

Warren Tavern

$$ | AMERICAN | Built in 1780 and reportedly one of the country's oldest taverns, this restored colonial neighborhood pub in the quaint and historic gaslight district was once frequented by George Washington and Paul Revere. After a blustery walk through the Navy Yard, grab a seat by the fireplace and warm yourself with hearty chowder, lobster mac, or short rib shepherd's pie and a Sam Adams draft. **Known for:** beer selection; short rib shepherd's pie; historical atmosphere. $ Average main: $21 ⊠ 2 Pleasant St., Charlestown ☎ 617/241–8142 ⊕ www.warrentavern.com Ⓜ Community College.

☕ Coffee and Quick Bites

Emack & Bolio's

$ | CAFÉ | Emack & Bolio's has been rocking the Boston frozen treat scene since the 1970s. Diet meets decadence at this smoothie bar/ice-cream parlor that serves in-house microbrewed soda and floats, ice-cream pizzas, and chocolate confections like the chocolate-dipped Twinkie. **Known for:** vegan ice cream; outrageous cones; decadent frozen treats. $ Average main: $5 ⊠ 100 City Sq., Charlestown ⊹ On Freedom Trail near Old Iron Sides ☎ 617/337–3571 ⊕ www.emackandbolios.com.

The Shop at Dovetail

$ | AMERICAN | This grab-and-go counter service shop offers up sandwiches heaping with meats and cheeses, as well as salads and wraps, soups, and cookies. The housemade chips are the perfect crunchy side. **Known for:** unique cold beverages; Spicy Italian sandwich; great service. $ Average main: $10 ⊠ 1 1st Ave., Charlestown ⊕ www.dovetailcharlestown.com/menu/shop.

Sorelle Bakery & Cafe

$ | BAKERY | When you need a break, duck into this hot little bakery for piping hot coffees, teas, and cocoa, or you can take yours chilled to perfection. If you're hungry, dig into one of their well-known bagel or pressed sandwiches, filled croissants, or a freshly made salad with a side of homemade soup du jour. **Known for:** iced coffees; pastries; bagel sandwiches. $ Average main: $10 ⊠ 100 City Sq., Charlestown ☎ 617/242–5980 ⊕ www.sorellecafe.com Ⓜ North Station.

Tradesman Coffee Shop & Lounge

$$ | AMERICAN | Serving locally roasted Barrington Gold Coffee, this coffee shop runs the gamut of grab-and-go java—from cinnamon maple latte to Americano—along with several dine-in options for its 32-seat bar. Sweet snacks include 14 types of mini-doughnuts. **Known for:** wood-fired pizza; Fruity Pebbles doughnut; brisket burger. $ Average main: $18 ⊠ 50 Hood Park Dr., Charlestown ⊕ www.tradesmantown.com.

Zume's Coffee House

$ | CAFÉ | This welcoming locally owned coffee shop has plenty of cozy chairs, local art–filled walls, cheerful purple ceilings, and piping hot mugs of freshly brewed coffee served by friendly baristas. The breakfast and lunch crowds love the grab-and-go sandwiches, such as the house-made burritos and English muffins, but there are also plenty of sweet treats like made-to-order tea cakes, energy bars, brownies, and decorated sugar cookies. **Known for:** tea cakes; homemade

English muffin sandwiches; nitrobrew. $ *Average main: $5* ✉ *221 Main St., Charlestown* ☎ *617/242–0038* ⊕ *www. zumescoffeehouse.com* Ⓜ *Community College.*

Nightlife

The historic waterfront along the harbor and Mystic River affords Charlestown sweeping views of the USS *Constitution,* the Navy Yard and Admiralty, and Boston itself, to which Charlestown is linked by bike paths and the Prison Point and Zakim Bridges. Bunker Hill's needle monument presides over a quiet, elegant neighborhood, while Main Street and City Square attract visitors to casual restaurants and lively taverns.

BARS

The Anchor Boston

BEER GARDENS | Nestled just 20 feet from the oceanfront, The Anchor is an open-air public gathering space, performing arts venue, and wine and beer garden. The two-story venue is full of swings, huge pillows set against stone terraces, lounge sets, and a grassy lawn for relaxing and sipping your cocktail. ✉ *1 Shipyard Park, Charlestown* ⊕ *www.theanchorboston. com.*

Blackmoor Bar & Kitchen

BARS | Watch the sun set over the Zakim Bridge as you peruse the extensive list of 34 rotating draughts, elite bottled beers, cask ale, draught wine, craft spirits, and custom cocktails. Located along the Freedom Trail at the end of the Charlestown Bridge, this watering hole is a favorite among locals to hang out and watch the game (expect crowds). ✉ *1 Chelsea St., Charlestown* ☎ *617/580–8166* ⊕ *www. blackmoorbar.com.*

Tavern at the End of the World

BARS | At the end of your Charlestown trip, hit up this pub with a 50-plus beer list and classic pub fare with an Irish flare. With a backdrop of live music

and traditional Irish *seisiún* (informal sessions), it's the spot to grab a lager with a snack of curry fries or satisfy a huge hunger with a shepherd's pie and the perfect Guinness pour. ✉ *108 Cambridge St., Charlestown* ☎ *617/241–4999* ⊕ *www.tavernattheendoftheworld.com* Ⓜ *Sullivan.*

⬤ Shopping

GIFTS

Place & Gather

SOUVENIRS | This home and boutique shop is the perfect stop along the Freedom Trail for gifts galore. Treat yourself to home accents like candles and vases or New England items such as lobster trays. ✉ *26 Common St., Charlestown* ☎ *617/580–8362* ⊕ *www.placeandgather. com.*

CLOTHING

Slate

WOMEN'S CLOTHING | This corner shop is the sister store to Martha's Vineyard's long-time fashion and lifestyle staple. The inventory supports local artisans, emerging designers, and ethical brands for clothing, jewelry, and home accessories, along with books, cheeky note cards, and clean beauty products. ✉ *54 High St., Charlestown* ⊕ *slatemv.com.*

FOOD

Main Street Pasta & Wine

FOOD | Thanks to its co-owners' past kitchen experience at L'Espalier, this pasta shop opened to much fanfare. You'll leave with everything you need to make a meal—fresh pasta, meatballs, sauce, and a bottle of wine (or beer) from upstairs. ✉ *40 Main St., Charlestown.*

Chapter 6

DOWNTOWN AND THE WATERFRONT

Updated by
Leigh Harrington

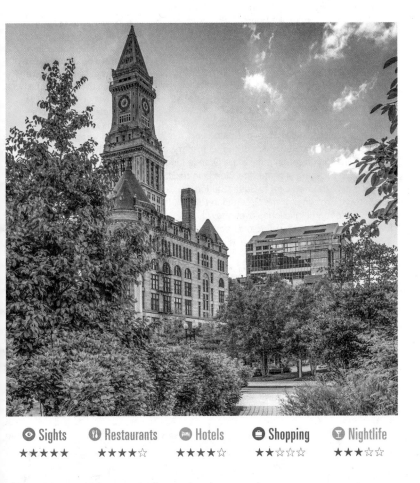

◉ Sights	🍴 Restaurants	🛏 Hotels	🛍 Shopping	🍸 Nightlife
★★★★★	★★★★☆	★★★★☆	★★☆☆☆	★★★☆☆

NEIGHBORHOOD SNAPSHOT

TOP EXPERIENCES

■ **Swim with sea life:** Touch a shark, watch Myrtle the Turtle feed, and see many of the ocean's creatures at the New England Aquarium.

■ **Revolutionary history:** Explore some of the Freedom Trail's most interactive sites, including Old South Meeting House and the Old State House.

■ **Savor Asia's authentic flavors:** Whether you prefer Cambodian, Vietnamese, or Cantonese, Chinatown is a great place to dine.

■ **Splendid waterfront views:** Stroll along the Harborwalk for gorgeous panoramas of Charlestown and East Boston, as well as fancy yachts, ferries, and maybe a harbor seal.

■ **See a show:** Most of the city's stages occupy Downtown's Theater District, and there's always something playing, from opera to Broadway musicals.

GETTING HERE AND AROUND

Travelers can access Downtown Boston very easily, as it is centrally situated. Each of the T's four main subway lines run through it: take the Orange Line to Downtown Crossing or State, the Blue Line to State or Aquarium, the Red Line to South Station or Downtown Crossing, or the Green Line to Park. If you're up for burning calories over a few hours, walking can be a great way to explore the neighborhood, with all its winding roads and historic sites to see along the way.

For the waterfront, get off at Aquarium and walk southeast, or South Station and walk northeast. You can also use the waterfront as a departure and arrival point when traveling by sea. A few ferry services and Boston Water Taxi (☎ *617/261–6620*) operate out of Rowes Wharf, and Long Wharf, and feature dozens of stops around Boston Harbor.

Driving in downtown is not recommended unless absolutely necessary. Parking is nonexistent, and traffic can crawl no matter the time of day.

QUICK BITES

■ **Clover Food Lab.** Famous for its meat-free menu and eco-conscious approach, Clover is an easy pit stop for food along the Freedom Trail. Expect local, organic ingredients in ever-changing options, but the chickpea fritters are a must-sample staple. ✉ *27 School St., Downtown* ⊕ *www. cloverfoodlab.com* Ⓣ *Park, State.*

■ **Dewey Square Food Trucks.** On weekday mornings and afternoons, locally operated food trucks congregate at Dewey Square plaza on the Rose Kennedy Greenway, ready to serve Financial District professionals an eat-it-while-you-walk or picnic meal. Typically, 8 to 10 different options offer variety from curry to Korean. ✉ *Summer St. at Congress St., Financial District* ⊕ *www.rosekennedygreenway.org/food-trucks* Ⓣ *South Station.*

■ **Sal's Pizza.** Grab a slice of cheese (be warned: one slice is actually two, and if you order two, you get four) and a soda from this legendary, small local chain, and take it to-go for a picnic on Boston Common, right across the street. ✉ *150 Tremont St., Downtown* ⊕ *www.sals. com* Ⓣ *Park, Boylston.*

Boston's commercial and financial districts are concentrated in a maze of streets laid out with little logic. They are, after all, only village lanes that happen to be lined with modern, 40-story office buildings. That's not to say the past has been erased; Downtown is one of the city's most historic 'hoods, and here beats the heart of the Freedom Trail.

Take the Orange Line to Downtown Crossing, or the Green Line to Park and walk east, or take the Red Line to South Station and walk west. Downtown is bordered by State Street to the north, Chinatown to the south, Tremont Street and Boston Common on the west, and Boston Harbor wharves on its eastern edge. Be prepared: the tangle of streets can be confusing. If you get lost, don't worry. These streets are also typically short, so you'll be able to reorient yourself quickly. In the meantime, you just might stumble upon something fun and historic.

Here's an interesting fact about Downtown: It's Boston's original landmass, along with the North End. Back in 1630, when Boston's founder, John Winthrop, sailed through, the place looked nothing like it does today. Look at an old map of the then-called Shawmut Peninsula, and you'll understand. Boston was a low-lying, swampy mess, before landfill projects created the Back Bay and significant portions of Chinatown, the South End, and South Boston, in the 19th century.

Washington Street (aka Downtown Crossing) is Downtown's main commercial thoroughfare. The block reeks of history—and sausage carts. Street vendors, flower sellers, and gaggles of teenagers, businesspeople, and shoppers throng the pedestrian mall. Shops like Primark and Macy's have been helping to revitalize the area after a dormant period.

Downtown

◉ Sights

Benjamin Franklin Statue/Boston Latin School

PUBLIC ART | FAMILY | This stop on the Freedom Trail, in front of Old City Hall, commemorates the noted revolutionary, statesman, and inventor. His likeness also marks the original location of the Boston Latin School, the country's oldest public school (founded in 1635). Franklin attended Boston Latin with three other signers of the Declaration of Independence—Samuel Adams, John Hancock, and Robert Treat Paine—but he has the dubious distinction of being the only one of the four not to graduate. ■TIP→ This is Freedom Trail stop 6. ⊠ 45 School St.,

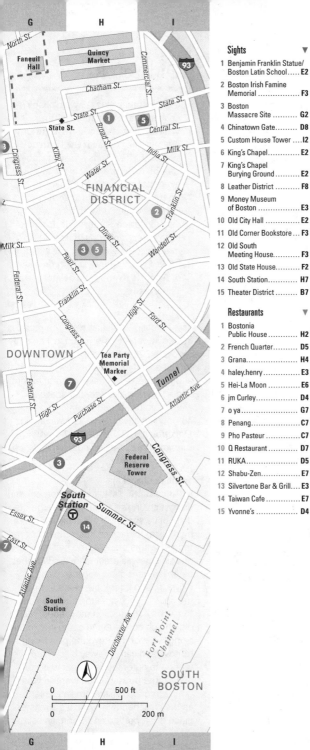

Sights ▼

1 Benjamin Franklin Statue/
Boston Latin School.....**E2**

2 Boston Irish Famine
Memorial **F3**

3 Boston
Massacre Site **G2**

4 Chinatown Gate.........**D8**

5 Custom House Tower **I2**

6 King's Chapel............**E2**

7 King's Chapel
Burying Ground **E2**

8 Leather District **F8**

9 Money Museum
of Boston **E3**

10 Old City Hall **E2**

11 Old Corner Bookstore ...**F3**

12 Old South
Meeting House...........**F3**

13 Old State House.........**F2**

14 South Station............**H7**

15 Theater District **B7**

Restaurants ▼

1 Bostonia
Public House **H2**

2 French Quarter.........**D5**

3 Grana.....................**H4**

4 haley.henry **E3**

5 Hei-La Moon **E6**

6 jm Curley................**D4**

7 o ya **G7**

8 Penang..................**C7**

9 Pho Pasteur **C7**

10 Q Restaurant **D7**

11 RUKA....................**D5**

12 Shabu-Zen...............**E7**

13 Silvertone Bar & Grill....**E3**

14 Taiwan Cafe **E7**

15 Yvonne's **D4**

Quick Bites ▼

1 Chacarero **F5**

2 Clover Food Lab..........**E3**

3 Dewey Square
Food Trucks **G6**

4 George Howell
Coffee....................**D5**

5 Gracenote Coffee **F7**

6 Great Taste Bakery......**E7**

7 High Street Place
Food Hall.................**H5**

8 Sal's Pizza................**C5**

9 Sam LaGrassa's..........**E3**

10 Tasty Burger.............**D4**

11 Tatte Bakery & Café **F2**

12 Tea Do....................**E7**

13 Thinking Cup **C5**

Hotels ▼

1 The Godfrey Hotel **D5**

2 Hilton Boston Downtown/
Faneuil Hall................**I3**

3 Hyatt Regency
Boston **D6**

4 Kimpton Nine Zero
Hotel......................**E3**

5 The Langham,
Boston **H4**

6 Moxy **B7**

7 Omni Parker House......**E3**

8 Revere Hotel **A8**

9 The Ritz-Carlton,
Boston **C6**

10 W Boston **B7**

Downtown ☎ *617/635–3911* ⊕ *www.thefreedomtrail.org* Ⓜ *Park.*

Boston Irish Famine Memorial

MONUMENT | Dedicated in 1998 with this memorial and a small park, artist Robert Shure's two sculptures—one depicting an anguished family on the shores of Ireland, the other a determined and hopeful Irish family stepping ashore in Boston—are a tribute to the rich immigrant past of this most Irish of American cities. ✉ *School St. at Washington St., Downtown* Ⓜ *State, Downtown Crossing.*

Boston Massacre Site

MONUMENT | FAMILY | A circle of cobblestones in front of the Old State House commemorates the Boston Massacre, which happened about 20 feet away. To recap: it was on the snowy evening of March 5, 1770, that nine British soldiers fired in panic upon a taunting mob of more than 75 colonists who were upset over British occupation and taxation. Five townsmen died. In the legal action that followed, the defense of the accused soldiers was undertaken by John Adams and Josiah Quincy, both of whom vehemently opposed British oppression but were devoted to the principle of a fair trial. All but two of the nine regulars charged were acquitted; the others were branded on the hand for the crime of manslaughter. Paul Revere lost little time in capturing the "massacre" in a dramatic engraving that soon became one of the Revolution's most potent images of propaganda. ■ **TIP→ This is Freedom Trail stop 10.** ✉ *206 Washington St., Downtown* ⊕ *www.thefreedomtrail.org* Ⓜ *State.*

Custom House Tower

NOTABLE BUILDING | One of Boston's most recognizable buildings, the gorgeous 1847 Custom House resembles a Greek Revival temple and features an iconic tower that was added much later, in 1915. This addition gave the building notoriety at the time as the city's tallest. Where the skyscraper once operated as a federal building, today, Marriott owns it

as a hotel and vacation club. The public is invited into the Custom House's recently renovated 26th-floor observation deck for unparalleled views of Downtown and Boston Harbor daily at 2 pm, except Friday. Entrance is free, but space is limited, so call ahead for a ticket at least 48 hours in advance. ✉ *3 McKinley Sq., Downtown* ☎ *617/310–6300* ⊕ *www.marriot.com* ⚲ *Call 48 hours in advance.* Ⓜ *State, Aquarium.*

★ King's Chapel

HISTORIC SIGHT | FAMILY | Both somber and dramatic, King's Chapel looms large. Its distinctive shape wasn't achieved entirely by design; for lack of funds, it was never topped with a steeple. The first chapel on this site was erected in 1688 for the establishment of an Anglican place of worship, and it took five years to build the solid Quincy-granite structure seen today. As construction proceeded, the old church continued to stand within the rising walls of the new, the plan being to remove and carry it away piece by piece when the outer stone chapel was completed. The builders then went to work on the interior, which remains essentially as they finished it in 1754; it's a masterpiece of proportion and Georgian calm (in fact, its acoustics make the use of a microphone unnecessary for Sunday sermons). The pulpit, built in 1717, is the oldest pulpit in continuous use on the same site in the United States. To the right of the main entrance is a special pew once reserved for condemned prisoners, who were trotted in to hear a sermon before being hanged on the Common. The chapel's bell is Paul Revere's largest and, in his judgment, his sweetest sounding. For a behind-the-scenes look at the bell or crypt, take a guided tour. You won't be disappointed. ■ TIP➜ This is Freedom Trail stop 5. ⊠ 58 Tremont St., Downtown ☎ 617/523–1749 ⊕ www.kings-chapel.org ⌫ $5 Ⓜ Park, State, Government Center.

King's Chapel Burying Ground
CEMETERY | FAMILY | Legends linger in this oldest of the city's cemeteries, its first proper burying ground. A handy map of famous grave sites is posted a short walk down the left path. Notable people buried here include Elizabeth Pain, the model for Hester Prynne in Nathaniel Hawthorne's The Scarlet Letter; William Dawes Jr., who rode out to warn of the British invasion the night of Paul Revere's famous ride; and John Winthrop, the first governor of Massachusetts, along with several generations of his descendants. ■ TIP➜ This is Freedom Trail stop 5. ⊠ 50 Tremont St., Downtown ☎ 617/523–1749 ⊕ www.kings-chapel.org Ⓜ Park, State, Government Center.

Money Museum of Boston
HISTORY MUSEUM | Although this small museum is only a few years old, the items it houses are not. Call ahead and schedule a private or small group tour for a peek at American currency that dates back as far as the colonial era; exhibits include money made in Boston, the United States, and other parts of the world. Informative and personalized tours are led by a coin and currency expert. ⊠ 41 Bromfield St., Downtown ⊹ Enter through Colonial Trading Company ☎ 617/451–0665

⊕ moneymuseumofboston.org ⌫ Donations requested, depending on group size. Ⓜ Park.

Old City Hall
NOTABLE BUILDING | Built in 1865, Old City Hall is a historic site and served as the municipal seat of government for 38 of Boston's mayors, including famous ones like John "Honey Fitz" Fitzgerald, James Curley, and Kevin White. In its courtyard, find Richard S. Greenough's bronze statue of Benjamin Franklin and a mural marking the original site of the Boston Latin School. Today, Old City Hall is an office building. While you can't really venture too far inside the building, do go up and check out the murals around its entrance. ⊠ 45 School St., Downtown ⊕ www.oldcityhall.com Ⓜ State, Park.

Old Corner Bookstore
NOTABLE BUILDING | Through these doors, between 1845 and 1865, passed some of the century's literary lights: Henry David Thoreau, Ralph Waldo Emerson, and Henry Wadsworth Longfellow—even Charles Dickens paid a visit. Many of their works were published here by James T. "Jamie" Fields, who in 1830 had founded the influential firm Ticknor and Fields. In the 19th century, the graceful, gambrel-roof, early-Georgian structure—built in 1718 on land once owned by religious rebel Anne Hutchinson—also housed the city's leading bookstore. There's a plaque on the wall to read more about its history, but today, somewhat sadly, the building is home to a fast-food joint. ■ TIP➜ This is Freedom Trail stop 7. ⊠ 1 School St., Downtown ⊕ www.thefreedomtrail.org Ⓜ State.

★ Old South Meeting House
NOTABLE BUILDING | FAMILY | This is the second-oldest church building in Boston (although the building is no longer used for religious services), and were it not for Longfellow's celebration of Old North in "Paul Revere's Ride," it might well be the most famous. Today, visitors can learn about its history through exhibits and

Old South Meeting House is Boston's second-oldest church building; it's also where the spark was lit for the infamous Boston Tea Party.

audio programs. Some of the fiercest of the town meetings that led to the Revolution were held here, culminating in the gathering of December 16, 1773, which was called by Samuel Adams to confront the crisis of three ships, laden with dutiable tea, anchored at Griffin's Wharf. The activists wanted the tea returned to England, but the governor would not permit it—and the rest is history. The Voices of Protest exhibit celebrates Old South as a forum for free speech from Revolutionary days to the present. ■TIP→ **This is Freedom Trail stop 8.** ☒ *310 Washington St., Downtown* ☎ *617/720–1713* ⊕ *www. revolutionaryspaces.org* ⊡ *$15 (includes dual admission to Old State House)* Ⓜ *State, Downtown Crossing.*

★ Old State House
NOTABLE BUILDING | FAMILY | This colonial-era landmark has one of the most recognizable facades in Boston, with its gable adorned by a brightly gilded lion and silver unicorn, symbols of British imperial power. This was the seat of the colonial government from 1713 until the Revolution, and after the evacuation of the British from Boston in 1776 it served the independent Commonwealth until its replacement on Beacon Hill was completed in 1798. The Declaration of Independence was first read in public in Boston from its balcony. John Hancock was inaugurated here as the first governor under the new state constitution. Today, it's an interactive museum with exhibits, artifacts, and 18th-century artwork, and tells the stories of Revolutionary Bostonians through costumed guides. ■TIP→ **This is Freedom Trail stop 9.** ☒ *206 Washington St., Downtown* ☎ *617/720–1713* ⊕ *www. revolutionaryspaces.org* ⊡ *$15 (includes dual admission to Old South Meeting House)* Ⓜ *State, Government Center.*

🍴 Restaurants

Downtown, professionals and execs keep the lunch business booming. While 15 to 20 years ago, the streets would get quiet after 6 pm, it's not so today. Dinner and drinks have become a thing, and the neighborhood has followed suit featuring a number of social hot spots with fantastic culinary options after dark.

Bostonia Public House

$$$ | AMERICAN | FAMILY | Airy and classic in atmosphere, this modern restaurant focuses on two things: food and local history (it is, after all, situated in a historic 1902 building). The menu features elevated takes on comfort food; at lunch expect more sandwiches. **Known for:** long bar with lots of seating; live music in the evenings; fantastic weekend brunch. ⑤ *Average main: $30* ⊠ *131 State St., Downtown* ☎ *617/948–9800* ⊕ *www. bostoniapublichouse.com* Ⓜ *Aquarium.*

Grana

$$$ | ITALIAN | FAMILY | Grand and resplendent in appearance—it *is* located in a luxury hotel and former Federal Reserve Bank, after all—Grana features upscale yet casual Italian dishes for lunch and weekend brunch that invite you to dig in. The only drawback to this place is that it isn't open for dinner. **Known for:** signature focaccia bread with a half-dozen different topping options; shareable tea cocktail; family-style three-course brunch. ⑤ *Average main: $26* ⊠ *The Langham, Boston, 250 Franklin St., Downtown* ☎ *617/956–8765* ⊕ *www.langhamhotels. com/en/the-langham/boston/dine/grana* ☾ *No dinner* Ⓜ *State, South Station.*

★ haley.henry

$$$ | WINE BAR | Charcuterie, tinned fish, ceviche: You can eat well at this excellent Downtown wine bar that's small in size but big in reputation. Definitely make a reservation before showing up; it can be busy, even on a Wednesday night. **Known for:** staff knows their stuff; incredible service; wine from small, independent producers. ⑤ *Average main: $35* ⊠ *45 Province St., Downtown* ☎ *617/208–6000* ⊕ *www.haleyhenry.com* ☾ *Closed Sun.– Mon.* Ⓜ *Downtown Crossing, Boylston.*

jm Curley

$$ | AMERICAN | You're guaranteed a tasty meal at this lively bar restaurant that can really get packed. Beer, American comfort food, and sandwiches—like a killer burger and a Nashville hot chicken—are on the menu, as well as a solid lineup of cocktails. **Known for:** tasty snacks, especially the fried pickles; local beers on draft; a secret back-room steak house. ⑤ *Average main: $24* ⊠ *21 Temple Pl., Downtown* ☎ *617/338–5333* ⊕ *www. jmcurleyboston.com* Ⓜ *Park, Boylston.*

RUKA

$$ | FUSION | If you've never heard of *chifa* cuisine (yeah, it's a real thing), you'll wonder why not after having a meal at RUKA, where the kitchen creates dishes inspired by Cantonese-Peruvian and Japanese culinary traditions. The menu features bountiful sushi options, raw bar items, snacks, and wok-prepared dishes. **Known for:** colorful, artful vibes; interesting sushi options; unique Asian-Peruvian fusion cuisine. ⑤ *Average main: $20* ⊠ *The Godfrey Hotel, 505 Washington St., Downtown* ☎ *617/266–0102* ⊕ *www. rukarestobar.com* ☾ *Closed Sun.–Mon.* Ⓜ *Downtown Crossing.*

Silvertone Bar & Grill

$$ | AMERICAN | Devotees of this retro-cool basement restaurant with strong cocktails and reasonable prices swear by the no-fuss menu options, such as a truly addictive macaroni and cheese, meat loaf with mashed potatoes, and steak tips. The wine list is compact but varied and has one of the lowest markups in the city. **Known for:** comfort food; laid-back feel; strong cocktails. ⑤ *Average main: $20* ⊠ *69 Bromfield St., Downtown* ☎ *617/338–7887* ⊕ *www.silvertonedowntown.com* Ⓜ *Park.*

Yvonne's

$$$$ | CONTEMPORARY | For a big, brassy, bountiful night out in an iconic Boston building, head to this reimagined supper club inside the ornate former 1862 Locke-Ober restaurant. The buffed and

beautiful sink into plush chairs in the book-packed library or at the original mahogany mirrored bar to swill down ice-cold martinis and large format drinks. **Known for:** historic setting; large-format cocktails and shared feasts; glamorous supper club concept. $ Average main: $45 ⊠ 2 Winter Pl., Downtown ☎ 617/267–0047 ⊕ www.yvonnesboston.com Ⓜ Park.

● Coffee and Quick Bites

★ Chacarero

$ | **CHILEAN** | This place is famous among the city's working professionals, who willingly wait in long lines for the signature Chilean-style sandwich, a delicious combination of green beans, chicken, muenster cheese, tomatoes, and an avocado spread on fresh bread. There are a few other offerings, including empanadas and rice pudding. **Known for:** signature Chilean sandwich; tasty orange cake; bread baked fresh daily. $ Average main: $13 ⊠ 101 Arch St., Downtown ☎ 617/542–0392 ⊕ chacarero.com ⏱ Closed Sat.–Sun. Ⓜ South Station, Downtown Crossing.

★ Clover Food Lab

$ | **VEGETARIAN** | After more than a decade, locals still love this vegetarian restaurant's chickpea fritters, not to mention the daily changing menu of freshly prepared sustainable and local veg- and vegan-friendly sandwiches and plates. Boston and Cambridge feature a number of Clover locations, but this one is bright and airy with huge windows that open onto School Street. ■TIP➡ **Awesome place to stop for lunch along the Freedom Trail. Known for:** housemade juice sodas and George Howell coffee; sourcing ingredients locally and sustainably; chickpea fritter sandwich. $ Average main: $12 ⊠ 27 School St., Downtown ⊕ www.cloverfoodlab.com Ⓜ Park, State.

Dewey Square Food Trucks

$ | **FAST FOOD** | **FAMILY** | On weekday mornings and afternoons, locally operated food trucks congregate at Dewey Square plaza on the Rose Kennedy Greenway, ready to serve Financial District professionals an eat-it-while-you-walk or picnic meal. Typically, four to five different options offer variety from curry to Korean. **Known for:** always changing options; easily accessible outdoor seating; multiple local food trucks in a gorgeous park location. $ Average main: $12 ⊠ Rose Kennedy Greenway, Dewey Sq., Financial District ⊕ www.rosekennedygreenway.org/foodtrucks Ⓜ South Station.

George Howell Coffee

$ | **CAFÉ** | If you like a premium coffee, head to this fancier-than-mainstream café with origins in Massachusetts. Original, fair-trade roasts are used to make all types of drip coffee and espresso drinks. **Known for:** avocado toast and baked goods; premium coffee roasts; usually having open tables. $ Average main: $10 ⊠ 505 Washington St., Downtown ☎ 857/957–0217 ⊕ www.georgehowellcoffee.com Ⓜ Downtown Crossing, Boylston.

★ High Street Place Food Hall

$ | **FAST FOOD** | **FAMILY** | If you can't agree among your traveling partners what to eat where, this food hall features 20 different local vendors featuring delicious and top-quality foods of all varieties. Gourmet doughnuts from Blackbird, porchetta sandwiches from Pennypacker's, Jewish deli eats from Mamaleh's, sushi at Fuji, and so much more are here. **Known for:** live DJs in the evening; tons of options from local vendors; open anytime you're hungry. $ Average main: $15 ⊠ 100 High St., Downtown ⊕ www.highstreetplace.com ⏱ Closed Sun. Ⓜ South Station, Downtown Crossing.

Sal's Pizza

$ | **PIZZA** | **FAMILY** | Some would argue that this small, local, independent chain may have the best Italian-style pizza in

Boston. Families on the go or solitary travelers looking for a quick bite should stop in for a slice and a soda. **Known for:** great meal deals; convenient location across from Boston Common and Freedom Trail start; pizza by the (large) slice. ⑤ *Average main: $12* ✉ *150 Tremont St., Downtown* ☎ *617/227–1010* ⊕ *www.sals. com* Ⓜ *Park, Boylston.*

Sam LaGrassa's

$ | SANDWICHES | FAMILY | It's unlikely you'll simply happen upon this famed Boston sandwich joint, tucked away as it is, but the hefty sandwiches (they weigh pounds) are worth the trouble of looking. The line typically snakes out the door, but while you're standing in it, you can savor the deli-like smells and browse the meats behind the counter. **Known for:** huge portions; a long line that moves fast; pastrami and corned beef made in-house. ⑤ *Average main: $15* ✉ *44 Province St., Downtown* ☎ *617/357–6861* ⊕ *www.samlagrassas.com* ⊘ *Closed weekends. No dinner* Ⓜ *Park.*

Tasty Burger

$ | BURGER | FAMILY | This local burger joint (there are a few of them, actually) channels a malt shop from the 1950s while serving milkshakes, beer and wine, and soda, the latter in some uncommon flavors like Fresca and Cheerwine. The star of the menu is, of course, the burger, which comes in the most basic version or more daring renditions like a spicy jalapeño or brûléed gorgonzola. **Known for:** thick milkshakes; value pricing; delicious burgers. ⑤ *Average main: $9* ✉ *48 Winter St., Downtown* ☎ *617/303–5055* ⊕ *www. tastyburger.com* Ⓜ *Park, Downtown Crossing.*

★ Tatte Bakery & Café

$ | ISRAELI | This upscale bakery and café takes pastries to the next level. From tea cakes to the Jerusalem bagel, expect hearty baked goods with an air of elegance and influenced by the owner's Israeli heritage. **Known for:** signature nut tarts that are as pretty as they are tasty;

convivial atmosphere; Owner Or's take on traditional North African shakshuka, served with challah bread. ⑤ *Average main: $12* ✉ *125 Summer St., Downtown* ☎ *617/488–9525* ⊕ *www.tattebakery. com* Ⓜ *South Station.*

Thinking Cup

$ | CAFÉ | Across from Boston Common, Thinking Cup caters to a mixed crowd of area professionals and students from nearby Emerson College. Rarely is the coffeehouse not packed with caffeine addicts looking for their next fix of Stumptown coffee, whether it's in the form of a single origin pour-over or a macchiato. **Known for:** awesome sandwiches, especially the Jittery Hen, made with coffee-braised chicken; no Wi-Fi access; signature lattes: the hazelnut is made with roasted hazelnut paste, and the honey-cinnamon with a house-made syrup. ⑤ *Average main: $10* ✉ *165 Tremont St., Downtown* ☎ *617/482–5555* ⊕ *www.thinkingcup.com* Ⓜ *Boylston, Park.*

Hotels

The Godfrey Hotel

$$$ | HOTEL | This chic, bustling boutique hotel is popular with business folk, who appreciate the ease of walking to the nearby Financial District. **Pros:** Frette linens; complimentary bikes and yoga mats; ideal for business travelers. **Cons:** expensive valet parking; no airport shuttle; added daily "urban fee" of $30. ⑤ *Rooms from: $350* ✉ *505 Washington St., Downtown* ☎ *617/804–2000, 855/649–4500* ⊕ *www.godfreyhotel-boston.com* ⇄ *242 rooms* ⦿ *No Meals* Ⓜ *Downtown Crossing.*

Hilton Boston Downtown/Faneuil Hall

$$ | HOTEL | If you're looking for comfortable downtown lodging, you'll find it at this classic business hotel located inside a 1920s art deco skyscraper, complete with mahogany paneling and soft gold lighting. **Pros:** 24-hour fitness and business centers; clean, quiet, and 100%

smoke-free; ideal for business travelers. **Cons:** pets welcome for $50 nonrefundable fee; doesn't have a Hilton Honors lounge; $15 daily Wi-Fi fee. $ *Rooms from: $275* ⊠ *89 Broad St., Downtown* ☎ *617/556–0006* ⊕ *www.hilton.com* ⇨ *403 rooms* ⓞ| *No Meals* Ⓜ *State.*

Hyatt Regency Boston

$$$$ | **HOTEL** | **FAMILY** | Hyatt Regency Boston sits amid the colorful Downtown Crossing neighborhood right on the edge of the Theater District and just steps away from world-renowned cultural attractions, businesses, and universities like Suffolk and Emerson. **Pros:** steps from Financial District and historic Downtown; 52-foot heated, indoor saline swimming pool; good for business travelers, with a 24-hour business center and free Wi-Fi. **Cons:** views of office buildings from guest rooms; thin walls; $30 daily destination fee. $ *Rooms from: $400* ⊠ *1 Ave. de Lafayette, Downtown* ☎ *617/912–1234* ⊕ *www.hyatt.com/ en-US/hotel/massachusetts/hyatt-regency-boston/bosto* ⇨ *502 rooms* ⓞ| *No Meals* Ⓜ *Downtown Crossing.*

★ Kimpton Nine Zero Hotel

$$$ | **HOTEL** | **FAMILY** | This Kimpton boutique hotel is sleek, sleek, sleek—all smooth lines, neutral tones, wood, and leather, and then bam! sudden bursts of vibrant color and pop art. **Pros:** in-room spa therapy available; late-afternoon hosted lobby wine reception (daily, 5–6 pm); complimentary bikes and kid's scooters. **Cons:** daily $25 amenities fee; no airport shuttle; smallish rooms. $ *Rooms from: $350* ⊠ *90 Tremont St., Downtown* ☎ *617/772–5800, 866/906–9090* ⊕ *www. ninezero.com* ⇨ *190 rooms* ⓞ| *No Meals* Ⓜ *Park, Government Center.*

★ The Langham, Boston

$$$$ | **HOTEL** | One of Boston's most luxurious hotels just got more so: an extensive renovation to the 1922 Renaissance Revival building has both preserved its heritage as the former Federal Reserve Bank of Boston and

elevated it into a contemporary luxury retreat. **Pros:** concierge who specializes in Boston's universities; glass-enclosed, heated indoor pool; lavish rooms. **Cons:** far from Seaport District and Fenway neighborhoods; cost is prohibitive to some; a bit of a walk to public transportation. $ *Rooms from: $600* ⊠ *250 Franklin St., Downtown* ☎ *617/451–1900* ⊕ *www. boston.langhamhotels.com* ⇨ *312 rooms* ⓞ| *No Meals* Ⓜ *South Station.*

Omni Parker House

$$$ | **HOTEL** | **FAMILY** | There's more than a century and a half of rich and varied history within these walls, where JFK proposed to Jackie and Charles Dickens gave his first reading of *A Christmas Carol*. **Pros:** overflowing with history; great location on the Freedom Trail; in-room fitness kits. **Cons:** thin-walled rooms can be noisy; area parking is very expensive; small rooms, some of which are a bit dark. $ *Rooms from: $320* ⊠ *60 School St., Downtown* ☎ *617/227–8600, 800/843–6664* ⊕ *www.omniparkerhouse. com* ⇨ *551 rooms* ⓞ| *No Meals* Ⓜ *Park.*

The Ritz-Carlton, Boston

$$$$ | **HOTEL** | **FAMILY** | The city's only Ritz is puttin' on the ritz with freshly renovated guest rooms inspired by nature and luxury. **Pros:** excellent service; great on-site bar; overlooks Boston Common. **Cons:** food service is expensive; steep valet parking costs; fee to access Equinox Sports Club, unless you're staying on Club Level. $ *Rooms from: $800* ⊠ *10 Avery St., Downtown* ☎ *617/574–7100, 800/542–8680* ⊕ *www.ritzcarlton.com* ⇨ *193 rooms* ⓞ| *No Meals* Ⓜ *Boylston.*

ⓨ Nightlife

BARS

Avery Bar

BARS | Whether you're staying at The Ritz or just stopping by for a drink, the decadent and modern Avery Bar serves some serious, handcrafted cocktails, including a few without alcohol. While this is a hotel lobby bar to be sure, the experience is anything but. The warm ambience attracts a fortysomething crowd, and there are a few select small plates for anyone who's hungry. ⊠ *The Ritz-Carlton Boston, 10 Avery St., Downtown* ☎ *617/574–7176* Ⓜ *Downtown Crossing, Chinatown.*

Beantown Pub

BARS | Beantown Pub cleverly posits itself to be "the only pub in the world where you can drink a cold Sam Adams while viewing a cold Sam Adams." And it's true, since this casual bar sits on the Freedom Trail, across Tremont Street from the Granary Burying Ground where the Founding Father is interred. The bar is a fine place to watch multiple sports events on television, shoot pool, or people-watch. There's also a standard pub menu, usually served until midnight. No kids are allowed after 6 pm. ⊠ *100 Tremont St., Downtown* ☎ *617/426–0111* ⊕ *www.beantownpub. com* Ⓜ *Park, Downtown Crossing.*

★ **The Fed**

BARS | This sumptuous nightlife spot is billed as a "British-inspired cocktail bar with a sophisticated New England twist." Sink into swivel, leather high-top stools at the bar, barrister chairs, or banquettes, and order up fancy food made casual, including the signature three-cheese toastie. They serve excellent craft cocktails and two dozen wines by the glass. In nice weather, The Fed features an outdoor terrace. ⊠ *The Langham, Boston, 250 Franklin St., Downtown* ☎ *617/956–8765* ⊕ *www.langhamhotels. com/en/the-langham/boston/dine/the-fed* ☞ *Reservations recommended* Ⓜ *State, South Station.*

Good Life

BARS | This funky bar in a heritage flatiron building mixes exotic martinis and fresh-juice cocktails and boasts a whopping selection of international vodkas. The basement level lounge draws eclectic crowds for dancing and live music. ⊠ *28 Kingston St., Downtown*

☎ *617/451–2622* ⊕ *www.goodlifebar.com* Ⓜ *Downtown Crossing, South Station.*

★ **The Last Hurrah**

COCKTAIL LOUNGES | Whiskey, wine, and loads of atmosphere: they're all staples within this historic bar at the Omni Parker House hotel, where mahogany club chairs and silver-tray service might make you feel like a Boston Brahmin, even if only for a dram or two. Be sure to order Boston Cream Pie in the place where it was invented. ⊠ *60 School St., Downtown* ☎ *617/305–1888* ⊕ *www.omnihotels.com/hotels/boston-parker-house/dining/the-last-hurrah* Ⓜ *Park.*

★ **Mariel**

COCKTAIL LOUNGES | Fitzgerald's *The Beautiful and Damned* meets the breezy tropics within this Havana-inspired nightlife spot. Mariel best serves those who appreciate good food and drink, a fun vibe, and a vivacious atmosphere—it gets louder as it gets later. Think arepas, plantain dumplings, gulf shrimp, Cuban-style pizza, fresh juices, and mojitos. ⊠ *10 Post Office Sq., Downtown* ☎ *617/333–8776* ⊕ *www.marielofficial. com* Ⓜ *State.*

Performing Arts

FILM

Orpheum Theatre

CONCERTS | At more than 170 years old, this midsize historic theater has hosted everything from vaudeville and film to opera and concerts. To visit the Orpheum today, you must have a ticket to an event. ⊠ *1 Hamilton Place, Downtown* ☎ *617/482–0106* ⊕ *crossroadspresents. com/pages/orpheum-theatre* Ⓜ *Park.*

Shopping

Historically, shopping has been the biggest reason to visit the Downtown Crossing area of the Downtown neighborhood, although its heyday was in the early part of the 20th century. Then and now, stores collect where Washington and Summer Streets meet and disperse from there. Today, you can find off-price clothing and shoe retailers, department stores like Macy's and Primark, and loads of jewelers.

BOOKS

★ Brattle Book Shop

BOOKS | Bibliophiles can't get enough of this old-timey book store that has been in operation since 1825 and is, literally, chockablock with books floor to ceiling and stuffed into corners. The owner Ken Gloss, who regularly tours with *Antiques Roadshow*, fields queries from passionate book lovers about out-of-print, rare, antique, and foreign-language tomes. If you're simply in need of a read for the ride home, browse the rolling carts in Brattle's adjacent outdoor lot, where books of all genres go for $5, $3, or just $1. ⊠ *9 West St., Downtown* ☎ *617/542–0210* ⊕ *www.brattlebookshop.com* Ⓜ *Downtown Crossing.*

SPECIALTY SHOPS

Appelboom

OTHER SPECIALTY STORE | Dutch luxury pen specialist Appelboom has opened its second brick and mortar location in what used to be Bromfield Pen Shop. You can find all major fountain pen brands, rollerballs, and ballpoints, as well as all types of accessories, from inks to paper goods. ⊠ *49 Bromfield St., Downtown* ☎ *617/482–9053* ⊕ *www.appelboom. com* Ⓜ *Park.*

JEWELRY

Jewelers Exchange Building

JEWELRY & WATCHES | Back in the mid-20th century when Downtown Crossing was truly a shopping mecca, this building drew crowds for its selection of precious gems and metals. Today, this building still bustles with its array of more than 75 independent jewelry artisans, who sell luxury watches, engagement rings, engraved silver, and much more. ⊠ *333 Washington St., Downtown* Ⓜ *Downtown Crossing, Park.*

★ Skylight Jewelers

JEWELRY & WATCHES | This independently owned jewelry store features custom creations, from gorgeous engagement rings to signature carved moonstone jewelry. Men's jewelry is a specialty. ⊠ *44 School St., Downtown* ☎ *617/426–0521* ⊕ *skylightjewelers.com* Ⓜ *State.*

Chinatown, Theater District, and Leather District

The heart of Asian-American life in Boston beats in Chinatown, with its authentic restaurants, cultural festivals, markets, and, of course, thousands of residents. Reportedly, it's the third largest Chinatown in the United States, after those in San Francisco and Manhattan, although today's neighborhood runs the spectrum of many Far East cultures, from Thai to Taiwanese, Korean to Cambodian. Before the 1870s, the area was resettled a few times as immigrant groups moved in and out: Syrian, Irish, Jewish, Italian. Chinese laborers arrived and settled here after 1870, and their families kept coming through the 1950s. Today, Beach Street serves as Chinatown's main street. The neighborhood is bounded by Essex, Washington, Lincoln and Marginal Streets; the Tufts Medical Center complex occupies approximately one third of the area.

Just west of Chinatown, the majority of Boston's historic stages reside in the Theater District, which means the area is a hot spot for ballet, opera, Broadway tours, stand-up comedy, and other performing arts productions. Emerson College students keep the vibe young.

And, then, to the east of Chinatown, a very small enclave known as the Leather District is bounded by Kneeland Street, Essex Street, Atlantic Avenue, and Lincoln Street. Before its 19th-century brick warehouses (now residential lofts) boomed with leather and textile merchants, it was known as South Cove, a soggy area that was filled in with land during the 1830s. Today, the Leather District features a few destination standouts, including the city's best sushi restaurant and South Station.

Sights

Chinatown Gate

NOTABLE BUILDING | Two foo lions ward off evil for those who pass through the massive, traditional paifang gate that signals your entrance to Chinatown. It was donated to the Asian residents of Boston by Taiwan, in the early 1980s. You'll likely see red lanterns hanging from it; they signify good luck. The main square around the gate acts as a gathering place for the neighborhood's residents, who meet to socialize or play games. The gate is situated at Beach Street, and it also marks the end of the Greenway. ⊠ *Beach St. at Hudson St., Chinatown* Ⓜ *South Station.*

Leather District

NEIGHBORHOOD | Opposite South Station and inside the angle formed by Kneeland Street and Atlantic Avenue is a corner of Downtown that has been relatively untouched by high-rise development: the old Leather District. For those who like to get a sense of history through place, this is probably the best place in downtown Boston to get an idea of what the city's business center looked like in the late 19th century as the wholesale supply area for raw materials in the days when the shoe industry was a regional economic mainstay. Today, a few leather firms remain, but most warehouses now contain expensive loft apartments. ⊠ *Bordered by Kneeland St., Atlantic Ave., and Lincoln St., Chinatown* Ⓜ *South Station.*

South Station

TRAIN/TRAIN STATION | This gorgeous colonnaded granite structure is to Boston what Grand Central Station is to New York. Behind its grand 1900s facade, you'll find an airy, modern transit center that services the MBTA commuter rail for lines originating west and south of the city, the Red and Silver subway lines, and regional Amtrak trains. Thanks to its eateries, coffee bars, newsstand, and other shops, waiting for a train here can actually be a pleasant experience. South Station's bus terminal for Greyhound, Peter Pan, and other bus lines, is right next door. ■TIP→ **South Station is a great launching point for exploring a variety of neighborhoods, including Downtown, Chinatown, and the Seaport.** ⊠ *700 Atlantic Ave., Downtown* ⊕ *www.south-station. net* Ⓜ *South Station.*

Theater District

HISTORIC DISTRICT | Bounded by Washington and West Streets, Marginal Road, and Charles Street South, the Theater District is fertile ground for Boston's performing arts scene—traditional, avant-garde, and otherwise. Each theater—the Wang, the Shubert, the Majestic, the Colonial, the Wilbur, the Paramount, the Modern, the Charles Playhouse, and the Opera House—has a history all its own and most have been restored within the last two decades. Emerson College and its campus occupy a large part of the neighborhood, and student interest brings in some acts from around the world. Night owls can enjoy stand-up shows at a few comedy clubs or feel the beat at a variety of dance and nightclubs. ⊠ *Theater District* Ⓜ *Boylston.*

Restaurants

When it comes to cuisine, Old World and New World traditions mingle in Chinatown, although the emphasis is definitely on the former. Restaurants are a big draw for this neighborhood, and today, Chinese establishments are interspersed with Vietnamese, Cantonese, Korean, Japanese, Thai, Taiwanese, and Malaysian eateries, to name a few. Many places are open after midnight. On Sunday, Bostonians often head here for dim sum.

French Quarter

$$$ | CAJUN | Tucked in next to the Opera House, the French Quarter's marquee signage fits right in. This ode to Louisiana features a menu of popcorn shrimp, fried okra, sticky chicken, and crab-crusted catfish, and toasts the Southern experience with a Vieux Carré and much more. **Known for:** good service; excellent cocktails; pre- or post-theater spot. $ *Average main: $26* ✉ *545 Washington St., Downtown* ☎ *617/542–5555* ⊕ *www.frenchquarterboston.com* Ⓜ *Downtown Crossing.*

★ Hei La Moon

$ | CHINESE | FAMILY | This Cantonese dim sum palace occupies two floors; its contemporary space is decked out with golden chandeliers and ultra-violet decor. Carts of dim sum delicacies are the star attraction here, but diners can also find a menu of Chinese dishes, including eight styles of soup, hot-pot dinners, moo shi, kung pao, lo mein, and egg foo yong. **Known for:** inexpensive prices; hot pot; dim sum. $ *Average main: $10* ✉ *83 Essex St., Chinatown* ☎ *617/338–8813* ⊕ *www.heilamoon.com* Ⓜ *South Station.*

★ o ya

$$$$ | SUSHI | Despite o ya's tucked-away location and hidden door, the place isn't exactly a secret: critics from the *New York Times, Bon Appétit,* and *Food & Wine* have all named this improvisational sushi spot among the best in the country. The chef-owner plates a 20-course nightly omakase dinner with sushi and cooked preparations. **Known for:** expensive prices; advance reservations a must; delicate, beautiful, sophisticated sushi. $ *Average main: $250* ✉ *9 East St., Chinatown* ☎ *617/654–9900* ⊕ *o-ya.*

restaurant/o-ya-boston ۞ *Closed Sun.– Mon.* Ⓜ *South Station.*

Penang

$ | MALAYSIAN | If you've never tried Malaysian cuisine before, start with Penang's Hainan chicken, roti, and coconut rice, all favorite menu items. The restaurant is fairly spacious—a rarity for restaurants in the neighborhood—and boasts a unique wooden interior. **Known for:** tasty Hainan chicken; great service; one of the only Malaysian restaurants in the region. $ *Average main: $17* ✉ *685 Washington St., Chinatown* ☎ *617/451–6372* ⊕ *www.penangboston. us* Ⓜ *Chinatown.*

Pho Pasteur

$ | VIETNAMESE | Day or night, patrons pack this Vietnamese staple of the Chinatown neighborhood known for its steaming bowls of pho. A lengthy menu offers plenty of alternatives, vermicelli dishes, traditional Vietnamese preparations, and about 20 options for vegetarians. **Known for:** unique espresso and soda beverages, plus smoothies; millennial crowd; traditional Vietnamese pho. $ *Average main: $14* ✉ *682 Washington St., Chinatown* ☎ *617/482–7467* ⊕ *www.phopasteurboston.net* Ⓜ *Chinatown, Boylston.*

Q Restaurant

$$$ | ASIAN FUSION | For a more upscale Chinatown experience, look no farther than this sleek Asian outpost with a full cocktail menu, extensive sushi bar, and addictive Mongolian-style hot pot menu featuring rich, robust broths served with a fleet of herbs, chilis, and ginger for further seasoning to taste. Order whatever vegetables, seafood, meats, and noodles you want to cook at the table, from paper-thin slices of Wagyu rib eye to shelled shrimp. **Known for:** good cocktails; long wait times for tables; flavorful, Mongolian-style hot pot. $ *Average main. $35* ✉ *660 Washington St., Chinatown* ☎ *857/350–3968* ⊕ *www.thequsa.com* Ⓜ *Chinatown.*

Shabu-Zen

$$$ | ASIAN FUSION | Hot pot is the name of the game at this neighborhood spot tucked into the heart of Chinatown. As you sit around a central high-top bar, you can dip thinly sliced wagyu beef, pork cheek, or a sampling of seafood into your selection of nearly a dozen different types of broth. **Known for:** serves alcohol; service is top-quality and attentive; excellent options for vegetarians. $ *Average main: $28* ⊠ *16 Tyler St., Chinatown* ☏ *617/292–8828* ⊕ *www.shabuzen.com* Ⓜ *Chinatown.*

Taiwan Cafe

$$ | TAIWANESE | Unsurprisingly, this Chinatown restaurant specializes in the cuisine culture of Taiwan, and has for 40-plus years. The big challenge is selecting what to eat from the massive menu of authentic dishes, although the tofu and house-special fried pork chop over rice are two of the best. **Known for:** house-special fried pork chop; open late; huge menu. $ *Average main: $20* ⊠ *34 Oxford St., Chinatown* ☏ *617/426–8181* ⊕ *www.ordertaiwancafe.com* Ⓜ *Chinatown.*

☕ Coffee and Quick Bites

★ Gracenote Coffee

$ | CAFÉ | Gracenote roasts top-shelf coffee beans using its own unique process here in Massachusetts, and then serves it in a teeny Leather District storefront just across the border from Chinatown. The flavor is well worth the slightly out-of-the-way jaunt to this hipster haven for pour-overs and espresso drinks that are the focus of the menu. **Known for:** extensive variety of milk alternatives; really friendly baristas; unmatched coffee. $ *Average main: $6* ⊠ *108 Lincoln St., Chinatown* ⊕ *www.gracenotecoffee.com* Ⓜ *South Station.*

Great Taste Bakery

$ | CHINESE | Just before you reach the Chinatown Gate, this Hong Kong–style take-out bakery offers you red bean buns, milk cake, fruit puffs, and custard tarts, among other sweet and savory baked goods. Prices are a bargain, but there's nowhere to sit, so plan to take your treats to go. **Known for:** low prices; authentic flavors; Hong Kong–style custard tarts. $ *Average main: $5* ⊠ *61 Beach St., Chinatown* ☏ *617/426–6688* ⊟ *No credit cards* Ⓜ *South Station, Chinatown.*

Tea Do

$ | CHINESE | You may have to wait in line to get into this Chinatown destination for cold drinks, but the fruity popping bubbles and green tea, aloe vera, and milk bubble tea are worth the wait. If you really want to step up your game, try the cheese-foam tea or the brown sugar tiger milk. **Known for:** lots of flavors; tasty boba; long lines. $ *Average main: $9* ⊠ *8 Tyler St., Chinatown* ☏ *617/988–8002* ⊕ *www.teadocafe.com* Ⓜ *South Station, Chinatown.*

🛏 Hotels

Moxy

$$ | HOTEL | One of Boston's newest hotels under the Marriott umbrella features a sleek exterior and artful flair (say, like custom murals by well-known street artists), and come nightfall, there's a boisterous, rave-like nightlife scene. **Pros:** 24th-floor rooftop lounge for guest-only use; floor-to-ceiling windows in every room; Bar Moxy work-fun space featuring board games, free Wi-Fi, coffee, cocktails, and food. **Cons:** lots of street noise; small rooms; not good for families. $ *Rooms from: $299* ⊠ *240 Tremont St., Theater District* ☏ *617/793–4200* ⊕ *www.marriott.com/hotels/travel/bos-ox-moxy-boston-downtown* ⇥ *340 rooms* ⦿ *No Meals* Ⓜ *Boylston, Chinatown.*

Revere Hotel

$$$ | **HOTEL** | This stylish spot embraces New England history with a twist— you'll notice artwork tied to Paul Revere throughout the hotel, like a steampunk sculpture constructed out of recycled metals by a local artist. **Pros:** rooftop pool and bar has amazing city views; balconies in every room; dog-friendly hotel, complete with bedding and a puppy menu of snacks. **Cons:** elevators can get congested; for less mobile folks, it's a bit of a walk to Freedom Trail sites; $30 guest amenity fee per day. *Rooms from: $350 ✉ 200 Stuart St., Theater District ☎ 617/482–1800 ⊕ www.reverehotel.com ➴ 356 rooms ❍ Free Breakfast Ⓜ Arlington, Boylston.*

W Boston

$$$ | **HOTEL** | Across the street from its sister property, Moxy Hotel, this towering Theater District staple caters to the see-and-be-seen crowd and is fronted by a metal-and-glass awning outfitted with soft, color-changing neon lights that cast a cheeky glow on passersby. **Pros:** expansive on-site Bliss spa; signature W feather-top beds; free electric-car charging stations. **Cons:** late-night street noise; expensive parking; lobby can be loud. *Rooms from: $399 ✉ 100 Stuart St., Theater District ☎ 617/261–8700 ⊕ www.whotels.com/boston ➴ 238 rooms ❍ No Meals Ⓜ Boylston, Tufts Medical Center.*

ⓨ Nightlife

BARS

4th Wall

BARS | This local hangout tries to be seen as a dive bar, but it's much nicer and too new to be called one. The menu features bar bites, hearty entrées, and a burger of the week, all made from scratch in the kitchen, while the bar serves craft beers on draft, craft cocktails, and vodka-soaked gummy bears. To find the 4th Wall from Tremont Street, look for the small, brick building with a gable roof squeezed in by much taller surrounding buildings. ✉ 228 Tremont St., Theater District ☎ 857/957–0909 ⊕ www.4thwall-restaurant.com Ⓜ Chinatown, Boylston.

Offsuit

COCKTAIL LOUNGES | Incredibly unique and thoughtful beverages are the stars at this small, under-the-radar cocktail lounge tucked into the Leather District near Chinatown. A recent concoction called the Praying Mantis pairs cachaça and gin with snap peas, green Jolly Ranchers, lime cordial, mint, and sour cream. Offsuit allows a few reservations per night, but most traffic is walk-in, and all table service is limited to 90 minutes. ✉ 5 Utica St., Chinatown ☎ 781/855–6111 ⊕ www.offsuitboston.com Ⓜ South Station.

★ Shojo

BARS | Fun, lively and contemporary, Shojo puts a shine on its little corner of Chinatown. This family-owned, edgy nightspot serves Asian-inspired imaginative craft cocktails using ingredients like Thai chili-infused vodka, cucumber ice, and yuzu, while the kitchen sends out tasty, modern, and chef-focused small plates that put a spin on traditional Asian preparations. ✉ 9 Tyler St., Chinatown ☎ 617/423–7888 ⊕ www.shojoboston.com Ⓜ Chinatown.

W Lounge

BARS | Vibrant purples and metallics set the tone at this chic, but accessible, bar and lounge in the W Hotel. The resident DJ—and he's legit—curates music (Thursday through Saturday) based on the crowd, while patrons warm up by the fireplace and nosh on small bites and signature cocktails. ✉ W Hotel, 100 Stuart St., Theater District ☎ 617/261–8700 Ⓜ Boylston, Chinatown.

COMEDY

Nick's Comedy Stop

COMEDY CLUBS | Boston's oldest comedy club has been yukking it up since 1977—Jay Leno reportedly got his start here. The lineup in this intimate venue is always funny, whether you catch a local comic on the weekend, or, occasionally, a well-known one. ⊠ *100 Warrenton St., Theater District* ⊕ *www.nickscomedystop.com* Ⓜ *Boylston.*

The Wilbur
COMEDY CLUBS | Inside this 1914-built, American-style stage, some of the country's funniest comics—like Tracy Morgan, Whitney Cummings, and Jenny Slate—get audiences laughing and laughing. On nights when comedy is off the bill, The Wilbur hosts more intimate musical performances by some serious national talent. ⊠ *246 Tremont St., Theater District* ☎ *617/248–9700* ⊕ *www.thewilbur.com* Ⓜ *Boylston.*

🎭 Performing Arts

THEATER
Boch Center Wang Theatre and Shubert Theatre
CONCERTS | The historic Wang Theatre, which opened in 1925 and holds an audience of 3,500, and its 1910 little sister, the Shubert Theatre, partner up to create this performance-space complex dedicated to national and international productions, dance companies, concerts, and headlining comics. ■ **TIP→ Check out the schedule online, and order your tickets before you come to town.** ⊠ *265 and 270 Tremont St., Theater District* ☎ *800/982–2787 Wang Theatre, 866/348–9738 Shubert Theatre* ⊕ *www.bochcenter.org* Ⓜ *Boylston.*

Charles Playhouse
THEATER | FAMILY | The Charles Playhouse celebrated its 175th anniversary in 2014 with a $2 million renovation. The vintage stage—also formerly serving as a church, Prohibition-era speakeasy, and jazz club—has been hosting a long-running local favorite: *Blue Man Group* since 1995. The uniquely exhilarating production features a trio of deadpan performance artists painted vivid cobalt as they pound drums, share eureka moments, spray

sloppy good will, and freely dispense toilet paper. ■ **TIP→ First-timer alert: dress casual, especially if you're seated down front.** ⊠ *74 Warrenton St., Theater District* ☎ *617/426–6912 general box office, 800/258–3626 Blue Man Group tickets* ⊕ *boston.broadway.com/theatre/charles-playhouse* ⊠ *$45–$95* Ⓜ *Boylston.*

★ Citizens Bank Opera House
THEATER | FAMILY | The 2,700-seat, vaudville-era Beaux-Arts building has been lavished with $35 million worth of gold leaf, lush carpeting, and rococo ornamentation. Today, it is the city's premier destination for touring Broadway companies as well as the home theater for the Boston Ballet and all its productions, including its famous *The Nutcracker.* ⊠ *539 Washington St., Theater District* ☎ *617/695–6955 Boston Ballet tickets, 800/982–2787 Broadway show tickets* ⊕ *www.bostonoperahouse.com* Ⓜ *Boylston, Chinatown, Downtown Crossing.*

Emerson Colonial Theater
THEATER | Welcome to Boston's oldest continuously operated theater, where musical magic was created, performed and transformed by the likes of Stephen Sondheim, Ethel Merman, and George and Ira Gershwin, before traveling to Broadway to become "official"—tryouts included *Porgy and Bess, Follies, Grand Hotel,* and *La Cage aux Folles.* Today, the Colonial continues to present Broadway tours and headline bands and musicians. ■ **TIP→ The Colonial hosts historical tours typically once monthly; reserve tickets online.** ⊠ *106 Boylston St., Theater District* ☎ *888/616–0272 for tickets* ⊕ *www.emersoncolonialtheatre.com* Ⓜ *Boylston.*

Emerson Cutler Majestic Theatre
THEATER | This gorgeous beaux arts theater and historic landmark was built with opera performances in mind, so it's fitting that Boston Lyric Opera calls it home for some performances today. You'll also see smaller traveling productions. It's owned by Emerson College,

which uses the stage for ArtsEmerson, its presenting arm that focuses on contemporary theater from around the globe. ✉ *219 Tremont St., Theater District* ☎ *617/824–8400* ⊕ *www.emersontheatres.org* Ⓜ *Boylston.*

Emerson Paramount Center

THEATER | Look for the orange-, red-, and yellow-lit marquee on Washington Street, and you'll find the Paramount. Three performance spaces make up this 1930s-era complex owned by Emerson College. Its main stage features an art deco vibe and performing artists from all over. Smaller, alternative productions—think classic and art films, professional puppet shows, circus arts—can also take place in a black box theater or a screening room. ArtsEmerson schedules all events here. ✉ *559 Washington St., Theater District* ☎ *617/824–8400* ⊕ *www.emersontheatres.org* Ⓜ *Downtown Crossing, Boylston, Park.*

Waterfront

You won't hear the sound of crashing waves thanks to Boston's protected and relatively calm inner harbor, but the lean stretch of coastline running from South Station to the North End is one of the prettiest, most serene escapes you'll encounter in this city. And, it manages to slow the pace of the bustling, driven Financial District behind it.

Along the Waterfront, you'll encounter wharf after wharf of harbor activity: private vessels, luxury yachts, harbor cruises, ferries, and more. Long Wharf, Central Wharf with the New England Aquarium, and Rowes Wharf are the three most prominent. Other attractions in this neighborhood include the Boston Harborwalk, the Rose Kennedy Greenway, and the lesser-known gems just offshore, the Boston Harbor Islands. Many upscale hotels and restaurants make the most of the expansive water views.

The Boston Harborwalk ◉

The walking path along Boston's shoreline stretches 43 miles. In the North End, Downtown, the Waterfront, the Seaport, and South Boston, marked signs point the way—plus you can find maps online. The public can hop on and off at their leisure, using the Harborwalk for exercise and other types of recreation. In the Waterfront, the trail navigates the city's many wharves; it also features art exhibits, educational panels, stationary viewfinders, and open green space (⊕ *www.bostonharborwalk.org*).

◉ Sights

Boston Harbor Islands National Recreation Area

ISLAND | **FAMILY** | Comprising 34 tiny islands and peninsulas, this is one of the city's best hidden gems—and it's literally out of sight. Stretching from South Boston (Castle Island) to the coastlines of South Shore towns Hingham and Hull, each island is different, but most feature abundant nature with miles of lightly traveled trails, shoreline, sea life, and wild plants. The focal point is 39-acre Georges Island and its partially restored pre–Civil War Fort Warren that once held Confederate prisoners. Pets and alcohol are not allowed on the Harbor Islands. ■**TIP**➔ **Ferries shuttle visitors from Boston to Georges and Spectacle Islands daily during summer months. Plan to spend a whole day exploring!** ✉ *Boston Harbor Islands National and State Park Welcome Center, 191 W. Atlantic Ave., Waterfront* ☎ *617/223–8666* ⊕ *www.bostonharborislands.org* ⊗ *Closed mid-Oct.–mid-May* Ⓜ *Aquarium.*

Located in the Boston Harbor Islands National Recreation Area, the 105-acre Spectacle Island is just 4 miles offshore of downtown Boston and accessible by ferry.

Christopher Columbus Park (*Waterfront Park*)

CITY PARK | This green space bordering the harbor and several of Boston's restored wharfs is a pleasant oasis of benches and a long arborlike shelter twinkling with colorful strands of lights at night. Lewis Wharf and Commercial Wharf (north of the park), which long lay nearly derelict, had been transformed into condominiums, offices, restaurants, and upscale shops by the mid-1970s. There are sprinklers, lawn games, summer outdoor movie nights, a playground, and even free Wi-Fi. The Rose Kennedy Rose Garden is enclosed by a wrought-iron fence in the center of the park. ⊠ *Atlantic Ave., bordered by Atlantic Ave., Commercial Wharf, and Long Wharf, North End* ☎ *617/635–4505* ⊕ *www.foccp.org* Ⓜ *Aquarium.*

Long Wharf

HISTORIC SIGHT | Long Wharf starts east of Atlantic Avenue, and it serves as the launching point for many of the city's water tours, sails, and cruises. Halfway down the wharf, you can have dinner at Chart House, a nice seafood restaurant, but note that the historic building it houses was once John Hancock's counting house and still contains his vault. The New England Aquarium sits next door, at Central Wharf. ⊠ *Long Wharf, Waterfront* Ⓜ *Aquarium.*

★ New England Aquarium

AQUARIUM | **FAMILY** | As interesting and exciting as it is educational, this aquarium is a must for those who are curious about what lives in and around the sea. The building's glass-and-steel exterior is constructed to mimic fish scales, and seals bark and swim in the outdoor tank. Inside the main facility, more than 30,000 animals of 800 different species frolic in simulated habitats.

In the semi-enclosed outdoor space of the New Balance Foundation Marine Mammal Center, visitors can enjoy the antics of northern fur seals and sea lions while gazing out at Boston Harbor.

Waterfront

A   **B**   **C**   **D**   **E**

Christopher Columbus Park

Boston Harbor Islands National & State Park

Quincy Market

Chatham

Long Wharf

Long Wharf

Aquarium

State St.

Long Wharf

State St.

U.S. Custom House

New England Aquarium

Central Wharf

Central St.

Milk St.

Broad St.

Milk St.

Custom House St.

India St.

Rose Kennedy Greenway

India Wharf

Boston Inner Harbor

Water St.

Milk St.

Broad St.

Franklin St.

Atlantic Ave.

Wharf District Park

FINANCIAL DISTRICT

Oliver St.

Batterymarch St.

Wendell St.

Rowe's Wharf

Franklin St.

High St.

Franklin St.

High St.

Oliver St.

Foster's Wharf

93

Fort Point Channel

Pearl St.

High St.

Ford St.

Purchase St.

KEY

- **1** Sights
- **1** Restaurants
- **1** Quick Bites
- **1** Hotels
- Ⓣ Subway station

Tea Party Memorial Marker

Tunnel

Old Northern Ave.

U.S. Federal Courthouse

Congress St.

Atlantic Ave.

Evelyn Moakley Bridge

0   300 ft

0   100 m

The real showstopper, though, is the four-story, 200,000-gallon ocean-reef tank. Ramps winding around the tank lead to the top level and allow you to view the inhabitants from many vantage points. Up top, the Yawkey Coral Reef Center features a seven-tank exhibit gallery that gives a close-up look at animals that might not be easily seen on the reef. Don't miss the five-times-a-day feedings; each lasts nearly an hour and takes divers 24 feet into the tank.

Get up close to a variety of species of sharks and rays at the Trust Family Foundation Shark and Ray Touch Tank, the largest of its kind on the East Coast.

Add on to the day at the aquarium's IMAX theater, which takes you on virtual journeys from the bottom of the sea to the depths of outer space in 3-D films. ■ TIP➔ **Planning to see an IMAX film or go whale-watching in addition to visiting the New England Aquarium? Ask about combo tickets to save some money.** ⊠ *1 Central Wharf, Waterfront* ☎ *617/973–5200* ⊕ *www.neaq.org* ⊠ *$32; $10 IMAX; $65 whale watch* Ⓜ *Aquarium.*

Rose Kennedy Greenway

CITY PARK | FAMILY | This one linear mile of winding parks marks the path the highway once took through the city (à la the Big Dig). A walk through shows off a wide variety of flora and fauna from the North End to Chinatown. Lawn furniture and games, seasonal farmers' and artists' markets, art installations, water features, live performances, free Wi-Fi, a beer garden, and more make it a lively spot, especially in warmer months. There's a one-of-a-kind, hand-carved carousel; and the food truck scene has grown into a bustling lunchtime destination. ⊠ *Waterfront* ✛ *Between New Sudbury St. in North End and Beach St. in Chinatown; along Atlantic Ave.* ⊕ *www.rosekennedygreenway.org* Ⓜ *State, Haymarket, Chinatown, Aquarium.*

Rowes Wharf

MARINA/PIER | Get a feel for "lifestyles of the rich and famous" at Rowes Wharf, where a six-story arched rotunda frames gorgeous views of Boston Harbor complete with mega-yachts and a water-set gazebo. Well-heeled patrons stay and dine at Boston Harbor Hotel and its upscale restaurants. ■ TIP➔ **During summer months, stop by any weekday night for free live music performances or film screenings, hosted by the hotel.** ⊠ *Rowes Wharf, Waterfront* Ⓜ *Aquarium, South Station.*

🍴 Restaurants

Chart House

$$$$ | AMERICAN | This may be one of the oldest U.S. buildings you'll ever eat in; John Hancock—yes, *that* John Hancock—called this place his counting house back in the mid-18th century. Today, it's a seafood restaurant perched on Long Wharf right over Boston Harbor, offering grilled, baked, or blackened fish, prepared seafood dishes, and steaks. **Known for:** excellent selection of crafted mocktails; fresh fish options; historic location with views. Ⓢ *Average main: $37* ⊠ *60 Long Wharf, Waterfront* ☎ *617/227–1576* ⊕ *www.chart-house.com* Ⓜ *Aquarium.*

Granary Tavern

$$$ | AMERICAN | This place has a lively atmosphere day or night, with the sounds of revelry bouncing off its exposed brick walls and beams in a building originally designed by historic architect Charles Bulfinch. The kitchen serves up decent, if over-priced, comfort food, and if you're looking for a late afternoon lunch and a couple of drinks, this is your spot. **Known for:** historic digs that enhance the mood; lively atmosphere in a great location; pricey food. Ⓢ *Average main: $30* ⊠ *170 Milk St., Waterfront* ☎ *617/449–7110* ⊕ *www.granarytavern.com* Ⓜ *Aquarium.*

Legal Sea Foods

$$$ | SEAFOOD | FAMILY | What began as a tiny restaurant adjacent to a Cambridge fish market has grown to important regional status, with more than 30 East Coast locations, including almost a dozen in Boston. The hallmark is the freshest possible seafood, whether you have it wood-grilled, in New England chowder, or doused in an Asia-inspired sauce. **Known for:** family-friendly setting; locations all over town; classic, fresh New England seafood. $ *Average main: $30* ⊠ *Long Wharf, 255 State St., Waterfront* ☎ *617/742–5300* ⊕ *www.legalseafoods.com* M *Aquarium.*

Nebo Cucina & Enoteca

$$$ | ITALIAN | FAMILY | Its name, Nebo, is an acronym for "North End Boston," which is the neighborhood where the first iteration of this local restaurant operated for a time. Today, it serves rustic Italian dishes from the owners' *nonna* in a classy, corner spot on the waterfront. **Known for:** 10 different styles of pizza on housemade dough; all-Italian wine list, many by the glass; zucchini lasagna that beat Bobby Flay in his own game on Food Network's *Throwdown.* $ *Average main: $30* ⊠ *520 Atlantic Ave., Waterfront* ☎ *617/723–6326* ⊕ *www.neborestaurant.com* ☾ *Closed Sun.* M *South Station.*

★ Rowes Wharf Sea Grille

$$$$ | SEAFOOD | Sophisticated and pristine yet unpretentious, this restaurant pairs nautical flair with fresh seafood, fitting for its setting overlooking Boston Harbor. Seafood selections are mainly from nearby Atlantic waters and favor Asian flavors. **Known for:** extraordinary seafood towers; afternoon tea service; lovely views of Boston Harbor beyond Rowes Wharf. $ *Average main: $45* ⊠ *70 Rowes Wharf, Waterfront* ☎ *617/856–7744* ⊕ *www.roweswharfseagrille.com* M *Aquarium, South Station.*

State Street Provisions

$$$ | AMERICAN | Right on the edge of Boston Harbor, this restaurant serves tasty, tavern-style food—seafood, salads, burgers, and crispy pizza—for a fraction of the cost of some of its neighbors. The atmosphere is lively and unpretentious, the cocktails are craft-made, and a tasty brunch is served on the weekends until mid-afternoon. **Known for:** crispy thin-crust pizzas; raw bar featuring East Coast oysters; burger served on an English muffin. $ *Average main: $25* ⊠ *255 State St., Waterfront* ☎ *617/863–8363* ⊕ *www.statestreetprovisions.com* M *Aquarium.*

★ Trade

$$$ | GREEK FUSION | Trade celebrates the culinary heritage of the Mediterranean region, and more specifically, Greece, with a curated menu by James Beard Award–winning chef-owner Jody Adams. Think perfectly charred flatbreads and pita that fly out of the open-hearth oven, eggplant- and feta-inspired dishes, lamb meatballs, and locally caught fish prepared Greek-style. **Known for:** extensive Greek spirits list; boisterous after-work, professional crowd; lemon-thyme roasted half-chicken. $ *Average main: $27* ⊠ *540 Atlantic Ave., Waterfront* ☎ *617/451–1234* ⊕ *www.trade-boston.com* ☾ *Closed Sun.–Mon.* M *South Station.*

☕ Coffee and Quick Bites

James Hook & Co.

$$$ | SEAFOOD | FAMILY | This Waterfront seafood shanty leaves all its frills for its lobster-loaded rolls; they're served with mayo or with butter, in a bun, and wrapped with foil so you can sit for a minute or eat it on the go. Other specialties include lobster mac and cheese, whole boiled lobster, stuffed clams, and the shrimp and corn chowder. **Known for:** whole-cooked lobsters; rustic vibe and no-frills seating; lobster rolls on the go. $ *Average main: $31* ⊠ *440 Atlantic Ave., Waterfront* ☎ *617/423–5501* ⊕ *www.jameshooklobster.com* M *South Station.*

★ Kane's Donuts

$ | BAKERY | FAMILY | A favorite among Financial District 9-to-5ers, this local mom and pop doughnut shop sells crave-worthy flavors, from the standard honey dip and chocolate glazed to the more elaborate crème brûlée and maple bacon. Kane's also offers 10 different seriously delicious gluten-free varieties. **Known for:** gluten-free options; the perfect morning coffee break; fluffy doughnuts. $ *Average main: $6* ✉ *90 Oliver St., Waterfront* ☎ *857/317–2654* ⊕ *www.kanesdonuts.com* Ⓜ *State, South Station.*

🛏 Hotels

★ Boston Harbor Hotel at Rowes Wharf

$$$$ | HOTEL | Boston has plenty of landmarks, but none are as synonymous with hospitality as Boston Harbor Hotel. **Pros:** free Wi-Fi and in-room tablet; premier views of Boston Harbor or the city; water shuttle to Logan Airport. **Cons:** the spa books up early, so make an advance reservation; not convenient to the Back Bay, South End, or Fenway neighborhoods; pricey. $ *Rooms from: $800* ✉ *70 Rowes Wharf, Waterfront* ☎ *617/439–7000, 800/752–7077* ⊕ *www.bostonharborhotel.com* ⤴ *232 rooms* ⑩ *No Meals* Ⓜ *Aquarium, South Station.*

Boston Marriott Long Wharf

$$$$ | HOTEL | FAMILY | Families favor this spot that looks like a big brick ship docked in Boston Harbor for its proximity to the New England Aquarium, Faneuil Hall Marketplace, and the North End. Guest rooms open to a five-story atrium, and some have views of the park, harbor, or aquarium. **Pros:** beautiful upper-level swimming pool with harbor views; centrally located for family interests; free Wi-Fi. **Cons:** far from the Back Bay; parking is difficult to find; surrounding area is packed with tourists. $ *Rooms from: $600* ✉ *296 State St., Waterfront* ☎ *617/227–0800* ⊕ *www.marriott.com* ⤴ *415 rooms* ⑩ *No Meals* Ⓜ *Aquarium.*

Harborside Inn

$$$ | HOTEL | With rates that are considerably lower than most Waterfront hotels, this hotel with an understated charm is an exceptional value. **Pros:** free Wi-Fi; close to key tourist sites; inexpensive. **Cons:** no turndown service; no valet; no on-site restaurant. $ *Rooms from: $325* ✉ *185 State St., Waterfront* ☎ *617/723–7500, 888/723–7565* ⊕ *www.harborsideinnboston.com* ⤴ *116 rooms* ⑩ *No Meals* Ⓜ *Aquarium.*

InterContinental Boston

$$$$ | HOTEL | Notice the two opulent, 22-story towers wrapped in blue glass facing Boston's waterfront, and you'll have found the InterContinental hotel. **Pros:** rooms have panoramic views; Miel restaurant and its seasonal waterfront dining terrace; close to the Financial District and South Station. **Cons:** far from Newbury Street and Back Bay shopping; soundproofing needs improvement; no airport shuttle service. $ *Rooms from: $400* ✉ *510 Atlantic Ave., Waterfront* ☎ *617/747–1000, 866/493–6495* ⊕ *www.icbostonhotel.com* ⤴ *424 rooms* ⑩ *No Meals* Ⓜ *South Station.*

🍸 Nightlife

★ Rowes Wharf Bar

BARS | Never mind the elegant setting and the extraordinary water views, this is a classic cocktail lover's bar. On the menu, there are punches, fizzes, slings, and juleps to start, before you move on to sparkling cocktails and spirited specialties, bourbon, whiskeys, and single malts. If you're one to really sit and savor, do so over Macallan or Louis XIII de Remy Martin. To keep the buzz at bay, the food menu features a few appetizers as well as oysters. ✉ *70 Rowes Wharf, Waterfront* ☎ *617/439–7000* Ⓜ *South Station.*

Trillium Garden

BEER GARDENS | BYOF (F is for food) for an afternoon or evening spent at Trillium Brewing's seasonal beer garden smack dab in the middle of the Rose Kennedy Greenway and directly across from Boston Harbor Hotel. The place is generally mobbed, especially considering it's both dog and kid friendly, leaving hardly an excuse to stay away. On tap: a rotating variety of beer crafted by the Boston-based brewery. ⊠ *High St. at Atlantic Ave., Waterfront* ⊕ *www.trilliumbrewing. com/pages/greenway* Ⓜ *Aquarium.*

☃ Activities

Boston Harbor Cruises

BOAT TOURS | **FAMILY** | From whale watches out to Stellwagen Bank National Marine Sanctuary to cruises around Boston's inner harbor at sunset to the "Codzilla" speedboat ride, this long-running water tour company features about a dozen different ways to experience and learn about Boston Harbor. ⊠ *1 Long Wharf, Waterfront* ☎ *877/733–9425* ⊕ *www.bostonharborcruises.com* ☞ *From $25* Ⓜ *Aquarium.*

Classic Harbor Line

BOAT TOURS | Hop aboard one of the teak-decked classic sailing vessels that are anchored at Boston Harbor's Rowes Wharf for a day sail, evening champagne cruise, or the occasional brunch or live music cruise. ⊠ *60 Rowes Wharf, Waterfront* ☎ *212/913–9991* ⊕ *www.classicharborline.com* ☞ *$38–$70* ☉ *Closed Nov.– Apr.* Ⓜ *South Station, Aquarium.*

THE BACK BAY AND SOUTH END

7

Updated by
Cheryl Fenton

👁 Sights	🍴 Restaurants	🛏 Hotels	🛍 Shopping	🍸 Nightlife
★★★★★	★★★★☆	★★★★☆	★★★★★	★★★★☆

NEIGHBORHOOD SNAPSHOT

TOP EXPERIENCES

■ **Stroll down Newbury Street:** Join the throngs of students, locals, and visitors window-shopping on Newbury Street.

■ **Tour the Boston Public Library:** Admire the architecture, revel in the artistry, and even enjoy an excellent lunch at the Boston Public Library—all without taking out a single book.

■ **Ride a Swan Boat:** Visit the Public Garden on a sunny summer day and take in the scenery from your seat on the Swan Boat, and don't forget to check out the bronze statues of the ducklings from Robert McCloskey's classic *Make Way for Ducklings*.

■ **Embrace the arts:** Enjoy a play, concert, or art installation at the "people's" art-and-culture complex, Boston Center for the Arts.

■ **Shop 'til you drop:** Shop Columbus Avenue and Tremont Street for the perfect additions to your home decor and head to the artsy SoWa Open Market on the weekends.

■ **See South End architecture:** Walk the streets around Rutland Square, Union Park, and Bay Village. Architecture buffs will love the Victorian and Italianate row houses harking back to the neighborhood's 19th-century roots.

GETTING HERE

There are myriad parking garages in the Back Bay. Take the Orange Line to the Back Bay station or the Green Line to Copley for the heart of the shopping areas. The Arlington stop on the Green Line is the most convenient to the Public Garden. ■ **TIP→ To stay oriented, remember that the north–south streets are arranged in alphabetical order, from Arlington to Hereford.**

The South End is easily accessible by the T; take the Orange Line to Back Bay and head south on Dartmouth Street to Columbus Avenue, or jump off the Silver Line at Union Park Street or East Berkeley Street to access the neighborhood.

QUICK BITES

■ **J.P. Licks.** Stop in for a tasty scoop of ice cream or a freshly brewed cup of joe. ✉ *1106 Boylston St., Back Bay* ⊕ *jplicks.com* Ⓣ *Back Bay.*

■ **Pavement Coffeehouse.** Grab a homemade bagel and coffee at this hip spot. ✉ *286 Newbury St., Back Bay pavementcoffeehouse.com* Ⓣ *Hynes, Copley.*

■ **Trident Booksellers & Cafe.** You can enjoy breakfast all day and pick up a bestseller or magazine at this bookstore/café. ✉ *338 Newbury St., Back Bay* ⊕ *www.tridentbookscafe.com* Ⓣ *Hynes.*

PLANNING YOUR TIME

■ If you're not a shopper, you can cover the Back Bay in about two hours. If you are, allow at least half a day to cover Newbury Street and the shops at Copley Place and the Pru Center. Around the third week of April, magnolias arrive and the flowers are magnificent along Comm Ave. In May the Public Garden bursts with color, thanks to its flowering dogwood trees and thousands of tulips.

■ A few hours is perfect to explore the South End; add a few more hours for a show at Boston Center for the Arts or to dine at one of the area's excellent restaurants.

In the roster of famous American neighborhoods, the Back Bay stands with New York's Park Avenue and San Francisco's Nob Hill as a symbol of propriety and high social standing. Before the 1850s it truly was a bay, a tidal flat that formed the south bank of a distended Charles River. The filling in of land along the isthmus that joined Boston to the mainland (the Neck) began in 1850, and resulted in the creation of the South End.

Though the name says it, it's hard to believe that this broad street grid running from the Public Garden up elegant Beacon Street and Commonwealth Avenue, divided by a center strip of statues and magnolia trees, was, until the 1830s, landfilled dockland. Anchored by 200 Clarendon Street (formerly the John Hancock Tower) and the Prudential, the Back Bay is studded with beautiful churches around Copley Square and lively Newbury Street.

Today, the Back Bay is a mix of the historic and the new, happily coexisting in one of the city's loveliest areas, with everything from landmarks, like Trinity Church, and green spaces, such as the Esplanade, to a multitude of hip bars and fine-dining restaurants. Adjacent to the Back Bay, the South End nonetheless has its own identity, with stunning Victorian row houses, art galleries galore, Boston's largest gay community, and plenty of unique shops and restaurants of every type.

The Back Bay

To the north a narrow causeway called the Mill Dam (later Beacon Street) was built in 1814 to separate the Back Bay from the Charles. By the late 1800s, Bostonians had filled in the shallows to as far as the marshland known as Fenway, and the original 783-acre peninsula had been expanded by about 450 acres. Thus the waters of the Back Bay became the neighborhood of the Back Bay.

Heavily influenced by the then-recent rebuilding of Paris according to the plans of Baron Georges-Eugène Haussmann, the Back Bay planners created thoroughfares that resemble Parisian boulevards. The thorough planning included service alleys behind the main streets to allow provisioning wagons to drive up to basement kitchens. (Now they're used for waste pickup and parking.)

The Swan Boats have been an iconic part of Boston Public Garden since 1877.

Today the area retains its posh spirit, but mansions are no longer the main draw. Locals and tourists alike flock to the commercial streets of Boylston and Newbury to shop at boutiques, galleries, and the usual mall stores. Many of the bars and restaurants have patio seating and bay windows, making the area the perfect spot to see and be seen while indulging in ethnic delicacies or an invigorating coffee. The Boston Public Library, Symphony Hall, and numerous churches ensure that high culture is not lost amid the frenzy of consumerism.

◉ Sights

Arlington Street Church

CHURCH | Opposite the Park Square corner of the Public Garden, this church was erected in 1861—the first to be built in the Back Bay. Though a classical portico is a keynote and its model was London's St. Martin-in-the-Fields, Arlington Street Church is less picturesque and more Georgian in character. Note the 16 Tiffany stained-glass windows. During the year preceding the Civil War the church was a hotbed of abolitionist fervor. Later, during the Vietnam War, this Unitarian-Universalist congregation became famous as a center of peace activism. ⊠ *351 Boylston St., Back Bay* ☎ *617/536–7050* ⊕ *www. ascboston.org* ✎ *Guided and self-guided tours $5* ⊘ *Closed Tues.* Ⓜ *Arlington.*

★ Boston Public Garden

GARDEN | FAMILY | America's oldest botanical garden is replete with gorgeous formal plantings, a 4-acre lagoon famous since 1877 for its foot-pedal–powered (by a captain) Swan Boats (⊕ *swanboats. com*), and the *Make Way for Ducklings* bronzes sculpted by Nancy Schön, a tribute to the 1941 classic children's story by Robert McCloskey.

Keep in mind that Boston Public Garden and Boston Common are two separate entities with different histories and purposes and a distinct boundary between them at Charles Street. The Common has been public land since Boston was founded in 1630, whereas the Public Garden belongs to a newer Boston,

Back Bay Mansions

If you like nothing better than to imagine how the other half lives, you'll suffer no shortage of old homes to sigh over in Boston's Back Bay. Most, unfortunately, are off-limits to visitors, but there's no law against gawking from the outside. Stroll Commonwealth, Beacon, and Marlborough Streets for the best views.

Of particular note are the Burrage Mansion (⊠ 314 Commonwealth Ave.); the Oliver Ames Mansion (⊠ 355 Commonwealth Ave.); and the Ames-Webster Mansion (⊠ 306 Dartmouth St.), which can all be admired from the outside, at a respectable distance, of course.

For details on lectures, films, and other events offered in some mansions that are now home to respected institutions, such as the French Cultural Center (⊠ 53 Marlborough St.) and the Goethe-Institut (⊠ 170 Beacon St.), check out the Boston Globe's art section or calendar listings.

occupying what had been salt marshes on the edge of the Common. By 1837 the tract was covered with an abundance of ornamental plantings donated by a group of private citizens. Near the Swan Boat dock is what has been described as the world's smallest suspension bridge, designed in 1867 to cross the pond at its narrowest point. The beds along the main walkways are replanted every spring. The tulips during the first two weeks of May are especially colorful, and there's a sampling of native and European tree species. ⊠ Bound by Arlington, Boylston, Charles, and Beacon Sts., Back Bay ☎ 617/522–1966 Swan Boats ⊕ friendsofthepublicgarden.org ⊠ Swan Boats $4 Ⓜ Arlington.

★ **Boston Public Library**

LIBRARY | FAMILY | This venerable institution is a handsome temple to reading and a valuable research library, as well as an art gallery of sorts, and you don't need a library card to enjoy it. At the main entrance hall of the 1895 Renaissance Revival building, take in the immense stone lions by Louis St. Gaudens, the vaulted ceiling, and the marble staircase. The corridor at the top of the stairs leads to Bates Hall, one of Boston's most sumptuous interior spaces. This is the main reading room, 218 feet long with a barrel vault ceiling 50 feet high. The murals at the head of the staircase, depicting the nine muses, are the work of the French artist Pierre Puvis de Chavannes; those in the room to the right are Edwin Austin Abbey's interpretations of the Holy Grail legend. Upstairs, in the public areas, is John Singer Sargent's mural series Triumph of Religion. The library offers free art and architecture tours. The McKim building contains a Renaissance-style courtyard inspired by Rome's Palazzo della Cancelleria. A covered arcade furnished with chairs rings a fountain; you can bring books or lunch into the peaceful courtyard. ⊠ 700 Boylston St., at Copley Sq., Back Bay ☎ 617/536–5400 ⊕ www.bpl.org Ⓜ Copley.

Boylston Street

STREET | Less posh than Newbury Street, this broad thoroughfare is the southern commercial spine of the Back Bay, lined with interesting restaurants and shops, and where you'll find the Boston Marathon finish line. Also located here is the Boston Marathon Bombing Memorial, composed of light spires and stone

The Boston Public Library is a stunning cathedral of books.

pillars, which pays homage to the Boston Marathon bombing victims at the sites where they were killed on April 15, 2013. ✉ *Back Bay*.

Charles River Reservation

CITY PARK | **FAMILY** | Runners, bikers, and in-line skaters crowd the Charles River Reservation at the Esplanade along Storrow Drive, the Memorial Drive Embankment in Cambridge, or any of the smaller and less-busy parks farther upriver. Here you can cheer a crew race, rent a canoe or a kayak, learn to sail, or simply sit on the grass, sharing the shore with packs of hard-jogging university athletes, in-line skaters, moms with strollers, dreamily entwined couples, and intense academics. ✉ *Back Bay* ☎ *617/727–4708* ⊕ *www. mass.gov/eea/agencies/dcr/massparks/ region-boston/charles-river-reservation. html* Ⓜ *Charles/MGH, Chinatown, Copley*.

Church of the Covenant

CHURCH | This 1867 Gothic Revival church, a National Historic Landmark at the corner of Newbury and Berkeley Streets, has one of the largest collections of liturgical windows by Louis Comfort Tiffany in the country. It's crowned by a 236-foot-tall steeple—the tallest in Boston—that Oliver Wendell Holmes called "absolutely perfect." Inside, a 14-foot-high Tiffany lantern hangs from a breathtaking 100-foot ceiling. The church is now Presbyterian and United Church of Christ. ✉ *67 Newbury St., enter at church office, Back Bay* ☎ *617/266–7480* ⊕ *www.cotcbos.org* Ⓜ *Arlington*.

Commonwealth Avenue Mall

PROMENADE | The mall that extends down the middle of the Back Bay's Commonwealth Avenue, which serves as the green link between the Public Garden and the public parks system, is studded with statuary. One of the most interesting memorials, at the Exeter Street intersection, is a portrayal of naval historian and author Samuel Eliot Morison seated on a rock as if he were peering out to sea. The Boston Women's Memorial, installed in 2003, sculpted by Meredith Bergmann, is between Fairfield

The Boston Marathon

The Boston Marathon is held on the third Monday of April, which is also known as Patriots' Day in Massachusetts, a state holiday that commemorates the first battles of the Revolutionary War in 1775. Though it missed being the country's first marathon by a year (the first, in 1896, went from Stamford, Connecticut, to New York City), the Boston Marathon is arguably the nation's most prestigious. Why? It's the only marathon in the world for which runners have to qualify; it's the world's oldest continuously run marathon; and it's been run on the same course since it began.

The marathon passes through Hopkinton, Ashland, Framingham, Natick, Wellesley, Newton, Brookline, and Boston; only the last few miles are run in the city proper, which has a festival atmosphere. Throngs of supporters and fans come out to cheer on the racers and eat and drink at restaurants and bars along the route. Some spectators have returned to the same spot for generations, bringing their lawn chairs and barbecues.

In 2013, a horrific bombing near the race's finish line killed three people and injured scores of others. The tragic event shocked Boston and the nation, but runners and supporters have returned in even bigger numbers. Located near the finish line is the poignant Boston Marathon Bombing Memorial, composed of light spires and stone pillars, which pays homage to the victims. Security, however, has gotten tighter during the race, especially in Boston proper. Driving is impossible anywhere near the route and the T is packed, so plan accordingly.

and Gloucester Streets. Statues of Abigail Adams, Lucy Stone, and Phillis Wheatley celebrate the progressive ideas of these three women and their contributions to Boston's history.

A dramatic and personal memorial near Dartmouth Street is the Vendome Hotel Fire Memorial, dedicated to the nine firemen who died in a 1972 blaze at the Back Bay's Vendome Hotel, which, now office space, is across the street. The curved black-granite block, 29 feet long and waist high, is etched with the names of the dead. A bronze cast of a fireman's coat and hat is draped over the granite. ⊠ *Commonwealth Ave. between Arlington St. and Massachusetts Ave., Back Bay* Ⓜ *Arlington, Copley.*

Copley Place

STORE/MALL | Two modern structures dominate Copley Square—200 Clarendon (also still referred to by its former name, the Hancock) off the southeast corner and the even more assertive Copley Place skyscraper on the southwest. An upscale, glass-and-brass urban mall built between 1980 and 1984, Copley Place includes two major hotels: the high-rise Westin and the Marriott Copley Place. Dozens of shops, restaurants, and offices are attractively grouped on several levels, surrounding bright, open indoor spaces. ⊠ *100 Huntington Ave., Back Bay* ⊕ *www.simon.com/mall/copley-place* Ⓜ *Copley.*

Copley Square

PLAZA/SQUARE | FAMILY | Every April thousands find a glimpse of Copley Square the most wonderful sight in the world: this is where the runners of the Boston Marathon end their 26.2-mile race. The civic space is defined by three monumental older buildings. One is the stately, bowfront 1912 Fairmont Copley Plaza

Back Bay - West of Dartmouth Street

KEY
- ① Sights
- ① Restaurants
- ① Quick Bites
- ① Hotels
- Ⓣ Subway station

Back Bay - East of Dartmouth Street

Charles River

Arthur Fiedler Footbridge

0   500 ft
0   150 m

BACK BAY

Commonwealth Avenue Mall

Exeter Street Theater

Old South Church

Copley

Copley Square

Boston Public Library

Copley Place

Prudential Center

Back Bay

hotel, which faces the square on St. James Avenue and serves as a dignified foil to its companions, two of the most important works of architecture in the United States: Trinity Church—Henry Hobson Richardson's masterwork of 1877—and the Boston Public Library, by McKim, Mead & White. The 200 Clarendon (Hancock) Tower looms in the background. To honor the runners who stagger over the marathon's finish line, bronze statues of the Tortoise and the Hare engaged in their mythical race were cast by Nancy Schön, who also did the much-loved *Make Way for Ducklings* group in the Public Garden. From May through October, a popular farmers' market draws crowds. ⊠ *Bounded by Dartmouth, Boylston, and Clarendon Sts. and St. James Ave., Back Bay* Ⓜ *Copley.*

Emmanuel Church

CHURCH | Built in 1860, this Back Bay Gothic Episcopal church is popular among classical music lovers—every Sunday morning at 10, from September to May, as part of the liturgy, a Bach cantata, and music by Schütz, Mendelssohn, and others, including music written by living composers, is performed; guest conductors have included Christopher Hogwood and Seiji Ozawa. From May to September, the Chapel Choir, comprised of both professional and volunteer singers, performs. ⊠ *15 Newbury St., Back Bay* ☎ *617/536–3355* ⊕ *www.emmanuel-boston.org* Ⓜ *Arlington.*

Esplanade

PROMENADE | FAMILY | Near the corner of Beacon and Arlington Streets, the recently redone Arthur Fiedler Footbridge crosses Storrow Drive to the 3-mile-long Esplanade and the Hatch Memorial Shell. The free concerts here in summer include the Boston Pops' immensely popular televised July 4 performance. For shows like this, Bostonians haul lawn chairs and blankets to the lawn in front of the shell; bring a takeout lunch from a nearby restaurant, find an empty spot—no mean feat, so come early—and you'll feel right at home. An impressive stone bust of the late maestro Arthur Fiedler watches over the walkers, joggers, picnickers, and sunbathers who fill the Esplanade's paths on pleasant days. Here, too, is the turn-of-the-20th-century Union Boat Club Boathouse, headquarters for the country's oldest private rowing club. You can also access the park by crossing the Frances Appleton Pedestrian Bridge linking the Beacon Hill neighborhood to the Esplanade. ⊠ *Back Bay* ⊕ *www. esplanadeassociation.org.*

Exeter Street Theatre

NOTABLE BUILDING | This massive Romanesque structure was built in 1884 as a temple for the Working Union of Progressive Spiritualists. Beginning in 1914, it enjoyed a long run from 1914 to 1984 as a movie theater, then served a turn as a bookstore. Today, it's home to a private school. ⊠ *26 Exeter St., at Newbury St., Back Bay* ⊕ *www.fst.org/exeter.htm* Ⓜ *Copley.*

First Baptist Church

CHURCH | This 1872 structure, at the corner of Clarendon Street and Commonwealth Avenue, was architect Henry Hobson Richardson's first foray into Romanesque Revival. It was originally erected for the Brattle Square Unitarian Society, but Richardson ran over budget and the church went bankrupt and dissolved. In 1882, the building was bought by the Baptists. The figures on each side of its 176-foot soaring tower were sculpted by Frédéric Auguste Bartholdi, the sculptor who designed the Statue of Liberty. The friezes represent four points at which God enters an individual's life: baptism, communion, marriage, and death. The tower is undergoing a huge restoration project to help it weather the years to come. Call ahead on a weekday and you may be given an informal tour. ⊠ *110 Commonwealth Ave., Back Bay* ☎ *617/267–3148* ⊕ *www.firstbaptistboston.org* ◪ *Free* Ⓜ *Copley.*

The First Church of Christ, Scientist

CHURCH | The world headquarters and mother church of the Christian Science faith mixes the traditional with the modern—marrying Bernini to Le Corbusier by combining an old-world basilica with a sleek office complex designed by I. M. Pei & Partners and Araldo Cossutta, Associated Architects. Mary Baker Eddy's original granite First Church of Christ, Scientist (1894) has since been enveloped by a domed Renaissance Revival basilica, added to the site in 1906, and both church buildings are now surrounded by the offices of the Christian Science Publishing Society, where the *Christian Science Monitor* is produced, and by Cossutta's complex of church-administration structures completed in 1973. You can hear all 13,000-plus pipes of the church's famed Aeolian-Skinner organ during Sunday services.

The outer reflection pool, small fountains, and surrounding area received a major face lift recently to include more walkways and sitting areas. There's still more planning for new indoor and outdoor space development on the horizon, so church tours are on hold until completion. ⊠ *275 Massachusetts Ave., Back Bay* ☎ *617/450–2000* ⊕ *www.christianscience.com/church-of-christ-scientist/the-mother-church-in-boston-ma-usa* ⊠ *Free* Ⓜ *Hynes, Symphony.*

Gibson House Museum

HISTORIC HOME | Through the foresight of an eccentric bon vivant, this house provides an authentic glimpse into daily life in Boston's Victorian era. One of the first Back Bay residences (1859), the Gibson House is relatively modest in comparison with some of the grand mansions built during the decades that followed; yet its furnishings, from its 1795 Willard clock to the raised and gilded wallpaper to the multipiece faux-bamboo bedroom set, seem sumptuous to modern eyes. Unlike other Back Bay houses, the Gibson family home has been preserved with all its Victorian fixtures and furniture intact. The house serves as the meeting place for the New England chapter of the Victorian Society in America; it was also used as an interior for the 1984 Merchant Ivory film *The Bostonians.* ◼TIP➡ **The museum is only open to the public by hourly guided tours Wednesday through Sunday 1 pm to 3 pm, and Thursday 3 pm to 5 pm through advance ticket purchase only.** ⊠ *137 Beacon St., Back Bay* ☎ *617/267–6338* ⊕ *www.thegibsonhouse.org* ⊠ *$10* ⊘ *Closed Mon. and Tues.* Ⓜ *Arlington.*

Hatch Memorial Shell

CITY PARK | FAMILY | Situated on the wonderfully scenic Charles River Esplanade, this acoustic and artful concert venue—100 feet wide and wood inlaid—annually hosts the Boston Pops' famous July 4 concert and dozens of other free, summer classical-orchestra performances, music festivals, film screenings, and other events. It's called a shell, well, because it looks like one. ⊠ *Esplanade, David G. Mugar Way at Beacon St., Beacon Hill* ✛ *Access Hatch Shell from Arthur Fiedler Footbridge, at Arlington and Beacon Sts.* ☎ *617/626–1250* ⊕ *www.hatchshell.com* Ⓜ *Charles/MGH, Arlington.*

Mary Baker Eddy Library

LIBRARY | FAMILY | One of the largest single collections by and about an American woman is housed at this library, located on the Christian Science Plaza. The library also includes two floors of exhibits, which celebrate the power of ideas and provide context to the life and achievements of Mary Baker Eddy (1821–1910).

The library is also home to the fascinating Mapparium, a huge stained-glass globe whose 30-foot interior can be traversed on a footbridge, where you can experience a unique sound-and-light show while viewing an accurate representation of the world from 1935. The Hall of Ideas showcases quotes from the world's greatest thinkers, which travel around the room and through a virtual fountain.

In the Quest Gallery, explore how Mary Baker Eddy founded a church and a college, and at the age of 87, launched the *Christian Science Monitor* newspaper. ✉ *210 Massachusetts Ave., Back Bay* ☎ *617/450–7000* ⊕ *www.marybakereddylibrary.org* 🎟 *Hall of Ideas and 3rd-fl. library free, exhibits $6* Ⓜ *Prudential*.

Massachusetts Historical Society

LIBRARY | The first historical society in the United States (founded in 1791) has paintings, a library, and a 12-million-piece manuscript collection from 17th-century New England to the present. Among these manuscripts are the Adams Family Papers, which comprise more than 300,000 pages from the letters and diaries of generations of the Adams family, including papers from John Adams and John Quincy Adams. Casual visitors are welcome, but if you'd like to examine the papers within the library in depth, call ahead. The Society also offers a variety of programs and special exhibits. ✉ *1154 Boylston St., Back Bay* ☎ *617/536–1608* ⊕ *www.masshist.org* 🎟 *Free* ☾ *Closed Sun.* Ⓜ *Hynes*.

Newbury Street

STREET | Eight-block-long Newbury Street has been compared to New York's 5th Avenue, and certainly this is the city's poshest shopping area, with branches of Chanel, Tiffany & Co., Valentino, Max Mara, Longchamp, and other top names in fashion. But here the pricey boutiques are more intimate than grand, and people live above the trendy restaurants and ubiquitous hair salons, giving the place a neighborhood feel. Toward the Massachusetts Avenue end, cafés proliferate and the stores get funkier, ending with Newbury Comics and Urban Outfitters. ✉ *From Arlington St. to Massachusetts Ave., Back Bay* ⊕ *www.newburystboston.com* Ⓜ *Hynes, Copley*.

Old South Church

CHURCH | Members of Old South Meeting House, of Tea Party fame, decamped to this new site in 1873, a move not without controversy. In an Italian Gothic style inspired by the art critic John Ruskin and with an interior decorated with Venetian mosaics and stained-glass windows, the "new" structure could hardly be more different from the plain meetinghouse they vacated. The sanctuary is free and open to the public seven days a week. ✉ *645 Boylston St., Back Bay* ☎ *617/536–1970* ⊕ *www.oldsouth.org* Ⓜ *Copley*.

Prudential Center

STORE/MALL | **FAMILY** | The 52-story Prudential Tower, or "the Pru," dominates the acreage between Boylston Street and Huntington Avenue. Its enclosed shopping mall anchored by Saks Fifth Avenue is home to over 60 stores and restaurants and is connected by a glass bridge to the more upscale Copley Place. The popular food emporium, Eataly, located in the Pru, offers a great spot for a quick bite or DIY fixings for an Italian feast. As for the Prudential Tower itself, the architectural historian Bainbridge Bunting made an acute observation when he called it "an apparition so vast in size that it appears to float above the surrounding district without being related to it." Later modifications to the Boylston Street frontage of the Prudential Center effected a better union of the complex with the urban space around it, but the tower itself floats on, vast as ever. In 2023, the top three floors of the Pru will welcome a new re-imagination of the famed SkyWalk, an incredible vantage point to view all of Boston with 360 degrees of observation from above. ✉ *800 Boylston St., Back Bay* ☎ *800/746–7778* ⊕ *www.prudentialcenter.com* Ⓜ *Prudential Center, Copley Station*.

Symphony Hall

PERFORMANCE VENUE | While Boston's Symphony Hall—the home of the Boston Symphony Orchestra and the Boston Pops—is considered among the best in the world for its sublime acoustics, it's also worth visiting to enjoy its other merits. The stage is framed by an enormous organ facade and an intricate golden proscenium. Above the second balcony are 16 replicas of Greek and Roman statues, which, like the rest of the Hall, marry the acoustic and aesthetic by creating niches and uneven surfaces to enhance the acoustics of the space. Although acoustical science was a brand-new field of research when Professor Wallace Sabine planned the interior, not one of the 2,500 seats is a bad one—the secret is the box-within-a-box design. ⊠ *301 Massachusetts Ave., Back Bay* ☎ *888/266–1200 box office, 617/638–9390 tours* ⊕ *www.bso.org* Ⓜ *Symphony.*

★ **Trinity Church**

CHURCH | In his 1877 masterpiece, architect Henry Hobson Richardson brought his Romanesque Revival style to maturity; all the aesthetic elements for which he was famous come together magnificently—bold polychromatic masonry, careful arrangement of masses, sumptuously carved interior woodwork—in this crowning centerpiece of Copley Square. A full appreciation of its architecture requires an understanding of the logistical problems of building it here. The Back Bay is a reclaimed wetland with a high water table. Bedrock, or at least stable glacial till, lies far beneath wet clay. Like all older Back Bay buildings, Trinity Church sits on submerged wooden pilings. But its central tower weighs 9,500 tons, and most of the 4,500 pilings beneath the building are under that tremendous central mass. The pilings are checked regularly for sinkage by means of a hatch in the basement.

Richardson engaged some of the best artists of his day—John La Farge, William Morris, and Edward Burne-Jones among them—to execute the paintings and stained glass that make this a monument to everything that was right about the pre-Raphaelite spirit and the nascent aesthetic of Morris's Arts and Crafts movement. Along the north side of the church, note the Augustus Saint-Gaudens statue

of Phillips Brooks—the most charismatic rector in New England, who almost single-handedly got Trinity built and furnished. The shining light of Harvard's religious community and lyricist of "O Little Town of Bethlehem," Brooks is shown here with Christ touching his shoulder in approval. For a nice respite, try to catch one of the Friday organ concerts beginning at 12:15. Free drop-in guided tours are held throughout the week. ⊠ *206 Clarendon St., Back Bay* ☎ *617/536–0944* ⊕ *trinitychurchboston.org* ☜ *Entrance free, guided and self-guided tours Tues.– Fri., $10* ⊗ *Closed Mon.* Ⓜ *Copley.*

200 Clarendon (The Hancock Tower)

NOTABLE BUILDING | In the early 1970s, the tallest building in New England became notorious as the monolith that rained glass from time to time. Windows were improperly seated in the sills of the blue rhomboid tower, designed by I. M. Pei. Once the building's 13 acres of glass were replaced and the central core stiffened, the problem was corrected. Bostonians originally feared the Hancock's stark modernism would overwhelm nearby Trinity Church, but its shimmering sides reflect the older structure's image, actually enlarging its presence. Renamed from the John Hancock Tower to 200 Clarendon in 2015, the building is mostly offices and remains off limits to the public. ⊠ *200 Clarendon St., Back Bay* ⊕ *www.200clarendon.com* Ⓜ *Copley.*

🍴 Restaurants

Easily the ritziest section of Boston, the Back Bay is where you'll find historic landmarks such as Copley Square and the Boston Public Library rubbing shoulders with stylish boutiques like Valentino and Max Mara. The restaurant scene follows suit with landmark steak houses and seafood spots sharing sidewalk space with more chic, more global options. But don't feel like you have to win the lottery to eat in this area. While lots of fine-dining establishments dot the

neighborhood, you'll also find plenty of affordable spots, including Irish taverns, burrito and burger joints, and Eataly, a massive Italian food emporium in the Prudential Center with groceries, bakeries, and seafood, cheese, and meat markets, a dozen eateries, and public café tables to sit at and enjoy takeout.

The Banks Fish House

$$$$ | SEAFOOD | Diving head first into dishes like cuttlefish ink spaghetti, rare tuna steak with roasted eggplant, and salmon with pork belly and spring peas, chef Robert Sisca pays homage to New England's long-standing fishing tradition. While the ocean's bounty is its main theme, he doesn't leave landlubbers stranded; there are a few chicken and turf dishes as well. **Known for:** fresh seafood; traditional lobster bake; baked fresh breads. $ Average main: $45 ✉ 406 Stuart St., Back Bay ☎ 617/399–0015 ⊕ thebanksboston.com Ⓜ Back Bay.

Buttermilk & Bourbon

$$$ | SOUTHERN | Buttermilk & Bourbon is chef Jason Santos's take on New Orleans fare, with dishes like beignets topped with powdered sugar, buttermilk biscuits paired with house-made sausage gravy, and fried chicken and waffles brought to your table in the cool lower-level space. Weekend brunch offers banana-cinnamon French toast, duck confit hash, and s'mores bacon. **Known for:** fun scene; buttermilk fried chicken; Southern cuisine. $ Average main: $25 ✉ 160 Commonwealth Ave., Back Bay ☎ 617/266–1122 ⊕ www.buttermilkbourbon.com Ⓜ Back Bay.

Café Landwer

$ | MEDITERRANEAN | Steps from the Boston Marathon finish line on Boylston Street, a coveted seat on the outdoor patio is worth the wait. If the weather isn't permitting, snag a spot inside this brasserie-vibe café inside the Charlesmark Hotel and be prepared to feast. **Known for:** patio space; hummus bowls; shakshuka. $ Average main: $16 ✉ 653 Boylston St., Back Bay ☎ 857/250-2902 ⊕ landwercafe.com Ⓜ Copley.

The Capital Grille

$$$$ | STEAKHOUSE | A carnivore's utopia awaits within the clubby, dark-wood walls of this beloved steak house favored by those on expense accounts. Adjust your starched napkin and tuck into such staples as lobster and crab cakes, a massive shellfish platter, and succulent meats such as the 24-ounce dry-aged porterhouse. **Known for:** stellar wine list; swell crowd; clubby feel. $ Average main: $40 ✉ 900 Boylston St., Back Bay ☎ 617/262–8900 ⊕ www.thecapitalgrille. com Ⓜ Hynes.

Contessa

$$$$ | ITALIAN | While the sweeping Back Bay views and neoclassical–meets–art deco decor are something to behold, the menu is just as captivating at this new crown jewel atop the luxurious hotel The Newbury. Fanciful dishes such as melt-in-your-mouth squash carpaccio, spicy lobster capellini, and a signature 40-oz. dry-aged bistecca fiorentina are as dazzling as the crowd, a blend of well-heeled locals, city socialites, and trend-seeking singles (mostly at the buzzy bar). **Known for:** squash carpaccio; year-round rooftop dining; see-and-be-seen crowd. $ Average main: $40 ✉ The Newbury, 3 Newbury St., Rooftop, Back Bay ☎ 617/741–3404 ⊕ contessatrattoria. com Ⓜ Arlington.

★ Davio's Northern Italian Steakhouse

$$$$ | ITALIAN | Comfy armchairs and a grand, high-ceilinged dining room give diners a heightened sense of self-importance, beginning with lunch when the city's power elite stop in for great pastas (half portions are available), prime aged steaks, and oversize salads. For dinner, some patrons snag quick, pretheater bites at the bar while others opt for a more leisurely experience, lingering over sophisticated Italian dishes like tagliatelle Bolognese and succulent grilled veal chops with creamy potatoes and

port wine sauce. **Known for:** generous portions; elegant setting and service; delectable Italian classics. ⑤ *Average main: $41 ☒ 75 Arlington St., Back Bay* ☎ *617/357–4810* ⊕ *www.davios.com* ⊗ *No lunch weekends* Ⓜ *Arlington.*

★ Deuxave

$$$ | **MODERN AMERICAN** | At the corner of two avenues (Commonwealth and Massachusetts), which is how this restaurant got its name *(deux* is French for "two"), you'll find this snazzy, dark-wood enclave serving sophisticated dishes like spice-crusted ahi tuna and braised pork belly, pan-seared Atlantic halibut, and organic chicken with parsnip and foie gras agnolotti. Make sure to pair your meal with a bottle from the thoughtfully crafted and surprisingly affordable wine list served by an attentive staff. **Known for:** nine-hour French onion soup; reasonably priced wine list; modern French food. ⑤ *Average main: $35 ☒ 371 Commonwealth Ave., Back Bay* ☎ *617/517–5915* ⊕ *www.deuxave.com* ▱ *No credit cards* Ⓜ *Hynes.*

Eataly

$$ | **ITALIAN** | An epicenter for all things Italian, this powerhouse is all about one word: *mangia.* There are four restaurants, a marketplace, wine shop, cooking school, and seven to-go counters, so you can find anything you want to eat or drink here, and maybe discover a few things you didn't know you needed (perhaps a snack size of Piave Stravecchio DOP, a hard cheese from the Belluno province in northeastern Italy). **Known for:** huge selection of Italian takeaways; several dining choices; new third-floor roof deck at Terra. ⑤ *Average main: $20 ☒ Prudential Center, 800 Boylston St., Back Bay* ☎ *617/807–7300* ⊕ *eataly.com* Ⓜ *Prudential Center.*

★ Grill 23 & Bar

$$$$ | **STEAKHOUSE** | Pinstripe suits, dark paneling, Persian rugs, and waiters in white jackets give this single-location steak house a posh tone, and the kitchen places a premium on seasonal, organic ingredients and sustainable and humanely raised meats; the divine coconut cake is worth saving room for dessert. Two bars, a big, buzzing one overlooking Berkeley Street and a quieter, smaller one on the second floor by the cozy fireplace, serve excellent drinks, specialty Scotches, and bar bites, along with the full menu. **Known for:** Brandt family beef; party-dress vibe; locally owned steak house. ⑤ *Average main: $40 ☒ 161 Berkeley St., Back Bay* ☎ *617/542–2255* ⊕ *grill23.com* ⊗ *No lunch* Ⓜ *Back Bay/ South End.*

Ostra

$$$$ | **SEAFOOD** | Boston has plenty of great seafood restaurants, but this sophisticated option near the Theater District turns out delicate and exquisitely prepared catches of the day fit for a king (and some say costing a king's ransom). Settle in with a seasonal cocktail in the sleek, pearl-white dining room before tucking into any one of the caviars or glistening raw fish tartares followed by a simply prepared entrée, whether it's a grilled sea bream in trevisano leaf or broiled Maine twin lobster. **Known for:** elegant setting; top-notch service; exquisite seafood dishes. ⑤ *Average main: $42 ☒ 1 Charles St., Back Bay* ☎ *617/421–1200* ⊕ *ostraboston.com.*

Porto

$$$ | **MEDITERRANEAN** | In a pristine white space next to the Prudential Center, beloved local chef/co-owner Jody Adams takes Mediterranean fare up a notch, with starters like Spanish octopus, local burrata, and meatballs, and entrées like whole roasted branzino and house-made pastas wowing diners. Other popular dishes include grilled lamb chops and saffron mussels. **Known for:** bountiful raw bar; elegant Back Bay setting; artful seafood preparations. ⑤ *Average main: $35 ☒ Ring Rd., next door to Saks Fifth Ave., Back Bay* ☎ *617/536–1234* ⊕ *www. porto-boston.com.*

Ramsay's Kitchen

$$$$ | MODERN AMERICAN | Celebrity chef Gordon Ramsay's newest venture within the Mandarin Oriental hotel offers a taste of his most well-known dishes along with a few local twists. While his famous beef Wellington sits front-and-center as a no-brainer choice entrée, he also gives a properly placed nod to local seafood with jumbo lump crab cakes and lobster, as well as clam bouillabaisse, Boston lager-steamed mussels, crispy skin salmon, and fish and chips. **Known for:** celebrity chef of Hell's Kitchen fame; traditional New England dishes made upscale; beef Wellington. ⑤ *Average main: $45* ✉ *774 Boylston St., Back Bay* ☎ *857/289–0771* ⊕ *www.gordonramsayrestaurants.com/en/us/ramsays-kitchen* Ⓜ *Copley.*

Rochambeau

$$$ | BISTRO | This two-story French-inspired bistro and café offers a stylish spot to sip a latte and enjoy a quiche in the morning, power lunch at midday, or dine on dishes like duck l'orange or the plate of the day, such as lemon chicken tagine or trout almandine at night. The weekend brunch menu includes classics, like croque madame, with ham, Gruyère and bechamel on brioche, topped with a sunny-side-up egg, and a to-die-for cinnamon skillet bread. **Known for:** onsite to-go café; buzzy scene; first-floor bar scene. ⑤ *Average main: $35* ✉ *900 Boylston St., Back Bay* ☎ *617/247–0400* ⊕ *rochambeauboston.com* Ⓜ *Back Bay.*

★ Saltie Girl

$$$ | SEAFOOD | Step into this Back Bay raw bar specializing in snappy cocktails and luscious preparations of all things seafood and you'll fall hook, line, and sinker for everything on the menu, including platters of fresh-shucked oysters on crushed ice, torched salmon belly with charred avocado, smoked fish that would make a New York deli owner proud, seafood-topped toasts, and a butter-drenched warm lobster roll overflowing with fresh meat. Rounding out the menu are tins of domestic and imported gourmet shellfish and fish (including caviar) served in all their oily goodness with bread, butter, smoked salt, lemon, and sweet pepper jam. **Known for:** large tinned seafood selection; hip crowd; creative seafood dishes. ⑤ *Average main: $25* ✉ *279 Dartmouth St., Back Bay* ☎ *617/267–0691* ⊕ *saltiegirl.com.*

★ Select Oyster Bar

$$$$ | SEAFOOD | Snug quarters and no desserts can't quell the stream of diners pouring into this uptown enclave eager to savor oysters and seductive seafood combinations like salmon crudo with pistachio oil, Maine lobster cabbage-kale Thai salad, and blue prawns à la *plancha*. With 70% of the restaurant's catch coming from New England, plus a thoughtful libations list and polished service, you have all the ingredients for a good time, whether you're sitting at the bar, at the front communal table, or in the three-season alfresco area out back. **Known for:** 20% pretax service charge automatically added to each bill; cozy, relaxed atmosphere; lip-smacking seafood dishes. ⑤ *Average main: $36* ✉ *50 Gloucester St., Back Bay* ☎ *857/293–8064* ⊕ *www.selectboston.com* Ⓜ *Hynes.*

Sonsie

$$$ | AMERICAN | Café society blossoms along Newbury Street, particularly at Sonsie, where a well-heeled crowd sips coffee up front or angles for places at the bar. Lunch and dinner dishes veer toward basic bistro fare with an American twist, such as kale Caesar salad with grilled chicken and pan-roasted salmon with potatoes, chard, and beet "ketchup." The restaurant is terrific for weekend brunch, when the light pours through the long windows, and is at its most vibrant in warm weather, when the open doors make for stellar people-watching. **Known for:** sceney vibe; Sunday brunch; American bistro favorites. ⑤ *Average main: $28* ✉ *327 Newbury St., Back Bay* ☎ *617/351–2500* ⊕ *sonsieboston.com* Ⓜ *Hynes.*

Stephanie's on Newbury

$$$ | **AMERICAN** | Here's comfort food at its best—sophisticated enough for adults (lobster pot pie), yet simple enough for kids (burgers and pasta). The attractive space has plenty of booths for spreading out in, and the great patio is a lively spot in summer. **Known for:** large portions; people-watching from the patio; burgers. ⑤ *Average main: $30* ✉ *190 Newbury St., Back Bay* ☎ *617/236–0990* ⊕ *www.stephaniesonnewbury.com* Ⓜ *Copley.*

Summer Shack

$$$ | **SEAFOOD** | **FAMILY** | Boston uberchef Jasper White's casual New England seafood restaurant is a boisterous, bright, fun eatery next to the Prudential Center (he also has one in Cambridge and at Mohegan Sun in Connecticut), where creamy clam chowder and fried Ipswich clams share menu space with golden crab cakes and cedar-planked, maple-lemon–glazed salmon. In addition to a handful of chicken and meat dishes for those not into seafood, White features some of the most succulent lobsters in the city (he has a patented process for cooking them). **Known for:** succulent lobster; fun, casual atmosphere; fresh seafood. ⑤ *Average main: $28* ✉ *50 Dalton St., Back Bay* ☎ *617/867–9955* ⊕ *www.summershackrestaurant.com* Ⓜ *Hynes.*

Uni

$$$$ | **ASIAN FUSION** | Inside the tasteful boutique Eliot Hotel lies an innovative *izakaya* (informal Japanese gastropub), owned by Boston star chefs-partners Ken Oringer and Tony Messina, who offer boldly flavored renditions of Asian street food—Sai Oua lettuce wraps; Mai duck carnitas; Wagyu beef dumplings; shrimp teriyaki fried rice; and dozens of tempting sashimi and nigiri choices. Although the bites can add up price-wise, the menu has a sprinkling of inexpensive dishes, like fried chicken bao bun and blistered shishito peppers. **Known for:** trendy feel; small plate format; creative raw fish options. ⑤ *Average main: $45* ✉ *Eliot Hotel, 370 Commonwealth Ave., Back Bay* ☎ *617/536–7200* ⊕ *www.uni-boston.com* ⊙ *No lunch* Ⓜ *Hynes.*

☕ Coffee and Quick Bites

Georgetown Cupcake

$ | **BAKERY** | Inspired by a grandma's confections, these cupcakes are heavenly. It's tough to choose between flavors like chocolate ganache, red velvet, double milk chocolate birthday, salted caramel, and the list goes on. **Known for:** gluten-free treats available; creative cupcakes; nice seating area. ⑤ *Average main: $4* ✉ *83 Newbury St., Back Bay* ☎ *617/927–2250* ⊕ *georgetowncupcake.com* Ⓜ *Copley.*

Levain Bakery

$ | **BAKERY** | Challenging the typical cookie weight limit, Levain's freshly baked cookies are the perfect two-person dessert, although it can be tough to share with flavors like chocolate chip walnut, dark chocolate chocolate chip, oatmeal raisin, and dark chocolate peanut butter chip tempting your sweet tooth. The banana chocolate chip loaf is moist, and the country boule breaks with the perfect outer crisp. **Known for:** housemade breads; moist loaf cakes; huge shareable cookies. ⑤ *Average main: $6* ✉ *180 Newbury St., Back Bay* ☎ *617/390–7799* ⊕ *levainbakery.com* Ⓜ *Copley.*

Pavement Coffeehouse

$ | **AMERICAN** | Enjoy coffee, snacks, and Wi-Fi access in this hip basement spot, one of several scattered about the city. Tea lovers needn't feel left out—there are plenty of excellent options, including jade oolong and chamomile medley. **Known for:** amazing hand-crafted bagels; lots of vegan options; roasting their own coffee beans. ⑤ *Average main: $10* ✉ *286 Newbury St., Back Bay* ☎ *617/859–9515* ⊕ *www.pavementcoffeehouse.com* Ⓜ *Hynes, Copley.*

Trident Booksellers & Café

$ | **AMERICAN** | Folks gather at the two-story Trident Booksellers & Café to review literary best sellers, thumb through the superb magazine selection, and chow down on items from the perpetual breakfast menu. The restaurant also serves lunch and dinner and has an excellent beer and wine selection. **Known for:** variety of events, from trivia to talks; lemon-ricotta–stuffed French toast; beloved local bookstore. $ *Average main: $15* ✉ *338 Newbury St., Back Bay* ☎ *617/267–8688* ⊕ *www.tridentbookscafe.com* Ⓜ *Hynes.*

🛏 Hotels

The Back Bay and the South End are what locals call the "well-heeled" sections of Boston, meaning money talks here—think the likes of Mandarin Oriental or Fairmont Copley Plaza. The streets are lined with upscale, stylish hotels (old and new), boutique hotels, and inns.

Boston Marriott Copley Place

$ | **HOTEL** | **FAMILY** | It's busy-busy, with throngs of tourists and business travelers, but you can't beat the location of this 38-story megahotel, which sports three entrances—a street-level door, a glass sky bridge from the Prudential Center, and a walk-in from the Copley mall—ensuring that you rarely have to go outside to shop or eat, which is especially nice in winter. **Pros:** good service; comfortable beds; prime Copley Square location. **Cons:** not for those who want an intimate, boutique experience; massive in size; chaotic lobby. $ *Rooms from: $185* ✉ *110 Huntington Ave., Back Bay* ☎ *617/236–5800, 800/228–9290* ⊕ *www.marriott.com* 🛏 *1,147 rooms* ⦿ *No Meals* Ⓜ *Copley, Back Bay.*

Boston Park Plaza

$$$ | **HOTEL** | **FAMILY** | Step into a true piece of Boston history at the esteemed Park Plaza, one of the city's most identifiable landmarks since 1927, but don't

worry—while the hotel is historic, modern updates make it an upscale place to stay, and it's an ideal spot for tourists looking for old-world charm and excellent service. **Pros:** access to the Lynx 20,000-square-foot health club; TopGolf swing suite in gym; tons of historic value. **Cons:** guest rooms vary in size; facilities fee per room, per night; bathrooms are small. $ *Rooms from: $300* ✉ *50 Park Plaza, at Arlington St., Back Bay* ☎ *617/426–2000, 800/225–2008* ⊕ *www.bostonparkplaza.com* 🛏 *1,060 rooms* ⦿ *No Meals* Ⓜ *Arlington.*

Charlesmark Hotel

$$ | **HOTEL** | Hipsters and romantics who'd rather spend their cash on a great meal than a hotel bill have put this late 19th-century former residential row house in the heart of the Back Bay on the map. **Pros:** discount at ground floor restaurant; free Wi-Fi; all rooms have safes and refrigerators. **Cons:** no valet; no turndown service; some might feel crowded by compact rooms and hallways. $ *Rooms from: $250* ✉ *655 Boylston St., Back Bay* ☎ *617/247–1212* ⊕ *www.thecharlesmarkhotel.com* 🛏 *40 rooms* ⦿ *Free Breakfast* Ⓜ *Copley.*

The Colonnade Hotel

$$ | **HOTEL** | **FAMILY** | The conveniently located Colonnade Hotel offers clean, modern environs injected with hues of khaki, chocolate, and chrome. **Pros:** roof-deck pool; across from Prudential Center shopping; close to Hynes Convention Center. **Cons:** on summer days the pool is packed by 11 am; parking is expensive; Huntington Avenue gets clogged with rush-hour traffic. $ *Rooms from: $269* ✉ *120 Huntington Ave., Back Bay* ☎ *617/424–7000, 800/962–3030* ⊕ *www.colonnadehotel.com* 🛏 *285 rooms* ⦿ *No Meals* Ⓜ *Back Bay, Prudential Center.*

Copley Square Hotel

$$$ | **HOTEL** | The chic, newly renovated Copley Square Hotel offers cushy mattresses, mini fridges, high speed Wi-Fi, and eco-friendly toiletries—not too

shabby for a place that opened in 1891 and has provided respite to a century of celebrities like Babe Ruth, Ella Fitzgerald, and Billie Holiday. **Pros:** free Wi-Fi; epic celebrity history; cool scene. **Cons:** rooms facing Huntington Avenue can be noisy; not ideal for couples seeking peace and quiet; no food or beverage service. ⑤ *Rooms from: $350* ✉ *47 Huntington Ave., Back Bay* ☎ *617/536–9000* ⊕ *www.copleysquarehotel.com* ⇗ *143 rooms* ⦿| *No Meals* Ⓜ *Copley, Back Bay.*

★ The Eliot Hotel

$$ | **HOTEL** | One of the city's best small hotels, located on posh Commonwealth Avenue, expertly merges the old blue-blood Boston aesthetic with modern flair (like contemporary rugs mingling with crystal chandeliers); everyone from well-heeled Sox fans to traveling CEOs to tony college parents have noticed. **Pros:** top-notch restaurant; beautiful rooms; great location near Fenway and Newbury Street. **Cons:** some complain of elevator noise; parking is expensive; can be pricey. ⑤ *Rooms from: $235* ✉ *370 Commonwealth Ave., Back Bay* ☎ *617/267–1607, 800/443–5468* ⊕ *www.eliothotel.com* ⇗ *95 rooms* ⦿| *No Meals* Ⓜ *Hynes.*

★ Fairmont Copley Plaza

$$$ | **HOTEL** | **FAMILY** | Since 1912, this decadent, unabashedly romantic hotel has welcomed guests in style, immediately impressing as they enter under the huge black awning, flanked by golden lion statues, into the lobby decked out in Italian marble, stunning coffered ceilings, and gorgeous crystal chandeliers. **Pros:** prime Back Bay location, centrally located in Copley Square; luxurious gym; 24-hour daily in-room dining. **Cons:** valet parking is expensive; due to the historical nature, room sizes vary greatly; small bathrooms. ⑤ *Rooms from: $350* ✉ *138 St. James Ave., Back Bay* ☎ *617/267–5300, 866/540–4417* ⊕ *www.fairmont.com/copley-plaza-boston* ⇗ *383 rooms* ⦿| *No Meals* Ⓜ *Copley, Back Bay.*

Four Seasons Hotel Boston

$$$$ | **HOTEL** | **FAMILY** | This Public Garden–facing spot keeps a surprisingly low profile in Boston—and that's OK by the jeans-clad millionaires and assorted business types who cluster in the glossy lobby or use the courtesy car. **Pros:** close to Newbury Street and the Public Garden; signature Four Seasons service; pet-friendly. **Cons:** wait to get into restaurants can be long; valet service can be slow; pricey during peak times. ⑤ *Rooms from: $710* ✉ *200 Boylston St., Back Bay* ☎ *617/338–4400, 800/819–5053* ⊕ *www.fourseasons.com/boston* ⇗ *273 rooms* ⦿| *No Meals* Ⓜ *Arlington.*

Hilton Boston Back Bay

$$ | **HOTEL** | Rooms at the Back Bay Hilton are relatively spacious, with elegant marble baths, plush "Serenity" bedding, Suite Dreams mattresses, and cozy, down-filled comforters. **Pros:** oversize showers; good 7th-floor fitness center; indoor pool. **Cons:** not pet-friendly; parking is expensive; room service is not 24/7. ⑤ *Rooms from: $290* ✉ *40 Dalton St., Back Bay* ☎ *617/236–1100, 888/874–0663* ⊕ *www.bostonbackbay.hilton.com* ⇗ *395 rooms* ⦿| *No Meals* Ⓜ *Prudential, Hynes.*

★ The Inn @ St. Botolph

$$ | **B&B/INN** | **FAMILY** | The posh yet homey 16-room Inn @ St. Botolph follows an edgy hotel model—no front desk, no restaurant, no keys, and no valet (there is, however, an office on-site that is staffed 24/7). **Pros:** short walk from the South End, Copley Square, and the Back Bay; free Wi-Fi; self-service laundry on-site. **Cons:** no traditional front desk check-in services; may be too "off the beaten path" for some; limited DIY parking nearby. ⑤ *Rooms from: $279* ✉ *99 St. Botolph St., Back Bay* ☎ *617/236–8099* ⊕ *www.innatstbotolph.com* ⇗ *16 rooms* ⦿| *Free Breakfast* Ⓜ *Prudential.*

The Lenox Hotel

$$ | **HOTEL** | **FAMILY** | A good alternative to chain-owned, big-box Back Bay hotels, the boutique family-owned Lenox offers top-notch service, three food and beverage outlets, 24-hour room service, a fitness center, and a business center in an ideal location. **Pros:** complimentary bottled water; historic/architectural charm; mini-refrigerator in every room. **Cons:** no minibar; costly parking; some bathrooms are small. ⑤ *Rooms from: $285* ⊠ *61 Exeter St., Back Bay* ☎ *617/536–5300, 800/225–7676* ⊕ *www.lenoxhotel.com* ⇨ *214 rooms* �‖ *No Meals* Ⓜ *Back Bay, Copley.*

Loews Boston Hotel

$$$ | **HOTEL** | **FAMILY** | The former headquarters of the Boston Police Department houses the sleek Loews Boston Hotel, which boasts a cool glass-and-marble lobby and a stylish restaurant, Precinct Kitchen + Bar, and manages to combine the building's history with 21st-century amenities. **Pros:** fitness center with Peloton; great for families with children; pet-friendly. **Cons:** parking is expensive; restaurant is pricey; bar-side rooms can be loud. ⑤ *Rooms from: $300* ⊠ *154 Berkeley St., Back Bay* ☎ *617/266–7200, 855/495–6397* ⊕ *www.loewshotels.com/boston-hotel* ⇨ *222 rooms* �‖ *No Meals* Ⓜ *Back Bay.*

Mandarin Oriental, Boston

$$$$ | **HOTEL** | The Mandarin Oriental manages to combine classic New England elegance with the luxurious touches the brand is known for around the world, including top-notch service, amenities galore, and public areas adorned with museum-quality art, while large guest rooms include contemporary Asian design and oversize bathrooms with soaking tubs and separate walk-in showers. **Pros:** creative kids programs; very quiet; good-size rooms. **Cons:** rates are exorbitant; valet parking is expensive; small fitness center. ⑤ *Rooms from: $795* ⊠ *776 Boylston St., Back Bay* ☎ *617/535–8888* ⊕ *www.mandarinoriental.com/boston* ⇨ *150 rooms* �‖ *No Meals* Ⓜ *Prudential, Copley, Back Bay.*

Newbury Guest House

$$ | **B&B/INN** | Located in the heart of Boston's most fashionable shopping street, a homey feel and personalized service are at the soul of this elegant and historic 1882 brownstone, which features natural pine flooring, blue Victorian furnishings, and prints from the Museum of Fine Arts. **Pros:** cozy and homey; free Wi-Fi; perfect base for shopping. **Cons:** small bathrooms; limited parking; rooms go quickly year-round. ⑤ *Rooms from: $298* ⊠ *261 Newbury St., Back Bay* ☎ *617/670–6000, 800/437–7668* ⊕ *www.newburyguesthouse.com* ⇨ *35 rooms* �‖ *Free Breakfast* Ⓜ *Back Bay, Hynes, Copley.*

The Newbury Boston

$$$$ | **HOTEL** | **FAMILY** | Standing guard at the corner of fashionable Newbury Street and the Public Garden, the old-school elegant former Taj Boston had a top-to-bottom facelift in 2020, with a fresh, contemporary look and amenities that include exclusive Byredo bath products, Frette robes and linens, in-room Nespresso Vertuo espresso-maker, and access to the Library and Fitness Center, along with preferred seating at the Street Bar and chic see-and-be-seen rooftop restaurant Contessa. **Pros:** white-glove service; amazing views; proximity to shopping, dining, and the park. **Cons:** pricey to park; not all rooms face the park; all this luxury will cost you. ⑤ *Rooms from: $400* ⊠ *1 Newbury St., Back Bay* ☎ *617/536–5700* ⊕ *www.thenewburyboston.com* ⇨ *315 rooms* �‖ *No Meals* Ⓜ *Arlington.*

Westin Copley Place Boston

$$$ | **HOTEL** | If the idea of sleeping in an upscale mall appeals to you, the Westin is a great bet; it boasts its own pod of retail shops and restaurants and is also connected by a covered skywalk to Copley Place (more high-end shopping) and the Hynes Convention Center. **Pros:** great location close to shopping and tourist spots; pet-friendly; on-site dining options. **Cons:** pool area is nothing special; some

say it's overpriced; big and busy feeling. Ⓢ *Rooms from: $300* ✉ *10 Huntington Ave., Back Bay* ☎ *617/262–9600, 888/937–8461* ⊕ *www.westincopleyplaceboston.com* ⇗ *945 rooms* ⦿ *No Meals* Ⓜ *Copley, Back Bay.*

Ⓨ Nightlife

BARS

Bukowski Tavern

BARS | Served by a no-nonsense bar staff, this narrow barroom has a literary flair and more than 100 brews for your sipping (or chugging) pleasure. You'll see many a beer nerd hanging out at the bar, but hungry folks also come to the funky joint for the creative burgers, hot dogs, and other comfort foods. ✉ *50 Dalton St., Back Bay* ☎ *617/437–9999* ⊕ *bukowski-tavern.com* Ⓜ *Hynes.*

★ OAK Long Bar + Kitchen

BARS | This stunning flagship bar in the 1912 Fairmont Copley Plaza hotel is a see-and-be-seen hot spot, with the original sky-high coffered ceilings, catbird views over Copley Square, and top-notch bartenders. Inside, coveted barstools are filled with an upscale crowd, while outside in warm weather, patrons can sit at outdoor tables while perusing a menu of signature martinis, single malts, shareable platters, and desserts. People-watch and enjoy a panorama that encompasses the Boston Public Library and Trinity Church in this historic spot. ✉ *Fairmont Copley Plaza, 138 St. James Ave., Back Bay* ☎ *617/267–5300* ⊕ *oaklongbarkitchen.com* Ⓜ *Copley.*

Sonsie

BARS | The crowd spilling through French doors onto the sidewalk café in warm weather consists of trendy cosmopolitans, fun-loving professionals, local sports celebs, and scenesters who have flocked to the contemporary spot for decades. The sophisticated jazz-rock soundtrack remains at a civilized volume as you dine, sip, and people-watch.

Order any of the martinis that earn a solid rep among the locals, and follow with a brick oven pizza off their late night menu. ✉ *327 Newbury St., Back Bay* ☎ *617/351–2500* ⊕ *sonsieboston.com* Ⓜ *Hynes.*

MUSIC CLUBS

The Red Room at Cafe 939

LIVE MUSIC | By day a Berklee College coffee and snack bar, the Cafe by night opens its tidy, scarlet, 200-capacity concert space. Run, booked, and played by students, it's an ideal all-ages venue for aspiring student bands and indies on the rise; everyone from Hozier to Karmin has played here. Refreshments are light (soft drinks, noodles), and so is the cover charge, which varies based on the event. There are a dozen eateries within 200 yards. ✉ *939 Boylston St., Back Bay* ☎ *617/747–2261* ⊕ *www.berklee.edu/cafe939* Ⓜ *Hynes.*

🎭 Performing Arts

MUSIC

Berklee Performance Center

CONCERTS | The main stage for the internationally renowned Berklee College of Music, the "BPC" is best known for its jazz and pop programs, but also hosts folk, world, and rock acts, and pop stars like Talking Heads, Aimee Mann, Snarky Puppy, and Melody Gardot. Bargain alert: the BPC stages a wealth of excellent student and faculty shows and showcases sets and clinics by visiting artists that cost next to nothing. While the performance center is 1,215 seats strong, it's an intimate locale for any show. ✉ *136 Massachusetts Ave., Back Bay* ☎ *617/266–7455 box office, 617/747–2261 performance center* ⊕ *www.berklee.edu/BPC* Ⓜ *Hynes.*

Boston Philharmonic Orchestra

MUSIC | The charismatic Benjamin Zander—whose signature preconcert chats help audiences better understand the blockbuster symphonies they're about to hear—heads up the Boston Philharmonic. Performances at Harvard's Sanders Theatre, the New England Conservatory's Jordan Hall, Symphony Hall, and a variety of other locales often encompass symphonies by Beethoven, Mahler, Shostakovich, and Brahms, plus lots of concertos. ☎ 617/236–0999 ⊕ www.bostonphil.org.

Boston Pops

MUSIC | Under the agile baton of Keith Lockhart, Boston Pops (largely Boston Symphony musicians) perform a bracing blend of American standards, movie themes, and contemporary vocal numbers (with top-tier guests) during May and June at Symphony Hall, plus 40 festive holiday-season concerts. Outdoor concerts on July 3 and 4 at the Hatch Memorial Shell are followed by concerts at the Boston Symphony Orchestra's summer home, Tanglewood, in Lenox, Massachusetts, in July and August. The free outdoor concerts are packed; be sure to arrive early with blankets, folding chairs, and a picnic. ☎ 617/266–1200, 888/266–1200 box office ⊕ www.bso. org.

Boston Symphony Orchestra

MUSIC | Founded in 1881, the Boston Symphony is one of America's oldest and most venerable orchestras, with dynamic Latvian conductor Andris Nelsons at the helm. Its home season at Symphony Hall runs from September through April. In July and August the music migrates to Tanglewood, the orchestra's bucolic summer home in the Berkshire Mountains in Lenox, Massachusetts. Including tours to Carnegie Hall and China, and the Boston Pops concerts, the BSO performs more than 250 concerts annually. ☒ 301 Massachusetts Ave., Back Bay ☎ 617/266–1200, 888/266–1200 box office ⊕ www. bso.org Ⓜ Symphony.

New England Conservatory's Jordan Hall

CONCERTS | One of the world's acoustic treasures, the New England Conservatory's Jordan Hall is ideal for solo and string

quartet recitals yet spacious enough for chamber and full orchestras. The pin-drop intimacy of this all-wood, 1,050-seat hall is in demand year-round for ensembles visiting and local. The New England Philharmonic and Boston Baroque perform here regularly. Dozens of free faculty and student concerts, jazz and classical, are a best-kept secret. ■ TIP→ The lobby box office is no longer open for purchasing tickets. All tickets must be purchased online. ☒ 30 Gainsborough St., Back Bay ☎ 617/585–1260 box office ⊕ necmusic. edu Ⓜ Symphony.

Odyssey Opera of Boston

OPERA | Odyssey Opera, under the able leadership of founder and conductor Gil Rose, presents classic and modern operas at various venues throughout the city, including the Strand Theatre, Calderwood Pavilion at Boston Center for the Arts, Jordan Hall, B.U. Theatre, and Suffolk University's Modern Theatre. ☒ Jordan Hall, 30 Gainsborough St., Boston ☎ 617/826–1626 ⊕ www.odysseyopera.org Ⓜ Symphony.

★ Symphony Hall

CONCERTS | One of the world's best acoustical concert halls—some say the best—has been home since 1900 to the Boston Symphony Orchestra (BSO) and the Boston Pops. Led by conductor Keith Lockhart, the Pops concerts take place in May and June and around the winter holidays. The hall is also used by visiting orchestras, chamber groups, soloists, and local ensembles. Rehearsals and daytime concerts for students are open to the public, with discounted tickets. If you can't attend a concert, you can still see the magnificent hall on a free guided tour. Visit the venue's website for dates and times. ☒ 301 Massachusetts Ave., Back Bay ☎ 617/266–1492 ⊕ www.bso. org Ⓜ Symphony.

THEATER
Huntington Theatre Company

THEATER | Boston's largest resident theater company consistently performs a high-quality mix of 21st-century plays and classics under the artistic direction of Loretta Greco, and commissions playwrights to produce original dramas. The Huntington performs at two locations: its own newly renovated theater at Boston University and the South End's Calderwood Theatre Pavilion. ⊠ *Boston University Theatre, 264 Huntington Ave., Back Bay* ☎ *617/266–7900 box office* ⊕ *www.huntingtontheatre.org* Ⓜ *Symphony.*

🛍 Shopping

This is the neighborhood of the elegant Mandarin Oriental hotel—so need we say more about the shops you'll find here? Just in case: elegant, chic, modern, stylish. It's also home to Newbury Street, Boston's version of L.A.'s Rodeo Drive. It's a shoppers' paradise, from high-end names, such as Valentino and MaxMara, to budget-conscious H&M and Zara, to tiny specialty shops, such as The Fish & Bone, Newbury Comics, and MUJI. There are also plenty of up-to-the-minute art galleries, salons, and trendy jewelry and hat shops thrown into the mix.

Parallel to Newbury Street runs Boylston Street, where you'll find just a few standout shops, such as Pompanoosuc Mills (hand-crafted furnishings), scattered among restaurants and convenience stores.

ANTIQUES

Brodney Antiques & Jewelry

ANTIQUES & COLLECTIBLES | In addition to plenty of porcelain and silver, Brodney claims to have the biggest selection of estate jewelry in New England. Shoppers will also find plenty of antiques, furniture, clocks, paintings, and more. ⊠ *176 Newbury St., Back Bay* ☎ *617/536–0500* ⊕ *www.brodney.com* Ⓜ *Copley.*

ART GALLERIES

Childs Gallery

ART GALLERIES | The large selection of works for sale in this gallery, established in 1937, includes paintings, prints, drawings, watercolors, and sculpture from the 1500s to the present. For a special memento with more weight than a Red Sox hat, pick out a piece from the gallery's impressive collection of Boston expressionism and Boston School impressionism art. ⊠ *168 Newbury St., Back Bay* ☎ *617/266–1108* ⊕ *www.childsgallery.com* Ⓜ *Copley.*

Copley Society of Art

ART GALLERIES | After more than a century, this nonprofit membership organization continues to present the works of well-known and aspiring New England artists, as well as out-of-town and foreign members. Styles of artists range from traditional and academic realists to contemporary and abstract painters, photographers, and sculptors. Each year, the gallery hosts between 15 and 20 exhibitions. ⊠ *158 Newbury St., Back Bay* ☎ *617/536–5049* ⊕ *www.copleysociety.org* Ⓜ *Copley.*

Gallery NAGA

ART GALLERIES | Specializing in contemporary paintings since 1977, primarily oil, watercolor, acrylic, and mixed media, this striking gallery in the neo-Gothic stone Church of the Covenant also displays sculpture, and furniture beyond your everyday tables and chairs. ⊠ *67 Newbury St., Back Bay* ☎ *617/267–9060* ⊕ *www.gallerynaga.com* Ⓜ *Arlington.*

Pellas

ART GALLERIES | As a contemporary art gallery located in Boston, Pellas Gallery's primary goal is to discover the best new emerging artists with a focus on local talent. Challenge your concept of "art" by exploring the rotating NFT collections. ⊠ *114 Newbury St., Back Bay* ☎ *424/394–2184* ⊕ *pellasgallery.com.*

Vose Galleries

ART GALLERIES | Established in 1841, Vose specializes in 19th- and 20th-century American art, including the Hudson River School, Boston School, and American impressionists. Over the five floors of galleries, visitors will find New England's largest inventory of American realist paintings, displayed in living and dining room settings furnished with antiques for a homelike scene for viewing. ✉ *238 Newbury St., Back Bay* ☎ *617/536–6176* ⊕ *www.vosegalleries.com* ☉ *Closed Sun. and Mon.* Ⓜ *Copley, Hynes.*

BEAUTY
Bella Santé

SPAS | For top-notch facials, body scrubs, and massages, as well as medical-grade treatments and peels, head to this elegant, tranquil day spa. In addition to a well-trained staff, you'll find pristine facilities, including a locker room stocked with a bevy of tonics, lotions, and hair products. First-time guests receive a discount on select treatments. ✉ *38 Newbury St., Back Bay* ☎ *617/424–9930* ⊕ *www.bellasante.com* Ⓜ *Arlington.*

G2O Spa + Salon

SPAS | Boston's largest all-encompassing spa and salon covers three floors and 17,000 square feet of pampering. Beyond massage and facials, hair and nails, new tricks are always up their robe sleeves, including a Flotation Pod, guided Virtual Reality Meditation, and LED Light Therapy. The Experience Room combines herbal-infused steam, color light therapy, ice fog, and tropical showers that can be enjoyed solo or shared with up to six guests. Healing salt therapies are another focus, with a Himalayan Salt Stone Massage, Himalayan Salt Rejuvenation body treatment, and Boston's only Salt Cave. ✉ *33 Exeter St., Back Bay* ☎ *617/262–2220* ⊕ *g2ospasalon.com.*

Spa at the Mandarin Oriental, Boston

SPAS | A soothing sanctuary of calm and rejuvenation awaits at this 16,000 square-foot spa with a menu of luxurious treatments, including massages, facials, manicures, and pedicures. Guests can also relax in the steam room (it houses a huge quartz crystal said to draw off negative energy), the vitality pool with soothing jets, and the "Experience" shower, where colored lights and warm and cold sprays mimic an Arctic mist, tropical rain, or island storm. The spa also offers CBD massages, wraps, and rituals. ✉ *Mandarin Oriental Boston, 776 Boylston St., Back Bay* ☎ *617/535–8888* ⊕ *www.mandarinoriental.com.*

BOOKS
★ Trident Booksellers & Café

BOOKS | This two-story shop with windows overlooking Newbury Street is known as much for its eclectic collection of books and magazines as its all-day breakfast menu. Follow the pack and order either the lemon-ricotta-stuffed French toast or homemade corned beef hash and then settle in with a favorite read. Feel free to stay through lunch, dinner, and beyond, as the store's open until midnight daily, making it a popular spot with students. A full slate of events, from game nights to author talks, is scheduled almost daily. ✉ *338 Newbury St., Back Bay* ☎ *617/267–8688* ⊕ *www.tridentbookscafe.com* Ⓜ *Hynes.*

CLOTHING
Betsy Jenney

WOMEN'S CLOTHING | This small, personal store showcases well-made, comfortable lines that cater to women who cannot walk into a fitted size-4 suit—in other words, most of the female population. The designers found here, such as Nicole Miller, Autumn Cashmere, and Cambio, are fashionable yet realistic. ✉ *114 Newbury St., Back Bay* ☎ *617/536–2610* ⊕ *www.betsyjenney.com* Ⓜ *Copley.*

Chanel

WOMEN'S CLOTHING | This spacious 10,000-square-foot branch of the Parisian couture house (complete with custom sofas upholstered in Chanel tweed and a 20-foot-high strand of cascading glass beads) carries suits, separates, bags, shoes, cosmetics, and, of course, a divine selection of little black dresses. ✉ *6 Newbury St., Back Bay* ☎ *617/859–0055* ⊕ *www.chanel.com/en_US/fashion.html* Ⓜ *Arlington.*

Freebird

SHOES | While the boots you usually see in Boston are made to tackle the snow, this new outpost for boots is kicking that notion to the curb. With sizes ranging from tiny tots to adults, they offer the best in hand-crafted leather Western boots, booties, and bold strappy sandals. ⊠ *201 Newbury St., Back Bay* ☎ *617/729–2150* ⊕ *freebirdstores.com.*

Lit Boutique

WOMEN'S CLOTHING | If there's a style trend out there, this small women-led, minority-owned shop sells it. Full of flirty frocks from the likes of Free People, For Love & Lemons, and Blank NYC, along with accessories like jewelry, hair clips, and bags, the packed racks of fun pieces can add confidence to chic shoppers' closets. ⊠ *223 Newbury St., Back Bay* ☎ *617/421–8637* ⊕ *litboutique.com.*

Ministry of Supply

MIXED CLOTHING | Inspired by the temperature-regulating materials used for NASA's astronaut clothes, three MIT students started this men's and women's clothing store that features stretchy, moisture-wicking, wrinkle-free, machine-washable slacks, shirts, blouses, blazers, and jackets designed by a former Theory designer (think clean and elegant). Interested in creating a bespoke blazer on-site? The store's 3-D print knitting machine can finish a garment in about two hours. ⊠ *303 Newbury St., Back Bay* ☎ *617/236–4253* ⊕ *www.ministryofsupply.com* Ⓜ *Hynes.*

JEWELRY

Shreve, Crump & Low

JEWELRY & WATCHES | Since 1796, Shreve has specialized in high-end treasures, including gems and handcrafted platinum rings, as well as men's and women's watches and high-quality antiques. But don't get the impression that you can't afford anything here: one of the store's best-selling items is a $99 ceramic pitcher called "The Gurgling Cod," in honor of the state fish. ⊠ *39 Newbury St., Back Bay* ☎ *617/267–9100* ⊕ *www.shreve-crumpandlow.com* Ⓜ *Arlington.*

Small Pleasures

JEWELRY & WATCHES | From Victorian-era tourmaline cocktail rings to mint-condition pocket watches, vintage lovers should not miss the antique and estate jewelry that fills these cases. The staff is notably helpful and informed. The shop also offers jewelry and watch repair, restringing, and custom jewelry design. ⊠ *Copley Pl., 142 Newbury St., Back Bay* ☎ *617/267–7371* ⊕ *www.small-pleasures.com* Ⓜ *Copley.*

MUSIC STORES

Newbury Comics

MUSIC | This renowned pop-culture store carries vinyl, CDs, DVDs, novelty tees, quirky gifts, and an especially good lineup of independent pressings. You'll find three other locations nearby: two in Cambridge (Harvard Square and the CambridgeSide Galleria), as well as one inside Faneuil Hall Marketplace. ⊠ *348 Newbury St., Back Bay* ☎ *617/236–4930* ⊕ *www.newburycomics.com* Ⓜ *Hynes.*

SHOPPING CENTERS

Copley Place

MALL | An indoor shopping mall in the Back Bay, Copley Place includes such high-end shops as Christian Dior and Louis Vuitton. It is anchored by the pricey but dependable Neiman Marcus and offers a few dining options, such as Legal Sea Foods and Caffè Nero. ⊠ *100 Huntington Ave., Back Bay* ☎ *617/262–6200* ⊕ *www.simon.com/mall/copley-place* Ⓜ *Copley, Back Bay.*

Prudential Center

MALL | A skywalk connects Copley Place to the Prudential Center. The Pru, as it's often called, contains popular chain stores such as Vineyard Vines, Canada Goose, Kate Spade, and Sephora and is anchored by Saks 5th Avenue. The giant food hall, Eataly, offers plenty of options for eating, from to-go sandwiches to sit-down dining, as well as shopping for items like olive oil and wine. ✉ *800 Boylston St., Back Bay* ☎ *800/746–7778* ⊕ *www.prudentialcenter.com* Ⓜ *Prudential.*

SPECIALTY STORES

The Fish & Bone

OTHER SPECIALTY STORE | This boutique is dedicated to all things cat and dog. Choose from the enormous selection of collars, toys, and food. Of note, none of the food the shop carries has artificial dyes, flavors, or preservatives. ✉ *217 Newbury St., Back Bay* ☎ *857/753–4176* ⊕ *www.thefishandbone.com* Ⓜ *Arlington.*

THRIFT SHOPS

Castanet Designer Consignment

OUTLET | Chanel purses, Rick Owens jackets, and Hermès bracelets have all graced this jam-packed couture-quality consignment shop, located on the second floor, which finds gently worn gems from fashion lovers across the country. Its picky choices are your gain. ✉ *175 Newbury St., 2nd fl., Back Bay* ☎ *617/536–1919* ⊕ *www.shopcastanet. com* Ⓜ *Arlington.*

Revolve

OUTLET | Come here to snag the perfect designer dress, a vintage Chanel bag, or some Manolo Blahnik heels to complete your outfit. The store receives designer booty every day, which they sell for about one-third of the retail price. Handbag hounds regularly stop in to peruse the store's generous selection. ✉ *262 Newbury St., Back Bay* ☎ *617/262–0720* ⊕ *www.revolveboutiques.com.*

The South End

The South End lost many residents to the Back Bay in the late 19th century, but in the late 1970s, middle-class professionals began snapping up town houses at bargain prices and restoring them. Solidly back in fashion now, the South End's redbrick row houses in various states of refurbished splendor now house a diverse population, the city's largest gay community, and some excellent shops and restaurants.

◉ Sights

Bay Village

NEIGHBORHOOD | This pocket of early-19th-century brick row houses, near Arlington and Piedmont Streets, is a fine, mellow neighborhood (Edgar Allan Poe was born here). Its window boxes and short, narrow streets make the area seem a toylike reproduction of Beacon Hill. Note that, owing to the street pattern, it's difficult to drive to Bay Village, and it's easy to miss on foot. ✉ *Bounded (roughly) by Arlington, Stuart, Charles, and Marginal Sts., South End* ⊕ *www. bayvillage.net.*

Boston Center for the Arts

ARTS CENTER | Of Boston's multiple arts organizations, this nonprofit arts-and-culture complex is one of the most lively and diverse. Here you can see the work of budding playwrights, check out rotating exhibits from contemporary artists, or stop in for a curator's talk and other special events, including book fairs, dance, and kids programming. BCA houses several performance spaces, a community music center, the Mills Art Gallery, and studio space for some 40 Boston-based contemporary artists. ✉ *539 Tremont St., South End* ☎ *617/426–5000* ⊕ *www. bcaonline.org* 🆓 *Free* ☉ *Closed Sun.– Tues.* Ⓜ *Back Bay/South End.*

Cathedral of the Holy Cross

CHURCH | This enormous 1875 Gothic cathedral dominates the corner of Washington and Union Park Streets. The main church of the Archdiocese of Boston and therefore the seat of Cardinal Seán Patrick O'Malley, Holy Cross is also New England's largest Catholic church. It's also home to an 1875 Hook & Hastings pipe organ, the largest instrument ever built by that company.

South End

BACK BAY

SOUTH END

Sights ▼

1 Bay Village F1
2 Boston Center
   for the Arts F3
3 Cathedral of the
   Holy Cross F5
4 Rutland Square C4
5 Union Park F4

Restaurants ▼

1 B&G Oysters F4
2 Barcelona Wine Bar ... F3
3 Black Lamb E4
4 Coppa G4
5 The Franklin Café G4
6 Frenchie F4
7 Kava Neo-Taverna F4
8 Mistral F1
9 Myers + Chang H4
10 Oishii Boston H4
11 Shore Leave H3
12 SRV B5
13 Toro D7

Quick Bites ▼

1 The Buttery F4
2 Flour Bakery + Café E6
3 Picco F3

✉ *1400 Washington St., South End*
☎ *617/542–5682* ⊕ *holycrossboston.com*
Ⓜ *Back Bay.*

Rutland Square

PLAZA/SQUARE | Reflecting a time when the South End was the most prestigious Boston address, this slice of a park is framed by lovely Italianate bowfront houses. ✉ *Rutland Sq. between Columbus Ave. and Tremont St., South End.*

Union Park

NEIGHBORHOOD | Cast-iron fences, Victorian-era town houses, and a grassy area all add up to one of Boston's most charming slices of a neighborhood. ✉ *Union Park St. between Shawmut Ave. and Tremont St., South End.*

🍴 Restaurants

Home to lovely Victorian brownstones, art galleries, and the city's most diverse crowd, the South End is Boston's cultural engine. It's also ground zero for local foodies, who flood the scores of ethnic resto-bars that morph from neighborhood bistros into packed hot spots as the evening progresses. Some of the city's most popular restaurants inhabit the small square between Berkeley Street and Massachusetts Avenue to the west, and Harrison Avenue and Columbus Avenue to the north.

B&G Oysters

$$$ | SEAFOOD | B&G Oysters' chef Barbara Lynch (of No. 9 Park, the Butcher Shop, Sportello, DRINK, and Menton fame) offers a style-conscious seafood restaurant with fresher than fresh oysters from both coasts; creative, seasonal dishes; and New England classics, including one of the best lobster rolls in the city. Designed to imitate the inside of an oyster shell, the iridescent bar glows with silvery, candlelit tiles and a sophisticated crowd that in warm weather fills the hidden outdoor patio strung with tiny white lights. **Known for:** delicate portions; stylish setting; excellent wine list. $ *Average*

main: $30 ✉ *550 Tremont St., South End* ☎ *617/423–0550* ⊕ *www.bandgoysters. com* Ⓜ *Back Bay.*

Barcelona Wine Bar

$$$ | SPANISH | While diving right into the monumental cheese and charcuterie menu seems like a solid starter bet, save some room for the outstanding tapas at this lively wine bar. Favorites on repeat with its young sophisticated diners include blistered shishitos, *patatas bravas*, chorizo with figs, spicy empanadas, and sauteed mussels. **Known for:** lively atmosphere; extensive wine list; flavorful shared plates. $ *Average main: $30* ✉ *525 Tremont St., South End* ☎ *617/266–2600* ⊕ *barcelonawinebar. com.*

Black Lamb

$$$ | MODERN AMERICAN | Black Lamb's chefs call the American brasserie "a love letter to the South End." Translation: they pour their hearts into the menu to captivate the palates of all who dine there, with dishes such as duck breast frites, lamb burger, roasted cauliflower with anchovies, and day boat scallops. **Known for:** flavorful takes on classics; inventive cocktail program; creative kids menu. $ *Average main: $30* ✉ *571 Tremont St., South End* ☎ *617/982–6330* ⊕ *blacklamb-southend.com.*

Coppa

$$$ | ITALIAN | A small *enoteca* with a whole lot of personality, Coppa is the definition of a neighborhood staple. James Beard–winning chefs Ken Oringer and Jamie Bissonnette have made this the South End spot to share Italian plates, charcuterie, and a spritz on the outdoor patio. **Known for:** carbonara and pizza; amari menu; intimate setting. $ *Average main: $28* ✉ *253 Shawmut Ave., South End* ☎ *617/391–0902* ⊕ *www.coppaboston.com.*

The Franklin Café

$$ | AMERICAN | With a full menu served until 1:30 am, The Franklin has jumped to the head of the class by keeping things simple yet effective, from the well-crafted cocktails to the homey cuisine: think skillet-smoked mussels, lasagna, and steak frites. The vibe tends to feel more like a bar than a restaurant (hence the many bartender awards), so be forewarned that it can get loud and the wait for a table (there are only seven booths and two tables) can be long. **Known for:** neighborhood feel; open late; gastropub fare. ⑤ *Average main: $22* ✉ *278 Shawmut Ave., South End* ☎ *617/350–0010* ⊕ *www.franklincafe.com* ☽ *No lunch* Ⓜ *Union Park.*

Frenchie

$$$ | FRENCH | Step down into this charming wine bistro and you'll feel like you've been transported to Paris, with a menu of classic French fare dressed up a bit, such as escargot toast or foie gras on brioche, paired with one of two dozen wines by the glass, all served with a smile by an attentive staff. The wall-length bar is a buzzy spot in the evenings, while those looking for a romantic nook choose the garden-side solarium. **Known for:** lively atmosphere; cozy solarium in back; authentic French food. ⑤ *Average main: $35* ✉ *560 Tremont St., South End* ☎ *857/233–5941* ⊕ *www.frenchieboston.com* Ⓜ *Back Bay.*

★ Kava Neo-Taverna

$$$ | GREEK | This sweet little white-washed taverna serves authentic Greek cuisine, with many ingredients imported directly from the Mediterranean, such as the feta, fish, and octopus. Order some crisp white wine off the hard-to-find Greek wines and liquors list to sip with a parade of home-style dishes, from tasty meze plates to entrées like grilled lamb chops. **Known for:** taverna feel; high-quality ingredients; authentic Greek favorites. ⑤ *Average main: $27* ✉ *315 Shawmut Ave., South End* ☎ *617/356–1100* ⊕ *www.kavaneotaverna.com* ☽ *No lunch weekdays.*

★ Mistral

$$$$ | FRENCH | Since 1997, Boston's fashionable set has flocked to this long-popular South End restaurant with polished service and upscale yet unpretentious French-Mediterranean cuisine. While seasonal tweaks do occur, fail-safe favorites like burgundy style escargot, parfait of Hudson Valley foie gras, tuna tartare, duck with cranberries, and Dover Sole Meunière are part of a menu that rarely changes—but no one's complaining. **Known for:** superb service; white-cloth, country French decor; sophisticated Mediterranean cuisine. ⑤ *Average main: $42* ✉ *223 Columbus Ave., South End* ☎ *617/867–9300* ⊕ *mistralbistro.com* ☽ *No lunch* Ⓜ *Back Bay.*

★ Myers + Chang

$$ | CHINESE | Pink and orange dragon decals cover the windows of this all-day Chinese café, where Joanne Chang (of Flour bakery fame) taps her familial cooking roots to create shareable platters of creative dumplings, wok-charred udon noodles, and stir-fries brimming with fresh ingredients and plenty of hot chili peppers, garlic, fresh herbs, crushed peanuts, and lime. The staff is young and fun, and the crowd generally follows suit. **Known for:** fabulous cocktails; great service; Asian soul food. ⑤ *Average main: $22* ✉ *1145 Washington St., South End* ☎ *617/542–5200* ⊕ *www.myersandchang.com* Ⓜ *Back Bay.*

Oishii Boston

$$$ | JAPANESE | Although the entrance to this superb sushi restaurant may elude you, simply follow the crowds of raw-fish fans streaming into the sleek, gray, industrial space, to find edible aquatic enchantment in the form of Tokyo-style soft-shell crab, lobster tempura, and Chilean sea bass. The vibe is stylish and so are the diners. **Known for:** quiet atmosphere; minimalist decor; high-end Japanese sushi. ⑤ *Average main: $35* ✉ *1166 Washington St., South End*

☎ 617/482–8868 ⊕ www.oishiiboston. com ⊘ Closed Mon. Ⓜ East Berkeley.

Shore Leave

$ | SUSHI | As you walk down the stairs to this subterranean hot spot, rattan cane pendant lamps, a tiki bar, and a striking tropics-to-Japan mural wall light the way to plates of tasty nigiri, creative rolls, and bar bites (the burgers and tots are local favorites). Named after a sailor's leisure time on dry land, the bar's drinks create the perfect escape, with rum Old Fashioneds, highballs, and punches on the long menu. **Known for:** impressive sake list; fun, tropical hideaway vibe; innovative sushi. Ⓢ *Average main: $15* ✉ 11 William E Mullins Way, South End ☎ 617/530–1775 ⊕ shoreleaveboston. com ⊘ Closed Sun. and Mon.

SRV

$$$ | ITALIAN | SRV, short for Serene Republic of Venice, bills itself as a *bacaro*, or Italian wine bar, which in the South End translates into a happening cocktail scene. The chic set gathers to sip on aperitifs like Aperol Spritz and negroni *bianco* before tucking into tantalizing small plates and hand-crafted pastas made from flour the chefs mill themselves from durum wheat berries. **Known for:** cocktail party buzz; casual, fun feel; Venetian bar bites. Ⓢ *Average main: $30* ✉ 569 Columbus St., South End ☎ 617/536–9500 ⊕ www.srvboston.com ⊘ No lunch.

★ Toro

$$$ | SPANISH | Chefs Ken Oringer and Jamie Bissonnette's tapas joint, which now has an outpost in Manhattan, is a lively, popular spot where the Barcelona-inspired small plates, such as the *jamon* and queso, salt cod croquettes, and grilled corn with cotija cheese, are hefty enough to make a meal out of a few. The traditional or vegetarian paella is also perfect for sharing with a hungry crowd. **Known for:** cozy, small dining room; cult following; excellent traditional tapas. Ⓢ *Average main: $35*

✉ 1704 Washington St., South End ☎ 617/536–4300 ⊕ www.toro-restaurant. com Ⓜ Massachusetts Ave.

☕ Coffee and Quick Bites

The Buttery

$ | CAFÉ | Neighborhood denizens swear by the counter-service whoopie pies, coffee, and buttery biscuits at this daytime destination for snacks, but the biggest buzz is saved for the back-room bistro, which boasts a hefty wine list and down-to-earth dinner options like meatloaf and shrimp *fra diavolo*. Housemade breakfast sandwiches keep locals returning, as do seasonal soups, gourmet sandwiches, and scratch pastries from their own pastry kitchen. **Known for:** favorite among locals; great breakfast sandwiches; cozy vibe. Ⓢ *Average main: $10* ✉ 314 Shawmut Ave., South End ☎ 617/482–1015 ⊕ www.southendbuttery.com.

★ Flour Bakery + Café

$ | AMERICAN | FAMILY | When folks need coffee, a great sandwich, or an irresistible sweet, like a pecan sticky bun, lemon tart, or double chocolate cookie—or just a place to sit and chat—they pay a visit to one of owner Joanne Chang's 10 Flour bakeries, including this one in the South End. A communal table in the middle acts as a gathering spot, around which diners enjoy morning pastries, homemade soups, hearty bean and grain salads, and specialty sandwiches, which change seasonally. **Known for:** delicious salads and sandwiches; laid-back setting; scrumptious sweets. Ⓢ *Average main: $11* ✉ 1595 Washington St., South End ☎ 617/267–4300 ⊕ www.flourbakery. com Ⓜ Massachusetts Ave.

Picco

$ | PIZZA | FAMILY | With a name that's short for Pizza and Ice Cream Company, Picco is perfect for both kids and kids at heart. This South End spot combines an upscale, trendy feel with an old-fashioned soda fountain and a changing list of homemade ice cream flavors that might include chocolate malt chip, prickly pear sorbet, and honey. **Known for:** homemade pizza dough with locally milled flour; homemade ice cream and floats; fun vibe. $ *Average main: $15* ⊠ *513 Tremont St., South End* ☎ *617/927–0066* ⊕ *www. piccorestaurant.com* ▭ *No credit cards.*

🍴 Hotels

The Revolution Hotel

$$ | **HOTEL** | An affordable option in a sea of sky-high rates, this art-filled hotel is an intriguing mix of luxurious touches—like pillow-top beds and a Peloton bike in the gym—and more downscale amenities, like shared bathrooms and tiny rooms. **Pros:** whimsical original artwork; inexpensive; on-site restaurant. **Cons:** small rooms; some rooms have shared bathrooms; inconvenient parking. $ *Rooms from: $200* ⊠ *40 Berkeley St., South End* ☎ *617/848–9200* ⊕ *therevolutionhotel.com* ➴ *177 rooms* ⦿ *No Meals* Ⓜ *Back Bay.*

Staypineapple

$$ | **B&B/INN** | This small property, part of a small brand of hotels, has a fresh, contemporary style with lots and lots of yellow accents along with complimentary Wi-Fi, plush pillow-top beds, and marble bathrooms with walk-in glass showers. **Pros:** can't beat the price; friendly staff; the South End is a prime location for foodies. **Cons:** rooms can be noisy; might be too quirky for some; area parking is brutally hard or expensive. $ *Rooms from: $225* ⊠ *26 Chandler St., South End* ☎ *857/444–6111, 800/842–3450* ⊕ *www. staypineapple.com/south-end-boston* ➴ *56 rooms* ⦿ *No Meals* Ⓜ *Back Bay.*

🌟 Nightlife

Sedate tree-lined streets of newly reappointed brick town houses cast demure impressions, but the South End is a truly lively area with cafés, restaurants, theaters, parks, and recreational enclaves.

BARS

Clerys

PUBS | Open-windowed, multiroomed Clerys can be your neighborhood bar, Irish pub, dance hall, sports hub, trivia game spot, or even the home for local Georgia Bulldogs sports fans. Expect long lines on weekend nights in this high-traffic club near Copley Square; its several rooms bustle with young professionals. Food is limited to bar snacks, such as nachos, wings, and sliders. ⊠ *113 Dartmouth St., South End* ☎ *617/262–9874* ⊕ *www.clerysboston. com* Ⓜ *Copley.*

Club Café

CAFÉS | This smart multiroom club and restaurant for the Boston LGBTQ+ community and their allies is livelier than ever going into its fourth decade. Behind a stylish restaurant, patrons dance in the "video lounge" or watch classic music videos, cult flicks, and TV shows. There are trivia, karaoke, and Edge Boston events weekly; Napoleon Cabaret hosts singers nightly. A weekly Sunday Tea from 6 to 10 pm is free. ⊠ *209 Columbus Ave., South End* ☎ *617/536–0966* ⊕ *www.clubcafe.com* Ⓜ *Back Bay/South End.*

★ Darryl's Corner Bar & Kitchen

BARS | This longtime neighborhood soulfood and jazz hangout still looks spiffy, and features real Southern cooking and live bands nearly nightly at light cover charges. Come for favorites like mac and cheese or glorified chicken and waffles, and on Sunday there is an all-you-can-eat blues brunch starting at 11 am. ⊠ *604 Columbus Ave., South End* ☎ *617/536–1100* ⊕ *www.dcbkboston.com* Ⓜ *Massachusetts Ave.*

Delux Café

BARS | This unpretentious, cozy bar on a quiet corner attracts old-timers and young professionals with modest drinks and affordable comfort food. The quesadillas are worth the wait for a table. Yellowing posters, dim lights, and a '60s soundtrack add to the quirky, retro vibe (did we mention it's covered in Elvis memorabilia?). The wine list features a couple of reds, whites, and sparklers. ⊠ *100 Chandler St., South End* 🕾 *617/338–5258* ⊕ *thedelux.com* ⚲ *Cash only* Ⓜ *Back Bay/South End.*

The Franklin Café

BARS | A neighborhood institution, The Franklin's renowned for creative cocktails, local microbrews, fine wines, and modern American food. There's no sign: just look for the white martini logo (or folks waiting for a dinner table) to know you're there. A full menu is served until 1:30 am every single night of the week, and the bar is open until 2 am. ⊠ *278 Shawmut Ave., South End* 🕾 *617/350–0010* ⊕ *www.franklincafe.com* Ⓜ *Back Bay.*

★ J. J. Foley's Cafe

BARS | Family-owned-and-operated since 1909, J. J. Foley's Cafe (or "Foley's," as regulars call it) is one of the most authentic Irish bars in Boston. There's an intimate dining room, as well as a more casual bar area where everyone from former Boston mayors to Justin Timberlake have enjoyed a pint. Better yet, it's open until 2 am. The pub food is great; order a sky-high plate of nachos if you dare. ⊠ *117 E. Berkeley St., South End* 🕾 *617/728–9101* ⊕ *www.jjfoleyscafe.com* Ⓜ *Tufts Medical Center.*

★ Jacque's Cabaret

CABARET | There's nothing traditional about Jacque's Cabaret, an institution for more than 60 years. Nightly drag-queen shows draw bachelorette parties and locals looking to swill cocktails from plastic cups. Be sure to make reservations if you're going in a group, and don't show up late; they may give your table away if you aren't seated before showtime. Because of a long-running licensing dispute with sleepy Bay Villagers, the whole carnival shuts down nightly at midnight. ⊠ *79 Broadway, Theater District* 🕾 *617/426–8902* ⊕ *www.jacques-cabaret.com* Ⓜ *Arlington.*

The Trophy Room

COCKTAIL LOUNGES | Tucked under the Staypineapple Boston inn, this gay bar is popular with the local after-work crowd, who enjoy live performances from local artists and apps like nachos and chicken fingers. Casually dressed locals drop by for the large beer list and classic breakfast dishes during the hopping weekend brunches starting at noon, which feature long, tall mimosas and bloodies. ⊠ *26 Chandler St., South End* 🕾 *617/482–4428* ⊕ *www.trophyroomboston.com* Ⓜ *Back Bay/South End.*

MUSIC CLUBS

★ The Beehive

LIVE MUSIC | An underground bohemian bistro featuring delicious food, libations, and live music nightly, The Beehive is nestled under the historic Cyclorama building. Nightly live music includes a mix of jazz, blues, R&B, electronica, reggae, latin, country, cabaret, and burlesque, while patrons enjoy craft cocktails and wines and dine on Mediterranean meze platters, daily special pastas, and comfort entrées. If jazz is your jam, don't miss the weekend live jazz brunch from 10 am to 3 pm; Sunday night features blues. ⊠ *541 Tremont St., South End* 🕾 *617/423–0069* ⊕ *www.beehiveboston.com* Ⓜ *Back Bay.*

🎭 Performing Arts

DANCE

Boston Ballet

BALLET | The city's premier dance company performs at the Boston Opera House. Shows have included *Romeo and Juliet*, classic Balanchine, and *La Sylphide*. And, of course, if you're visiting during the holidays, be sure to score seats to *The Nutcracker*. ⊠ *19 Clarendon St., South End* 🕾 *617/695–6955* ⊕ *www.bostonballet.org* Ⓜ *Back Bay.*

Boston Dance Alliance

MODERN DANCE | This group serves as a clearinghouse for an amazing array of local dance companies' classes, performances, and workshops. Visit the alliance's website for upcoming performances and venues. ⊠ *19 Clarendon St., South End* ☎ *617/456–6295* ⊕ *www.bostondancealliance.org* Ⓜ *Back Bay.*

MUSIC

Boston Gay Men's Chorus

MUSIC | With an aim to "inspire change, build community, and celebrate difference," the Boston Gay Men's Chorus has a repertoire that ranges from holiday favorites to show tunes to chamber selections to pop hits. With more than 300 members, the group performs at the New England Conservatory's Jordan Hall. ⊠ *539 Tremont St., South End* ☎ *617/542–7464* ⊕ *www.bgmc.org* Ⓜ *Back Bay.*

THEATER

Huntington Theatre Company

THEATER | Boston's largest resident theater company consistently performs a high-quality mix of 21st-century plays and classics under the artistic direction of Loretta Greco, and commissions playwrights to produce original dramas. The Huntington performs at two locations: its own newly renovated theater at Boston University and the South End's Calderwood Theatre Pavilion. ⊠ *Boston University Theatre, 264 Huntington Ave., Back Bay* ☎ *617/266–7900 box office* ⊕ *www.huntingtontheatre.org* Ⓜ *Symphony.*

🛍 Shopping

If you like to shop, you'll have a blast in this area, which focuses on home furnishings and accessories, with a heavy accent on the unique and handmade. At the northern tip of the South End, where Harrison Avenue and Washington Street lead to Chinatown, are several Chinese supermarkets. South of Washington Street is the "SoWa" District, home to a large number of art galleries. From May through October, the excellent SoWa Open Market on Sunday is a great excursion, packed with artists, food trucks,

and a farmers' market. Chic home-furnishings, restaurants, bakeries, and gift shops line Tremont Street, starting at Berkeley Street.

ART GALLERIES

Alpha Gallery

ART GALLERIES | This gallery specializes in paintings, drawings, watercolors, and mixed media works from contemporary American and foreign artists. It also has a fine selection of master prints and works from 20th-century American masters. The gallery exhibits emerging, mid-career, and established artists, as well as special shows of master artists such as Pablo Picasso, Fairfield Porter, Max Beckmann, and others. ⊠ *450 Harrison Ave., Suite 55, South End* ☎ *617/536–4465* ⊕ *www.alphagallery.com* Ⓜ *Silver Line MBTA.*

Bromfield Gallery

ART GALLERIES | Tucked among dozens of art studios in the artsy SoWa (South of Washington) area, this artist-run, members-only gallery mounts monthly shows featuring contemporary art in all forms, including printmaking, video, acrylic, ink drawing, and pastels. ⊠ *450 Harrison Ave., South End* ☎ *617/451–3605* ⊕ *www.bromfieldgallery.com* Ⓜ *Tufts Medical Center.*

CLOTHING

CouCou

CHILDREN'S CLOTHING | When you want your tot to stand out sartorially, head to this globally sourced boutique packed with a thoughtfully curated selection of clothes; you'll also find toys and crafts, as well as a playroom in the back of the store. CouCou has also started carrying women's collections. ⊠ *24 Union Park St., South End* ☎ *617/936–4082* ⊕ *coucou-boston.com* ☾ *Closed Mon.*

Flock

MIXED CLOTHING | This boho-chic boutique brims with cotton T-shirts, floral dresses, and vintage-inspired jewelry, along with whimsical gift items, like handmade keepsake boxes filled with colorful images and antique baubles. ✉ *274 Shawmut Ave., South End* ☎ *617/391–0222* ⊕ *www.flockboston.com* Ⓜ *Back Bay.*

SAULT New England

MIXED CLOTHING | In the heart of the South End, shoppers can step down into this small boutique celebrating the history of fashion in New England. Shoppers will find a selection of preppy staples mixed in with current trends for all genders. The boutique recently partnered with Brooks Brothers to carry the latest collection of men's spring/summer styles designed by Michael Bastian. ✉ *577 Tremont St., South End* ☎ *857/9434* ⊕ *saultne.com.*

HOME FURNISHINGS

Gifted

SOUVENIRS | Enchanting homemade gifts from a rotating group of more than 60 artists (including the owner, Marie Corcoran) fill this dreamy boutique. Scoop up dainty charm and gemstone pendants, vegan handbags, men's handpainted ties, or a cute caterpillar wooden wall clock for that special little one in your life. This store has something for everyone, including you. ✉ *2 Dartmouth St., South End* ☎ *617/716–9924* ⊕ *gifted-boston. myshopify.com* Ⓜ *Back Bay.*

Hudson Interior Designs

HOUSEWARES | Jill Goldberg offers full-scale, in-home design services, but you can also pick up custom furniture and cool home goods, such as decorative throw pillows, marbleized pottery bowls, rugs, and luscious-smelling candles, at the store. ✉ *12 Union Park St., South End* ☎ *617/292–0900* ⊕ *hudsonboston.com* Ⓜ *Back Bay, Prudential.*

Lekker Home

HOUSEWARES | Dutch design with contemporary panache pervades the neighborhood's coolest furniture and home goods store. This is a great place to pick up a sleek dining set, the perfect accent table, some funky china, or a statement pendant light. ✉ *38 Wareham St., South End* ☎ *617/737–7307* ⊕ *www.lekkerhome. com* Ⓜ *Back Bay.*

SoWa Open Market

MARKET | From May through October, the excellent SoWa Open Market on Sunday (affectionately known as "SoWa Sundays") is a great excursion packed with artists, food trucks, and a farmers' market. Held 11 am to 4 pm, it has 100-plus weekly outdoor tent vendors, along with 100-plus indoor artist studios, galleries, and retail shops; food trucks; a vintage flea market; Outdoor Oasis Café & Bar; and rotating DJs. ✉ *500 Harrison Ave., Back Bay* ☎ *857/362–7692* ⊕ *www. sowaboston.com/sowa-open-market.*

THRIFT SHOPS

★ Boomerangs – Special Edition

SECOND-HAND | Stepping into this cozy secondhand boutique feels like you could be in the salon of a very wealthy couple, who just happen to be unloading their cache of designer clothes and housewares. Jade satin flats, beaded Armani tops, and vintage dresses and jewelry—all at a fraction of their original cost—are the sorts of treats you'll find sharing space with menswear, books, and silver-plated serving dishes. All proceeds go to the AIDS Action group. There are also branches in Cambridge and Jamaica Plain. ✉ *1407 Washington St., South End* ☎ *617/456–0996* ⊕ *shopboomerangs.org* Ⓜ *Back Bay.*

FENWAY AND KENMORE SQUARE

8

Updated by
Kim Foley MacKinnon

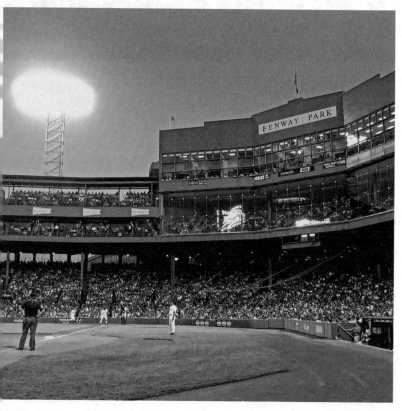

● Sights	⑪ Restaurants	🛏 Hotels	● Shopping	⒴ Nightlife
★★★★☆	★★★★☆	★★★☆☆	★★☆☆☆	★★★★☆

FENWAY PARK

Take yourself out to a ball game at legendary Fenway Park.

For baseball fans a trip to Fenway Park is a religious pilgrimage. The Boston Red Sox have played here since 1912. The oldest Major League Baseball ballpark is one of the last of its kind, a place where the scoreboard is hand-operated and fans endure uncomfortable seats.

For much of the ballpark's history Babe Ruth's specter loomed large. The team won five titles by 1918 but endured an 86-year title drought after trading away the Sultan of Swat. The Sox "reversed the curse" in 2004, defeating the rival Yankees in the American League Championship Series after being down 3–0 in the series (an unheard of comeback in baseball) and sweeping the St. Louis Cardinals in the World Series. The Red Sox won again in 2007 against the Colorado Rockies; against the Cardinals in 2013, the first time since 1918 that the team cinched the series in its hometown; and once more in 2018 against the Los Angeles Dodgers. The curse is no more.

FENWAY PARK TOURS

If you can't see the Sox, you can still see the Green Monster up close by going on a tour of the park. The one-hour Fenway walking tour runs year-round, and if you go on the last tour on a home-game day, you can watch batting practice. Tours run hourly from 9 am (10 am November through March) to 5 pm (or three hours before game time) and cost $21. Check the site for info on premium tours. ☎ 617/226–6666 ⊕ mlb.com/redsox/ballpark/tours.

THE NATION

The Red Sox have the most enthusiastic fans in baseball. Knowledgeable and dedicated, they follow the team with religious-like intensity.

THE GREEN MONSTER

Fenway's most dominant feature is the 37-foot-high wall that looms over left field. It's just over 300 feet from home plate and in the field of play, so deep fly balls that would have been outs in other parks sometimes become home runs. The Monster also stops line drives that would have been over the walls of other stadiums.

THE MUSIC

Fans sing "Take Me Out to the Ballgame" during the seventh-inning stretch in every ballpark, but at Fenway they also sing Neil Diamond's "Sweet Caroline" at the bottom of the eighth. If the Sox win, the Standells' "Dirty Water" blasts over the loudspeakers.

THE CURSE

In 1920 the Red Sox traded pitcher Babe Ruth to the Yankees, where he became a home-run-hitting baseball legend. Some fans—most famously *Boston Globe* columnist Dan Shaughnessy, who wrote a book called *The Curse of the Bambino*—blamed this move for the team's 86-year title drought, but others will claim that "The Curse" was just a media-driven storyline used to explain the team's past woes. Still, fans who watched a ground ball roll between Bill Buckner's legs in the 1986 World Series or saw Aaron Boone's winning home run in the 2003 division series swear the curse was real.

THE WEATHER

If you plan on catching a game at Fenway in the spring, bring warm clothes or a blanket. It can get chilly, especially in the stands. April lows are in the 40s, and in May it can still get down to 50 degrees.

Iconic Sox mark the park walls.

VISIT THE NATION

Not lucky enough to nab tickets ahead of time? Try your luck at Gate E 90 minutes before the game, when a handful of tickets are sold. There's a one-ticket limit, so everyone in your party must be in line.

If that doesn't yield results, you can still experience the Nation. The game with other fans. A favorite is the **Cask 'n Flagon**, at Brookline Avenue and Lansdowne Street, across the street from Fenway.

The closest you can get to Fenway without buying a ticket is the **Bleacher Bar** (✉ *82A Lansdowne St.*). There's a huge window in the center field wall overlooking the field. Get here early—it starts filling up a few hours before game time.

NEIGHBORHOOD SNAPSHOT

TOP REASONS TO GO

■ **Root for the home team:** Cheer on the only team in the eyes of Red Sox Nation at Fenway Park.

■ **Immerse yourself in art:** See masterpieces at the Museum of Fine Arts and the Isabella Stewart Gardner Museum.

■ **Listen to beautiful music:** Relish the perfect acoustics of a concert at Symphony Hall.

■ **Sip suds:** Head to Trillium, outside Time Out Market, for local brews.

■ **Explore the outdoors:** Enjoy the outdoors in the Emerald Necklace parks.

GETTING HERE

The Green Line is the best way to get to Fenway; get off at the Kenmore or Fenway stop for a short walk to the ballpark. Also know that it *is* possible to drive around this part of town. With a little hunting, on-street parking can usually be found on nongame days; if not, many lots and garages are within reasonable walking distance of Fenway Park.

PLANNING YOUR TIME

Although this area can be walked through in a couple of hours, art lovers could spend a week here, thanks to the glories of the MFA and the Isabella Stewart Gardner Museum.

■ TIP→ **Avoid Tuesday, when the Gardner is closed.**

If you're visiting between spring and early fall, take a tour of Fenway Park—or better yet, catch a game.

The Fenway and Kenmore Square area is generally safe, and is home to thousands of college students attending Boston University, Wheelock, Simmons, and Emmanuel, to name only a few of the nearby institutions. While the main strips—Beacon Street, Commonwealth Avenue, and Brookline Avenue—can be choked with pedestrians during game day, the marshy area of the Fens is quiet and poorly lighted: avoid walking there alone at night.

QUICK BITES

■ **Blackbird Doughnuts.** It's hard to resist sampling more than one doughnut at this artisanal shop, which offers flavors like Boston Cream and Cake Batter. ⊠ *20 Kilmarnock St., Fenway* ⊕ *www.blackbird-doughnuts.com/fenway.*

■ **Bleacher Bar.** Nothing beats a dog and a beer at Fenway when you're enjoying the game on a warm summer's night. If you don't have a ticket, you can enjoy the same vibe at this hidden bar with a view into center field, and enough historical Red Sox memorabilia to open its own museum. ⊠ *82A Lansdowne St., Fenway* ⊕ *www.bleacherbarboston.com.*

■ **Saloniki Greek.** Two-time James Beard–award winning chef Jody Adams offers classic Greek bites—think pitas, salads, and other favorites. ⊠ *4 Kilmarnock St., Fenway* ⊕ *www.salonikigreek.com.*

■ **Time Out Market Boston.** Some of Boston's top chefs have outlets at this open concept food hall; there's also a couple of bars and lots of space to spread out. ⊠ *401 Park Dr., Fenway* ⊕ *www.timeoutmarket.com/boston.*

The Back Bay Fens marshland gave this neighborhood its name, but two celebrated institutions give it its character: Fenway Park, which in 2004 saw the triumphant reversal of an 86-year drought for Boston's beloved Red Sox, and the Isabella Stewart Gardner Museum, the legacy of a high-living Boston Brahmin who attended a concert at Symphony Hall in 1912 wearing a headband that read "Oh, You Red Sox." Not far from the Gardner is another major cultural magnet: the Museum of Fine Arts. Kenmore Square, a favorite haunt for Boston University students, adds a bit of youthful flavor to the mix.

After the outsize job of filling in the bay had been completed, it would have been small trouble to obliterate the Fens with gravel and march row houses straight through to Brookline. But the planners, deciding that enough pavement had been laid between here and the Public Garden, hired vaunted landscape architect Frederick Law Olmsted to turn the Fens into a park. Olmsted applied his genius for heightening natural effects while subtly manicuring their surroundings; today the Fens park consists of irregularly shaped reed-bound pools surrounded by broad meadows, trees, and flower gardens.

The Fens marks the beginning of Boston's Emerald Necklace, a loosely connected chain of parks designed by Olmsted that extends along Fenway, Riverway, and Jamaicaway to Jamaica Pond, the Arnold Arboretum, and Franklin Park.

◉ Sights

Along the fens unclaimed by the Back Bay, where Olmstead's Emerald Necklace winds along museum row, you'll find ball fields, the Kelleher Rose Garden, and extensive, lovingly maintained victory gardens in the shadow of Fenway Park and lively upper Boylston Street. Along "Avenue of the Arts" (aka Huntington Avenue) are Symphony Hall, the New England Conservatory, Northeastern University, the Museum of Fine Arts, and the Isabella Stewart Gardner Museum. In the middle are Berklee College of Music, Boston Conservatory, and the Massachusetts Historical Society.

★ Boston Red Sox

SPORTS VENUE | FAMILY | The Boston Red Sox may be New England's most storied professional sports team of all time. For 86 years, the club suffered a World Series drought, a streak of bad luck that fans attributed to the "Curse of the Bambino," which was spelled in 1920 when the Sox sold Babe Ruth to the New York Yankees. All that changed in 2004, when a maverick squad broke the curse in a thrilling seven-game semifinals series against the Yankees, followed by a four-game sweep of St. Louis in the finals. Repeat World Series wins in 2007, 2013, and 2018 have cemented Bostonians' sense that the universe is back in order. Today, home games are played at Fenway Park from April to October. ⊠ *Fenway Park, 4 Jersey St., Kenmore Square* ⊕ *www.mlb.com/redsox/tickets/single-game-tickets* Ⓜ *Kenmore Square, Fenway.*

★ Emerald Necklace Conservancy

CITY PARK | FAMILY | The six large public parks known as Boston's Emerald Necklace stretch seven miles from the Back Bay Fens to Franklin Park in Dorchester, and include Arnold Arboretum, Jamaica Pond, Olmsted Park, and the Riverway. The linear parks, designed by master landscape architect Frederick Law Olmsted more than 100 years ago, remain a well-groomed urban masterpiece. ⊠ *125 The Fenway, The Fenway* ☎ *617/522–2700* ⊕ *www.emeraldnecklace.org.*

★ Fenway Park

SPORTS VENUE | FAMILY | Fenway Park is Major League Baseball's oldest ballpark and has seen some stuff since its 1912 opening. For one, it's the home field for the Boston Red Sox, which overcame the "Curse of the Bambino" to win World Series championships in 2004, 2007, 2013, and 2018. Ticket-holding Sox fans can browse display cases mounted inside Fenway Park before and during a ballgame; these shed light on and show off memorabilia from particular players and eras of the club team's history. Fenway offers hour-long behind-the-scenes guided walking tours of the park; there are also specialized tour options. ⊠ *4 Jersey St., Gate D, Kenmore Square* ☎ *617/226–6666 tours* ⊕ *www.mlb.com/redsox/ballpark/tours* ⊠ *$21* Ⓜ *Kenmore, Fenway.*

★ Isabella Stewart Gardner Museum

ART MUSEUM | A spirited society woman, Isabella Stewart came in 1860 from New York to marry John Lowell Gardner, one of Boston's leading citizens. "Mrs. Jack" promptly set about becoming the most un-Bostonian of the Proper Bostonians. She built a Venetian palazzo to hold her collected art. Her will stipulated that the building remain exactly as she left it—paintings, furniture, down to the smallest object in a hall cabinet—and so it has remained.

A Good Walk

With Boston's two major art museums on this itinerary, a case of museum fatigue could set in. However, both the Museum of Fine Arts and the Isabella Stewart Gardner Museum are surrounded by the sylvan glades of Fenway—a perfect oasis and time-out location when you're suffering from gallery overload. From the intersection of Massachusetts and Huntington Avenues, with the front entrance of Symphony Hall on your right, walk down Huntington Avenue. On your left is the New England Conservatory of Music and, on Gainsborough Street, its recital center, Jordan Hall. Between Huntington Avenue and Fenway is the **Museum of Fine Arts (MFA)** and, just around the corner, the **Isabella Stewart Gardner Museum.**

If you prefer to pay homage to the Red Sox: from Symphony Hall, go north on Mass. Ave., turn left on Comm. Ave., and continue until you reach **Kenmore Square**; from here it's a 10-minute walk down Brookline Avenue to Jersey Street and **Fenway Park.** If you get hungry, the Time Out Market Boston food hall offers plenty of tasty choices and is just down the street from Fenway Park.

Gardner's palazzo includes such masterpieces as Titian's *Europa,* Giotto's *Presentation of Christ in the Temple,* and John Singer Sargent's *El Jaleo.* Eight balconies adorn the majestic Venetian courtyard, and themed rooms include Raphael, Spanish Cloister, Gothic, Chinese Loggia, and a magnificent Tapestry Room for concerts, where Gardner entertained Henry James and Edith Wharton.

On March 18, 1990, the Gardner was the target of a sensational art heist. Thieves disguised as police officers stole 12 works, including Vermeer's *The Concert.* None of the art has been recovered. Because Mrs. Gardner's will prohibited substituting other works for any stolen art, empty expanses of wall identify spots where the paintings once hung. The heist is the subject of a 2021 Netflix documentary, *This is a Robbery.*

The modern Renzo Piano–designed addition houses a music hall, exhibit space, and conservation labs. ⊠ *25 Evans Way, The Fenway* ☎ *617/566–1401* ⊕ *www. gardnermuseum.org* 🖃 *$20* ⊘ *Closed Tues.* Ⓜ *Museum.*

Kenmore Square

PLAZA/SQUARE | Two blocks north of Fenway Park is Kenmore Square, where you'll find shops, restaurants, and the city's emblematic sign advertising Citgo gasoline. The red, white, and blue neon sign from 1965 is so thoroughly identified with the area that historic preservationists fought, successfully, to save it. The old Kenmore Square punk clubs have given way to a block-long development of pricey stores and restaurants, as well as brick sidewalks, gaslight-style street lamps, and tree plantings. In the shadow of Fenway Park between Brookline and Ipswich is Lansdowne Street, a nightlife magnet for the trendy, who have their pick of dance clubs and pregame bars. The urban campus of Boston University begins farther west on Commonwealth Avenue, in blocks thick with dorms, shops, and restaurants. ⊠ *Convergence of Beacon St., Commonwealth Ave., and Brookline Ave., The Fenway* Ⓜ *Kenmore.*

Sights ▼

1 Emerald Necklace
  Conservancy **G6**
2 Fenway Park **E3**
3 Isabella Stewart
  Gardner Museum....... **E7**
4 Kenmore Square........ **F2**
5 Museum of Fine Arts ... **F7**

Restaurants ▼

1 Audubon Boston........ **C3**
2 Citizen Public House
  & Oyster Bar **E4**
3 Eventide.................. **E4**
4 Sweet Cheeks Q **D4**

Quick Bites ▼

1 Blackbird Doughnuts... **D4**
2 Bleacher Bar............. **E3**
3 Saloniki Greek........... **D4**
4 Time Out Market
  Boston **D4**

Hotels ▼

1 Hotel
  Commonwealth **F2**
2 The Verb Hotel **E4**

Fenway and Kenmore Square

★ Museum of Fine Arts

ART MUSEUM | FAMILY | The MFA's collection of approximately 450,000 objects was built from a core of paintings and sculpture from the Boston Athenæum, historical portraits from the city of Boston, and donations by area universities. The MFA has more than 70 works by John Singleton Copley; major paintings by Winslow Homer, John Singer Sargent, Fitz Henry Lane, and Edward Hopper; and a wealth of American works ranging from native New England folk art and Colonial portraiture to New York abstract expressionism of the 1950s and 1960s.

More than 30 galleries contain the MFA's European painting and sculpture collection, dating from the 11th century to the 20th. Contemporary art has a dynamic home in the MFA's dramatic I. M. Pei–designed building.

The MFA is open until 10 pm on Friday. Save time and purchase your tickets online in advance as lines can get quite long. The museum requires you to check any bag larger than 11 inches by 15 inches (even purses). ⊠ *465 Huntington Ave., The Fenway* ☎ *617/267–9300* ⊕ *www. mfa.org* ✑ *$27* ⊘ *Closed Tues. and Wed.* Ⓜ *Museum.*

🍴 Restaurants

This area adjacent to Fenway Park and Boston University is a trendy, bustling spot with a variety of restaurants along tree-lined streets that specialize in barbecue, oysters, tacos, and faculty-friendly bistro fare.

Audubon Boston

$$ | AMERICAN | While close to Fenway Park, Audubon feels more like a neighborhood joint than a tourist spot, though it does fill up on game days. Service is outstanding and matches the delicious dishes, many of which are made for sharing. **Known for:** Taco Tuesdays; excellent service; heated patio. ⑤ *Average main:* *$18* ⊠ *838 Beacon St., Kenmore Square* ☎ *617/421–1910* ⊕ *www.audubonboston. com* Ⓜ *Kenmore.*

Citizen Public House & Oyster Bar

$$$ | AMERICAN | All you want and expect from a modern public house, this spot has burgers, steak frites, and, as the name promises, plenty of oysters. In addition, the bar offers more than 200 whiskeys, along with plenty of craft beers and wines. **Known for:** oysters; pig roasts; classy vibe. ⑤ *Average main:* *$25* ⊠ *1310 Boylston St., The Fenway* ☎ *617/450–9000* ⊕ *www.citizenpub.com* Ⓜ *Kenmore.*

Eventide

$ | SEAFOOD | This casual seafood spot, where you order at the counter, is an outpost of the famous Portland, Maine, restaurant of the same name. Offering reasonable prices for excellent fare, this is a fun option in Fenway without a lot of fuss. **Known for:** brown-butter lobster roll; casual setting; fresh seafood. ⑤ *Average main: $15* ⊠ *1321 Boylston St., The Fenway* ☎ *617/545–1060* ⊕ *www. eventideoysterco.com* ⊘ *Closed Mon. and Tues.* Ⓜ *Fenway.*

★ Sweet Cheeks Q

$$ | SOUTHERN | Red Sox fans, foodies, and Fenway residents flock to this meat-lover's mecca, where Texas-style barbecue is the name of the game. Hefty slabs of dry-rubbed heritage pork, great northern beef brisket, and plump chickens cook low and slow in a jumbo black smoker, then come to the table heaped on a tray lined with butcher paper, along with homemade sweet pickles, shaved onion, and your choice of "hot scoops" (collard greens, mac and cheese) or "cold scoops" (coleslaw, potato salad). **Known for:** scrumptious sides; jeans and T-shirt atmosphere; finger-licking barbecue. ⑤ *Average main: $22* ⊠ *1381 Boylston St., The Fenway* ☎ *617/266–1300* ⊕ *www.sweetcheeksq.com* ⊘ *Closed Mon. No lunch Tues.–Fri.* Ⓜ *Fenway.*

☕ Coffee and Quick Bites

Blackbird Doughnuts

$ | **AMERICAN** | Creative, delicious, and irresistible, the sweet treats from Blackbird Doughnuts have a cult following—even rock star Adele praised them when in town for a concert. One of several outposts in the city, the Fenway location is tiny and it's a good idea to get there early before your fave flavor sells out. **Known for:** creative, unusual flavors; turn your doughnut into an ice cream sandwich with soft-serve; fan favorite Boston Cream. ⑤ *Average main: $4 ⊠ 20 Kilmarnock St., The Fenway* ☏ *617/482–9000* ⊕ *www.blackbirddoughnuts.com/fenway* Ⓜ *Fenway.*

Bleacher Bar

$ | **AMERICAN** | This Fenway restaurant is famous for its enormous garage window which looks into Fenway Park, especially cool on game days, but it's also a fun place to relax with friends, nosh on nachos or fries, and catch all sorts of sporting events on the TV. **Known for:** beers and burgers; sports fans; sneaky way to see a Red Sox game. ⑤ *Average main: $17 ⊠ 82A Lansdowne St., The Fenway* ☏ *617/262–2424* ⊕ *www.bleacherbarboston.com* Ⓜ *Kenmore.*

Saloniki Greek

$ | **GREEK** | Chef Jody Adams's fast-casual Greek concept offers classic flavors and everything from lamb meatballs to meze plates in a lively, fun atmosphere. Pitas stuffed with lamb, pork, chicken thighs, or Impossible meatballs fly out of the kitchen, while sides like zucchini-feta fritters and grilled Halloumi are hard to put down. **Known for:** The George, a lamb meatball rollup; Greek fries; pita bread cooked in front of you. ⑤ *Average main: $15 ⊠ 4 Kilmarnock St., The Fenway* ☏ *617/266–0001* ⊕ *www.salonikigreek.com* Ⓜ *Fenway.*

Time Out Market Boston

$$ | **INTERNATIONAL** | A food hall curated by the media company known for its magazines and books, Time Out Market Boston features more than a dozen eateries run by some of Boston's most acclaimed chefs, plus two bars, a demo cooking area, and communal seating. The 25,200-square-foot space is a fun place to sample everything from sweet treats at Union Square Donuts to meatballs at chef Michael Schlow's, by one of the city's most acclaimed chefs. **Known for:** fun vibe; located in historic building; variety of eateries. ⑤ *Average main: $18 ⊠ 401 Park Dr., The Fenway* ☏ *978/393–8088* ⊕ *www.timeoutmarket.com/boston* Ⓜ *Fenway.*

🛏 Hotels

If you have tickets for a Red Sox baseball game at Fenway Park, this is the area you want to stay in. If you're a museum hound, you'll also be able to walk to the Museum of Fine Arts and the Isabella Stewart Gardner Museum as well as to Downtown. Boston University is a stone's throw from here and lots of students means lots of visiting parents. Book early.

★ Hotel Commonwealth

$$$$ | **HOTEL** | Luxury and service without pretense make this hip spot a solid choice. **Pros:** down bedding; perfect locale for Red Sox fans; free Wi-Fi. **Cons:** small gym; pricey rates; area is absolutely mobbed during Sox games. ⑤ *Rooms from: $500 ⊠ 500 Commonwealth Ave., Kenmore Square* ☏ *617/933–5000, 866/784–4000* ⊕ *www.hotelcommonwealth.com* ⤳ *245 rooms* ⑩ *No Meals* Ⓜ *Kenmore.*

The Verb Hotel

$$$ | **HOTEL** | A rock and roll reimagining of a classic midcentury hotel, the stylish Verb is filled to the brim with carefully curated music memorabilia. **Pros:** stylish pool scene; C. O. Bigelow bath products in the showers; free Wi-Fi. **Cons:** one-way cooling/heating system; valet only parking option; no elevator to second floor. ⑤ *Rooms from: $398* ✉ *1271 Boylston St., The Fenway* ☎ *855/695–6678* ⊕ *www.theverbhotel.com* ↝ *93 rooms* ⑩ *Free Breakfast* Ⓜ *Fenway*.

Nightlife

BARS

House of Blues

LIVE MUSIC | Around the corner from Fenway Park and girded with bars and restaurants, the city's juggernaut among nightclubs books a wide array of bands into its barnlike music hall. Tickets are $25–$45, with VIP box seats usually $15–$20 more. The Foundation Room (an upscale VIP lounge) opens to the public for an additional fee, and promises "high-class debauchery." ✉ *15 Lansdowne St., The Fenway* ☎ *888/693–2583* ⊕ *www.houseofblues.com* Ⓜ *Kenmore*.

BOWLING ALLEYS AND POOL HALLS

Lucky Strike Fenway

GATHERING PLACES | This multistory complex has something for everyone. Home to Cheeky Monkey Brewing Co. on the first floor, 150 games of all kinds and a bar and restaurant on the second floor, and 25 pool tables, 12 plasma screens, 16 bowling lanes, and an 800-square-foot video wall on the third floor, it's impossible to be bored. ✉ *145 Ipswich St., The Fenway* ☎ *617/437–0300* ⊕ *www.jilliansboston.com* Ⓜ *Kenmore*.

Performing Arts

MUSIC

MGM Music Hall at Fenway

CONCERTS | This 5,000-seat live performance venue opened next to Fenway Park in 2022. It covers 91,500 square feet over four levels and has hosted artists such as Ray LaMontagne and Arcade Fire. ✉ *2 Lansdowne St., The Fenway* ⊕ *crossroadspresents.com/pages/mgm-fenway-music-hall* Ⓜ *Kenmore*.

9

BROOKLINE AND JAMAICA PLAIN

Updated by
Kim Foley MacKinnon

⦿ Sights	⑪ Restaurants	🛏 Hotels	🛍 Shopping	☯ Nightlife
★★★☆☆	★★★☆☆	★★☆☆☆	★★★☆☆	★★☆☆☆

NEIGHBORHOOD SNAPSHOT

TOP REASONS TO GO

■ **Check out the Larz Anderson Auto Museum:**
Classic car aficionados will want to see the oldest
automobile collection in the United States.

■ **Visit the Frederick Law Olmsted National
Historic Site:** America's preeminent landscape architect's home and office make for a fascinating tour.

■ **Sample beer at the Samuel Adams Brewery:** Tour
the home of Boston's own award-winning beers, and
down some free samples.

■ **Explore the Arnold Arboretum:** The 281-acre
Arboretum offers a breath of fresh air, with more than
4,000 plants and trees, a visitor center, and walking
paths.

■ **Walk around or boat on Jamaica Pond:** Part of
Boston's Emerald Necklace, Jamaica Pond is an
outdoor oasis for locals and visitors alike.

GETTING HERE

Although driving to these suburbs is relatively
painless, they're not called the "streetcar suburbs"
for nothing. To reach the Arnold Arboretum in
Jamaica Plain, take the Orange Line to the end at
Forest Hills. To access the restaurants and shops in
Jamaica Plain, get off a few stops earlier at the
Green Street stop. Brookline is accessible via the C
and D lines of the Green Line.

PLANNING YOUR TIME

Timing all depends on which areas you decide to
explore. Each neighborhood merits a half day,
especially factoring in travel time from Boston proper
and a leisurely lunch or dinner.

Generally, most of these neighborhoods are safe,
particularly in the areas where these attractions
reside. But use common sense: stick to well-lighted
areas and avoid walking alone late at night.

QUICK BITES

■ **Brassica Kitchen + Cafe.**
Across from the Forest
Hills T stop, this spot is a
hip place to dine and drink
that's famous for its fried
chicken. ✉ *3710 Washington
St., Jamaica Plain* ⊕ *www.
brassicakitchen.com*
Ⓣ *Forest Hills.*

■ **J.P. Licks.** Treat yourself
to a few scoops of what
is arguably some of the
Boston area's best ice
cream. ✉ *659 Centre St.,
Jamaica Plain* ⊕ *www.
jplicks.com* Ⓣ *Green Street.*

■ **Otto Pizza.** This outpost
of the popular Portland,
Maine, pizzeria offers
creative pies, along with
slices, perfect for a quick
snack. ✉ *289 Harvard St.,
Brookline* ⊕ *www.otto-
portland.com* Ⓣ *Coolidge
Corner.*

■ **Zaftigs Delicatessen.**
This modern Jewish deli
serves breakfast all day and
classics like chicken matzo
ball soup. ✉ *335 Harvard St.,
Brookline* ⊕ *www.zaftigs.
com* Ⓣ *Coolidge Corner.*

The expansion of Boston in the 1800s went beyond the Back Bay and the South End. As the working population of the Downtown district swelled and public transportation grew, outlying suburbs became part of the city proper. Today, most of these neighborhoods are technically in the city of Boston, yet have managed to keep their own distinct personalities and charms.

Among the streetcar suburbs are Jamaica Plain and Brookline—rural retreats barely more than a century ago that are now popular and densely settled neighborhoods. Jamaica Plain is a hip, young neighborhood with a strong lesbian and ecofriendly population; brunch and a wander through the neighborhood's quirky stores or through the Arnold Arboretum make for a relaxing weekend excursion. Jamaica Plain also borders Franklin Park, an Olmsted creation of more than 500 acres, noted for its zoo. Farther west, Brookline is composed of a mixture of the affluent and students.

Brookline

Located 4 miles from downtown Boston, Brookline is mainly a residential area, but there are significant reasons to visit, from the birthplace of JFK, to the home and office of landscape architect Frederick Law Olmsted, to great local restaurants. Surrounded by Boston on three sides, Brookline truly feels like part of the city, though like other outlying towns, it started out as an agricultural community in the 17th century.

◉ Sights

Frederick Law Olmsted National Historic Site

HISTORIC HOME | Frederick Law Olmsted (1822–1903) is considered the nation's preeminent creator of parks. In 1883, while immersed in planning Boston's Emerald Necklace of parks, Olmsted set up his first permanent office at Fairsted, an 18-room farmhouse dating from 1810, to which he added another 18 rooms for his design offices. Plans and drawings on display include the U.S. Capitol grounds, Stanford University, and Mount Royal Park in Montréal. You can also tour the design rooms (some now in use as an archive library) where Olmsted and staff drew up their plans; highlights include a 1904 "electric blueprint machine," a kind of primitive photocopier.

The 1¾-acre site incorporates many trademark Olmstedian designs, including

Frederick Law Olmsted lived and worked at Fairsted, this circa 1810-residence, while he was planning Boston's Emerald Necklace; the home is now a National Historic Site.

areas of meadow, wild garden, and woodland; Olmsted believed body and spirit could be healed through close association with nature. The site became part of the National Park Service in 1980; Olmsted's office played an influential role in the creation of this federal agency. Call ahead to inquire about house tour hours, which change with the seasons, though the grounds are open year-round. ✉ *99 Warren St., Brookline* ☏ *617/566–1689* ⊕ *www.nps.gov/frla/index.htm* ✉ *Free* ⊗ *Interior closed Dec.–mid-Apr.* Ⓜ *Brookline Hills.*

John F. Kennedy National Historic Site

HISTORIC HOME | This was the home of the 35th president from his birth on May 29, 1917, until 1921, when the family moved to nearby Naples and Abbottsford Streets. Rose Kennedy provided the furnishings for the restored 2½-story, wood-frame structure. You can pick up a brochure for a walking tour of Kennedy's school, church, and neighborhood. To get here, take the MBTA Green Line to Coolidge Corner and walk north on

Harvard Street four blocks. The house is scheduled to reopen from renovations in Spring 2023; from November through May it is open by appointment only. ✉ *83 Beals St., Brookline* ☏ *617/566–7937* ⊕ *www.nps.gov/jofi* ✉ *Free* Ⓜ *Coolidge Corner.*

★ Larz Anderson Auto Museum

OTHER MUSEUM | Almost every year from 1899 to 1948 wealthy socialites Larz and Isabel Anderson bought a car, which they kept at their Brookline estate in a castle-like carriage house built in 1888 (originally to stable horses). After Isabel's death in 1948, the building was turned into a museum. Today, visitors can see 14 of their cars in this special collection. ✉ *15 Newton St., Brookline* ☏ *617/522–6547* ⊕ *larzanderson.org* ✉ *$12* ⊗ *Closed Mon. and Tues.* Ⓜ *Forest Hills.*

Larz Anderson Park

CITY PARK | FAMILY | Brookline's largest park was once the home of wealthy socialites Larz and Isabel Anderson, who left the estate to the town in 1951. It's now home to a large lawn at the top of the hill, playing fields, a pond, a seasonal outdoor ice rink, and the Larz Anderson Auto Museum. The top of the hill offers great views of Boston. ⊠ *23 Newton St., Brookline* ⊕ *From Forest Hills T station, take Bus 51 toward Cleveland Circle and get off at Clyde and Whitney Sts. The park is a 5-min walk* ☎ *617/879–5650* ⊕ *www.brooklinema.gov/Facilities/ Facility/Details/Larz-Anderson-Park-87* Ⓜ *Forest Hills.*

🍴 Restaurants

Going to Brookline is a nice way to get out of the city without really leaving town. Although it's surrounded by Boston on three sides, Brookline has its own suburban flavor, seasoned with a multitude of historic—and expensive—houses and garnished with a diverse ethnic population that supports a string of sushi bars, gastropubs, and kosher restaurants. Most Brookline eateries are clustered in the town's commercial centers: Brookline Village, Washington Square, Longwood, and bustling Coolidge Corner.

Blossom Bar/Sichuan Garden

$$ | **CHINESE** | In 1997, Ran Duan's parents opened Sichuan Garden, and today their son—an award-winning bartender—has added the Blossom Bar inside, where wildly creative cocktails with ingredients like avocado and toasted coconut bring in rave reviews. Longtime restaurant fans will be happy that all their favorite classic dishes, like Kung Pao chicken and Dan Dan noodles, are still on the menu. **Known for:** cocktails you won't find anywhere else; a mix of classic and American Chinese dishes; knowledgeable staff. Ⓢ *Average main: $22* ⊠ *295 Washington St., Brookline* ⊕ *www.blossombar-brookline.com* Ⓜ *Brookline Village.*

FuGaKyu

$$$ | **JAPANESE** | The name in Japanese means "house of elegance," and the gracious and efficient service hits the mark at this flagship location, along with the interior's tatami mats, rice-paper partitions, and wooden ships circling a moat around the sushi bar. The extensive menu is both elegant and novel, with thick slabs of super-fresh sashimi, inventive maki rolls, and plenty of cooked items, like beef fried rice or chicken curry, for those not into seafood or raw fish. **Known for:** attentive service; private, screened-in booths; excellent sushi and sashimi. Ⓢ *Average main: $30* ⊠ *1280 Beacon St., Brookline* ☎ *617/734–1268* ⊕ *www. fugakyu.net* ⊗ *Closed Mon.* Ⓜ *Coolidge Corner.*

Prairie Fire

$$ | **ITALIAN** | It's all about the fire here, with wood-fired vegetables, wood-fired pizzas, and wood-oven-roasted chicken among the highlights. There is also a small raw bar menu, with items like oysters and red snapper ceviche, and a selection of pastas and entrees, such as grilled *tautog* (blackfish) and porchetta, to round out the menu. **Known for:** amazing craft beer list; enthusiastic staff; seasonal beer garden in back. Ⓢ *Average main: $22* ⊠ *242 Harvard St., Coolidge Corner* ⊕ *prairiefirebrookline.com* ⊗ *Closed Mon.* Ⓜ *Coolidge Corner.*

The Publick House

$$ | **AMERICAN** | What started as a simple neighborhood beer bar has reached cult-like status for Brookline-ites and beyond. Serving an impressive amount of out-of-the-ordinary and artisanal beers—with almost two dozen on tap—the bar also offers tasty sandwiches, smaller entrées, and main dishes, of which the most beloved is the mac and cheese, customizable with additions including bacon, tomato, mushrooms, peas, egg, asparagus, shrimp, hot dog, and truffle cream. **Known for:** great pub fare; chummy feel; standout beer selection. Ⓢ *Average main: $22* ⊠ *1648 Beacon St., Brookline* ☎ *617/277–2880* ⊕ *publickhousebrookline.com* ⊗ *Closed Mon.* Ⓜ *Washington Sq.*

Brookline

0   1/4 mi

0   1/4 km

KEY

1 Sights

1 Restaurants

1 Quick Bites

1 Hotels

Ⓣ Subway station

Taberna de Haro

$$ | **SPANISH** | With a cozy saffron-yellow interior and an outdoor patio that fills up in warm weather, this tapas bar has a mostly Spanish wine list (more than 320 bottles, 60 of which are Sherry and Manzanilla). Authentic hot and cold tapas and *raciones* (medium-size plates) include such classics as a tortilla Españo-la, shrimp in garlic oil, braised eggplant, and octopus, along with favorite entrées like paella. **Known for:** warm atmosphere; bountiful Sherry and Manzanilla selec-tion; authentic Spanish tapas. $ *Average main: $22* ✉ *999 and 1001 Beacon St., Brookline* ☎ *617/277–8272* ⊕ *www. tabernaboston.com* ◷ *Closed Sun.* Ⓜ *Coolidge Corner.*

🍵 Coffee and Quick Bites

Otto Pizza

$ | **PIZZA** | **FAMILY** | Usually packed, Otto Pizza delivers on tasty, delicious classics like cheese, pepperoni, or margherita, but where it really shines is with oddball combinations—like butternut squash, ricotta, and cranberry, or pulled pork and mango. Diners can enjoy sit-down service, paired with a beer or glass of wine, or get a slice to go. **Known for:** lively vibe; friendly service; creative toppings. $ *Average main: $15* ✉ *289 Harvard St., Brookline* ⊕ *www.ottoportland.com* Ⓜ *Coolidge Corner.*

Zaftigs Delicatessen

$ | **AMERICAN** | **FAMILY** | This contemporary version of a Jewish delicatessen offers genuinely lean corned beef, chicken matzo ball soup, and a lovely whitefish salad plate. If you believe breakfast is the most important meal, you'll be happy to know it's served all day, so you can skip the hour-long weekend brunch waits elsewhere and enjoy the area's best pancakes and stuffed French toast any weekday. **Known for:** great breakfasts; friendly service; contemporary Jew-ish food. $ *Average main: $17* ✉ *335*

Harvard St., Brookline ☎ *617/975–0075* ⊕ *www.zaftigs.com* Ⓜ *Coolidge Corner.*

🛏 Hotels

If you don't want to pay Boston or Cam-bridge prices, then staying in Brookline is your best bet. Located 4 miles from Boston, Brookline is an easy T ride into the city.

Courtyard by Marriott Boston Brookline

$$$ | **HOTEL** | **FAMILY** | If you don't mind the anonymity and predictability of a chain hotel—and don't mind staying outside Boston proper—this is a decent choice. **Pros:** 1 mile from Fenway Park and Long-wood Medical Center; roomy bathrooms; free Wi-Fi. **Cons:** dull decor; too far of a walk to downtown Boston for some people; staff can be indifferent. $ *Rooms from: $350* ✉ *40 Webster St., Brookline* ☎ *617/734–1393, 866/296–2296* ⊕ *www. marriott.com/bosbl* ⇥ *188 rooms* ⦙⦙ *No Meals* Ⓜ *Beacon St.*

🎭 Performing Arts

FILM

★ Coolidge Corner Theatre

FILM | This lovingly restored art deco theater presents an eclectic and exciting selection of world cinema, including first-run art films, documentaries, and classics. Two intimate screening rooms offer occasional special programming highlighting experimental films. The independent nonprofit art house also holds book readings, private events, and midnight screenings of cult movies. One of Coolidge's signature programs is Science on Screen, a creative pairing of films with introductions by renowned sci-ence experts; the program has expanded to more than 50 independent theaters nationwide. ✉ *290 Harvard St., Brookline* ☎ *617/734–2501, 617/734–2500 recorded info* ⊕ *www.coolidge.org* Ⓜ *Coolidge Corner.*

🛍 Shopping

BOOKS

★ Brookline Booksmith

BOOKS | Since 1961 this independent bookseller has anchored Harvard Street and enriched the Coolidge Corner community with poetry readings, book clubs, and author talks. Browse the well-edited selection of best sellers, hardcovers, and paperbacks, as well as the area toward the back packed with cards and fun gifts that range from cutting boards and tea towels to leather notebooks and printed scarves. The well-read booksellers can always offer great suggestions. ■ **TIP→ Head downstairs for thousands of used books.** ✉ *279 Harvard St., Brookline* ☎ *617/566–6660* ⊕ *www.brooklinebooksmith-shop.com* Ⓜ *Coolidge Corner.*

GIFTS

Boston General Store

SOUVENIRS | This is the sort of shop every neighborhood should have—a warm, welcoming space filled with beautifully crafted, locally sourced products. Bamboo pet brushes share room with handwoven French market baskets, fruit and flower cocktail syrups, vintage fabric neckties, and fragrances from a Boston-area perfumer who uses only botanicals (no synthetics!) to create her scents. It's hard to walk out empty-handed. ✉ *305 Harvard St., Coolidge Corner* ☎ *617/232–0103* ⊕ *www.bostongeneralstore.com.*

Jamaica Plain

Before Prohibition, Jamaica Plain was home to a thriving beer industry, the remnants of which can be seen in the neighborhood's 19th-century brick breweries, long since converted to offices and lofts. That said, Sam Adams and Turtle Swamp are two great places that pay homage to that history, with lively breweries and beer gardens. Other attractions in this slightly funkier part of Boston include open spaces, like the Arnold Arboretum and Jamaica Pond (part of the Emerald Necklace), and plenty of independent restaurants, bars, and shops. It's easy enough to get to "JP", as locals call it, via the Orange Line on the MBTA.

◎ Sights

★ Arnold Arboretum of Harvard University

GARDEN | **FAMILY** | This 281-acre living laboratory contains more than 4,000 kinds of woody plants, most from the hardy north temperate zone. The rhododendrons, azaleas, lilacs, magnolias, and fruit trees are eye-popping when in bloom, and something is always in season from April through September. The Larz Anderson bonsai collection contains individual specimens imported from Japan. In the visitor center there is a 40-to-1 scale model of the arboretum (with 4,000 tiny trees). If you visit during May, Lilac Sunday (usually held on Mother's Day) is a celebration of blooming trees, and is the only day picnicking is allowed in the Arboretum. ✉ *125 Arborway, at Centre St., Jamaica Plain* ✥ *Take MBTA Orange Line (Forest Hills stop) or Bus 39 from Copley Sq. to Custer St. stop in Jamaica Plain (3 blocks away)* ☎ *617/524–1718* ⊕ *www.arboretum.harvard.edu* 🎫 *Donations accepted* Ⓜ *Forest Hills.*

Jamaica Pond and Boat House

CITY PARK | **FAMILY** | Part of Boston's Emerald Necklace, Jamaica Pond is a delightful way to escape from the city and enjoy nature. A 1.5-mile paved path running entirely around the large pond—which is actually a glacial kettle hole—is a big draw for walkers and joggers. The pond is stocked with trout and salmon each year and those with a permit can fish. From May to October, Courageous Sailing operates out of the Boat House and provides lessons and equipment for

The 281-acre Arnold Arboretum of Harvard University contains more than 4,000 plants like rhododendrons, azaleas, lilacs, magnolias, and fruit trees.

rowing and sailing, except when youth classes are in session; call ahead to confirm. One-hour kayak and sailboat rentals are $20; rowboats are $15, or $10 with a fishing license—cash or check only. ✉ *Jamaica Way and Pond St., Jamaica Plain* ☎ *617/522–5061* ⊕ *courageous-sailing.org/jamaica-pond* ⊙ *Closed Wed.* Ⓜ *Stony Brook, Green.*

Samuel Adams Boston Brewery
BREWERY | Tour the Boston beer company's Jamaica Plain facility, where it conducts research and develops new products. There are a few different tours (21+ only) at different price points, all including samples and a souvenir glass. Smell and taste the components of brewing (hops, malt, and barley), look at the flavoring process, and hear about—perhaps even see—new beers in development. Tours run Thursday through Monday and you must book online. Whether you take a tour or not, you can enjoy a beer in the Boston Tap Room, which is open daily,

or the Beer Garden, in nice weather.
■**TIP**➔ **Parking is limited, so consider taking the T to Stony Brook.** ✉ *30 Germania St., Jamaica Plain* ☎ *617/368–5080* ⊕ *www.samueladams.com* ⊙ *No tours Tues. and Wed.* Ⓜ *Stony Brook.*

🍴 Restaurants

This diverse neighborhood is filled with cutting-edge artists, graduate students, political idealists, and yuppie families. Once a more scruffy part of Boston, it is much more gentrified—but no less creative—to this day.

Brassica Kitchen + Cafe
$$ | AMERICAN | This tiny spot, tucked into a row of businesses across from the Forest Hills T station, is a lively restaurant and bar with legions of fans. The decor is cozy and warm, with counters, tabletops, and shelves made from antique woods repurposed from an old farmhouse. **Known for:** excellent

Jamaica Plain

BROOKLINE

Willow Pond

Olmsted Park

Wards Pond

Jamaica Pond

JAMAICA HILLS

Arboretum

JAMAICA PLAIN

Arnold Arboretum of Harvard University

FOREST HILLS

Jackson Square

Stony Brook

EGLESTON SQUARE

Green Street

Johnson Park

Franklin Park

TO FRANKLIN PARK ZOO

Forest Hills

FOREST HILLS

Forest Hills Cemetery

Lemuel Shattuck Hospital

203

KEY	
①	Sights
①	Restaurants
①	Quick Bites
Ⓣ	Subway station

0   1/4 mi
0   1/4 km

service; neighborhood favorite; creative and playful menu. [$] *Average main: $18* ✉ *3710 Washington St., Jamaica Plain* ☎ *617/477–4519* ⊕ *www.brassicakitchen. com* ⊘ *No dinner Sun.–Tues.* Ⓜ *Forest Hills.*

El Oriental de Cuba

$ | **CUBAN** | This cozy spot with wooden tables and walls full of artwork—featuring tropical fruit, Cuban street life, and magazine covers—serves a large variety of authentic Cuban food, including a restorative chicken soup, a classic Cuban sub, superb rice and beans (opt for the red beans over the black), and sweet "tropical shakes." Breakfast options include various preparations of eggs with ham, chorizo, or cheese, and espresso or iced coffee with milk. *Tostones* (twice-fried plantains) are beloved during cold New England winters by the city's many Cuban transplants, who will also find such dishes as oxtail, braised beef tongue, and mofongo (fried mashed green plantains with pork rinds and garlic oil). **Known for:** generous menu selection; homey setting; simple, quality Cuban cuisine. [$] *Average main: $16* ✉ *416 Centre St., Jamaica Plain* ☎ *617/524–6464* ⊕ *elorientaldecuba.net* Ⓜ *Stony Brook.*

Ten Tables

$$$ | **MODERN AMERICAN** | This tiny candlelit space is an enchanting mix of elegance and chummy neighborhood revelry—both in the atmosphere and the food. Simple but high-quality dishes, such as chickpea fritters and seared salmon, are prepared expertly, and the menu changes frequently; fun theme nights include "Beerger Tuesday," when you can enjoy a burger, beer, and fries for just $18, and "Pasta Thursday," with a different featured pasta each week, accompanied by a serving of wine. **Known for:** locally sourced ingredients; snug feel; New England bistro fare. [$] *Average main: $30* ✉ *597 Centre St., Jamaica*

Plain ☎ *617/524–8810* ⊕ *tentables.net* ⊘ *Closed Mon. and Tues. No lunch.* Ⓜ *Stony Brook.*

Tres Gatos

$ | **SPANISH** | Tres Gatos not only serves delicious Spanish tapas, *pinchos* (appetizers), and paella; it also has a cool record- and bookstore in the back. Olives, stuffed dates, and tortilla Espanola are great starters, but the paella, made with shrimp, clams, chorizo, and rabbit is the star—there's also a vegetarian version. **Known for:** always feels like a celebration; brick and mortar shop beats online; great service. [$] *Average main: $17* ✉ *470 Centre St., Jamaica Plain* ☎ *617/477–4851* ⊕ *www.tresgatosjp.com* Ⓜ *Stony Brook.*

☕ Coffee and Quick Bites

J.P. Licks

$ | **AMERICAN** | For more than 40 years, J.P. Licks has been serving up delicious homemade ice cream and frozen yogurt, later adding its own roasted coffee and baked goods, in a fun, funky atmosphere. This is the original shop, but outposts can be found all over the city, all with the same great flavors and service. **Known for:** awesome ice cream cakes; low-key vibe; creative ice cream flavors. [$] *Average main: $7.25* ✉ *659 Centre St., Jamaica Plain* ☎ *617/524–6740* ⊕ *www. jplicks.com* Ⓜ *Green Street.*

▼ Nightlife

Great swaths of green—the Arboretum, Jamaica Pond, and Emerald Necklace stretching miles to Fenway—set JP apart from other streetcar suburbs. Centre Street runs the cultural gamut with Cuban, Mexican, Indian, Irish, Thai, and Dominican restaurants. Cafés and bars are wide open to the LGBTQ+ community and everyone else.

BARS

Midway Café

LIVE MUSIC | This very popular Jamaica Plain café books a lively mix of rock bands, DJs, and noise artists. There's punk, soul, R&B, and on Thursday a raucous lesbian dance party and "queeraoke"—straights welcome too. Cover varies nightly; check for show age-restrictions. ✉ *3496 Washington St., Jamaica Plain* ☎ *617/524–9038* ⊕ *www.midwaycafe.com* Ⓜ *Green Street, Forest Hills.*

BREWPUBS AND BEER GARDENS

Turtle Swamp Brewing

BEER GARDENS | This lively and fun brewery and beer garden boasts a dozen beers that can be enjoyed on-site—indoors or outside at picnic tables. The flagship brew is the aptly named Orange Line IPA. The brewery often hosts food trucks, so patrons can enjoy a pint with different types of food, though customers are also welcome to bring their own food to enjoy as well. ✉ *3377 Washington St., Jamaica Plain* ☎ *617/522–0038* ⊕ *turtleswampbrewing.com* Ⓜ *Green Street.*

THE SEAPORT, SOUTH BOSTON, AND EAST BOSTON

10

Updated by
Leigh Harrington

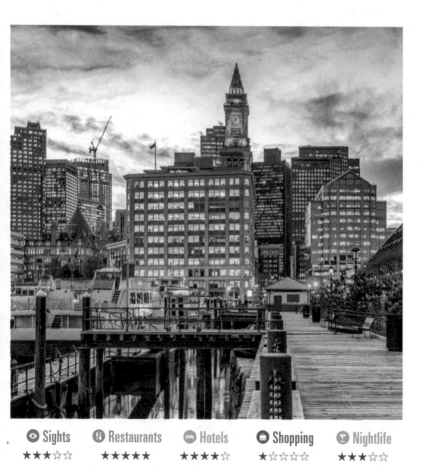

◉ Sights	⏀ Restaurants	🛏 Hotels	◗ Shopping	☻ Nightlife
★★★☆☆	★★★★★	★★★★☆	★☆☆☆☆	★★★☆☆

NEIGHBORHOOD SNAPSHOT

TOP EXPERIENCES

■ **Explore Camelot:** Visit the John F. Kennedy Presidential Library and Museum for a look into the life and legacy of Jack and Jackie.

■ **Appreciate an architectural marvel:** The Institute of Contemporary Art/Boston leans over Boston Harbor in opposition to physics.

■ **Take in stunning views:** The unparalleled, 360-degree views from Boston Harborwalk of the water and the city's other neighborhoods can't be beat.

■ **Eat out:** The Seaport District is known for its abundant culinary offerings, from gourmet local bakeries to top national steak houses.

■ **Swing it:** Geometrically unique swings for adults can be found at the Lawn on D. Snag a beer there, too.

GETTING HERE

Accessing the Seaport District is relatively easy, but the neighborhood is large. From South Station, you can walk anywhere along the Fort Point Channel, but for farther afield take the Silver Line. If you're headed to South Boston, take a Red Line train and get off at Andrew or Broadway. By car, both the Seaport and South Boston have a moderate amount of street (free after 8 pm and all day Sunday) and lot parking.

East Boston poses more of a challenge. It's long, lean, and residential, so the best way to explore is by vehicle. Taking public transit is not impossible; ride the Blue Line to Maverick, Wood Island, Orient Heights, or Suffolk Downs and be sure to know where you want to exit. Blue Line and Silver Line trains service Logan Airport.

GOOD TO KNOW

Travelers looking for a vibrant nightlife scene should visit South Boston after dark, particularly along Broadway, with its abundance of bars and restaurants.

QUICK BITES

■ **Bon Me.** Expect chef-crafted contemporary versions of Vietnamese street food. ⊠ *313 Congress St., Fort Point* ⊕ *www.bonmetruck.com* Ⓣ *South Station, Courthouse.*

■ **Yankee Lobster Co.** This family-owned fish market and take-out seafood shack has been serving the local catch since 1950. ⊠ *300 Northern Ave., Seaport District* ⊕ *www.yankeelobstercompany.com* Ⓣ *Silver Line Way.*

PLANNING YOUR TIME

■ You'll spend some time getting around the Seaport. Ambitious travelers can see two museums in a day, have a beer at Harpoon Brewery, and walk part of the Harborwalk. If you have only a few hours, plan an early dinner to enjoy top-notch dining and sunset water views.

■ Safety isn't a concern in the Seaport and South Boston. East Boston is also safe, but its once rough reputation follows it.

While distinctly different, the Seaport, South Boston, and East Boston have one major commonality: Boston Harbor. Historically, the Seaport has supported the textile and commercial fishing industries with its working piers. South Boston and Fort Independence have safeguarded the city from attack by sea since 1643. And, in East Boston, Donald McKay built record-setting clipper ships.

Today, a lot has changed. Over the last 15 years, the Seaport has transformed from an industrial no-man's-land to a vibrant, bustling extension of downtown Boston. Luxury hotels and residences, manicured micro-parks, upscale restaurants both local and national in name, and cutting-edge cultural institutions have all found homes here. Development projects remain in the works, so the face of the Seaport will continue to adjust for years to come.

Heavily populated South Boston has experienced its own renaissance, more so in the form of putting polish on existing multifamily homes and old-timey Irish bars rather than making room for new construction. The neighborhood's residents, both Southie lifers and young professional transplants, walk and walk: they walk to meals, they walk to Boston's best stretch of beaches, and they walk to and around Castle Island for exercise year-round.

Across the harbor, East Boston has been a haven for immigrants, first Italian and then Latino, and today's population reflects this heritage. Logan Airport is Eastie's crown jewel, but there are only a few other cultural sites to see unless you count the abundance of authentic Latin restaurants.

The Seaport

What's the appeal of the Seaport District? Bostonians have only been able to answer that question recently. As the neighborhood becomes developed, and its former life as a parking lot wasteland fades from peoples' minds, locals have realized its gorgeous potential, something the Moakley Courthouse, the Institute of Contemporary Art/Boston, and restaurateur-chef Barbara Lynch recognized more than a decade back.

Start your visit to the Seaport District at South Station, which is actually just across the Fort Point Channel in the heart of Downtown. From there, it's an easy walk to historical and cultural sites like the Boston Tea Party Ships & Museum, Fan Pier, and the Boston Children's Museum. If your destination is farther

Sights ▼

1 Black Falcon Pier....... **H6**

2 Boston
Children's Museum..... **A3**

3 Boston Harborwalk..... **D2**

4 Boston Tea Party
Ships & Museum **A2**

5 Fort Point Channel
Landmark District....... **B3**

6 Harpoon Brewery and
Beer Hall................. **F5**

7 Institute of
Contemporary Art/
Boston **D2**

8 John Joseph Moakley
United States
Courthouse **B2**

9 The Lawn on D **C6**

Restaurants ▼

1 The Barking Crab **B2**

2 Chickadee **G6**

3 Committee **C2**

4 Coquette **D5**

5 Davio's Northern
Italian Steakhouse...... **C1**

The Seaport

Ted Williams Tunnel

Boston
Main Channel

Rockland
Trust Bank
Pavilion

LIBERTY
WHARF

Seafood Way

Harbor St.

Northern Ave.

6th St.

B Street

Drydock Ave.

Black Falcon Ave.

Black Falcon
Pier

Reserved Channel

KEY

- 1 Sights
- 1 Restaurants
- 1 Quick Bites
- 1 Hotels
- 🚇 Subway station

afield, say the Boston Convention and Exhibition Center, Harpoon Brewery, the Seaport World Trade Center, or the Boston Design Center, head to South Station's subway concourse to catch the Silver Line.

■ TIP→ **The Silver Line operates three different branches (SL1, SL2, SL3) in the Seaport District and each has different destinations, so make sure you hop on the correct one.**

Of all of Boston's neighborhoods, the Seaport is the least "Bostonian" in appearance. In fact, with all its skyscrapers and shiny glass, the Seaport could have been plucked straight out of New York. It's new; it's fresh; it's young.

◉ Sights

Black Falcon Pier

MARINA/PIER | Surrounded by water on three sides, Black Falcon Pier is a stop on Boston's Harborwalk that seekers of amazing views won't want to miss. There's not much to do out this way at the end of the Seaport District except gaze at the fishing vessels, barges, and cruise ships navigating the inner harbor. Next door, the Boston Design Center offers shopping and dining options. ⊠ *Black Falcon Pier, Seaport* Ⓜ *Dry Dock, Black Falcon.*

★ Boston Children's Museum

OTHER MUSEUM | FAMILY | The country's second-oldest children's museum has always been ahead of the curve with creative hands-on exhibits, cultural diversity, and problem solving. Some of the most popular stops are also the simplest, like the bubble-making machinery and the two-story climbing maze. At the Japanese House you're invited to take off your shoes and step inside a Kyoto silk merchant's home. The *Boston Black* exhibit stimulates dialogue about ethnicity and community, and children can dig, climb, and build at the Construction Zone. In

the toddler PlaySpace, children under three can run free in a safe environment. There's also a full schedule of special exhibits, festivals, and performances. ⊠ *308 Congress St., Fort Point Channel* ☎ *617/426–6500* ⊕ *www.bostonchildrensmuseum.org* ⊠ *$18* Ⓜ *South Station.*

Boston Harborwalk

TRAIL | For the last 30-plus years, a number of agencies and organizations have been collaborating to create a waterfront walking path along Boston's shoreline—currently, it stretches 43 miles. Boston's Seaport District boasts a hearty portion of the Harborwalk, which winds from the Fort Point Channel, around Fan Pier, up Seaport Boulevard, and out and around the Black Falcon Cruise Terminal. Along the way, pedestrians can see art exhibits, stationary viewfinders, open green spaces, and incredible Boston Harbor views. Marked signs point the way, and maps can be found online. ⊠ *Seaport* ✛ *Congress St. Bridge by Children's Museum* ⊕ *www.bostonharborwalk.org* Ⓜ *South Station.*

★ Boston Tea Party Ships & Museum

OTHER ATTRACTION | FAMILY | Situated at the Congress Street Bridge near the site of Griffin's Wharf, this lively museum offers an interactive look at the past in a place as close as possible to the actual spot where the Boston Tea Party took place on December 16, 1773. Actors in period costumes greet patrons, assign them real-life colonial personas, and then ask a few people to heave boxes of tea into the water from aboard historical reproductions of the ships forcibly boarded and unloaded the night Boston Harbor became a teapot. There are 3-D holograms, talking portraits, and even the Robinson Half Tea Chest, one of two original tea chests known to exist. ■ TIP→ **Abigail's Tea Room (you don't need a museum ticket for entry) features a tea tasting of five tea blends that would have been aboard the ships.** ⊠ *Congress*

Boston Children's Museum is the country's second-oldest children's museum.

St. Bridge, Fort Point Channel ⊕ *www.bostonteapartyship.com* ✉ *$32* Ⓜ *South Station.*

Fort Point Channel Landmark District

NEIGHBORHOOD | This historic district, which was designated by the City of Boston in 2009, features the city's largest, most cohesive grouping of late 19th- and early 20th-century industrial loft buildings. The Boston Wharf Company owned and developed the area from 1836 to 1882. Today, the small, walkable, revitalized area sits between the Fort Point Channel and the Seaport District and is home to Boston Children's Museum, the Boston Tea Party Ships & Museum, working artist studios, and a variety of restaurants. ✉ *Bounded by Seaport Blvd., Summer St., Boston Wharf Rd., and Fort Point Channel.*

Harpoon Brewery and Beer Hall

BREWERY | Harpoon Brewery holds Massachusetts' first-ever brewing permit, obtained in 1986 by three college friends who wanted to create a fresh beer culture in their hometown. Today, Harpoon features guided tours of its Seaport District facility, sharing its story, fun facts, and samples with beer lovers from around the globe. Harpoon's on-site beer hall pours a rotating lineup of limited-edition and pilot beers, nonbrand beers, and ciders, and it serves handmade pretzels, pizzas, and paninis. ✉ *306 Northern Ave., Seaport* ☎ *617/456–2322* ⊕ *www.harpoonbrewery.com* ✉ *$5* Ⓜ *Silver Line Way, Harbor Street.*

★ Institute of Contemporary Art/Boston

ART MUSEUM | The ICA mounts temporary exhibits by the contemporary art world's brightest talents, as well as curated pieces from its permanent collection, all of which are as cutting edge as the breathtaking, cantilevered edifice jutting out over Boston Harbor that houses them. The ICA's fourth floor is where most happens: incredible art and stunning water views. The Poss Family Mediatheque serves as a great resting spot for families. Live programming, from film festivals to outdoor live music concerts take place regularly. Don't miss the

ICA Store on the ground level, where you can pick up an inventive trinket of your own. ✉ *25 Harbor Shore Dr., Seaport* ☎ *617/478–3100* ⊕ *www.icaboston.org* 🍴 *$15* 🕑 *Closed Mon.* Ⓜ *Courthouse.*

John Joseph Moakley United States Courthouse

NOTABLE BUILDING | Believe it or not, the public is welcomed in for a visit to this architectural wonder and federal house of justice. Galleries across the courthouse feature rotating exhibitions on a variety of themes, from maritime history to the judicial system. Don't miss Ellsworth Kelly's permanent installation *The Boston Panels* in the courthouse's entry rotunda. It's not uncommon to see a tall ship or a charter vessel docked outside, in season. You can also book an hour-long Discovering Justice tour. ✉ *Fan Pier, 1 Courthouse Way, Seaport* ☎ *617/261–2440.*

★ The Lawn on D

CITY PARK | FAMILY | Stop, rest awhile, and have some fun. That's the purpose of The Lawn on D, a free-to-all open green space that features a plethora of geometrical swings, games like bocce, corn hole, and ping-pong, and chairs for lounging. In warmer weather, you can often catch a live concert or film screening here, or a public art installation. A concession stand makes sure visitors are well-fed. The only catch? You can't bring Fido. ✉ *420 D St., Seaport* 🕑 *Closed Nov.–Apr., and during private events* Ⓜ *World Trade Center, Silver Line Way.*

🍴 Restaurants

As the Seaport District has grown over the last 15 years, so, too, has the quality of its dining options. A few humble "fish shacks" remain in operation as testaments to the area's lucrative industry, but accompanying them today are large-scale and upscale restaurants appealing to 9-to-5ers that now call the area home.

The Barking Crab

$$$ | SEAFOOD | FAMILY | Decked out in cheery colors of yellow, red, and green, this popular, somewhat touristy spot has the feel of a seaside clam shack located smack dab in the middle of Boston. An outdoor patio and lobster tent in summer features stunning views of the Financial District; in winter, dining retreats indoors to a warmhearted version of a waterfront dive, where you'll encounter a classic New England clambake or oysters and littlenecks from the raw bar, followed by meaty, golden crab cakes. **Known for:** lobster rolls; crowds in summer; water views. 💲 *Average main: $35* ✉ *88 Sleeper St., Fort Point Channel* ☎ *617/426–2722* ⊕ *www.barkingcrab.com* Ⓜ *Courthouse, South Station.*

★ Chickadee

$$$$ | MODERN AMERICAN | At the far eastern end of the city and tucked into the Innovation and Design Building, Chickadee is a restaurant you'd wish to stumble over. Make the trek on the Silver Line or simply walk to sample chef-owner John daSilva's curated seasonal menu, rife with unique preparations and locally sourced ingredients. **Known for:** whole-food focused; original, unique cocktails; free parking. 💲 *Average main: $39* ✉ *21 Drydock Ave., Seaport* ☎ *617/531–5591* ⊕ *www.chickadeerestaurant.com* 🕑 *Closed Sun.* Ⓜ *Drydock Avenue.*

Committee

$$$ | MODERN GREEK | Weekend brunch is a national sport at this popular restaurant known for its modern and inspired take on Greek cuisine and killer cocktails, but it's also open daily for dinner. Come and share meze plates with your dining companions, or, if you've really got a big appetite, dig into one of the "feasts," which may include a selection of grilled meats or a whole fish. **Known for:** sesame feta meze; trendy vibes; lively scene. 💲 *Average main: $30* ✉ *50 Northern Ave., Seaport* ☎ *617/737–5051* ⊕ *committee-boston.com* Ⓜ *Courthouse.*

★ Coquette

$$$$ | FRENCH | This new addition to the Seaport District has personality in spades, with pastel purple and bright red chandeliers, plumes of feathers in floral arrangements, and pink napkins on the table. The menu, too, is inspired, featuring French cuisine informed by global flavors meant to be ordered in abundance—two to three plates per diner. **Known for:** colorful decor; spinach dumplings; excellent cocktails. $ *Average main: $55* ✉ *450 Summer St., Seaport* ☎ *617/419–8140* ⊕ *www.frenchcoquette. com* Ⓜ *World Trade Center.*

Davio's Northern Italian Steakhouse

$$$$ | STEAKHOUSE | This popular Boston-born restaurant splits its focus between grilled all-natural steaks and chops and hearty, Italian-inspired dishes. Diners can't get enough of Davio's signature spring rolls, stuffed with Philly cheesesteak or chicken parm, and pasta is made in-house. **Known for:** interesting takes on spring rolls; à la carte steaks and decadent side dishes; excellent wine list. $ *Average main: $55* ✉ *50 Liberty Dr., Seaport* ☎ *617/261–4810* ⊕ *www.davios. com/seaport* Ⓜ *Courthouse.*

Legal Sea Foods—Harborside

$$$ | SEAFOOD | With a roof deck, patio, balcony, and floor-to-ceiling windows, Legal Sea Foods' flagship restaurant features abundant space for diners to take in panoramic views of Boston Harbor no matter the season or the weather, and this view certainly draws a crowd. The menu is classic seafood: from raw bar and sushi offerings to grilled fish, fried fish, and sandwiches, there is plenty to eat here—unless you're a landlubber. **Known for:** prime waterfront location; tasty seafood menu; Legal Sea Food's flagship restaurant. $ *Average main: $32* ✉ *270 Northern Ave., Seaport* ☎ *617/477–2900* ⊕ *www.legalseafoods. com/restaurants/boston-legal-harborside* Ⓜ *World Trade Center.*

Lolita Fort Point

$$$ | MEXICAN | Come for the tacos and margaritas; stay for the nightlife scene and at this lively Mexican joint on the water. In the moody dining room painted with murals and adorned with red chandeliers or on the bright waterfront patio, you'll start off with a granita palate cleanser, then dive into guacamole and a few sharing plates as you imbibe with the trendy, young Boston crowd. **Known for:** brunch on the patio; bar with stained glass backdrop; Mexican street corn. $ *Average main: $35* ✉ *253 Summer St., Fort Point Channel* ☎ *617/369-0931* ⊕ *www.lolitamexican.com.*

Menton

$$$$ | FRENCH | Barbara Lynch's luxurious, France-meets-Italy-inspired eatery is arguably the best restaurant in town (and also Boston's only Relais & Châteaux–awarded property, a prestigious honor). Named for a French town near Italy's border, Menton features just two multicourse menu options: prix-fixe or chef's tasting (with wine pairings if you so choose). **Known for:** opulent dishes; extravagant prices; excellent wine list. $ *Average main: $165* ✉ *354 Congress St., Fort Point Channel* ☎ *617/737–0099* ⊕ *www.mentonboston. com* ⊘ *Closed Mon. and Tues.* Ⓜ *South Station.*

Pastoral

$$ | ITALIAN | FAMILY | Satisfy your pizza craving with a crispy, wood-fired, thin-crust pie from this Fort Point neighborhood joint. A dozen and a half options run from the traditional margherita to more inventive options; note that the pies are smaller in size, so order a few. **Known for:** wood-fired, Neapolitan-style pizza; family-friendly; casual vibe. $ *Average main: $22* ✉ *345 Congress St., Fort Point Channel* ☎ *617/345–0005* ⊕ *www.pastoralfortpoint.com* ⊘ *Closed Sun. and Mon.* Ⓜ *South Station.*

★ Row 34

$$$ | **SEAFOOD** | Emphasizing oysters and local craft beers, this contemporary seafood restaurant has a boisterous energy contained only by its soaring ceilings. A neighborhood crowd comes for the excellent menu devoted to raw things, fried seafood, a variety of "rolls," and fish-based entrées. **Known for:** local oysters fresh from restaurant's own oyster farm; seafood—carnivores and vegetarians should head elsewhere; excellent selection of American craft beer. $ *Average main: $31* ✉ *383 Congress St., Seaport* ☎ *617/553–5900* ⊕ *www.row34. com* Ⓜ *World Trade Center.*

Sportello

$$ | **ITALIAN** | One of the city's most widely awarded chefs, Barbara Lynch serves rustic, hearty Italian food with her team in a casual setting, where diners sit and eat at one long, winding counter. Fare like burrata, lamb meatballs, foccacia, braised rabbit, and bolognese are plentiful and tasty, if on the pricey side of things. **Known for:** pasta made in-house daily, by hand; casual, modern vibe; top-quality ingredients. $ *Average main: $22* ✉ *348 Congress St., Fort Point Channel* ☎ *617/737–1234* ⊕ *www. sportelloboston.com* ◔ *Closed Mon. and Tues.* Ⓜ *South Station.*

Trillium Brewing Company

$$ | **AMERICAN** | **FAMILY** | When it comes to craft beer, a lot of Bostonians get excited about Trillium, so do as the locals do and quench your thirst in the ever-crowded ground-level tap room or sit for a quieter meal upstairs to enjoy a small menu of American fare that's meant to keep you reaching for more. The tap rotates with seasonal and standard Trillium beers, including ciders, sours, and IPAs. **Known for:** fantastic roof deck; hazy IPAs; fun, family-friendly atmosphere. $ *Average main: $20* ✉ *50 Thomson Pl., Fort Point Channel* ☎ *857/449–0083* ⊕ *www.trilliumbrewing.com* Ⓜ *Courthouse.*

★ Woods Hill Pier 4

$$$$ | **MODERN AMERICAN** | Featuring floor-to-ceiling windows and sweeping 270-degree views of the Boston Harbor waterfront, this sophisticated and lively restaurant serves up midsized plates that are meant to be shared—two to three per person. The well-curated menu features meat and produce from the owner's 360-acre New Hampshire farm, as well as handmade pasta and sustainably sourced seafood. **Known for:** panoramic views of Boston Harbor; pasture-raised, sustainable, and organic farm-to-table ingredients; a killer Sunday brunch. $ *Average main: $45* ✉ *300 Pier 4 Blvd., Seaport* ☎ *617/981–4577* ⊕ *www.woodshillpier4.com* ◔ *Closed Mon.* Ⓜ *Courthouse.*

☕ Coffee and Quick Bites

Bon Me

$ | **VIETNAMESE** | **FAMILY** | Bon Me's moniker is a whimsical take on Vietnam's signature sandwich, the banh mi, and the versions that this local fast-casual restaurant serves are authentic to its spirit, if not with traditional ingredients. Diners can create their own bowls (salad, noodle, or rice), selecting from a variety of proteins, veggies, and sauces. **Known for:** tasty proteins; spicy ginger lemonade that will flare your nostrils; customized bowls. $ *Average main: $11* ✉ *313 Congress St., Fort Point Channel* ☎ *857/350–4035* ⊕ *www.bonmetruck.com* Ⓜ *South Station, Courthouse.*

GreCo

$ | **MODERN GREEK** | **FAMILY** | As far as options for fast-casual meals along Seaport Boulevard go, this is one place you should stop. You'll get modern, Greek street food here, in the form of pita sandwiches, salads, and build-your-own meals, dressed with sauces, like housemade spicy feta and lemon yogurt, that are so good you'll be licking it off your fingers. **Known for:** build-your-own salads, pitas, and plates; delicious, authentic doughnut dessert; plenty of seating. $ *Average main: $12* ✉ *200 Pier 4 Blvd., Seaport* ☎ *617/572–3300* ⊕ *www.greco-boston.com* Ⓜ *World Trade Center.*

★ Tatte Bakery & Café

$ | BAKERY | FAMILY | This upscale bakery and café takes pastries to the next level. From tea cakes to the Jerusalem bagel, expect hearty baked goods with an air of elegance and influenced by the owner's Israeli heritage. **Known for:** traditional North African shakshuka; signature nut tarts that are as pretty as they are tasty; convivial atmosphere. $ *Average main: $12* ✉ *200 Pier 4 Blvd., Seaport* ☎ *617/765–7600* ⊕ *www.tattebakery.com* Ⓜ *Courthouse.*

★ Yankee Lobster Co.

$$ | SEAFOOD | FAMILY | There's nothing fresher than eating fish the same day it's caught, and that's what you get at this family-owned seafood shack. Open since 1950, the local favorite serves fresh oysters, crab cakes, fried oysters and clams, steamers, and lobster. **Known for:** lobster, lobster, lobster; being simple and authentic; limited seating options. $ *Average main: $20* ✉ *300 Northern Ave., Seaport* ☎ *617/345–9799* ⊕ *www.yankeelobstercompany.com* ⊗ *Closed Tues.* Ⓜ *Silver Line Way.*

🛏 Hotels

The Envoy Hotel

$$$$ | HOTEL | Visitors and locals like to hang out at The Envoy, where a design-forward aesthetic provides a comfortable yet stylish vibe. **Pros:** 24-hour fitness center includes Peloton bikes; excellent on-site restaurants and rooftop bar; beautiful views overlooking the Fort Point Channel. **Cons:** bar crowds can be loud and rowdy; no rollaway beds available; a bit fancy for kids. $ *Rooms from: $525* ✉ *70 Sleeper St., Seaport* ☎ *617/338–3030* ⊕ *www.theenvoyhotel.com* ⇆ *136 rooms* ‖◎‖ *No Meals* Ⓜ *Courthouse.*

★ Omni Boston Hotel at the Seaport

$$$ | HOTEL | Opened in 2021, this Omni hotel debuts a chic, modern counterpoint to its grande dame Downtown property, Omni Parker House. **Pros:** year-round, outdoor, heated pool with bar area; seven food and drink options on-site; brand-new accommodations. **Cons:** far from Back Bay and Beacon Hill shopping; tight restrictions on pet policy. $ *Rooms from: $350* ✉ *450 Summer St., Seaport* ☎ *617/476–6664* ⊕ *www.omnihotels.com* ⇆ *1,054 rooms* ‖◎‖ *No Meals* Ⓜ *World Trade Center, Silver Line Way.*

Renaissance Boston Waterfront Hotel

$$$ | HOTEL | Set near Boston's working fish piers, the Renaissance plays to a watery theme—in the modern lobby, blue-and-green glass orbs complement a suspended glass lighting fixture, and the spiral staircase was created to look like a nautilus shell. **Pros:** sleek lobby bar and lounge; close to airport transportation and convention center; indoor pool and 24-hour fitness center. **Cons:** no on-site restaurant; hordes of conventioneers; far from the Back Bay and Boston Common. $ *Rooms from: $325* ✉ *606 Congress St., Seaport* ☎ *617/338–4111, 888/796–4664* ⊕ *marriott.com/hotels/travel/boswf-renaissance-boston-waterfront-hotel* ⇆ *471 rooms* ‖◎‖ *No Meals* Ⓜ *World Trade Center.*

Seaport Hotel

$$$ | HOTEL | FAMILY | Adjacent to the World Trade Center and not far from the Boston Convention and Exhibition Center, the Seaport Hotel is awash with badge-wearing, convention-going suits. **Pros:** beautiful on-site gym and fitness center; pick your own pillow; complimentary bikes. **Cons:** slow elevators; swamped during conventions; far from the Back Bay and South End. $ *Rooms from: $375* ✉ *Seaport World Trade Center, 1 Seaport La., Seaport* ☎ *617/385–4000* ⊕ *www.seaportboston.com* ⇆ *428 rooms* ‖◎‖ *No Meals* Ⓜ *World Trade Center.*

The Westin Boston Seaport District

$$$ | HOTEL | The Westin is connected to the Boston Convention and Exhibition Center and provides comfortable accommodations and exceptional service. **Pros:** connected to the Boston Convention and Exhibition Center; pet-friendly for animals up to 50 lbs.; nice fitness center with a pool. **Cons:** clusters of meeting-goers; lobby can get hectic; not within walking distance of the Back Bay and South End. ⓢ *Rooms from: $350* ✉ *425 Summer St., Seaport* ☎ *617/532–4600* ⊕ *www.marriott.com* ⇨ *793 rooms* ⦿ *No Meals* Ⓜ *World Trade Center.*

 Nightlife

BARS

★ **Drink**

COCKTAIL LOUNGES | Barbara Lynch handles this elegant den as only a chef of worldwide acclaim would—like a restaurant. Behind the bar, tenders use herbs, infusions, and elixirs to custom-create a top-shelf libation for your palate; that is, there is no drink list. There are low, beamed ceilings and a wooden bar that snakes through the space, maximizing room for a discerning cocktail crowd. A limited menu features snacks and things, including a legendary burger. Drink is one of the best bars in Boston, and it's hugely popular, so you'll likely wait in line to get in, but once you do, there's room to breathe. ✉ *348 Congress St., Fort Point Channel* ☎ *617/695–1806* ⊕ *www.drinkfortpoint.com* Ⓜ *South Station.*

Kings

THEMED ENTERTAINMENT | Calling all gamers to this massive bar and restaurant that entertains with upscale-style bowling, billiards, air hockey, shuffleboard, foosball, and more. The '80s kids among us can wax nostalgic while playing the retro arcade games they remember from their childhood, including *Pac-Man*, *Super Mario Bros.*, and *Teenage Mutant Ninja Turtles*. The kitchen makes burgers, wings, tacos, and more. Kings' Draft Room serves up beers and sports. Anyone under age 18 must be accompanied by an adult, and no one under age 21 is admitted after 9 pm. ✉ *60 Seaport Blvd., Seaport* ☎ *617/401–0025* ⊕ *www.kingsde.com* Ⓜ *Courthouse.*

Lucky's Lounge

BARS | Located on a corner midway into the Fort Point area, this hangout was here well before anything else called the neighborhood home. Low-lit and subterranean, it replicates a Rat Pack–era speakeasy as much as it can in modern-day Boston. On the menu, find a mix of Southern-inspired dishes, Asian plates, and other snackable, shareable fare. Lucky's is known for its live music, too. ✉ *355 Congress St., Fort Point Channel* ☎ *617/357–5825* ⊕ *www.luckyslounge.com* Ⓜ *South Station.*

COMEDY CLUBS

Laugh Boston

COMEDY CLUBS | More than 300 people per show can share a laugh with the local comics and national headliners who take the stage at one of Boston's favorite comedy clubs. Doors are open to anyone ages 16 and older because comedic material is typically R-rated. There's a two-item minimum per person from the drink or food menu—can you really say no to a pitcher of Coors and a warm pretzel? ✉ *425 Summer St., Seaport* ☎ *617/725–2844* ⊕ *www.laughboston.com* Ⓜ *World Trade Center.*

⬤ **Shopping**

National and international brands like L.L. Bean, Away, and Outdoor Voices have set up along Seaport Boulevard, and a few local entrepreneurs have moved in, too. In summer, shop local at the Seaport Summer Market next to Seaport Common.

Built in 1801, Fort Independence is the centerpiece of Castle Island. It's open for free tours on summer weekends.

FOOD

Cardullo's Gourmet Shoppe

FOOD | Cardullo's has been a local stand-out for gourmet global food items for the last 70 years, although it recently opened its Seaport location, a bit of a departure from its Harvard Square origins. Artisan and international wines and beer, chocolates and sweets, jams, crackers, teas and coffee, cured meats, cheese, and foodstuffs made in the New England region stock the shelves. A deli counter serves awesome sandwiches-to-go. ✉ *99 Seaport Blvd., Seaport* ☎ *857/350–4579* ⊕ *www.cardullos.com* Ⓜ *Courthouse.*

South Boston

Never to be confused with the city's South End neighborhood, South Boston (Southie, as locals know it) still feels largely Irish and working class, even though the area has fully gentrified over the last two decades. In doing so, young professionals—drawn to Southie's waterfront, beaches, and green walking spaces—have bought condos in converted triple-deckers along Day Boulevard or up and down streets named for alphabet letters from A to P. The farther down the alphabet, the closer you are to historic Castle Island and Pleasure Bay.

Irish-Americans still hold sway here, as the city's raucous annual St. Patrick's Day parade and numerous Irish bars attest. Long-standing residents are hearty folk; every January 1 they follow tradition and run into the frigid waters off L Street Beach for a quick dip. Southie is also famously where Whitey Bulger held court over the Irish mob during the 1980s and early 1990s.

👁 Sights

Castle Island

HISTORIC SIGHT | FAMILY | Although it once was, Castle Island is no longer, well, an island. Today, this tip of South Boston is accessible by car and by foot from Day

F   G   H   I   J

1

Reserved Channel

South Boston

2

Fort
Independence

*Boston
Harbour*

E 1st St.
E 2nd St.
E 3rd St.

Shore Rd.
William J. Day Blvd.

Evans
Field

*dal of
onor
Park*

N St.

**CITY
POINT**

Castle
Island

Pleasure
Beach

*Pleasure
Bay*

E 4th St.
E 5th St.
E 6th St.
E 7th St.

O St.

P St.

Farrgut Rd.

Columbia Rd.

3

*M Street
Beach*

Head
Island

4

KEY

1 *Sights*

1 *Restaurants*

1 *Quick Bites*

1 *Hotels*

T *Subway
station*

*North
Dorchester
Bay*

5

6

*Thompson
Island*

0   1/4 mi

0   1/4 km

7

Boulevard. Castle Island's centerpiece is Fort Independence, built in 1801 (although there have been battlements on-site since 1644) and open for free tours on summer weekend afternoons. Castle Island is a popular spot for South Boston residents to walk their dogs, jog, or cycle, whether just around the island itself or along the water-set Pleasure Bay Loop. There's also a nice playground for kids. If you get peckish, stop by Sullivan's (known locally as Sully's). Open February through November, come to this Castle Island institution of more than 60 years for a hot dog and fries. Views of the harbor and its outlying islands are expansive. ⊠ *2010 Day Blvd., South Boston* 🕾 *617/727–5290* Ⓜ *Broadway (then catch Bus 9 or 11 going east).*

Castle Island Brewing Company

BREWERY | This taproom takes up an entire corner of the Cole Hersee Building. In nice weather, the garage windows in the front roll all the way up to reveal a contemporary rendezvous spot for craft beer lovers. Find signature brews, from IPAs to lagers, as well as some limited releases, on draft. Children are welcome if they're accompanied by adults. ⊠ *10 Old Colony Ave., South Boston* 🕾 *617/977–4017* ⊕ *castleislandbeer.com* Ⓜ *Broadway.*

★ John F. Kennedy Presidential Library and Museum

LIBRARY | The library-museum is both a center for serious scholarship and a focus for Boston's nostalgia for her native son. The stark, white building (another modernist monument designed by I. M. Pei) at this Dorchester Bay–enclosed site pays homage to the life and presidency of John F. Kennedy, as well as to members of his family, including his wife, Jacqueline, and brother Robert.

The library is the official repository of JFK's presidential papers and displays re-creations of his desk in the Oval Office and of the television studio in which

he debated Richard Nixon in the 1960 election. Permanent exhibits focus on his life before politics, the 1960 Presidential election, the Peace Corps, and the U.S. space program (currently under renovation). Two theaters show films about JFK's life. There's also a permanent display on the late Jacqueline Kennedy Onassis. The facility also includes a store and a small café. ⊠ *Columbia Point, Dorchester* 🕾 *617/514–1600* ⊕ *www.jfklibrary.org* 🖾 *$18* ⊘ *Closed Mon.–Wed.* Ⓜ *JFK/UMass, then free shuttle bus every 20 min.*

🍴 Restaurants

★ Cafe Polonia

$$ | POLISH | FAMILY | People come to Boston for certain things—colleges, Irish pubs, Fenway Park—and Polish food isn't usually one of them. But, if you do land here, this authentic Polish restaurant in Southie is a must-stop. **Known for:** pierogi, beet soup, stuffed cabbage and kielbasa; Polish beer; food worth traveling for. Ⓢ *Average main: $18* ⊠ *611 Dorchester Ave., South Boston* 🕾 *617/269–0110* ⊕ *www.cafepolonia.com* Ⓜ *Andrew.*

★ Fox & the Knife Enoteca

$$$ | MODERN ITALIAN | Chef-owner Karen Akunowicz steps up with hearty, traditional Italian food inspired by her time as a chef and pasta maker in Italy. Locals love it so much that in order to score a table, especially on the weekends, you have to book a reservation about a month or so out. **Known for:** award-winning chef; focaccia; excellent service. Ⓢ *Average main: $25* ⊠ *28 W. Broadway, South Boston* 🕾 *617/766–8630* ⊕ *www.foxandtheknife.com* ⊘ *Closed Mon.* Ⓜ *Broadway.*

Lincoln Tavern & Restaurant

$$ | AMERICAN | Young professionals living in the area will tell you that this place is a South Boston institution, and they flock here regularly, especially for brunch served every day of the week. Don't expect a quiet meal; the atmosphere here is loud and lively at all hours, and there's often a line at the door to get in. **Known for:** neighborhood favorite; brunch; bloody Marys. ⑤ *Average main: $21* ✉ *425 W. Broadway, South Boston* ☎ *617/765–8636* ⊕ *www.lincolnsouthboston.com* Ⓜ *Broadway.*

Moonshine 152

$$ | FUSION | Diners who appreciate flavor and spice will adore chef-owner Asia Mei's creative kitchen endeavors, which often mix up elements of American, Chinese, Mexican, Vietnamese, Thai, and Spanish cuisines. A lively local crowd comes for dinner and to get their hands on such crave-worthy dishes as the tofu-mushroom burger and various street tacos, but the menu does change frequently. **Known for:** friendly service; unpretentious atmosphere; interesting, flavorful dishes. ⑤ *Average main: $22* ✉ *152 Dorchester Ave., South Boston* ☎ *617/752–4191* ⊕ *www.moonshine152.com* ⊗ *Closed Mon.* Ⓜ *Broadway.*

Roza Lyons

$ | AMERICAN | This casual but upscale neighborhood bar and restaurant doesn't attract too much of a crowd, even though it should. The kitchen serves hearty American comfort food made with fresh ingredients. **Known for:** craft beer; steak and avocado salad; low-key amosphere. ⑤ *Average main: $17* ✉ *709 E. Broadway, South Boston* ☎ *617/902–9333* ⊕ *www.rozalyons.com* Ⓜ *Broadway.*

☕ Coffee and Quick Bites

Joseph's Bakery

$ | BAKERY | FAMILY | You won't get many frills at this traditional Italian-style bakery that's tucked a bit off the main drag, but you will get loads of sweets in the form of cream puffs, eclairs, pastry twists, Italian cookies, and loaves of *scali* bread (braided and coated in sesame seeds). There's also a deli that serves

sandwiches to go. **Known for:** pan pizza; brewed flavored coffee; Italian desserts. ⑤ *Average main: $8* ✉ *258 K St., South Boston* ☎ *617/268–1133* ⊕ *www.josephsdelisouthie.com.*

Sullivan's Castle Island

$ | FAST FOOD | FAMILY | Family-owned and established in 1951, this beach-style dairy bar—affectionately nicknamed Sully's—serves fried seafood, hot dogs, hamburgers, and soft-serve ice cream at Castle Island every spring, summer, and fall. Don't expect frills or indoor seating—there is no need since its surroundings provide sloping lawns, picnic tables, benches, and beach vistas for lunching. ■**TIP→ Fries don't automatically come as a side with sandwiches, so if you want them, make sure you order them. Known for:** long lines but quick service; fried seafood, burgers, and hot dogs; great views. ⑤ *Average main: $10* ✉ *2080 Day Blvd., South Boston* ☎ *617/268–5685* ⊕ *www.sullivanscastleisland.com* ⊗ *Closed in winter.*

Hotels

Cambria Hotel Boston

$$$ | HOTEL | One of very few lodgings in South Boston outside of the Seaport District, this hotel attracts a younger, trendy traveler with simple but well-appointed guest rooms, contemporary art, and snazzy dining and drinking options on-site. **Pros:** large, 24-hour fitness center; seasonal rooftop bar with spectacular views; easy walk to the South End, Back Bay, and Seaport District. **Cons:** no pets; no cribs, no extra beds available; far from most of Boston's universities. ⑤ *Rooms from: $315* ✉ *6 W. Broadway, South Boston* ☎ *617/752–6681* ⊕ *www.cambriaboston.com* ⇱ *159 rooms* ⊘ *No Meals* Ⓜ *Broadway.*

The 300-acre Belle Isle Marsh Reservation is all that remains of the salt marsh landscape that once covered Boston when the early settlers arrived.

East Boston

A drive into East Boston shows off street after street of multifamily homes and commercial squares laden with restaurants and markets catering to its varied ethnic communities, primarily Italian, Asian, and Latino. In the last few years, this waterfront neighborhood—"Eastie" as it's called by longtime locals—has begun to undergo a renaissance as modern, luxury apartments pop up on Jeffries Point. Any visitor to Boston who arrives by plane has been to Eastie—it's home to Logan International Airport. We'll let you in on a secret: East Boston features absolutely amazing views of Boston Harbor and the downtown skyline.

◉ Sights

Belle Isle Marsh Reservation
TRAIL | FAMILY | This 300-acre patch of remaining wetland environment is indicative of the salt marsh landscape that covered Boston when early settlers arrived and which today has been filled in. As you walk or run Belle Isle's gravel paths, listen to the sound of the marsh's diverse bird community, which includes the American kestrel, belted kingfisher, great blue heron, northern harrier, and saltmarsh sparrow. Boardwalks venture into the marsh for great viewing and photo ops. ⊠ *1399 Bennington St., East Boston* ☎ *617/727–5350* ⊕ *www.mass. gov/locations/belle-isle-marsh-reservation* Ⓜ *Suffolk Downs.*

Downeast Cider House Taproom
BREWERY | You've got to really look for the garage doors that mark the entrance to this zero-frills local taproom. Once you make it inside the industrial space, you can sample flights of Downeast's fresh, unfiltered cider varieties—many of which are only available at the cider house. Bring some food to eat if you want—none is served here—and your

dog. ⊠ *256 Marginal St., East Boston* ☏ *857/301–8881* ⊕ *www.downeastcider. com* ⊗ *Closed Mon.–Wed.* Ⓜ *Maverick.*

HarborArts & The Shipyard Gallery

MARINA/PIER | **FAMILY** | Whimsical murals on cement barriers, colorful wooden chairs mounted on the outside wall of a commercial building, large-scale sculpture: together these pieces and more generate an arty feel in the industrial setting of East Boston's working shipyard. HarborArts curates a rotating collection of works by local and international artists across 14 acres, completely open to the public for perusal. ⊠ *256 Marginal St., East Boston* ☏ *617/561–1400* ⊕ *www.bhsmarina.com/shipyard-gallery* Ⓜ *Maverick.*

ICA Watershed

ART MUSEUM | **FAMILY** | The Institute of Contemporary Art/Boston's seasonal outpost first opened in 2018 after renovations to a dilapidated former copper-pipe facility in East Boston's working shipyard and marina. Every summer, a single large-scale, immersive art installation makes the 15,000-square-foot space its own. A smaller gallery delves into the shipyard's history. ⊠ *256 Marginal St., East Boston* ⊕ *www.icaboston. org/ica-watershed* ⊗ *Closed Oct.–Apr.* ☞ *Water shuttle transportation from the ICA's Seaport location to the Watershed is included with general admission* Ⓜ *Maverick.*

Madonna Queen of the Universe National Shrine

RELIGIOUS BUILDING | A 35-foot golden and green statue of the Virgin Mary standing atop a globe dominates the Pope Paul VI Pilgrim Plaza that welcomes curious visitors and religious pilgrims to this Roman Catholic shrine. From its perch in Orient Heights, the shrine also boasts some pretty spectacular views of Logan Airport and the downtown skyline. Beneath the plaza, a sprawling sanctuary offers a quiet retreat, and some holy relics are on display. Masses are offered weekly in English, Spanish, and Portuguese. ⊠ *150 Orient Ave., East Boston* ☏ *617/569–8792* ⊕ *www.madonnaqueenshrine.com* Ⓜ *Orient Heights.*

Piers Park

CITY PARK | **FAMILY** | Sandwiched between Marginal Street and Boston Harbor, the gorgeous, landscaped, waterfront Piers Park features a grassy, green retreat from urban life and sweeping views of downtown Boston to the southwest. It is so named because of its many long piers that jut into the inner harbor. For a bit of historical knowledge: it's also in close proximity to the facility site where naval architect Donald McKay built his reputedly fast clipper ships. Take a stroll down the promenade and let the kiddos enjoy the large playground. ⊠ *95 Marginal St., East Boston* ☏ *617/561–6677* ⊕ *www. piersparksailing.org* Ⓜ *Maverick.*

🍴 Restaurants

Mirroring the makeup of its residents, East Boston's restaurant scene satisfies a variety of tastes, from the authentically ethnic to modern American. Foodies can dig into some of the city's best Latino and Italian fare, while closer to Eastie's coast, new, upscale restaurants serve up trendier, chef-driven options.

★ Angela's Cafe

$$ | **MEXICAN** | **FAMILY** | Colorful and airy, this East Boston Mexican restaurant reflects the culture of many living in the neighborhood, and its eponymous cook re-creates dishes from her native Puebla. Locals love it for its authenticity and extensive selection of small, snacky plates (mmm, *queso fundido*) and hearty main courses (*chilaquiles, mole poblano*). **Known for:** house-made guacamole; chicken and queso chilaquiles; brunch. Ⓢ *Average main: $18* ⊠ *1012 Bennington St., East Boston* ☏ *617/874–8251* ⊕ *www.angelascafeboston.com* Ⓜ *Orient Heights.*

East Boston

ADMIRALS HILL

Mary O'Malley State Park

Williams St.

Broadway

Park St.

Central Ave.

CHELSEA

Highland St.

Willow St.

Eastern Ave.

Marginal St.

Chelsea Creek

Condor St.

Chelsea St.

EAGLE HILL

Meridian St.

Marion St.

Trenton St.

Princeton St.

145

Bennington St.

Chelsea St.

4

East Boston Expwy.

Wood Island

CENTRAL SQUARE

Mystic River

CHARLESTOWN

Bremen Street Community Park

Airport

1

Border St.

London St.

EAST BOSTON

Orleans St.

Cottage St.

East Boston Memorial Park

Massachusetts Turnpike

90

Tomahawk Dr.

Terminal E

Charles R.

1A

Maverick

3

Sumner St.

Maverick St.

2

Webster St.

Marginal St.

JEFFRIES POINT

Jeffries St.

Logan International Airport

1

NORTH END

Atlantic Ave.

6

3 **4** **2**

Terminal A

Terminal B

93

Boston Inner Harbor

2

Aquarium

New England Aquarium

Sights ▼

1 Belle Isle Marsh Reservation.............. **I2**

2 Downeast Cider House Taproom **C6**

3 HarborArts & The Shipyard Gallery... **C6**

4 ICA Watershed.......... **C6**

5 Madonna Queen of the Universe National Shrine **G1**

6 Piers Park............... **C6**

Restaurants ▼

1 Angela's Cafe **G2**

2 Cunard Tavern **C6**

3 The Quiet Few........... **C6**

4 Rincon Limeño **D3**

Quick Bites ▼

1 Santarpio's Pizza........ **C5**

F G H I J

1

BEACHMONT

Waldemar Ave.

◆ Suffolk Downs
Race Course

Orient Ave.

5

Gladstone St.

**Suffolk
Downs** ⊤ St.

Bennington

*Belle Isle
Marsh
Reservation* **1**

Revere St.

I-90

Boardman St.

1

⊤ **Orient
Heights**

2

Saratoga St.
Bennington St.

Saratoga St.

Short Beach Creek

Kennedy Dr.

Morton St.

Revere St.

3

Constitution Beach

Main St.

*Belle Isle
Inlet*

Pleasant St.

Lincoln St.

Winthrop St.

Bowdin St.

Cross St.

*Ingleside
Park*

4

145

Pauline St.

WINTHROP

Court Rd.

Washington St.

College Park Rd.

5

Johnson Ave.

Terminal
C

6

*Snake
Island*

0 — 1/4 mi

0 — 1/2 km

KEY	
1	*Sights*
1	*Restaurants*
1	*Quick Bites*
1	*Hotels*
⊤	*Subway
station*

7

Hotels ▼

Cunard Tavern

$$ | **AMERICAN** | On this once industrial stretch of the Boston Harbor waterfront sits this gastropub, fittingly at the former site of the Cunard Steamship Company and Wharf. From within a contemporary and lively environment, peruse a Southern-inspired menu, regional craft beer, and wide windows that open onto the street. **Known for:** notable brunch; seasonal roof deck with great views and a walk-up window bar; high prices for what you get. ⑤ *Average main: $22* ⊠ *24 Orleans St., East Boston* ☎ *617/567–7609* ⊕ *www.cunardtavern.com* Ⓜ *Maverick.*

The Quiet Few

$ | **AMERICAN** | One look at the neighborhood bar's menu will have you holding back belly laughs, even as it's grumbling with hunger. Plates are interesting and well thought-out, with a flair for Frito corn chips. **Known for:** huge selection of whiskies, including flights and top-shelf, off-the-menu options; creative meals; very crowded during peak hours. ⑤ *Average main: $13* ⊠ *331 Sumner St., East Boston* ☎ *617/561–1061* ⊕ *www. thequietfew.com* Ⓜ *Maverick.*

Rincon Limeño

$$ | **PERUVIAN** | **FAMILY** | Authentic Peruvian food is beautifully presented in a wonderfully warm and inviting space. Sip a much-talked-about pisco sour while perusing the menu, which includes traditionally prepared dishes, seafood and ceviche, and smaller plates called *piqueos*. **Known for:** lemony ceviche mixto; anticuchos, a Peruvian classic; long lines, so making a reservation is advised. ⑤ *Average main: $23* ⊠ *409 Chelsea St., East Boston* ☎ *617/569–4942* ⊕ *www. rinconlimeno.com* Ⓜ *Wood Island.*

☕ Coffee and Quick Bites

Santarpio's Pizza

$ | **PIZZA** | **FAMILY** | Stepping into this family-owned East Boston pizza joint is like stepping into the 1980s, even though it first opened way back in 1903. Every table is full on a Saturday night at 7 pm, and don't be surprised to see a line that runs out the cramped front doorway. **Known for:** legendary pizza; really long lines during peak hours; unapologetically casual atmosphere. ⑤ *Average main: $15* ⊠ *111 Chelsea St., East Boston* ☎ *617/567–9871* ⊕ *www.santarpiospizza. com.*

🛏 Hotels

Hilton Boston Logan Airport

$$$ | **HOTEL** | **FAMILY** | Quiet rooms, competitive prices, and the only hotel actually connected to the airport make this Hilton a good choice for in-and-out visitors to Boston. **Pros:** attached via skywalk to Logan terminals A and E; most rooms have great views of downtown Boston; free shuttle to subway or water taxi. **Cons:** standard check-in time is late, at 4 pm; not walking distance to attractions, restaurants, or shopping; pay for Wi-Fi. ⑤ *Rooms from: $375* ⊠ *1 Hotel Dr., East Boston* ☎ *617/568–6700* ⊕ *www.bostonlogan.hilton.com* ➪ *604 rooms* ⊙ *No Meals* Ⓜ *Airport.*

Hyatt Regency Boston Harbor

$$$ | **HOTEL** | **FAMILY** | Half the rooms at this hotel have sweeping views of either the city skyline or the ocean; the other half overlook Logan Airport runways. **Pros:** close to airport; 24-hour airport shuttle; restaurant and bar on-site. **Cons:** late standard check-in, at 4 pm; daily destination fee; effort to get to downtown

sights. $ Rooms from: $375 ⊠ 101 Harborside Dr., East Boston ☎ 617/568–1234 ⊕ www.hyatt.com/en-US/hotel/massachusetts/hyatt-regency-boston-harbor/bosha ⇌ 270 rooms ¶○¶ No Meals Ⓜ Airport.

▼ Nightlife

Next Door Speakeasy & Raw Bar

BARS | In order to score 90 minutes at a table in this exclusive bar (the waitlist to get in is booked up months in advance), you must be dressed up, charm the person guarding the door, and most important, first find the entrance—it's not obviously marked. Craft cocktails have a flair for the dramatic, made with unique premium and small-label brands, creative liqueurs, and other interesting juices, syrups, and ingredients. The food is fantastic, but secondary to the cocktails. ⊠ 107 Porter St., East Boston ⊕ www.nextdooreastie.com ☞ No casual shorts, beachwear, flip-flops, tank tops, ripped pants, baseball caps, or hats. Ⓜ Maverick.

The Tall Ship Boston

BARS | This historic-style ship sidles up to an East Boston pier and features outdoor drinking, games like corn hole, live music, and more alfresco fun. The unique destination does offer some food in the form of raw oysters and a couple of snack boards, and drinks are slightly overpriced, but let's be honest: you're paying for the view. If you happen to be dining in the area, there's a free shuttle to the ship from local restaurants on the weekends. The ship is 21+ after 7 pm. ⊠ 1 East Pier Dr., Boston ☎ 617/307–7714 ⊕ www.tallshipboston.com Ⓜ Maverick.

Chapter 11

CAMBRIDGE AND SOMERVILLE

11

Updated by
Cheryl Fenton

◉ Sights	🧳 Restaurants	🛏 Hotels	🛍 Shopping	🍸 Nightlife
★★★★☆	★★★★★	★★☆☆☆	★★★★☆	★★★★★

NEIGHBORHOOD SNAPSHOT

TOP REASONS TO GO

■ **Take it all in:** Browse bookstores for new and used volumes, trawl the artsy boutiques, grab a cup of coffee, and people-watch in Harvard Square.

■ **Round the museum circuit:** Make a visit to the Harvard Art Museums, the Harvard Museum of the Ancient Near East, the Peabody and the Natural History Museum for artifacts and culture, and the MIT Museum.

■ **Be surprised by art at a tech university:** Visit MIT to wander its campus (full of hidden works of art), visit its museum, and see Pritzker Prize–winning architect Frank Gehry's Seuss-like Stata Center.

■ **Visit the country's first university:** Breathe the rarefied air of Harvard with an official tour (or an irreverent unofficial one) and a stroll around its famous "Yard."

■ **Walk the Charles River:** Follow Memorial Drive to spend some time along the famous river. The busy road is closed to traffic on Sunday from the last Sunday of April until the second Sunday of November.

GETTING HERE

Just minutes from Boston, Cambridge is easily reached by taking the Red Line train outbound to any stop past Charles/MGH station. There are stops at MIT (Kendall Square), Central Square, Harvard Square, Porter Square, Davis Square (actually in Somerville), and Alewife. Harvard Square is the best place to begin any visit to Cambridge, but driving (and parking) here is a small nightmare. Do yourself a favor and take the T. If you insist on driving, suck it up and park in a garage. (Street parking is usually limited to two hours, and most spots are permit only.) Driving is less of a pain in other parts of Cambridge, but you're still better off getting around via the T. Try to spend as much time as possible exploring on foot. This is a walking town, and you will want to spend more time exploring the sites than looking for a parking spot.

QUICK BITES

■ **Mr. Bartley's Burger Cottage.** This Harvard institution serves dozens of riffs on the humble burger. ⊠ *1246 Massachusetts Ave., Harvard Square* ⊕ *www.mrbartley. com* Ⓣ *Harvard.*

■ **Felipe's Taqueria.** A good bet for tasty Mexican food. ⊠ *21 Brattle St., Harvard Square* ⊕ *www.felipestaqueria.com* Ⓣ *Harvard.*

■ **Toscanini's.** Known for their coffee and homemade ice cream. ⊠ *159 1st St., Central Square* ⊕ *www.tosci. com* Ⓣ *Central.*

■ **Veggie Grill.** Popular for plant-based burgers, sandwiches, and bowls. ⊠ *57 John F. Kennedy St., Harvard Square* ⊕ *www. veggiegrill.com* Ⓣ *Harvard.*

PLANNING YOUR TIME

■ Most visitors don't go beyond Harvard Square and Harvard Yard, but Cambridge is a one-of-a-kind city filled with funky restaurants, independent shops, unique art, historic sites, and lots of independent bookstores. If you plan to visit Harvard's Natural History or Art Museums or explore other Cambridge neighborhoods like Kendall, Porter, Inman, and Central Squares, give yourself a day or two.

Boston's Left Bank—a super-liberal academic enclave—is a must-visit if you're spending more than a day or two in the Boston area. Cambridge is packed with world-class cultural institutions, quirky shops, restaurants galore, and tons of people-watching.

The city is punctuated at one end by the funky architecture of MIT (the Massachusetts Institute of Technology) and at the other by the grand academic fortress that is Harvard University. Civic life connects the two camps into an urban stew of 100,000 residents who represent nearly every nationality in the world, work at every kind of job from tenured professor to Uber driver, and are passionate about living on this side of the river.

The Charles River is the Cantabrigians' backyard, and there's virtually no place in Cambridge more than a 10-minute walk from its banks. Strolling, running, rollerblading, or biking is one of the great pleasures of Cambridge, and your views will include graceful bridges, the distant Boston skyline, crew teams rowing through the calm water (possibly training for October's annual Head of the Charles, the largest two-day regatta in the world), and the elegant spires of Harvard soaring into the sky.

No visit to Cambridge is complete without an afternoon (at least) in Harvard Square. It's a hub, a hot spot, and home to every variation of the human condition: Nobel laureates, homeless buskers, trust-fund babies, and working-class Joes. Farther along Massachusetts Avenue is Central Square, an ethnic melting pot of people and restaurants.

Ten minutes more brings you to MIT, with its eclectic architecture from postwar pedestrian to Frank Gehry's futuristic fantasyland. In addition to providing a stellar view, the Massachusetts Avenue Bridge, spanning the Charles from Cambridge to Boston, is also notorious in MIT lore for its Smoot measurements.

Cambridge

Harvard Square

In Cambridge all streets point toward Harvard Square. In addition to being the gateway to Harvard University and its various attractions, Harvard Square is home to the tiny yet venerable folk-music venue Club Passim (Bob Dylan played here, and Bonnie Raitt was a regular during her time at Harvard), first-run and vintage movie theaters, concert and lecture venues, and a tempting collection of eclectic, independent shops. Harvard Square is a multicultural microcosm. On a warm day street musicians coax exotic tones from their Andean pan flutes and *erhus,* Chinese stringed instruments, while cranks and local pessimists pass out pamphlets warning against all sorts of end-of-the-world scenarios. In the small plaza atop the main entrance to

Harvard Square
and Tory Row

the Harvard T station known as "the Pit," you'll find students and activists gathering alongside artists selling their work. It's a wonderful circus of humanity.

Porter Square is about a mile northwest of Harvard Square. The area consists of several blocks along Mass Ave. that have shopping and restaurants.

Harvard Square's Brattle Street, a long stretch that begins in the center of Harvard Square, is where you'll find several shops and eateries as you make your way down away from the Square. Follow it for the short walk to its legacy: historical Tory Row—the nickname given by purist Cantabrigians to the part of Brattle Street where many Loyalists had mansions at the time of the Revolutionary War.

VISITOR INFORMATION

CONTACTS Cambridge Visitor Information Booth. ⊠ Harvard Sq., near MBTA station entrance, Harvard Square ☎ 617/441–2884 ⊕ www.cambridgeusa. org Ⓜ Harvard.

 Sights

Brattle House

HISTORIC HOME | This charming yellow 18th-century, gambrel-roof Colonial once belonged to the Loyalist William Brattle. He moved to Boston in 1774 to escape the patriots' anger, then left in 1776 with the British troops. From 1831 to 1833 the house was the residence of Margaret Fuller, feminist author and editor of The Dial. Today it's the office of the Cambridge Center for Adult Education, and is listed on the National Register of Historic Places. ⊠ 42 Brattle St., Brattle Street ☎ 617/547–6789 ⊕ www.ccae.org Ⓜ Harvard.

The Brattle Theatre

FILM/TV STUDIO | For the last half century, The Brattle has served as the square's independent movie house, screening indie, foreign, obscure, and classic films, from nouveau to noir. Occupying a squat,

barnlike building from 1890, it is set improbably between a modern shopping center and a colonial mansion. The resident repertory company gained notoriety in the 1950s when it made a practice of hiring actors blacklisted as Communists by the U.S. government. Check the website for current offerings and events. ⊠ 40 Brattle St., Brattle Street ☎ 617/876–6837 ⊕ www.brattlefilm.org 🎟 Tickets from $12 Ⓜ Harvard.

Carpenter Center for the Visual Arts

ARTS CENTER | This gravity-defying mass of concrete and glass, built in 1963, is the only building in North America designed by the French architect Le Corbusier. It hosts Harvard's Department of Art, Film, and Visual Studies, exhibition spaces, and the Harvard Film Archive (currently closed until further notice), and is dedicated to artist-centered programming. The open floor plan provides students with five stories of flexible workspace, and the large, outward-facing windows ensure that the creative process is always visible and public. The center regularly holds free lectures, workshops, and receptions with artists.

At the top of the ramp, the Sert Gallery plays host to changing exhibits of contemporary works and has a café. The Main Gallery on the ground floor often showcases work by students and faculty. The Carpenter Center Bookshop, a collaboration with Berlin-based Motto Books, is one of the only local places to carry small-press contemporary art books, magazines, and journals, with an emphasis on international publications and limited-edition projects. ⊠ 24 Quincy St., Harvard Square ☎ 617/495–3251 ⊕ carpenter.center 🎟 Galleries free ⊘ Closed Mon. Ⓜ Harvard.

Christ Church Cambridge

CHURCH | This modest yet beautiful gray clapboard structure was designed in 1761 by Peter Harrison, the first architect of note in the colonies (he designed

King's Chapel). During the Revolution, members of its mostly Tory congregation fled for their lives. The organ was melted down for bullets and the building was used as a barracks during the Siege of Boston. (Step into the vestibule to look for the bullet hole left during the skirmish.) Today, the organ facade takes inspiration from the original 1762 gallery organ.

Martha Washington requested that the church reopen for services on New Year's Eve in 1775. The church's historical significance extends to the 20th century: Teddy Roosevelt was a Sunday-school teacher here (and famously fired because he remained Dutch Reformed rather than becoming an Episcopalian), and Martin Luther King Jr. spoke from the pulpit to announce his opposition to the Vietnam War. ⊠ *0 Garden St., Harvard Square* ☎ *617/876–0200* ⊕ *www.cccambridge. org* Ⓜ *Harvard.*

First Parish in Cambridge and the Old Burying Ground

CEMETERY | Next to the imposing church on the corner of Church Street and Mass Ave. lies the spooky-looking colonial Old Burying Ground. Known as the most historic cemetery in Cambridge, it was established around 1635 and houses 17th- and 18th-century tombstones of ministers, Continental Congressmen, authors, early Harvard presidents, and Revolutionary War soldiers. The wooden Gothic Revival church, known locally as "First Church" or "First Parish," was built in 1833 by Isaiah Rogers. The congregation dates to two centuries earlier, and has been linked to Harvard since the founding of the college. ⊠ *3 Church St., Harvard Square* ☎ *617/876–7772* ⊕ *www. firstparishcambridge.org* Ⓜ *Harvard.*

★ Harvard Art Museums

ART MUSEUM | This is Harvard University's oldest museum, and in late 2014, it became the combined collections of the Busch-Reisinger, Fogg, and Arthur M.

Sackler Museums. All three were united under one glorious, mostly glass roof, under the umbrella name Harvard Art Museums. Housed in a facility designed by award-winning architect Renzo Piano, the 204,000-square-foot museum is spread over seven levels, allowing more of Harvard's 250,000-piece art collection, featuring European and American art from the Middle Ages to the present day, to be seen in one place. Highlights include American and European paintings, sculptures, and decorative arts from the Fogg Museum; Asian art, Buddhist cave-temple sculptures, and Chinese bronzes from the Arthur M. Sackler collection; and works by German expressionists, materials related to the Bauhaus, and postwar contemporary art from German-speaking Europe from the Busch-Reisinger Museum.

In addition to the gallery spaces, there's a 300-seat theater, Jenny's Cafe, a museum shop, and the Calderwood Courtyard, plus conservation and research labs. ⊠ *32 Quincy St., Harvard Square* ☎ *617/495–9400* ⊕ *www.harvardartmuseums.org* ☒ *$20; free Sun.* Ⓜ *Harvard.*

Harvard Museum of the Ancient Near East

HISTORY MUSEUM | Formerly known as the Semitic Museum, this Harvard institution is an almost unknown gem, serving as an exhibit space for Egyptian, Mesopotamian, and ancient Near East artifacts and as a center for archaeological exploration. The museum's extensive temporary collections rotate, while more permanent exhibits include life-size casts of famous Mesopotamian monuments, authentic mummy coffins, and tablets containing the earliest forms of writing. Free lectures are held weekly, and the building also houses the Department of Near Eastern Languages and Civilizations. ⊠ *6 Divinity Ave., Harvard Square* ☎ *617/495–4631* ⊕ *hmane.harvard.edu* ☒ *Free; donations appreciated* ☉ *Closed Sat.* Ⓜ *Harvard.*

★ Harvard Museum of Natural History

SCIENCE MUSEUM | FAMILY | The Harvard Museum of Natural History (which exhibits specimens from the Museum of Comparative Zoology, the Harvard University Herbaria, and the Mineralogical and Geological Museum) reminds us nature is the original masterpiece. Cases are packed with zoological specimens, from tiny hummingbirds and deer mice to rare Indian rhinoceroses and one of the largest Amazon pirarucu ever caught. View fossils and skeletons alongside marvelous minerals, including a 1,600-pound amethyst geode. Harvard's world-famous Blaschka *Glass Flowers* collection is a creative approach to flora, with more than 4,300 hand-blown glass plant models. The museum combines historic exhibits drawn from the university's vast collections with new and changing multimedia exhibitions, such as *In Search of Thoreau's Flowers: An Exploration of Change and Loss* and *Lily Simonson: Painting the Deep,* plus a renovated Earth & Planetary Sciences gallery. ⊠ *26 Oxford St., Harvard Square* ☎ *617/495–3045* ⊕ *www.hmnh.harvard. edu* ⊠ *$15; ticket includes admission to adjacent Peabody Museum* Ⓜ *Harvard.*

★ Harvard Square

PLAZA/SQUARE | FAMILY | Tides of students, tourists, and politically charged proponents are all part of the nonstop pedestrian flow at this most celebrated of Cambridge crossroads. Harvard Square is where Massachusetts Avenue, coming from Boston, turns and widens into a triangle broad enough to accommodate a brick peninsula (above the T station). The restored 1928 kiosk in the center of the square once served as the entrance to the MBTA station, and is now home to lively street musicians and artists selling their paintings and photos on blankets. Harvard Yard, with its lecture halls, residential houses, libraries, and museums, is one long border of the square; the other three are composed of clusters of banks, retailers, and restaurants.

Time in the Square raises people-watching to a high art form. On an average afternoon you'll hear earnest conversations in dozens of foreign languages; see every kind of youthful uniform from slouchy sweats to impeccable prep; wander by street musicians playing guitars and flutes; and wonder at how students reading textbooks out in the sunshine can get any work done among the commotion.

The historic buildings are worth noting. It's a thrill to walk though the big brick-and-wrought-iron gates to Harvard Yard on up to Widener Library, the University's flagship library. More than 50 miles of bookshelves snake around this imposing neoclassical structure, designed by one of the nation's first major African American architects, Julian Abele. It holds more than 3.5 million volumes in 450 languages, but is unfortunately not open to the public.

Across Garden Street, through an ornamental arch, is Cambridge Common, decreed a public pasture in 1631. It's said that under a large tree that once stood in this meadow George Washington took command of the Continental Army on July 3, 1775. A stone memorial now marks the site of the "Washington Elm." Also on the Common is the Irish Famine Memorial by Derry artist Maurice Harron, unveiled in 1997 to coincide with the 150th anniversary of "Black '47," the deadliest year of the potato famine. At the center of the Common a large memorial commemorates the Union soldiers who lost their lives in the Civil War. On the far side of the Common is a fantastic park and newly renovated playground. ⊠ *Harvard Square* ⊕ *www. harvardsquare.com* Ⓜ *Harvard.*

Harvard University

COLLEGE | The tree-studded, shady, and redbrick expanse of Harvard Yard—the very center of Harvard University—has weathered the footsteps of Harvard students for hundreds of years. In 1636

Did You Know?

The Harvard Museum of Natural History's collection includes 21 million specimens, but only a small sample is on display. An active lecture and family program means there's plenty of opportunity to interact with another local species—the Harvard researcher.

Explore Harvard Square

History 101

If you want to revisit the city's Tory beginnings, walk past the **Wadsworth House**, a clapboard house on Massachusetts Avenue that dates from 1726, and enter the dignified hush of the Yard at **Harvard University**. Admire the exterior of **Widener Library** (only students and their guests are allowed inside); it houses one of the largest collections of books, historical materials, and journals in the academic world. Then circle back through the yard, crossing Massachusetts Avenue to view the **First Parish in Cambridge and the Old Burying Ground** on the corner of Church Street. Through the iron railing of the cemetery you can make out a number of tombstones. Buried here are the remains of 17th- and 18th-century Tory landowners, people who were enslaved, and soldiers. Continue up Garden Street to **Christ Church**, designed in 1761 and still an active parish. The Cambridge Common, across Garden Street, has a terrific playground in the back corner away from the university; this is a good spot to take a rest.

Retrace your steps along Massachusetts Avenue and cross the street near the First Parish church. Cut through Harvard Yard, bearing to your left, pass the modern Science Center (a good place for a bathroom break; restrooms are in the basement), and look for the striking Victorian architecture of Memorial Hall. Spend some time milling around the Yard and getting in touch with your inner undergrad.

the Great and General Court of the Massachusetts Bay Colony voted funds to establish the colony's first college, and a year later chose Cambridge as the site. Named in 1639 for John Harvard, a young Charlestown clergyman who died in 1638 and left the college his entire library and half his estate, Harvard remained the only college in the New World until 1693, by which time it was firmly established as a respected center of learning. Local wags refer to Harvard as WGU—World's Greatest University—and it's certainly the oldest and most famous American university.

Although the college dates from the 17th century, the oldest buildings in Harvard Yard are from the 18th century (though you'll sometimes see archaeologists digging here for evidence of older structures). Together the buildings chronicle American architecture from the colonial era to the present. Holden Chapel, completed in 1744, is a Georgian gem. The graceful University Hall was designed in 1815 by Charles Bulfinch. An 1884 statue of John Harvard by Daniel Chester French stands outside; ironically for a school with the motto of "Veritas" ("Truth"), the model for the statue was a member of the class of 1882 and not Harvard himself. Sever Hall, completed in 1880 and designed by Henry Hobson Richardson, represents the Romanesque revival that was followed by the neoclassical (note the pillared facade of Widener Library) and the neo-Georgian, represented by the sumptuous brick houses along the Charles River, many of which are now undergraduate residences. Memorial Church, a graceful steepled edifice of modified Colonial Revival design, was dedicated in 1932. Just north of the Yard is Memorial Hall, completed in 1878 as a memorial to Harvard men who died for the Union cause; it's High Victorian both inside and out. It also contains the

1,166-seat Sanders Theatre, which serves as the university's largest lecture hall, site of year-round concerts by students and professionals, and the venue for the festive Christmas Revels.

Many of Harvard's cultural and scholarly facilities are important sights in themselves, but most campus buildings, other than museums and concert halls, are off-limits to the general public.

The Harvard Information Center, in the Smith Campus Center, has a small exhibit space, distributes maps of the university area, and offers free student-led tours of Harvard Yard. The tour doesn't include visits to museums, and it doesn't take you into campus buildings, but it provides a fine orientation. The information center is open year-round (except during spring recess and other semester breaks). From the end of June through August, guides offer tours every half hour; however, it's best to call ahead to confirm times. You can also download a mobile tour on your smart phone. ⊠ *Bounded by Massachusetts Ave. and Mt. Auburn, Holyoke, and Dunster Sts., 1350 Massachusetts Ave., Harvard Square* ☎ *617/495–1573 Information Center* ⊕ *www.harvard.edu* Ⓜ *Harvard.*

Peabody Museum of Archaeology and Ethnology

HISTORY MUSEUM | With one of the world's outstanding anthropological collections, the Peabody Museum is among the oldest anthropology museums in the world. Its collections focus on Native American and Central and South American cultures and are comprised of more than 1.2 million objects. The Hall of the North American Indian is particularly outstanding, with art, textiles, and models of traditional dwellings from across the continent. The Mesoamerican room juxtaposes ancient relief carvings and weavings with contemporary works from the Maya and other peoples. Of special note is the museum's only surviving collection of objects acquired from Native

American people during the Lewis and Clark expedition. ⊠ *11 Divinity Ave., Harvard Square* ☎ *617/496–1027* ⊕ *www.peabody.harvard.edu* ⌲ *$15, includes admission to the adjacent Harvard Museum of Natural History* Ⓜ *Harvard.*

Porter Square

PLAZA/SQUARE | **FAMILY** | About a mile northwest of Harvard Square lies Porter Square, an area that consists of several blocks along Mass Ave. that boast shopping centers and eateries. As you walk north (away from Harvard) past the heart of Porter Square, you'll find pretty much every ethnic eatery imaginable, many of them excellent and far cheaper than Harvard Square restaurants. There are also quite a few unique shops along the way, including thrift shops and music stores. ⊠ *Porter Square* ⊹ *The Porter Square T stop is on the Red Line.*

Wadsworth House

HISTORIC HOME | On the Harvard University side of Harvard Square stands the Wadsworth House, a yellow clapboard structure built in 1726 as a home for Harvard presidents. It served as the first Massachusetts headquarters for George Washington, who arrived on July 2, 1775, just a day before he took command of the Continental Army. The building traded presidents in for students (such as Ralph Waldo Emerson) and visiting preachers as its boarders, and today, it houses Harvard's general offices. ⊠ *1341 Massachusetts Ave., Harvard Square* ⊕ *www.harvard.edu* ⊘ *Closed to the public.* Ⓜ *Harvard.*

🍴 Restaurants

Alden & Harlow

$$$ | **MODERN AMERICAN** | This boisterous subterranean restaurant with a 30-seat bar and industrial-chic design specializes in rustic, seasonal snacks and small plates layered with flavor. Whether it's brunch or dinner, start with an expertly made cocktail before you dig into a menu that includes little dishes like seared bluefin crudo, chicken-fried local rabbit, and sweet corn pancakes. **Known for:** terrific cocktails; boisterous feel; flavor-packed sharing plates. $ *Average main: $28* ✉ *40 Brattle St., Harvard Square* ☎ *617/864-2100* ⊕ *www.alden-harlow.com* ☉ *No lunch* Ⓜ *Harvard.*

★ Giulia

$$$ | **ITALIAN** | With exposed-brick walls and soft lighting, the heart and soul of this charming Italian restaurant is its communal pasta table at which chef Michael Pagliarini spends hours hand-rolling superlative pastas for dishes like buckwheat *pizzoccheri* and pasta *alla bolognese*. Plates such as house-made lamb sausage, monkfish piccata, warm semolina cakes, grilled barramundi, and Sardinian flatbread are original, generous, and, of course delicious. Known for its romantic nature, it's the perfect place for lovers to linger over a chocolate terrine and cappuccino. **Known for:** silky pastas; warm, softly lit space; excellent Italian food. $ *Average main: $30* ✉ *1682 Massachusetts Ave., Harvard Square* ☎ *617/441-2800* ⊕ *www.giuliarestaurant.com* ☉ *Closed Sun.*

★ Harvest

$$$$ | **AMERICAN** | Once a favorite of former Cambridge resident Julia Child, this sophisticated shrine to New England cuisine has been a perennial go-to spot for Harvard students when their parents are in town since 1975. The seasonal menu could feature Cape scallop crudo, fresh pasta with braised veal and pesto, or fresh Cape lobster with lemon hollandaise. **Known for:** expansive wine list; pretty patio dining area; elegant New England cuisine. $ *Average main: $40* ✉ *44 Brattle St., on walkway, Brattle Street* ☎ *617/868-2255* ⊕ *harvestcambridge.com* Ⓜ *Harvard.*

Henrietta's Table

$$$ | **AMERICAN** | Located in the Charles Hotel, this cheerful, country-style restaurant is named after chef-owner Peter Davis's pet pig, Henrietta. Davis is passionate about working with small area growers and purveyors, as well as harvesting veggies and honey from the restaurant's rooftop garden and hives, which is evident in his fresh, honest, wholesome, New England–style dishes like juicy Yankee pot roast, Pig Under a Brick, Ritz-crusted scrod, and creamy Maine crab-corn chowder. **Known for:** inviting, sunny setting; New England farm–sourced ingredients; epic weekend brunches. $ *Average main: $29* ✉ *1 Bennett St., Harvard Square* ☎ *617/661-5005* ⊕ *www.henriettastable.com* ☉ *No dinner Mon. and Tues.* Ⓜ *Harvard.*

The Hourly Oyster House

$$$ | **SEAFOOD** | This dimly lit, nautically inspired spot pays homage to the ocean in not only decor but tasty fare. Against a backdrop of sailing ships and vessels, antiqued mirrors, and chandelier bubble-like bulbs, day-time appetites fill up on beer-battered fish-and-chips, po'boys, and lobster rolls, while the dinner crowd enjoys entrées like *bucatini frutti di mare*, seared scallops, swordfish tacos, and an oyster bar that features dozens of the bivalve beauties, as well as a massive chilled grand seafood tower. **Known for:** chilled seafood tower; quick bar dining; cozy atmosphere. $ *Average main: $28* ✉ *15 Dunster St., Harvard Square* ☎ *617/765-2342* ⊕ *www.thehourlycambridge.com* Ⓜ *Harvard.*

Lê's

$ | **VIETNAMESE** | **FAMILY** | The Vietnamese noodle soup pho is the name of the game in this quick and casual eatery (it's set inside The Garage, a small mall in Harvard Square); at $11, it's a meal unto itself with chicken, shrimp, or beef, steaming hot in a big bowl. Fresh salads, rice plates, steamed vermicelli, seafood entrees, and stir-fries are offered, as well as crispy spring rolls, summer rolls, and Chinese chicken wings. **Known for:** low prices; fast service; terrific Vietnamese. $ *Average main: $11* ✉ *35 Dunster St.,*

Harvard Square ☎ *617/864–4100* ⊕ *lesrestaurantcambridge.cafecityguide.website* Ⓜ *Harvard.*

★ Orinoco

$ | LATIN AMERICAN | Don't miss this red clapboard, Pan–Latin American restaurant located down an alleyway in Harvard Square. Owner Andres Branger's dream to bring bountiful plates of super-fresh family fare from his home country of Venezuela to Cambridge (as well as Brookline Village and the South End) rewards diners with delectable, palm-size *arepas* (crispy, hot, corn-flour pockets stuffed with beans, cheese, chicken, or pork), *pabellon criollo* (moist shredded beef with stewed beans, rice, and plantains), and red chili adobo–marinated, charred *pollo* (chicken). **Known for:** generous portions; great value; Venezuelan specialties. ⑤ *Average main: $10* ⊠ *56 JFK St., Harvard Square* ☎ *617/354–6900* ⊕ *www.orinocokitchen.com* ⊙ *Closed Mon.*

Russell House Tavern

$$ | AMERICAN | The seasonally inspired menu at this New American tavern brings American classics to the table, featuring signatures like the R. House burger (with cheddar, bacon, and caramelized onions on an English muffin), a selection of tavern pizzas, and steak frites. **Known for:** lively Saturday night scene; small brick patio; New England classics. ⑤ *Average main: $20* ⊠ *14 JFK St., Harvard Square* ☎ *617/500–3055* ⊕ *www.russellhouse-cambridge.com* Ⓜ *Harvard.*

Waypoint

$$$$ | SEAFOOD | Chef-owner Michael Scelfo looked seaward to inform the menu of his second venture after Alden & Harlow. Named aptly for a plot on a map, Waypoint is his step forward on the path to coastal-inspired fare that includes an excellent raw bar with crudos, bivalves, and the celebrated caviar served with doughnut holes, along with whole-fish roasts, slow-roasted meats, indulgent seafood pasta dishes, and

inventive pizzas. **Known for:** hip, happening vibe; extensive absinthe offerings; lusty seafood-rich fare. ⑤ *Average main: $36* ⊠ *1030 Massachusetts Ave., Harvard Square* ☎ *617/864–2300* ⊕ *www.waypointharvard.com.*

☕ Coffee and Quick Bites

BerryLine

$ | CAFÉ | Two postdoctoral-fellowship students founded this tasty oasis that serves superlative soft frozen yogurt made from milk, cane sugar, fresh fruit, and other natural ingredients. The shop has featured well over 150 frozen yogurt flavors like rose, chocolate coconut, passion fruit, and green tea, and dedicated staff bakers create many of the homemade toppings, including the cheesecake chunks, chewy mochi bits, brownie bites, and honey-nut granola. **Known for:** homemade bakery toppings; fresh fruit add-ons; award-winning fro-yo. ⑤ *Average main: $3* ⊠ *3 Arrow St., Harvard Square* ☎ *617/868–3500* ⊕ *www.berryline.com.*

Cardullo's Gourmet Shoppe

$ | SANDWICHES | This snug, more than 70–year-old shop (family-owned and-operated up until a few years ago) in Harvard Square purveys exotic imports, including cheeses, chocolates, British biscuits, jams, olive oils, and mustards, along with sandwiches, cheeses, and charcuterie to go. You'll also find a generous assortment of champagnes and domestic caviar, fine wines, and assorted beers. **Known for:** made-to-order sandwiches and charcuterie; international gourmet sweet shop; New England goods. ⑤ *Average main: $9* ⊠ *6 Brattle St., Harvard Square* ☎ *617/491–8888* ⊕ *www.cardullos.com* ⊙ *No dinner* Ⓜ *Harvard.*

Felipe's Taqueria

$ | MEXICAN | Cafés abound on Brattle Street, but Felipe's is a good bet for fresh ingredients and authentic recipes that build out a quick hit menu of Mexican grab-and-go dishes. Start off with their *queso fundido* or guac, then fill up on heaping Super Burritos, Baja-style tacos, and chimichangas. **Known for:** cheap eats; Super Burritos; tacos. $ *Average main: $8* ⊠ *21 Brattle St., Brattle Street* ☎ *617/354–9944* ⊕ *www.felipestaqueria. com.*

L.A. Burdick Chocolates

$ | **AMERICAN** | This charming artisanal chocolatier is a staple for locals and tourists alike, who come for its famously adorable signature chocolate mice, chocolate bonbons, and chocolate bars. The elegant, life-changing hot cocoa may be just the thing to restore flagging spirits or weary feet with variations on the classic milk chocolate, including dark, spicy, and white. **Known for:** chocolate milk and penguins; cozy atmosphere; dreamy drinking chocolate. $ *Average main: $10* ⊠ *52 Brattle St., Brattle Street* ☎ *617/491–4340* ⊕ *www.burdickchocolate.com* Ⓜ *Harvard.*

Lizzy's Homemade Ice Cream

$ | **CAFÉ** | Barely bigger than a shoebox, this Harvard Square take-out parlor offers more than 50 fabulous flavor options like orange-pineapple and Charles River Crunch (a dark-chocolate ice cream with almond toffee nuggets), along with a small selection of frozen yogurts, "lite" ice creams, and sorbet, plus soda fountain favorites, including frappes and sundaes. Adult-only flavors include Bailey's and Rum Raisin, and for those looking for just "a tiny taste," the minicone, topped with a golf ball–size scoop, hits the spot. **Known for:** take-out service; Tofutti dairy-free treats; homemade ice cream. $ *Average main: $5* ⊠ *29 Church St., Harvard Square* ☎ *617/354–2911* ⊕ *www. lizzysicecream.com.*

Mr. Bartley's Gourmet Burgers

$ | **AMERICAN** | **FAMILY** | It may be perfect cuisine for the student metabolism: a huge variety of variously garnished thick burgers with sassy names (many of them after celebrities, like the Marcus Smart, the POTUS Biden, or the Megan Thee Stallion), deliciously crispy regular and sweet-potato fries, award-winning onion rings, and toppings like an egg or mac and cheese. There's also a competent veggie burger, along with comforting dinner fare like baked meat loaf, fried chicken, and franks and beans. **Known for:** thick frappes; loud atmosphere; creative burgers. $ *Average main: $17* ⊠ *1246 Massachusetts Ave., Harvard Square* ☎ *617/354–6559* ⊕ *www.mrbartley.com* ☉ *Closed Sun. and Mon.* Ⓜ *Harvard.*

Saloniki

$ | **GREEK** | Locally loved chef Jody Adams pays tribute to the humble Greek sandwich shop with Saloniki, bringing traditional Greek flavor and fresh ingredients in the form of pitas brimming with braised pork shoulder, crispy fried chicken, spicy lamb meatballs, and more. Vegetarians aren't left out with squeaky Halloumi, moussaka and meatballs made from Impossible meat, and griddled spanakopita. **Known for:** other locations in Fenway and Central Square; filling classics; souvlaki mixed grill. $ *Average main: $14* ⊠ *24 Dunster St., Harvard Square* ☎ *617/945–5074* ⊕ *salonikigreek. com* Ⓜ *Harvard.*

Veggie Grill

$ | **VEGETARIAN** | This California-based fast-food chain makes living that plant-based life a little easier. The extensive meat-free menu features burgers, sandwiches, entrée salads, tacos, burritos, and desserts sans meat, dairy, eggs, and other animal products, so you can fill up on tasty meals without sacrificing any dietary restrictions. **Known for:** vegan menu; heaping bowls; Beyond Burgers, Tacos, and Burritos. $ *Average main: $10* ⊠ *57 John F. Kennedy St., Harvard Square* ☎ *617/430–4004* ⊕ *www.veggiegrill.com* Ⓜ *Harvard.*

Hotels

★ The Charles Hotel

$$$ | HOTEL | FAMILY | It used to be that The Charles was *the* place to stay in Cambridge, and while other luxury hotels have since arrived to give it a little healthy competition, this Harvard Square staple is standing strong. **Pros:** two blocks from the T Red Line to Boston; on-site dining options; on-site 4,000-square-foot Corbu Spa & Salon. **Cons:** restricted pool hours for children; coffee pots and tea kettles are available by request only; great location comes at a price. ⑤ *Rooms from: $399* ✉ *1 Bennett St., Harvard Square* ☎ *617/864–1200, 800/882–1818* ⊕ *www. charleshotel.com* ⇆ *294 rooms* ⦿ *No Meals* Ⓜ *Harvard.*

Harvard Square Hotel

$$$ | HOTEL | Check in to Harvard Square Hotel for a modern aesthetic within a sophisticated Harvard University–owned space, just steps from the Square's plethora of shops, eateries, and bars. **Pros:** awesome location; front-view rooms overlook Harvard Square; complimentary Wi-Fi, tea, and coffee in the lobby café. **Cons:** no gym; no restaurant; parking costs extra. ⑤ *Rooms from: $319* ✉ *110 Mt. Auburn St., Harvard Square* ☎ *617/864–5200, 800/458–5886* ⊕ *www. harvardsquarehotel.com* ⇆ *73 rooms* ⦿ *No Meals* Ⓜ *Harvard.*

Irving House at Harvard

$ | B&B/INN | On a residential street three blocks from Harvard Square, this four-story gray clapboard guest house is a bargain. **Pros:** free Wi-Fi; good location and price; all-day coffee, tea, and snacks. **Cons:** four floors are not served by elevator; some rooms with shared baths; dining room is in the basement. ⑤ *Rooms from: $165* ✉ *24 Irving St., Harvard Square* ☎ *617/547–4600, 877/547–4600* ⊕ *www.irvinghouse.com* ⇆ *44 rooms* ⦿ *Free Breakfast* Ⓜ *Harvard.*

Sheraton Commander Hotel

$ | HOTEL | The stately 1927 Harvard Square landmark overlooking Cambridge Common park features classic furnishings (hello four-poster beds) in handsome, warm tones, but it's the hotel's signature bright-red neon sign towering overhead that really puts it on the map as a Cambridge classic. **Pros:** central Harvard Square location; pet-friendly; 24/7 gym. **Cons:** some rooms have views of the parking lot; it's an older building; small bathrooms. ⑤ *Rooms from: $189* ✉ *16 Garden St., Harvard Square* ☎ *617/547–4800, 800/325–3535* ⊕ *www. marriott.com* ⇆ *175 rooms* ⦿ *No Meals* Ⓜ *Harvard.*

🕐 Nightlife

Town meets gown at Harvard Square, and glitz meets not-so-nerdy MIT at biotech-booming Kendall Square. As Mass Ave. bends beyond the Charles, it connects both campuses and Porter Square's ethnic restaurants and jolly scenesters. Inman Square's music spots, Brattle Street's patrician serenity, and the bustle of Cambridgeside's mall and hotel pubs and dining rooms enrich the fabric.

BARS
Grendel's Den

BARS | This quintessential grad-student hangout is cavelike, low-lit, and brick-walled. During early evenings, tasty entrées like buffalo chicken dip, burritos, brisket nachos, and burgers are half-price with a $4-per-person drink (inside only; not on outdoor patio). Named after Grendel, the antagonist in the Old English poem *Beowulf*, there's nothing but neighborhood love here as you raise a pint in this half-century old hangout. ✉ *89 Winthrop St., Harvard Square* ☎ *617/491–1160* ⊕ *www.grendelsden. com* Ⓜ *Harvard.*

The Longfellow Bar

COCKTAIL LOUNGES | Named after famed architect Alexander Wadsworth Longfellow (nephew of poet Henry), this neighborhood bar and restaurant is located in the historic Café Algiers space directly above chef/owner Michael Scelfo's Alden & Harlow, a subterranean haunt adjacent to The Brattle Theatre. Bartenders pour creative cocktails, local craft brews, and a fluid list of edgy boutique wines by the bottle. The menu features bar food intended to be passed and shared. ⊠ *40 Brattle St., Harvard Square* ☎ *617/864–0001* ⊕ *longfellowharvard.com* Ⓜ *Harvard Sq.*

★ Toad

BARS | This is where local hipsters make their home. Bands, beers, and burgers sum up this snug and amiable little Porter Square hideaway attached to Christopher's. The bar is maple, the toads ceramic, and microbrews on tap are a dozen-plus. Nightly music comes in many a stripe Wednesday through Saturday nights, and sometimes in double bills at 5 and 9 pm. Record lovers unite on Saturday from 5 to 7:30 pm for vinyl sharing, drink sipping, and "favorite music?" chatting. ⊠ *1912 Massachusetts Ave., Porter Square* ☎ *617/497–4950 recording* ⊕ *www.toadcambridge.com* Ⓜ *Porter.*

MUSIC CLUBS

Club Passim

LIVE MUSIC | Joan Baez, Bob Dylan, Josh Ritter, Lake Street Dive—thousands of folkies have strummed and warbled their way through Club Passim, one of America's oldest (1958) and most renowned clubs for Americana and roots music. Audience participation is encouraged, so be ready to sing along. The ultra-cozy brick basement has a kitchen that's open for relaxed live-music dining (which is only available to ticket holders). If you travel with your guitar, call about open-mic nights. Classes and workshops at their school around the corner carry on folk traditions. Acoustic bands perform nightly; expect to pay a $5–$25 cover. ⊠ *47 Palmer St., Harvard Square* ☎ *617/492–7679 box office* ⊕ *www. passim.org* Ⓜ *Harvard.*

The Sinclair

LIVE MUSIC | Follow the retro neon sign to the music scene you've been waiting for. Bringing a long-awaited sophisticated rock music and dining venue to Harvard Square, The Sinclair's adventurous, near-nightly lineup of indie rock—with enticing flings into world, electronica, and jazz—often sells out. Its adjacent but quite separate restaurant and bar, with wanderlusty train and highway decor, a serious beverage list, creative mixology, and cuisine inspired by regional Americana at on-site Brato, is proving to be a winning formula. Accommodating 500, here's a party made to order for transient, academic, and streetwise grown-ups. ⊠ *52 Church St., Harvard Square* ☎ *617/547–5200* ⊕ *www.sinclaircambridge.com* Ⓜ *Harvard.*

🎭 Performing Arts

DANCE

José Mateo Ballet Theatre

BALLET | This troupe is building an exciting, contemporary repertory under Cuban-born José Mateo, the resident artistic director-choreographer. Performances, which include Dance Saturdays and an original *Nutcracker,* take place October through April at the Sanctuary Theatre, a beautifully converted Gothic revival church at Massachusetts Avenue and Harvard Street in Harvard Square. The vibe is intimate cabaret-style seating with 250 seats, each with its own perfect view. ⊠ *400 Harvard St., Cambridge* ☎ *617/945–1944* ⊕ *www.ballettheatre. org* Ⓜ *Harvard.*

FILM

The Brattle Theatre

FILM | A classic moviegoer's den with 230 seats and only one screen, The Brattle shows art house, new foreign, and indie films, classic movies, theme series, and directors' cuts. Tickets sell out for its Valentine's Day screenings of *Casablanca*; the Bugs Bunny Film Festival in February; March's *Underground Film Festival; Trailer Treats*, an annual fundraiser featuring classic and modern movie previews; and DocYard, a stunning series of documentaries. At Christmastime, expect seasonal movies like *It's a Wonderful Life* and *Holiday Inn*. Enjoy a rotating selection of local beers and wines. ⊠ *40 Brattle St., Harvard Sq., Cambridge* ☎ *617/876–6837* ⊕ *brattlefilm.org* Ⓜ *Harvard*.

Harvard Film Archive

FILM | Screening independent, foreign, classic, and experimental films rarely seen in commercial cinemas, the Harvard Film Archive is open to the public Friday through Monday. The 188-seat theater, with pristine film and digital projection, is located in the basement of the stunning brick-and-glass Carpenter Center for Visual Arts, Le Corbusier's only American building. A division of Harvard Library, this is one of the country's largest and most significant university-based motion picture collections—more than 36,000 global audiovisual items from almost every period in film history. Tickets are $10; seniors and students, $8. ⊠ *Carpenter Center for the Visual Arts, 24 Quincy St., Cambridge* ☎ *617/496–6750* ⊕ *harvardfilmarchive.org* Ⓜ *Harvard*.

MUSIC

★ Sanders Theatre

CONCERTS | This gilt-wood jewel box of a stage is the preferred venue for many of Boston's classical orchestras and the home of Harvard University's many ensembles. Located in Memorial Hall, 180-degree stage design and superb acoustics afford intimacy and crystal projection. A favorite of folk, jazz, and world-music performers, the 1,000-seat Sanders hosts the holiday favorite *Christmas Revels,* a traditional participatory Yule celebration. Winston Churchill, Martin Luther King Jr., Wynton Marsalis,

Leonard Bernstein, and Oprah Winfrey have appeared at this famed seat of oratory and music. ⊠ *Harvard University, 45 Quincy St., Harvard Sq., Cambridge* ☎ *617/496–2222 box office* ⊕ *www.fas. harvard.edu/~memhall/sanders.html* Ⓜ *Harvard*.

THEATER

★ American Repertory Theater

THEATER | Founded by Robert Brustein and since 2009 under the helm of Tony Award–winning director Diane Paulus, the ART is one of America's most celebrated regional theaters, winning Tonys for Broadway originals *All the Way* and *Once* as well as revivals of *The Glass Menagerie, Pippin,* and *The Gershwins' Porgy and Bess.* The ART often premieres new works and seeks to expand the boundaries of theater through productions such as *Waitress, Finding Neverland,* and *Natasha, Pierre & the Great Comet of 1812* among others. The Loeb Drama Center, home of the ART, houses two theaters: the Mainstage and The Ex, a smaller black box often staging productions by the irreverent Harvard-Radcliffe Dramatic Club. OBERON, the ART's "club theater" with flexible stage design, engages young audiences in immersive theater (and has attracted national acclaim for its groundbreaking model) with gay, alternative, and cutting-edge programming. ⊠ *64 Brattle St., Harvard Sq., Cambridge* ☎ *617/547–8300* ⊕ *americanrepertorytheater.org* Ⓜ *Harvard*.

Hasty Pudding Theatricals

THEATER | The oldest (1844) collegiate theatrical company in the United States still has all-male casts, though women participate in the troupe's staging and production. Its single annual madcap show plays at its theater in February and March, then tours to New York and Vegas. The troupe infamously honors actors as Man and Woman of the Year in an annual awards ceremony, complete with a celebrity roast and drag-queen and boa-laden party parade through the streets of Cambridge

Harvard University's Radcliffe Quad is surrounded by undergrad housing; it's about a 12-minute walk, or half a mile, from Harvard Square.

for the chosen woman. The 2021 honorees were Jason Bateman and Jennifer Garner. ✉ *Harvard Sq., 12 Holyoke St., Cambridge* ☎ *617/495–5205* ⊕ *www. hastypudding.org* Ⓜ *Harvard.*

🛍 Shopping

Cross over the Charles River to Cambridge, just as historic as Boston and where Harvard University's famous campus provides a beautiful backdrop for a unique and charming shopping experience. Massachusetts Avenue, Brattle Street, and Mt. Auburn Street shape the area known as Harvard Square, the place to go in Cambridge for just about anything.

A handful of chains and independent boutiques are clustered on Brattle Street.

BOOKS

Grolier Poetry Book Shop

BOOKS | A beloved hangout for T. S. Eliot and E. E. Cummings when they attended Harvard, this tiny shop founded in 1927 carries classic, modern, and contemporary in-print poetry from all over the world. ✉ *6 Plympton St., Harvard Square* ☎ *617/547–4648* ⊕ *www.grolier-poetrybookshop.org* Ⓜ *Harvard.*

Harvard Book Store

BOOKS | Time disappears as you browse the tables and shelves of this always-busy bookstore packed with new titles and used books, as well as remaindered books. Founded in 1932, the collection's diversity has made the store a favored destination for casual readers and academics alike, as they have plenty to discover within the floor-to-ceiling bookcases. You can also stock up on Harvard University gifts, or catch an author reading. ✉ *1256 Massachusetts Ave., Harvard Square* ☎ *617/661–1515* ⊕ *www.harvard. com* Ⓜ *Harvard.*

★ The Harvard Coop

BOOKS | What began in 1882 as a nonprofit service for students and faculty is now managed by Barnes & Noble College, a separate entity that manages college campus bookstores. Housed in the same location since 1906 and affectionately called The Coop (pronounced "coop," not "co-op"), the store sells books and textbooks (many discounted), school supplies, clothes, and accessories plastered with the Harvard emblem, as well as basic housewares geared toward dorm dwellers. If you need a public restroom, you'll find it here. And if you're looking for MIT swag, they have a location on that campus as well. ⊠ *1400 Massachusetts Ave., Harvard Square* ☎ *617/499–2000* ⊕ *store.thecoop.com* Ⓜ *Harvard.*

Raven Used Books

BOOKS | Looking for a stash of scholarly or literary used books? The Raven attracts local students eager to unload their university press titles. The store stocks approximately 15,000 carefully used books on topics ranging from social and political theory to art and architecture and buys more than 1,000 books weekly, with discounts ranging from 50% to 80% off the cover price. It's situated next to the Christian Science Reading Room, in case you need a quiet place to settle down with your purchases. ⊠ *23 Church St., Harvard Square* ☎ *617/441–6999* ⊕ *www.ravencambridge.com* Ⓜ *Harvard.*

CRAFTS

Cambridge Artists' Cooperative

CRAFTS | Unique, handcrafted ceramics, weavings, jewelry, paper, wood, and leatherwork fill this two-level artist-owned and-operated store, with more than 200 global artists represented—more than half of whom hail from New England. Spend time perusing the glass cases of artistic hand-crafted notions that greet you inside the front door, then stroll downstairs for wearable art in the forms of scarves, purses, and more. ⊠ *59A Church St., Brattle Street* ☎ *617/868–1434* ⊕ *www.cambridgeartistscoop.com* Ⓜ *Harvard.*

SPECIALTY SHOPS

Bonde Fine Wine Shop

WINE/SPIRITS | Challenging the very concept of a wine shop, Bonde is more like an experience, or a place you'll

"bond" with the vintages. Owner Bertil Jean-Chronberg (one of America's only master sommeliers) sells only eco-responsible wines, 95% of which are from American micromakers. His wine accessories are unique—think swordfish tusk wine stoppers custom-made for the shop and stunning champagne sabres—and the tiny display table transforms to eight-person "Wednesday Wine Tastings" with food pairings. ⊠ *54 Church St., Harvard Square* ☎ *617/945–2360* ⊕ *bondewines.com.*

★ Leavitt & Peirce

SOUVENIRS | A throwback to another era, this storied museum-like tobacco shop has been in the same location since 1883, when it served as a clubby gathering spot for young Harvard men, who puffed away while playing pool on the back billiard tables. While Harvard oars, hockey sticks, and photos still adorn the ivy-green walls, the store now caters to a broader clientele in search of quality smoking items, old-fashioned straight razors and shave brushes, chess and checker sets, and small gift items, such as beer steins. ⊠ *1316 Massachusetts Ave., Harvard Square* ☎ *617/547–0576* ⊕ *www.leavitt-peirce.com* Ⓜ *Harvard.*

Tory Row

The stretch of Brattle Street nicknamed Tory Row remains one of New England's most elegant thoroughfares. Elaborate mansions line both sides from where it meets JFK Street to Fresh Pond Parkway. Dubbed Tory Row because during the 1770s its seven mansions, on land that stretched to the river, were owned by staunch supporters of King George, these properties were appropriated by the patriots when they took over Cambridge in the summer of 1775. Many of the historic houses are marked with blue signs, and although only two (the Hooper-Lee-Nichols House and the Longfellow House National Historic Site) are fully open to the public, it's easy to imagine yourself back in the days of Ralph Waldo Emerson and Henry David Thoreau as you stroll the brick sidewalks. Mt. Auburn Cemetery, an exquisitely landscaped garden cemetery, is less than 2 miles down Brattle Street from Harvard Square.

⊙ Sights

Dexter Pratt House

COLLEGE | Also known as the "Blacksmith House," this yellow Colonial is now owned by the Cambridge Center for Adult Education. The tree itself is long gone, but this spot inspired Longfellow's lines: "Under a spreading chestnut tree, the village smithy stands." The blacksmith's shop, today commemorated by a granite marker, was next door, at the corner of Story Street. If you're lucky, you might be able to catch the celebrated Blacksmith House Poetry Series, which runs periodically throughout the year on Monday night. Tickets are $3. ⊠ *56 Brattle St., Tory Row* ⊕ *ccae.org/blacksmithpoetry* Ⓜ *Harvard.*

Elmwood

HISTORIC HOME | Shortly after its construction in 1767, this three-story Georgian house was abandoned by its owner, colonial governor Thomas Oliver. Also known as the Oliver-Gerry-Lowell House, it was home to the accomplished Lowell family for two centuries. Elmwood is now the Harvard University president's residence, ever since student riots in 1969 drove president Nathan Pusey from his house in Harvard Yard. ⊠ *33 Elmwood Ave., Tory Row* Ⓜ *Harvard.*

Henry Vassall House

HISTORIC HOME | Brattle Street's seven houses known as "Tory Row" were once occupied by wealthy families linked by friendship, if not blood. Portions of this house may have been built as early as 1636. In 1737 it was purchased by John Vassall Sr.; four years later he sold it to his younger brother Henry and his wife Penelope. It was used as a hospital during the Revolution, and the traitor Dr. Benjamin Church was held here as a prisoner. The house was remodeled during the 19th century. It's now a private residence, but from the street you can view the Colonial home with its black-shuttered windows and multiple dormers. ⊠ *94 Brattle St., Tory Row* Ⓜ *Harvard.*

Hooper-Lee-Nichols House

HISTORIC HOME | Now headquarters of the History Cambridge historical society, this is one of two Tory-era homes on Brattle Street fully open to the public; it's one of the older houses in Cambridge. The Emerson family gave it to the society in 1957. Built between 1685 and 1690, the house has been remodeled at least six times, but has maintained much of the original structure. The downstairs is elegantly, although sparsely, appointed with period books, portraits, and wallpaper. An upstairs bedroom has been furnished with period antiques, some belonging to the original residents. Tours are offered by appointment only. Check the website for special events including public art installations, and to see a virtual tour of the house. ⊠ *159 Brattle St., Tory Row* ☎ *617/547–4252* ⊕ *www.historycambridge.org* Ⓜ *Harvard.*

Longfellow House–Washington's Headquarters

HISTORIC HOME | Henry Wadsworth Longfellow, the poet whose stirring tales of the village blacksmith, Evangeline, Hiawatha, and Paul Revere's midnight ride thrilled 19th-century America, once lived in this elegant Georgian mansion. One of several original Tory Row homes on Brattle Street, the house was built in 1759 by John Vassall Jr., and George Washington lived here during the Siege of Boston from July 1775 to April 1776. Longfellow first boarded here in 1837 and later received the house as a gift from his father-in-law on his marriage to Frances Appleton, who burned to death here in an accident in 1861. For 45 years

It's Hip to Be Square

In Cambridge, any commercial area where three or more streets meet in a jumble of traffic and noise has been dubbed a "square." (There are literally dozens, though most are just simple intersections.) Harvard Square draws the most visitors, but several other neighborhood squares exude their own charm. These are a few of our favorites, if you want to see where real Cantabrigians hang out.

Central Square, at Massachusetts Avenue (known by locals as "Mass Ave."), Prospect Street, and Western Avenue, has burger and beer joints, ethnic eats, music clubs, vintage record stores, and consignment shops. Cambridge's city government is here, and Ben Affleck and Matt Damon used to live here. For good eats, check out Little Donkey (✉ 505 Massachusetts Ave.) or The Phoenix Landing (✉ 512 Massachusetts Ave.), which also has dancing after 9 pm. The Central Square T stop is on the Red Line.

Somerville's **Davis Square** is just over the border from northwest Cambridge and easily accessible on the Red Line. This funky neighborhood near Tufts University is packed with great eateries, lively bars, and candlepin bowling. Harvard Square can sometimes feel a little tired after midnight, but there's still a lot of energy here late at night. At the Somerville Theatre (✉ 55 Davis Sq.), you can enjoy cheap first-run matinee movies ($10), excellent popcorn, and even beer and wine with your feature. Check out the hilarious Museum of Bad Art in the basement before or after your flick. The Davis Square T stop is on the Red Line.

Inman Square, at the intersection of Cambridge and Hampshire Streets,

has a great cluster of restaurants, cafés, bars, and shops. This place is just plain cool. One highlight is Punjabi Dhaba (✉ 225 Hampshire St.) for late-night, cheap and tasty, counter-service Indian food with Bollywood music and outstanding people-watching. Sadly, there's no T service to Inman, but you can get here from Harvard Square or Central Square on foot; it's near the intersection of Hampshire and Cambridge Streets.

At **Kendall Square**, near the Massachusetts Institute of Technology (MIT) and the heart of the city's thriving biotech industry, you'll find an art-house multiplex that shows first-run films and a walkable garden on top of a parking garage. The square is also a stone's throw from the Charles. The Kendall Square/MIT T stop is on the Red Line.

Porter Square, about a mile northwest of Harvard Square on Mass Ave., has several shopping centers and, within the nearby Porter Exchange, Japanese noodle and food shops. As you walk north (away from Harvard) past the heart of Porter Square, you'll pass pretty much every ethnic eatery imaginable, many of them excellent and far cheaper than Harvard Square restaurants. Standouts include one of the city's supposed first Chinese restaurants, Changsho (✉ 1712 Massachusetts Ave.), and popular Greek Corner (✉ 2366 Massachusetts Ave.), but you'll also find Indian, Thai, Bangladeshi, Vietnamese, and Himalayan. There are also quite a few unique shops along the way. The Porter Square T stop is on the Red Line.

Longfellow wrote his famous verses here and filled the house with the exuberant spirit of his literary circle, which included Ralph Waldo Emerson, Nathaniel Hawthorne, and Charles Sumner, an abolitionist senator. Longfellow died in 1882, but his presence in the house lives on—from the Longfellow family furniture to the wallpaper to the books on the shelves (many the poet's own).

The home is preserved and run by the National Park Service; guided tours are offered Memorial Day through October. The formal garden is the perfect place to relax; the grounds are open year-round. Longfellow Park, across the street, is the place to stand to take photos of the house. The park was created to preserve the view immortalized in the poet's "To the River Charles." ⊠ *105 Brattle St., Tory Row* ☎ *617/876–4491* ⊕ *www.nps.gov/long* ⌨ *Free* ۞ *Closed Tues.–Thurs. and Nov.–Apr.* Ⓜ *Harvard.*

Mt. Auburn Cemetery

CEMETERY | A cemetery might not strike you as a first choice for a visit, but this one is an absolute pleasure, filled with artwork and gorgeous landscaping. Opened in 1831, it was the country's first garden cemetery, and its bucolic landscape boasts peaceful ponds, statues (including a giant sphinx), breathtaking mausoleums, and a panorama of Boston and Cambridge from Washington Tower. More than 90,000 people have been buried here—among them Henry Wadsworth Longfellow, Mary Baker Eddy, Winslow Homer, Amy Lowell, Isabella Stewart Gardner, and architect Charles Bulfinch. The grave of engineer Buckminster Fuller bears an engraved geodesic dome.

In spring, local nature lovers and bird-watchers come out of the woodwork to see the warbler migrations, the glorious blossoms, and blooming trees, while later in the year nature shows off its autumnal range of glorious color. Brochures, maps, and audio tours are

at the entrance, and the cemetery is a five-minute drive from the heart of Harvard Square. ⊠ *580 Mt. Auburn St., Mt. Auburn* ☎ *617/547–7105* ⊕ *www.mountauburn.org* Ⓜ *Harvard; then Watertown (71) or Waverly (73) bus to cemetery.*

Kendall Square/ Central Square

Harvard Square may be the center of the "People's Republic of Cambridge," but the Kendall Square neighborhood is the city's hard-driving capitalist core. Gritty industrial buildings share space with sleek office blocks and the sprawling Massachusetts Institute of Technology. Although the MIT campus may lack the ivied elegance of Harvard Yard, major modern architects, including Alvar Aalto, Frank Gehry, I. M. Pei, and Eero Saarinen, created signature buildings here. To balance out the Square's tech-driven bustle, there's a newly developed green space with more than five acres of walkways, urban gardens, lounge areas, playgrounds, and the like. Called Cambridge Commons, the green oasis weaves in and out of the massive buildings. To reach MIT, take the Red Line T to Kendall station; if you're headed for the MIT Museum on the western edge of the campus, the Central Square station is more convenient.

Central Square has its own draw of ethnic eateries, vintage vinyl shops, music clubs, late-night dance hot spots, and thrift shops worth exploring.

◉ Sights

Massachusetts Institute of Technology

COLLEGE | Founded in 1861, MIT moved to Cambridge from Copley Square in the Back Bay in 1916. Once dissed as "the factory," particularly by its Ivy League neighbor, Harvard University, MIT mints graduates that are the sharp

Designed by famed architect Frank Gehry, MIT's Ray and Maria Stata Center is home to various computer science labs.

blades on the edge of the information revolution. It's perennially in the top five of *U.S. News and World Report*'s college rankings. It has long since fulfilled the predictions of its founder, the geologist William Barton Rogers, that it would surpass "the universities of the land in the accuracy and the extent of its teachings in all branches of positive science." Its emphasis shifted in the 1930s from practical engineering and mechanics to the outer limits of scientific fields.

Architecture is important at MIT. Although the original buildings were obviously designed by and for scientists, many represent pioneering designs of their times. Kresge Auditorium, designed by Eero Saarinen, with a curving roof and unusual thrust, rests on three, instead of four, points. The nondenominational MIT Chapel, a circular Saarinen design, is lighted primarily by a roof oculus that focuses natural light on the altar and by reflections from the water in a small surrounding moat; it's topped by an

aluminum sculpture by Theodore Roszak. The serpentine Baker House, now a dormitory, was designed in 1947 by the Finnish architect Alvar Aalto in such a way as to provide every room with a view of the Charles River. Sculptures by Henry Moore and other notable artists dot the campus. The latest addition is the Green Center, punctuated by the splash of color that is Sol LeWitt's 5,500-square-foot mosaic floor.

The East Campus, which has grown around the university's original neo-classical buildings of 1916, also has outstanding modern architecture and sculpture, including the stark high-rise Green Building by I. M. Pei, housing the Department of Earth, Atmospheric, and Planetary Sciences. Just outside is Alexander Calder's giant stabile (a stationary mobile) *The Big Sail*. Another Pei work on the East Campus is the Wiesner Building, designed in 1985, which houses the List Visual Arts Center. Architect Frank Gehry made his mark on the campus with the

A	B	C
D	E	

1
Library
Park
Cambridge St.
Ellery St.
Dana St.
Ellsworth Ave.
Highland Ave.
Hampshire St.
Springfield St.
Houghton St.
Prospect St.
Webster Ave.
INMAN
SQUARE **①**

2
Chatham St.
Harvard St.
Maple Ave.
Fayette St.
Antrim St.
Inman St.
Amory St.
Tremont St.
Norfolk St.
Columbia St.
Lincoln St.
Windsor St.
Broadway
Elm St.
Hampshire St.
⑥
Willow

3
③
2A
⑦
Massachusetts Ave.
Hancock St.
Lee St.
Clinton St.
Bigelow St.
Inman St.
Prospect St.
Edward J.
Sennott
Park
Harvard St.
Market St.
Webster Ave

4
Franklin St.
Green St.
Essex St.
Norfolk St.
CENTRAL
SQUARE
Pine St.
Cherry St.
Windsor St.
Washington St.

5
Western Avenue
River Street
Ⓣ Central
Bishop Allen Dr.
Columbia St.
CAMBRIDGE
Portland St.
⑤
2A

6
Pleasant St.
Magazine Street
Pearl St.
Auburn St.
Green St.
Franklin St.
Brookline St.
Massachusetts Ave.
④
③
Windsor St.
Osborn St.
Albany St.
②
Erie St.
Landsdowne St.
Purrington St.

7
Hamilton St.
Allston St.
Sidney St.
Albany St.
0   800 ft
0   300 m
Vassar St.
MIT
Chapel

Sights ▼

1 Massachusetts Institute
   of Technology **F7**

2 MIT List
   Visual Arts Center **G6**

3 MIT Museum **D6**

Restaurants ▼

1 Catalyst **F5**

2 Glass House **H5**

3 Helmand **I4**

4 The Lexington
   at The Shed **J2**

5 Little Donkey **C5**

6 Oleana **D3**

7 Pammy's **A3**

Quick Bites ▼

1 All Star
   Sandwich Bar **D1**

2 Cafe Luna **E6**

3 Dado Tea **A3**

4 Toscanini's Ice Cream ... **I4**

Kendall Square and Central Square

NORTHPOINT

Lechmere

EAST CAMBRIDGE

KENDALL SQUARE

Stata Center

Massachusetts Institute of Technology (MIT)

Kendall

Longfellow Bridge

Charles River

Medford St.
South St.
Porter St.
Harding St.
Warren St.
Msgr. O'Brien Hwy
28
Winter St.
Gore St.
Cambridge St.
Otis St.
Thorndike St.
Spring St.
5th St.
4th St.
3rd St.
Hurley St.
Charles St.
Bent St.
Rogers St.
3rd St.
Bent St.
Binney St.
Fulkerson St.
6th St.
2nd St.
1st St.
Linskey Way
Athenaeum St.
Kendall St.
Broadway
Binney St.
Main St.
Ames St.
Amherst St.
Memorial Drive
Edwin Land Boulevard
Cambridge Parkway
1st St.
Jacobs St.
Morgan Ave.
Cardinal Medeiros Ave.
John F. Connelly field

KEY

- ① Sights
- ① Restaurants
- ① Quick Bites
- ① Hotels
- Ⓣ Subway station

cockeyed, improbable Ray and Maria Stata Center, a complex of buildings on Vassar Street. The center houses computer, artificial intelligence, and information systems laboratories, and is reputedly as confusing to navigate on the inside as it is to follow on the outside. East Campus's Great Dome, which looms over neoclassical Killian Court, has often been the target of student "hacks" and has at various times supported a telephone booth with a ringing phone, a life-size statue of a cow, and a campus police cruiser. Nearby, the domed Rogers Building has earned unusual notoriety as the center of a series of hallways and tunnels dubbed "the infinite corridor." Twice each winter the sun's path lines up perfectly with the corridor's axis, and at dusk students line the third-floor hallway to watch the sun set through the westernmost window. The phenomenon is known as "MIT-henge."

MIT maintains a welcome center located at 292 Main Street in Kendall Square, where you can pick up campus maps, grab some water, and charge your phone weekdays 9 to 6. ☒ *77 Massachusetts Ave., Kendall Square* ☎ *617/253–4795* ⊕ *www.mit.edu* Ⓜ *Kendall/MIT.*

MIT List Visual Arts Center

ARTS CENTER | Founded by Albert and Vera List, pioneer collectors of modern art, this MIT center has three galleries showcasing exhibitions of cutting-edge art and mixed media. Works from the center's collection of contemporary art, such as Thomas Hart Benton's painting *Fluid Catalytic Crackers* and Harry Bertoia's altarpiece for the MIT Chapel, are on view here and around campus. The center's website includes a map indicating the locations of more than 20 of these public works of art. ☒ *20 Ames St., Bldg. E 15, Kendall Square* ☎ *617/253–4680* ⊕ *listart.mit.edu* ☜ *Free* ۞ *Closed Mon.* Ⓜ *Kendall/MIT.*

MIT Museum

SCIENCE MUSEUM | FAMILY | A place where art, science, and technology meet, the MIT Museum boasts the world's largest collection of holograms, though young kids may prefer the moving gestural sculptures of Arthur Ganson. The robot room shows off inventions of MIT's renowned robotics lab and an extensive exhibit on artificial intelligence. Allow an hour or two for a visit and check the schedule for special programs and demonstrations by MIT researchers and inventors. ☒ *265 Massachusetts Ave., Kendall Square* ☎ *617/253–5927* ⊕ *mit-museum.mit.edu* ☜ *$10; free last Sun. of month, Sept.–June* Ⓜ *Kendall/MIT.*

🍴 Restaurants

Catalyst

$$$ | FRENCH FUSION | Chef-owner William Kovel's simple, approachable French-American cuisine translates to dishes like chicken liver mousse, squid ink cavatelli, pan-roasted blue cod, and house-made pastas. The dining room has views of the semi-open kitchen and the atrium with sweeping floor-to-ceiling windows. **Known for:** after-work crowd; huge U-shape bar; modern French dishes. ⑤ *Average main: $30* ☒ *300 Technology Sq., Kendall Square* ☎ *617/576–3000* ⊕ *www.catalystrestaurant.com* ۞ *Closed Sun.* Ⓜ *Kendall.*

Glass House

$$$ | AMERICAN | A nod to East Cambridge's place as the center of the nation's glass-making industry and home to its largest glass factory, Glass House is an eye-catching restaurant that offers tasty American cuisine that delivers a good balance between sea and land (think charred octopus and bone-in rib eye). While the cocktail menu is full of creative drinks and the draft beer selections are strong, the mocktail list is just as impressive, with several fruity and fizzy refreshing drinks. **Known for:** kids

menu; modern twists on classic dishes; Boston Harborfest five-time winner for best clam chowder. $ *Average main: $25* ⊠ *450 Kendall St., Kendall Square* ☏ *617/945–9450* ⊕ *www.glasshouse-cambridge.com* ⊘ *Closed Sat.–Mon.*

★ Helmand

$$$ | AFGHAN | The area's first Afghan restaurant, named after the country's most important river, welcomes you into its cozy Kendall Square confines with Afghan rugs, a wood-burning oven, and exotic, yet extremely approachable food that reflects the motherland's location halfway between the Middle East and India. Standouts, beyond the chewy warm bread, include magical names from a faraway land like *aushak* (leek-stuffed ravioli over yogurt with beef ragu and mint), *chapendaz* (marinated grilled beef tenderloin served with cumin-spiced hot pepper–tomato puree), and a vegetarian baked pumpkin platter. **Known for:** enveloping atmosphere; incredible breads; excellent Afghan fare. $ *Average main: $28* ⊠ *143 1st St., Kendall Square* ☏ *617/492–4646* ⊕ *helmandrestaurant.com* Ⓜ *Lechmere.*

The Lexington at The Shed

$$$ | MODERN AMERICAN | With three foodie destinations under one roof, The Shed is a dining hat trick right in the middle of Cambridge Crossing's Picnic Grove (a new green area in the heart of the city). The Lexington is chef/owner Will Gilson's shining star of the space, serving up dishes that highlight foods from The Herb Lyceum, a four-acre working farm in Groton operated by his family since the 1800s. **Known for:** amazing patio scene; crafty cocktails; fresh ingredients from the chef's family farm. $ *Average main: $25* ⊠ *100 N First St., Kendall Square* ☏ *617/945–1349* ⊕ *thelexingtoncx.com.*

Little Donkey

$$ | FUSION | Dream team James Beard Award–winning chef-owners Jamie Bissonnette and Ken Oringer (of Coppa and Toro fame) serve crazy-good small plates made from big, bold, unexpected combos: think foie gras with bee pollen, *manti* (Istanbul meat ravioli), and Wagyu tartare with caviar. While burgers are indulgent—patties gilded with foie gras—you can also enjoy empanadas with Impossible Burger for plant-based protein, as well as a light and refreshing raw bar. **Known for:** slushy and boozy drinks; fun atmosphere; bold-flavored small plates. $ *Average main: $22* ⊠ *505 Massachusetts Ave., Central Square* ☏ *617/945–1008* ⊕ *www.littledonkeybos.com.*

★ Oleana

$$$ | MEDITERRANEAN | With two restaurants (including Sofra in Cambridge) and two cookbooks to her name, chef-owner Ana Sortun continues to bewitch area diners with her intricately spiced eastern Mediterranean mezes (small plates) made with fresh-picked produce from her husband's nearby Siena Farms. Oleana's menu changes often, but look for the hot, crispy-fried mussels starter and Sultan's Delight (tamarind-glazed beef with smoky eggplant puree) along with large plates of Iskender lamb kebab and lemon chicken. **Known for:** mouthwatering small plates; deft use of spices; eastern Mediterranean menu. $ *Average main: $27* ⊠ *134 Hampshire St., Central Square* ☏ *617/661–0505* ⊕ *www.oleanarestaurant.com* Ⓜ *Central.*

Pammy's

$$$$ | MODERN ITALIAN | Perched between Central and Harvard Squares, this New American trattoria was created by husband and wife team Chris and Pam Willis. The rulebook goes out the window here as the menu takes traditional Italian flavors and turns them on their tails in a prix-fixe menu (à la carte is available only in the bar/lounge area), with items like Hiramasa crudo, 45-day–aged steak tartare, and sablefish with forbidden rice at the ready. **Known for:** prix-fixe menu only; strong cocktail program; unexpected flavor combos. $ *Average*

*main: $69 ⊠ 928 Massachusetts Ave.,
Central Square ☎ 617/945–1761 ⊕ www.
pammyscambridge.com ☽ Closed Sun.
☞ Walk-ins welcome in lounge area;
reservations required for dining prix-fixe
menu* Ⓜ *Central Square.*

☕ Coffee and Quick Bites

All Star Sandwich Bar

$ | AMERICAN | This brightly colored
place with about a dozen tables turns
out fresh, high-quality sandwiches and
burgers, all served with coleslaw, dill
pickle, and a smile. Beyond multiple beef
burgers, you'll find classics like crispy,
overstuffed Reubens, the Pastraminator,
and the famous Atomic Meatloaf Melt-
down, which has been highlighted on a
number of foodie networks. **Known for:**
creative combinations; simple setting;
chef-quality sandwiches. $ *Average
main: $14 ⊠ 1245 Cambridge St., Central
Square ☎ 617/868–3065 ⊕ www.allstar-
sandwichbar.com* Ⓜ *Central.*

Cafe Luna

$$ | AMERICAN | This Cambridge hot spot
is locally loved, which means there
are usually long waiting times but the
breakfast and lunch menus are worth
it. The omelet menu is far beyond your
basic egg and cheese, with combos such
as fig, prosciutto, and goat cheese, and
there's cinnamon swirl French toast, their
20-hour slow-cooked corned beef hash,
and the signature eggs Benedict. **Known
for:** slow-cooked corned beef; crowded
college scene; epic omelets. $ *Aver-
age main: $20 ⊠ 612 Main St., Kendall
Square ☎ 617/576–3400 ⊕ cafeluna-cen-
tralsq.com* Ⓜ *Kendall/MIT.*

Dado Tea

$ | CAFÉ | FAMILY | Named after the art of
the tea ceremony, the new-age feel to
this spacious outpost starts with organic
teas and coffee (displayed in canisters
behind the counter) and extends to
hearty meal options such as hot noodle
soup, cold noodle salads, multigrain

rice bowls, wraps, vegan dishes, and
smoothies. Linger over free Wi-Fi. **Known
for:** noodle bowls; bubble teas; loose leaf
organic teas. $ *Average main: $7 ⊠ 955
Massachusetts Ave., Harvard Square
☎ 617/497–9061 ⊕ www.dadotea.com
☽ No dinner* Ⓜ *Harvard.*

Toscanini's Ice Cream

$ | CAFÉ | If you're looking for serious ice
cream, head to Toscanini's. With flavors
such as gingersnap molasses, bourbon,
cranberry goat cheese, burnt caramel,
and green tea, this MIT establishment
has few equals, especially when it comes
to their microsundae—a teeny scoop
of ice cream topped with excellent
homemade hot fudge and real whipped
cream—a perfect option for kids and
adults eager for a guilt-free splurge (well,
almost). **Known for:** coffee drinks; unique
flavors; excellent homemade ice cream.
$ *Average main: $5 ⊠ 159 1st St.,
Central Square ☎ 617/491–5877 ⊕ www.
tosci.com ☽ Closed Mon. and Tues.*

🛏 Hotels

Boston Marriott Cambridge

$$$ | HOTEL | Traveling businesspeople
and families like the modern look and
efficiency of this 26-story high-rise hotel
in Kendall Square, mere steps from the
subway and MIT. **Pros:** top-floor rooms
have stunning views; on-site Starbucks;
24-hour fitness center. **Cons:** no dining
options; lots of business travelers and
people with children; has the "chain
hotel" feel. $ *Rooms from: $300 ⊠ 2
Cambridge Center, 50 Broadway, Kendall
Square ☎ 617/494–6600, 888/228–9290
⊕ www.marriotthotels.com/boscb � 444
rooms* ⑩ *No Meals* Ⓜ *Kendall/MIT.*

The Kendall Hotel

$$ | HOTEL | You might think a place in
such a high-tech neighborhood would
be all stainless steel and chrome; think
again: the Queen Anne–style Kendall
Hotel is homey and ultrafriendly, bright-
hued and lively—and it's convenient, with

a T stop just one block away. **Pros:** quiet rooms thanks to sound-proof windows; free Wi-Fi, hot Fireman's Gourmet buffet breakfast, and passes to local gyms; welcome snacks and nightly reception. **Cons:** no swimming pool; can feel cramped; crowded with tchotchkes. $ *Rooms from: $279* ⊠ *350 Main St., Kendall Square* ☎ *617/577–1300, 866/566–1300* ⊕ *www.kendallhotel.com* ⊃ *77 rooms* ¶⊙¶ *Free Breakfast* Ⓜ *Kendall/MIT.*

Kimpton Marlowe Hotel
$$$ | **HOTEL** | As you enter the private courtyard set back from bustling Kendall Square, say "hello" to Celeste, a 25-foot-tall armillary sculpture that serves as a centerpiece surrounded by plush couches that fill up in the evenings for live music and cocktails. **Pros:** family- and pet-friendly; wine tastings; music in the courtyard. **Cons:** amenity fee; short walk required to get to nearby non-chain restaurants; must request items like in-room Keurigs. $ *Rooms from: $349* ⊠ *25 Edwin H. Land Blvd., Cambridge* ☎ *617/868–8000, 800/825–7140* ⊕ *www.hotelmarlowe.com* ⊃ *237 rooms* ¶⊙¶ *No Meals* Ⓜ *Lechmere.*

Le Méridien Cambridge
$$ | **HOTEL** | When the Marriott chain took over the geek-chic Le Méridien Cambridge-MIT, with its tech-savvy rooms and surroundings, some fans worried the Cambridge spot would lose its charm; but the new owners only amped up the offerings—and added some luxe touches—by displaying cool interactive lobby art from MIT and refurbishing the guest rooms with platform beds, puffy white duvets, flat-screen TVs, and ergonomically designed furniture. **Pros:** pet-friendly up to two dogs per room; close to the T (Red Line Central) and restaurants; 24-hour fitness center. **Cons:** tons of tech people; not really walkable to Boston sights; pricey high-season rates. $ *Rooms from: $219* ⊠ *20 Sidney St., Kendall Square* ☎ *617/577–0200, 800/543–4300* ⊕ *www.lemeridien.com/*

cambridge ⊃ *210 rooms* ¶⊙¶ *No Meals* Ⓜ *Central, Kendall/MIT.*

★ The Royal Sonesta Boston
$$$ | **HOTEL** | **FAMILY** | Right next to the Charles River, the certified-green Sonesta has one of the best city skylines and sunset views in Boston. **Pros:** walk to the Museum of Science and the T to Downtown Boston; pet-friendly; nice pool and fitness center with Peloton. **Cons:** river-view guest rooms have much better view than Cambridge-view rooms; no air-conditioning in rooms; pay parking. $ *Rooms from: $379* ⊠ *40 Edwin Land Blvd., off Memorial Dr., Kendall Square* ☎ *617/806–4200, 800/766–3782* ⊕ *www.sonesta.com/boston* ⊃ *400 rooms* ¶⊙¶ *No Meals* Ⓜ *Lechmere.*

🍸 Nightlife

BARS
Cambridge Brewing Company
BREWPUBS | This collegial, cavernous microbrewery is the oldest brew pub in the greater Boston area and has been the happy haunt for MIT techies and craft-brew geeks since its 1989 founding. They push the boundaries of beer, from bourbon barrel-aging an imperial stout to creating the first true solera aging process in the United States for beer. Order CBC's Cambridge Amber, Charles River Porter, and Blunderbuss Barleywine fresh in pints, or go for a "tower" (an 83-ounce glass "yard"). In warm weather, try to nab a coveted patio table, a catbird seat for people-watching across bricky Kendall Square. Cheerful staff serve above-average pub grub, even at weekend "beerunches." ⊠ *1 Kendall Sq., Bldg. 100, at Hampshire St. and Broadway, Kendall Square* ☎ *617/494–1994* ⊕ *www.cambridgebrewingcompany.com* Ⓜ *Kendall/MIT.*

The Druid
BREWPUBS | You can feel like you're in Dublin here, sipping well-poured pints, eyeing the dusky atmosphere with wood

paneled walls, and eating black-and-white pudding or rib eye roasted in Guinness. Musicians jam Wednesday evening, Saturday late day, and Sunday afternoon. ✉ *1357 Cambridge St., Inman Square* ☎ *617/497–0965* ⊕ *www.druidpub.com* Ⓜ *Central, Harvard.*

★ Middlesex

DANCE CLUBS | For those looking to avoid Boston's ultra-sceney clubs, Middlesex is a welcoming, laid-back club for all sorts of people looking to dance the night away. Rolling settees, movable in varied seating configurations for trivia, games, and sports nights, are usually cleared by 9 pm, when a $10 cover kicks in for DJs spinning crowd-pleasing EDM and hip-hop. Feed on small plates and pressed sandwiches. The lounge is only open Thursday through Saturday, 5 pm–2 am. ✉ *315 Massachusetts Ave., Central Square* ☎ *617/714–4831* ⊕ *msexcambridge.com* Ⓜ *Central.*

The Plough & Stars

BREWPUBS | This genuine Irish pub has doubled as a bohemian oasis since 1969. Drink Guinness and Bass on tap and many Irish whiskies; hear light rock, Irish, or country music nightly, usually by 10:30 pm. Narrow and cozy, The Plough is a comfy, noisy den for locals and students, yet a fine place to have lunch alone. The cover charge varies, but the popular weekday beer and burger specials remain the same. Fun fact: literary magazine *Ploughshares* was founded here. ✉ *912 Massachusetts Ave., Central Square* ☎ *617/576–0032* ⊕ *www. ploughandstars.com* Ⓜ *Central, Harvard.*

COMEDY CLUBS
ImprovBoston

COMEDY CLUBS | This Central Square venue flips audience cues into situation comedy, complete with theme songs and commercials. Be careful when you go to the restroom—you might be pulled onstage. Performers may face off in improv competitions judged by audiences. Shows run Wednesday through Sunday, $15 to $25, at The Rockwell theater in Davis Square (with a full bar). ✉ *620 Mass. Ave, Suite 6, Central Square* ☎ *617/576–1253* ⊕ *www.improvboston.com* Ⓜ *Central.*

MUSIC CLUBS
Havana Club

DANCE CLUBS | Overlooking Central Square, this 5,400-square-foot ballroom dance floor hosts a kaleidoscope of DJs and live bands, and often free burritos or nachos. Three hundred people may show up to dance salsa, creating a lively scene for dancers at any level. Open Monday is for bachata (sultry midtempo Dominican dance), Friday and Saturday for salsa, and Tuesday blends both. With lessons at 8 or 9 pm, depending on the night, the joint really gets hopping by 9 or 10 pm. ✉ *288 Green St., Central Square* ☎ *617/312–5550* ⊕ *www.havanaclubsalsa.com* Ⓜ *Central.*

🎭 Performing Arts

DANCE
The Dance Complex

MODERN DANCE | Performances (and classes and workshops) by local and visiting choreographers take place at Odd Fellows Hall, an intimate space that draws a multicultural crowd within its seven studios. Styles range from classical ballet to contemporary and world dance, beginner street dance moves to advanced hip-hop. Occasionally, when weather permits, performers take to the streets for fun pop-up outdoor sets. ✉ *536 Massachusetts Ave., Central Square* ☎ *617/547–9363* ⊕ *www.dancecomplex.org* Ⓜ *Central.*

Global Arts Live

MODERN DANCE | As the metro area's premier presenter of worldwide music and dance, Global Arts Live has a truly global roster featuring exciting contemporary artists in their Boston debuts (like The Bad Plus and Freshlyground), as well as world music icons, such as South Africa's Ladysmith Black Mambazo and Ireland's Mary Black. Performances unfold at many venues, such as Brighton Music Hall, the Berklee Performance Center, The Sinclair, Somerville Theatre, and the Emerson Cutler Majestic Theatre. ✉ *720 Massachusetts Ave., Central Square* ☎ *617/876–4275* ⊕ *www.worldmusic.org* Ⓜ *Central.*

Multicultural Arts Center

ARTS CENTERS | The MAC in East Cambridge supports diversity within the performing arts, engaging with the community through jazz, dance, and visiting programs. The two spacious galleries showcase international visual arts, and the theater itself is a showstopper with ornate Victorian details and theater lighting. Galleries are open Tuesday to Friday from 10 am to 6 pm (Wednesday until 8pm), and free performances are held throughout the year, including outdoor summer programming at nearby Centanni Park. ✉ *41 2nd St., Cambridge* ☎ *617/577–1400* ⊕ *www.multiculturalartscenter.org* Ⓜ *Lechmere.*

FILM
Landmark's Kendall Square Cinema

FILM | This newly remodeled cinema's nine screens are devoted to first-run independent, avant-garde, and foreign films, and the concession stand offers hip goodies like coffee, empanadas, and homemade cookies. Their Kendall Bar now serves beer and wine. ■TIP➔ **1 Kendall Square stands where Hampshire Street meets Broadway, a 10-minute walk from the Kendall Square T station. Validated four-hour parking ($3) is available in an adjacent garage. If you're walking, be advised the area can get a bit desolate at night.** ✉ *1 Kendall Sq., Cambridge* ☎ *617/621–1202* ⊕ *www.landmarktheatres.com* ✉ *Tickets from $7* Ⓜ *Kendall/MIT.*

🛍 Shopping

Kendall and Central Squares have an eclectic mix of furniture stores, thrift shops, used-record stores, ethnic restaurants, and small, hip performance

venues. The best word to describe the area is bohemian at its best.

ANTIQUES
Cambridge Antique Market

ANTIQUES & COLLECTIBLES | Off the beaten track, this antiques hot spot has a selection bordering on overwhelming: five floors of goods from more than 150 dealers ranging from 19th-century furniture to vintage clothing, much of it reasonably priced. You can find everything from collectible magazines to China dolls, art work to fine silver. Head to the basement for a large selection of secondhand bikes. ✉ *201 Monsignor O'Brien Hwy., Cambridge* ☎ *617/868–9655* ⊕ *www.marketantique.com* Ⓜ *Lechmere.*

CLOTHING
The Garment District

OUTLET | Step into this warehouse-like building through the famous pink door and head to the second level to find a massive selection of vintage, used, and new clothing and accessories. Boston Costume, the sister business on the first floor, draws thrift pickers to the back room to paw through an 850-pound bale of clothes that's dumped on the floor each day (twice on Saturday and Sunday); items are sold for $2 per pound. Students crowd the entire store year-round, and everyone comes at Halloween for that perfect costume. They're also known for their vintage wears, dating back to the '50s for as retro as you please. ✉ *200 Broadway, Kendall Square* ☎ *617/876–5230* ⊕ *www.garment-district.com* Ⓜ *Kendall/MIT.*

Somerville

Just north of Cambridge lies Somerville, New England's most densely populated city. There is always something to see and do, as its eclectic mix of families, young professionals, and students will attest. Somerville is defined by its city squares, the most active of which are the expansive Davis and Union, Ball, and Magoun. Each offers a mix of ethnic restaurants, bars and shops, and small businesses to fit every taste and occasion. The latest center of art and industry is Assembly Row, a live-work-play urban environment along the Mystic River that has become a destination for even Bostonians typically hesitant to cross the Charles River. The ever-changing landscape seems to be bursting with new development every month.

◉ Sights

Assembly Row

NEIGHBORHOOD | What was once large barren fields and the former home of a Ford Assembly Plant is now a thriving destination neighborhood along the Mystic River. Assembly Row is an open-air community of live-work-play spaces all connected by waterfront walkways and parks. Retail abounds, with stores like the area's only Saks Off Fifth, Puma, Brooks Brothers, a J. Crew outlet, and more. For entertainment, check out the AMC movie theater, the famed LEGOLAND Discovery Center, and Lucky Strike, a 36,000-square-foot space with dining, bowling, games, and floor shuffleboard on the first floor and an island bar on the second.

There are 31 restaurants at Assembly, including the trendy River Bar (noted for its year-round fire pits), casual noodles and sake at Fuji, and award-winning barbecue at The Smoke Shop. The five-in-one fitness studio FitRow has you covered for whatever workout you desire, from boxing to cycling to pilates. Also here is the Row Hotel at Assembly Row, a boutique hotel with some of the best interior design around. ⊠ *355 Artisan Way, Somerville ⊕ assemblyrow.com* Ⓜ *Assembly.*

Bow Market

MARKET | FAMILY | Once a storage building, today's Bow Market provides small-scale storefronts to both established

and aspiring chefs, retailers, and artists from Somerville and Greater Boston. An afternoon is well spent among the 25 independent food, art, and retail shops set around a public courtyard in the heart of Union Square. Saus, maca, and Nibble Kitchen are just a few of the eateries, while shopping goes global with one-of-a-kind gifts at retailers including vintage records at Vinyl Index and artisanal Japanese arts and crafts at Crane & Turtle. On any given day, there could be a pop-up event like a book fair, jewelry shops, Etsy spotlights, and oysterfests. Grab a pint (or a freshly roasted Barrington coffee) at the market's Remnant Brewery, which boasts a garage door that opens whenever the weather permits. ⊠ *1 Bow Market Way, Somerville ⊕ bowmarketsomerville. com.*

LEGOLAND Discovery Center Boston

THEME PARK | FAMILY | Look for the giant Lego giraffe and you've found this mecca for building-block enthusiasts. There are more than 10 Build & Play Zones, including The LEGO City Indoor Play Zone, which is full of energy-expending climbing walls, slides, a jungle gym, and the Duplo Farm, which is perfect for tiny tots to spend some quiet discovery and building time. The 4-D Cinema brings LEGO movies to life with additional wind, rain, and snow effects, while the indoor rides and virtual reality experiences add in a little more interactive fun. Discover iconic Boston attractions and local buildings all made entirely out of LEGO bricks in the infamous MINILAND attraction that used more than 1.5 million. ⊠ *598 Assembly Row, Somerville ☎ 866/228–6439 ⊕ boston.legolanddiscoverycenter.com.*

🍴 Restaurants

Just 2 miles north of Boston, Somerville is known for its eclectic mix of students, families, and indie musicians, all of whom help inform the hip restaurant scene here, which centers on Davis and Union Squares. In addition to Spanish,

Somerville

Sights ▶

1 Assembly Row..................G1
2 Bow Market....................E3
3 LEGOLAND Discovery
  Center Boston................G1

Restaurants ▶

1 Boston Burger
  Company.......................B1
2 Bronwyn........................E3
3 Posto.............................B1
4 Redbones.......................B1
5 Rosebud American
  Kitchen & Bar................B1
6 Sarma............................E2

Quick Bites ▶

1 Diesel Cafe....................B1
2 Gracie's..........................E3
3 J.P. Licks........................B1
4 Mr. Crêpe.......................B1

Hotels ▶

1 The Row Hotel at
  Assembly Row...............G1

KEY

- ❶ Sights
- ❶ Restaurants
- ❶ Quick Bites
- ❶ Hotels
- 🚇 Subway station

Haitian, and Brazilian eateries, you'll find burger joints, barbecue, and tacos, along with a new sort of place—second restaurants from Boston's star chefs.

Boston Burger Company

$ | **BURGER** | When a basic burger won't do, this Davis Square dive satisfies. It's go big or go somewhere else thanks to thick patties covered in crazy toppings, such as the Artery Clogger (a deep-fried, beer-battered burger topped with bacon, cheese, and barbecue sauce) or the Mac Attack (four-cheese mac and cheese, plus bacon). **Known for:** thick, juicy burgers; huge milkshakes; fries with creative toppings. $ *Average main: $15 ⊠ 37 Davis Sq., Somerville* ☎ *617/440–7361* ⊕ *www.bostonburgercompany.com* Ⓜ *Davis Square.*

Bronwyn

$$$ | **GERMAN** | Harkening back to his German heritage, chef-owner Tim Wiechmann and his wife, Bronwyn, the restaurant's namesake, have brought a rib-sticking yet sophisticated taste of Central and Eastern Europe to Union Square. The menu here includes juicy hand-stuffed pork sausages served with powerfully seasoned sauces, hearty dumplings, noodle dishes (try the spaetzle with cheddar), the best wurst trio, Hirsch goulash, and sauerbraten. **Known for:** excellent beer list; medieval manor-like setting; hearty German specialties. $ *Average main: $25 ⊠ 255 Washington St., Somerville* ☎ *617/776–9900* ⊕ *www.bronwynrestaurant.com* ⊟ *No credit cards* ⊘ *Closed Mon. No lunch Sun.–Fri.*

★ Posto

$$$ | **ITALIAN** | A central wood-burning oven at this Davis Square spot churns out more than a dozen varieties of excellent tomato and "white" bubble-crusted pies (try the wood-fired apple, caramelized onions, fontina cheese, and gorgonzola pizza), while the kitchen crafts scrumptious starters and mains, like "nonna" meatballs, gnocchi with beef short ribs, and shrimp scampi. The central brick and glass-walled dining room (with sidewalk seating during fair weather) fills nightly, as this eatery succeeds at blending a classic Italian pizzeria, *enoteca*, and trattoria all together in a "farm chic" open-air concept. **Known for:** a huge variety of "white" pies; cheerful environment; wood-fired Italian cuisine. $ *Average main: $25 ⊠ 187 Elm St., Somerville* ☎ *617/625–0600* ⊕ *www.postoboston. com* ⊟ *No credit cards* ⊘ *No lunch.*

Redbones

$$ | **BARBECUE** | Weekend lines out the door of Redbones can only mean one thing: you're about to hit the epicenter of barbecue in Somerville. Piled high on plates since 1987, Redbones's meat-heavy menu has a dedicated following for its pulled pork and chicken, sliced brisket, and chopped burnt ends. **Known for:** funky vibe; good beer selection; authentic Southern barbecue. $ *Average main: $20 ⊠ 55 Chester St., Somerville* ☎ *617/628–2200* ⊕ *redbones.com* ⊘ *Closed Mon.* Ⓜ *Davis Square.*

Rosebud American Kitchen & Bar

$$ | **DINER** | Housed inside Davis Square's landmark renovated Worcester Lunch Car with neon aplenty, Rosebud is Americana realized: tufted booths, counter swivel stools, an old-fashioned diner vibe, and classic dishes with a few global surprises. Breakfast diners can't go wrong with the chicken and waffle combo or the "plain Jane" pancakes, while the dinner crowd enjoys dishes including pork shoulder rigatoni, Nashville hot chicken, house mac and cheese, and rice bowls. **Known for:** old-timey diner dishes; boozy milkshakes; seats inside an actual railcar. $ *Average main: $19 ⊠ 381 Summer St., Somerville* ☎ *617/629–9500* ⊕ *rosebudkitchen.com* Ⓜ *Davis Square.*

★ Sarma

$$$ | **MEDITERRANEAN** | The small meze plates at this locally loved Mediterranean joint are so good you might not want to share. Pair dishes like squash blossom *tiropita* (cheese pie) and lamb *manti*

(dumplings) with their expertly crafted cocktails or wine, and soak up the social atmosphere. **Known for:** excellent meze; Black Sea cornbread; vibrant, colorful decor. ⑤ *Average main: $30* ⊠ *249 Pearl St., Boston* ⊹ *Somerville* ☎ *617/764-4464* ⊕ *www.sarmarestaurant.com* Ⓜ *02145.*

☕ Coffee and Quick Bites

Diesel Cafe

$ | **CAFÉ** | Known as Somerville's "refueling station," this bright, window-y spot just got a new look but still boasts a retro vibe, bold local artwork, and spacious tables that draw in Davis Square hipsters, Tufts students, and LGBTQ+ sets. Be part of the rebel crowd over veggie-friendly fare, crafted salads, soups, wraps, house-made pastries, and gourmet coffee with tasty house-made syrups in flavors like turmeric, caramel, and vanilla. **Known for:** coffee drinks; local hangout; industrial no-nonsense vibe. ⑤ *Average main: $5* ⊠ *257 Elm St., Somerville* ☎ *617/629-8717* ⊕ *www. diesel-cafe.com* Ⓜ *Davis.*

Gracie's

$ | **CAFÉ** | This snow-white shop in Union Square makes microbatches of ice cream daily and serves it, if you wish, in a torched marshmallow-cream–lined cone. There are six All the Time Flavors (chocolate, sweet cream, black raspberry chip, mint chip, cookies and cream, salty whiskey) and six Sometimes Flavors. **Known for:** tiny location; dairy-free option available; daily-made creative ice creams. ⑤ *Average main: $5* ⊠ *22 Union Sq., Somerville* ☎ *617/764-5294* ⊕ *www. icecreamgracies.com.*

J.P. Licks

$ | **CAFÉ** | Vince Petryk started this Boston ice cream institution back in 1981, and today, there are 17 locations in and around Boston. With all their ice cream made in-house and kosher, J.P. Licks is most well-known for inventive flavors, such as Unicorn Crunch cake batter

with edible sequins and Cinnamon Toast Crunch. **Known for:** their own roasted coffee; Lixwiches ice cream cookie sandwiches; creative ice cream flavors. ⑤ *Average main: $5* ⊠ *4A College Ave., Somerville* ☎ *617/666–5079* ⊕ *www. jplicks.com* Ⓜ *Davis Square.*

Mr. Crêpe

$ | **CAFÉ** | Since 1999, this unpretentious, quick-serve creperie and café in the heart of Davis Square has been a local favorite. For the savory set, ingredients are layered together (think grilled veggies, fresh cheeses, and crispy greens), wrapped in very thin pancakes, and heated until warm and toasty. **Known for:** relaxed counter service; homemade soups; tasty crepes. ⑤ *Average main: $13* ⊠ *51 Davis Sq., Somerville* ☎ *617/623–0661* ⊕ *www. mrcrepe.com* Ⓜ *Davis Square.*

🛏️ Hotels

The Row Hotel at Assembly Row

$$$ | **HOTEL** | Part of Marriott's Autograph Collection, The Row's elegant calm pays homage to its past life as a Ford Motor Assembly Plant. **Pros:** 15 minutes by T from Boston and right next to Assembly Row; a communal pantry with ILLY coffee, tea, water, and snacks; wellness center with pool and on-demand fitness. **Cons:** busy scene; rooms can be loud; limited storage in standard rooms. ⑤ *Rooms from: $399* ⊠ *360 Foley St., Somerville* ☎ *617/628–1300* ⊕ *www. therowhotelatassemblyrow.com* ⇥ *158 rooms* ⊚ *No Meals.*

🍸 Nightlife

Once marginal, crowded Somerville is now very cool. Look at Davis Square: a hub for the T and bike paths, the square's alive with cafés, clubs, and a theater. It's a prime location for students and young thinkers to gather.

BARS
Backbar
BARS | If you can find the entrance to this tiny bar in Union Square, you'll be rewarded with top-notch cocktails from an ever-changing themed menu, plus bar bites and plenty of cool vibes. ⊠ *7 Sanborn Ct., Somerville, Boston* ☎ *617/249-3522* ⊕ *www.backbarunion. com* ☽ *Closed Mon.* Ⓜ *Union Square.*

★ The Burren
BARS | Your true-emerald Irish music pub pulls in devoted locals and all fans of *craic* (enjoyable environment). Enthusiastic staff and professional bartenders expertly pour Guinness on tap and serve comfort food (some of the best fish-and-chips in the area, bangers and mash, Irish stew, shepherd's pie). Dark decor, a tiny sunny west-facing patio, an old-wood library bar, and slate specials add to the allure of live Irish music—acoustic groups—most nights in both the Front and Back Rooms. ⊠ *247 Elm St., Somerville* ☎ *617/776–6896* ⊕ *www.burren.com* Ⓜ *Davis.*

The Independent
BARS | In Somerville's Union Square, this comfortable neighborhood bar is a good spot to hit for a pint, a whiskey-based cocktail with a quaint name, quality brews (20 drafts, 15 bottles), and a long listing of spirits that come together for a mad menu of house cocktails. ⊠ *75 Union Sq., Somerville* ☎ *617/440–6022* ⊕ *www.theindo.com* Ⓜ *Bus 86, 87, 91, CT2.*

Sacco's Bowl Haven
BOWLING | The '50s decor here "makes bowling the way it was, the way it is" in the heart of Davis Square. Its 10 lanes are open daily until 11 pm (10 pm Sunday, Monday, and Tuesday), and cost $30 per hour; there's a $4 fee to rent shoes. You can bowl away and enjoy pizza. ⊠ *45 Day St., Somerville* ☎ *617/776–0552* ⊕ *americanflatbread.com/locations/ somerville-ma.*

Trina's Starlite Lounge
BARS | Inventive cocktails wash down Southern comfort grub at this hip, retro joint packed with a younger crowd. The original drinks are just that—original—with concoctions like Nicolas Sage (gin, matcha, ginger sage syrup, and lemon) and the Fallen Angel (a spicy mango margarita with a barbecue-dusted rim). Their buttermilk fried chicken is well loved, and the mac and cheese with Ritz crackers and hot dogs is your new guilty pleasure. ⊠ *3 Beacon St., Somerville* ☎ *617/576–0006.*

Performing Arts

THEATER
★ Somerville Theatre
CONCERTS | What started as a vaudeville stage and movie house continues to cement itself as a keystone of Davis Square's growing culture through films and live entertainment (believe it or not, The Boss, Adele, and U2 have all played here). The 900-seat, five-screen theater recently celebrated its centennial and continues to delight with special evening events like silent movies set to live music as well as beloved film festivals. In the coffered-ceiling, stone-tiled foyer you may buy beer, wine, popcorn, and ice cream to enjoy during the show, whether it's a new release or an oldie but goodie. ⊠ *55 Davis Sq., Somerville* ☎ *617/625–5700* ⊕ *www.somervilletheatre.com* Ⓜ *Davis.*

Chapter 12

SIDE TRIPS FROM BOSTON

12

Updated by
Kim Foley MacKinnon

⊙ Sights	🍴 Restaurants	🛏 Hotels	🛍 Shopping	🍸 Nightlife
★★★★★	★★★★☆	★★★★☆	★★★★☆	★★★★☆

WELCOME TO SIDE TRIPS FROM BOSTON

TOP REASONS TO GO

★ **Early American history:** From Plymouth to Salem, Concord, and Lexington, you can visit colonial-reenactment museums, Revolutionary War battle sites, historic homes, and inns.

★ **Seafaring communities:** Set off on a whale-watch from Gloucester, warm yourself after a windy coastal walk in Rockport with clam chowder, and admire the dedicated routine of local fishermen.

★ **Literary heritage:** Nathaniel Hawthorne's House of the Seven Gables still stands in Salem. Liberate yourself with a swim in Thoreau's Walden Pond. In Concord, see where both Louisa May Alcott and Ralph Waldo Emerson penned their works.

★ **Cranberry bogs:** The bogs' red, green, gold, and blue colors dot Cape Cod and the Plymouth area.

★ **The *Mayflower II:*** The story of the Pilgrims' Atlantic crossing comes alive in Plymouth.

Visit Concord and Lexington and that history class from high school may suddenly come rushing back to you. The state's coast from Boston to Cape Ann is called the North Shore, visited for its beaches, quintessential New England seaside communities, and bewitching Salem. South of Boston lies more history in Plymouth and seaside scenery at Cape Cod.

1 **Lexington.** Where the British and the upstart colonists first fought.

2 **Concord.** A literary hot spot, Emerson, the Alcotts, and Thoreau all lived in Concord.

3 **Gloucester.** America's oldest seaport still has a vibrant harbor.

4 **Salem.** Famous for witches, writers, and the seafaring trade.

5 **Rockport.** Calling to artists for centuries, this scenic town is stunning.

6 **Plymouth.** Learn all about the Pilgrims' journey at several museums and memorials.

7 **Provincetown.** This town at the tip of the Cape Cod is a colorful spot for a day trip.

History lies thick on the ground in the towns surrounding Boston—from Pilgrims to pirates, witches to whalers, the American Revolution to the Industrial Revolution. The sights outside the city are at least as interesting as those on Boston's Freedom Trail. When you're ready to trade history lessons for beach fun, Cape Cod to the south and the North Shore to the northeast entice sand-and-sun seekers.

Rich in more than history, the areas surrounding Boston also allow visitors to retrace the steps of famous writers, bask in the outdoors, and browse shops in funky artist communities. The haunts of literary luminaries of every generation lurk throughout Massachusetts. Head to Concord to visit the place where Henry David Thoreau wrote his prophetic *Walden* and where Louisa May Alcott's *Little Women* brightened a grim time during the Civil War. Relive Nathaniel Hawthorne's vision of Puritan-era Salem.

The seaside towns of Massachusetts were built before the Revolution, during the heyday of American shipping. On the North Shore, Gloucester is the country's oldest seaport and Rockport has artists' studios and seafood spots. South of Boston, you'll find Plymouth and the *Mayflower II* and the town of Province-town on the tip of Cape Cod.

In a more contemporary vein, Boston and its suburbs have become a major destination for food and wine lovers.

Internationally acclaimed chefs, including Barbara Lynch, Tiffany Faison, and Ming Tsai, draw thousands of devoted, discerning foodies to their restaurants each year. The state's extensive system of parks, protected forests, beaches, and nature preserves satisfies everyone from the avid hiker to the beach bum.

MAJOR REGIONS
Northwest of Boston, Lexington and **Concord** embody the spirit of the American Revolution. Sites of the first skirmishes of the Revolutionary War, these two quintessential New England towns were also cradles of American literature; several historic homes and small museums here are dedicated to some of the country's first substantial writers—Ralph Waldo Emerson, Nathaniel Hawthorne, Louisa May Alcott, and Henry David Thoreau.

The slice of Massachusetts' Atlantic Coast known as the **North Shore** extends past Boston to the picturesque Cape Ann region just shy of the New Hampshire border. In addition to miles of woods and

Northwest of Boston

beaches, the North Shore's highlights include **Salem,** which thrives on a history of witches, writers, and maritime trades; **Gloucester,** the oldest seaport in America; and **Rockport,** rich with crafts shops and artists' studios. Bustling during the short summer season and breathtaking during the autumn foliage, the North Shore is calmer (and colder) between November and June. Since many restaurants, inns, and attractions operate on reduced hours, it's worth calling ahead off-season.

South of Boston will help you gain insight into what the earliest American settlers experienced. In **Plymouth,** learn how the Pilgrims raised food, built their homes, and survived under harsh conditions at Plimoth Patuxet Museums. As you may guess, November in Plymouth brings special events focused on Thanksgiving. And don't forget vacation-central: Cape Cod! **Provincetown,** on the tip of the Cape, is only 90 minutes by ferry from Boston.

Planning

When to Go

The dazzling foliage and cool temperatures make fall one of the best times to visit Massachusetts. Summer, especially late in the season when the water is a bit warmer, is ideal for beach vacations. Many towns save their best for winter—inns open their doors to carolers, shops serve eggnog, and lobster boats parade around Gloucester Harbor.

Budgeting Your Time

Though Massachusetts is relatively small, you can easily spend several weeks exploring it. If you have a few days, head to a town or two north and south of Boston, such as Concord, Plymouth, and Salem. With a week you may want to spend the entire time relaxing "down the Cape."

Getting Here and Around

AIR

Boston's Logan International Airport is the state's major airport. Trains, ferries, and small commuter flights take you to points around the state. If you're driving to Cape Cod, try to avoid the Friday late-afternoon-to-early-evening summer rush.

BOAT

Though Martha's Vineyard, Nantucket, and Cape Cod aren't covered in this chapter (except for Provincetown), they are popular getaway destinations from Boston. High-speed ferries provide transportation to Martha's Vineyard and Nantucket. The Bay State Cruise Co. and City Experiences by Hornblower run 90-minute ferry rides between Boston and Cape Cod's Provincetown from May through October; reservations are strongly recommended. For details on what to see and do in these destinations, see *Fodor's New England*.

CONTACTS Bay State Cruise Co.
☎ *877/783–3779* ⊕ *www.baystate-cruisecompany.com*. **Boston Harbor Cruises.** ✉ *Long Wharf, 1 Seaport La., Boston* ☎ *877/733–9425, 617/227–4321, 877/733–9425* ⊕ *www.bostonharbor-cruises.com*.

CAR

Outside Boston you need a car to explore the state. Expect heavy traffic heading in and out of the city at rush hour, generally from 6 am to 9 am and 4 pm to 7 pm.

From Boston to Lexington, pick up Route 2 West in Cambridge. Exit at Routes 4/225. Turn left on Massachusetts Avenue for the National Heritage Museum. For Lexington's town center, take the Waltham Street–Lexington exit from Route 2. Follow Waltham Street just under 2 miles to Massachusetts Avenue; you'll be just east of the Battle Green. The drive takes about 30 minutes. To continue to Concord, head farther west on Route 2. Or take Interstate 90 (the Massachusetts Turnpike) to Interstate 95 North, and then exit at Route 2, heading west. Driving time is 40–45 minutes from Boston.

The primary link between Boston and the North Shore is Route 128, which follows the coast northeast to Gloucester. To pick up Route 128 from Boston, take Interstate 93 North to Interstate 95 North to Route 128. If you stay on Interstate 95, you'll reach Newburyport. From Boston to Salem or Marblehead, follow Route 128 to Route 114 into Salem or continue to Marblehead. Driving from Boston to Salem takes about 35–40 minutes; to Gloucester, about 50–60 minutes.

To get to Plymouth, take the Southeast Expressway Interstate 93 South to Route 3 (toward Cape Cod); Exits 6 and 4 lead to downtown Plymouth and Plimoth Patuxet Museums, respectively. Allow about one hour or so.

TRAIN

The MBTA's commuter rail offers service to Ipswich, Rockport, Salem, and Gloucester. Travel times are usually 70 minutes or less, but times are limited.

CONTACT Massachusetts Bay Transportation Authority. ☎ *800/392–6100, 617/222–3200* ⊕ *www.mbta.com*.

Hotels

Although Boston has everything from luxury hotels to charming bed-and-breakfasts, the signature accommodation outside Boston is the country inn; less extravagant and less expensive are B&B establishments, many of them in private homes. Make reservations well in advance if traveling in the summer or during holidays. Smoking has been banned in all Massachusetts hotels.

HOTEL AND RESTAURANT PRICES

Hotel prices in the reviews are the lowest cost of a standard double room in high season. Restaurant prices in the reviews are the average cost of a main course at dinner, or if dinner is not served, at lunch.

What It Costs in U.S. Dollars

	$	$$	$$$	$$$$
RESTAURANTS				
	under $15	$15–$24	$25–$32	over $32
HOTELS				
	under $150	$150–$225	$226–$325	over $325

Restaurants

Massachusetts invented the fried clam, and it's served in many North Shore restaurants. Creamy clam chowder is another specialty. Eating seafood in the rough—from paper plates in seaside shacks—is a revered local custom. At country inns you'll find traditional New England dinners: double-cut pork chops, rack of lamb, game, local produce, and sometimes even the dubiously glorified New England boiled dinner (corned beef and cabbage with potatoes, carrots, turnips, and other vegetables).

Lexington

16 miles northwest of Boston.

Incensed against the British, American colonials burst into action in Lexington in April 1775. On April 18, patriot leader Paul Revere alerted the town that British soldiers were approaching. The next day, as the British advance troops arrived in Lexington on their march toward Concord, the minutemen were waiting to confront the redcoats in what became the first skirmish of the Revolutionary War.

These first military encounters of the American Revolution are very much a part of present-day Lexington, a modern suburban town that sprawls out from the historic sites near its center. Although the downtown area is generally lively, with ice cream and coffee shops, boutiques, and a great little movie theater, the town becomes especially animated each Patriots' Day (April 19 but celebrated on the third Monday in April), when costume-clad groups re-create the minutemen's battle maneuvers and Paul Revere rides again.

To learn more about the city and the 1775 clash, stop by the **Lexington Visitors Center.**

GETTING HERE AND AROUND

The Massachusetts Bay Transportation Authority (MBTA) operates bus service in the greater Boston area and serves Lexington.

ESSENTIALS

VISITOR INFORMATION Lexington Visitors Center. ⊠ *1605 Massachusetts Ave., Lexington* ☎ *781/862–1450* ⊕ *www. lexingtonchamber.org.*

◉ Sights

Buckman Tavern

HISTORIC SIGHT | While waiting for the arrival of the British on the morning of April 19, 1775, the minutemen gathered at this 1690 tavern. A half-hour tour takes in the tavern's seven rooms, which have been restored to the way they looked in the 1770s. Among the items on display is an old front door with a hole made by a British musket ball. ⊠ *1 Bedford St.,*

Lexington

KEY

① Sights

Sights

1 Buckman Tavern................**F2**
2 Hancock-Clarke
House.........▼........**F1**
3 Lexington Green
National Historic
Landmark................**F2**

▶

4 Minute Man
National
Historical Park.........**B1**
5 Munroe Tavern..........**G2**
6 Scottish Rite
Masonic Museum &
Library................**G2**

0 — 1/2 mi
0 — 1/2 km

← TO CONCORD

deCordova Sculpture
Park and Museum

Lexington ☎ 781/862–3763 ⊕ www. lexingtonhistory.org ☞ $12 ⊗ Closed Mon.–Fri. Dec.–Feb.

Hancock-Clarke House

HISTORIC SIGHT | On April 18, 1775, Paul Revere came here to warn patriots John Hancock and Sam Adams (who were staying at the house while attending the Provincial Congress in nearby Concord) of the advance of British troops. Hancock and Adams, on whose heads the British king had put a price, fled to avoid capture. The house, a parsonage built in 1698, is a 10-minute walk from Lexington Common. Inside is the *Treasures of the Revolution* exhibit, and outside, a colonial herb garden. ⊠ *36 Hancock St., Lexington* ☎ *781/862–3763* ⊕ *www.lexingtonhistory.org* ☞ *$12* ⊗ *Closed Mon.–Fri. Apr.–Memorial Day.*

Lexington Green National Historic Landmark

MILITARY SIGHT | It was on this 2-acre triangle of land, commonly referred to as simply the "Battle Green," on April 19, 1775, that the first confrontation between British soldiers, who were marching from Boston toward Concord, and the colonial militia known as the minutemen took place. The minutemen—so called because they were able to prepare themselves at a moment's notice—were led by Captain John Parker, whose role in the American Revolution is commemorated in Henry Hudson Kitson's renowned 1900 *Minuteman* statue. Facing downtown Lexington at the tip of the Battle Green, the statue is on a traffic island, making for a difficult photo op. ⊠ *Junction of Massachusetts Ave. and Bedford St., Lexington* ⊕ *www.lexingtonma.gov/battle-green* ☞ *Free.*

Minute Man National Historical Park

NATIONAL PARK | FAMILY | West of Lexington's center stretches this 1,000-acre park that also extends into nearby Lincoln and Concord. Begin your park visit at the Minute Man Visitor Center in Lexington to see the free multimedia presentation,

12

Side Trips from Boston LEXINGTON

Take a Tour ◉

Liberty Ride Trolley Tour. Ride along the historic Battle Road while your costumed guide recounts the exciting events of April 19, 1775, and the literary legacy that defined American identity and culture. This 90-minute trolley tour begins and ends at the Lexington Visitors Center. Purchase tickets online in advance. Runs mid-June through October. ⊠ *1605 Massachusetts Ave., Lexington* ☎ *781/862–1450* ⊕ *www. tourlexington.us/liberty-ride-trolley-tours* ☞ *$28* ⊗ *Closed Tues.–Thurs.*

"The Road to Revolution," a captivating introduction to the events of April 1775. Staffed by costumed park volunteers, the Whittemore House has a hands-on *Try on 1775!* exhibit where kids can wear colonial clothing and gather ingredients for a meal.

Continuing along Highway 2A toward Concord, you pass the point where Revere's midnight ride ended with his capture by the British; it's marked with a boulder and plaque, as well as an enclosure with wayside exhibits. You can also visit the 1732 Hartwell Tavern, a restored drover's (driver's) tavern staffed by park employees in period costume; they frequently demonstrate musket firing and militia drills and talk about life in colonial Massachusetts. ⊠ *Rte. 2A, ¼ mile west of Rte. 128, Lexington* ☎ *978/369–6993* ⊕ *www.nps.gov/mima.*

Munroe Tavern

HISTORIC SIGHT | As April 19, 1775, dragged on, British forces met fierce resistance in Concord. Dazed and demoralized after the battle at Concord's Old North Bridge, the British backtracked and regrouped at this 1695 tavern 1 mile east of Lexington Common, while the Munroe family hid in nearby woods. The troops then retreated through what is now the town of Arlington. After a bloody battle there, they returned to Boston. ⊠ *1332 Massachusetts Ave., Lexington* ☏ *781/862–3763* ⊕ *www.lexingtonhistory.org* ⌑ *$12* ⊘ *Closed weekdays Apr. and May.*

Scottish Rite Masonic Museum & Library
HISTORY MUSEUM | View artifacts from all facets of American life, put in social and political context. Specializing in the history of American Freemasonry and Fraternalism, the changing exhibits and lectures also focus on local events leading up to April 1775 and illustrate Revolutionary-era life through everyday objects such as blacksmithing tools, bloodletting paraphernalia, and dental instruments, including a "tooth key" used to extract teeth. ⊠ *33 Marrett Rd., Rte. 2A at Massachusetts Ave., Lexington* ☏ *781/861–6559* ⊕ *www.srmml.org* ⌑ *Donations accepted* ⊘ *Closed weekends.*

Concord

About 10 miles west of Lexington, 21 miles northwest of Boston.

The Concord of today is a modern suburb with a busy center filled with artsy shops, places to eat, and (recalling the literary history made here) old bookstores. Autumn lovers, take note: Concord is a great place to start a fall foliage tour. From Boston, head west along Route 2 to Concord, and then continue on to find harvest stands and apple picking around Harvard and Stow.

GETTING HERE AND AROUND
The MBTA runs buses to Concord. On the Commuter Rail, Concord is a 40-minute ride on the Fitchburg Line, which departs from Boston's North Station.

BUS AND TRAIN CONTACT MBTA.
☏ *617/222–3200, 800/392–6100* ⊕ *www.mbta.com.*

Tour by Phone

Cell-phone audio tours of various parts of Minute Man National Historical Park are available. They start at the visitor center, Hartwell Tavern, and Concord's North Bridge entrance—just look for the audio-tour signs and call ☏ *978/224–4905* for instructions.

ESSENTIALS
VISITOR INFORMATION Concord Visitor Center. ⊠ *58 Main St., Concord* ☏ *978/318–3061* ⊕ *concordma.gov/1920/Visitor-Center.*

Sights

Concord Museum
HISTORY MUSEUM | FAMILY | The original contents of Emerson's private study, as well as the world's largest collection of Thoreau artifacts, reside in this 1930 Colonial Revival building just east of the town center. The museum provides a good overview of the town's history, from its original Native American settlement to the present. Highlights include Native American artifacts, furnishings from Thoreau's Walden Pond cabin (there's a replica of the cabin itself on the museum's lawn), and one of the two lanterns hung at Boston's Old North Church to signal that the British were coming by sea. Those with kids should stop by the Family Station to get kid-friendly guides, scavenger hunts, and drawing sets. ⊠ *200 Lexington Rd., GPS address is 53 Cambridge Tpke., Concord* ☏ *978/369–9763* ⊕ *www.concordmuseum.org* ⌑ *$15* ⊘ *Closed Mon.*

Louisa May Alcott's Orchard House
HISTORIC HOME | The dark brown exterior of Louisa May Alcott's family home sharply contrasts with the light, wit, and energy so much in evidence within.

Named for the apple orchard that once surrounded it, Orchard House was the Alcott family home from 1857 to 1877. Here Louisa wrote *Little Women,* based in part on her life with her three sisters; and her father, Bronson, founded the Concord School of Philosophy—the building remains behind the house. Because Orchard House had just one owner after the Alcotts left, and because it became a museum in 1911, more than 80% of the original furnishings remain, including the semicircular shelf-desk where Louisa wrote *Little Women.* The only way to visit the house is by guided tour; reservations are recommended. ✉ *399 Lexington Rd., Concord* ☎ *978/369–4118* ⊕ *www. louisamayalcott.org* ✉ *$12.*

The Old Manse

HISTORIC HOME | The Reverend William Emerson, grandfather of Ralph Waldo Emerson, watched rebels and redcoats battle from behind his home, which was within sight of the Old North Bridge. The house, built in 1770, was occupied continuously by the Emerson family for almost two centuries, except for a 3½-year period during which Nathaniel Hawthorne rented it. Furnishings date from the late 18th century. Guided tours run throughout the day and last 45 minutes. The grounds are open year-round sunrise–sunset. ✉ *269 Monument St., Concord* ☎ *978/369–3909* ⊕ *www. thetrustees.org/places-to-visit/great-er-boston/old-manse.html* ✉ *Grounds free; house tours $12* ⊘ *Closed Tues.*

Old North Bridge

BRIDGE | A half mile from Concord Center, at this bridge, the Concord minutemen turned the tables on the British on the morning of April 19, 1775. The Americans didn't fire first, but when two of their own fell dead from a redcoat volley, Major John Buttrick of Concord roared, "Fire, fellow soldiers, for God's sake, fire." The minutemen released volley after volley, and the redcoats fled. Daniel Chester French's famous statue *The Minute Man* (1875) honors the country's first freedom fighters. The lovely wooded surroundings give a sense of what the landscape was like in more rural times. Guests who take the Liberty Ride trolley tour from Lexington Center will be treated to a quick stop at the bridge. ⊠ *Concord* ⊕ *www.nps.gov/mima.*

Ralph Waldo Emerson House

HISTORIC HOME | The 19th-century essayist and poet Ralph Waldo Emerson lived briefly in the Old Manse in 1834–35, then moved to this home, where he lived until his death in 1882. Here he wrote *Essays.* Except for artifacts from Emerson's study, now at the nearby Concord Museum, the Emerson House furnishings have been preserved as the writer left them, down to his hat resting on the newel post. You must join one of the half-hour-long tours to see the interior. ⊠ *28 Cambridge Tpke., at Lexington Rd., Concord* ☎ *978/369–2236* ⊕ *ralphwaldoemersonhouse.org* ▧ *$12* ⊘ *Closed Mon.–Wed. and Nov.–late-Apr.* ☞ *Call ahead for tour-scheduling information.*

Sleepy Hollow Cemetery

CEMETERY | This garden cemetery on the National Registry of Historic Places served as a place of inspiration and a final resting place for American literary greats like Louisa May Alcott, Ralph Waldo Emerson, Henry David Thoreau, and Nathaniel Hawthorne. Each Memorial Day Alcott's grave is decorated in commemoration of her death. ⊠ *Bedford St. (Rte. 62), 24 Court La. and Bedford St., Concord* ✛ *1 block east of Monument Sq. in Concord* ☎ *978/318–3233* ⊕ *www.friendsofsleepyhollow.org.*

★ Walden Pond

STATE/PROVINCIAL PARK | For lovers of Early American literature, a trip to Concord isn't complete without a pilgrimage to Henry David Thoreau's most famous residence. Here, in 1845, at age 28, Thoreau moved into a one-room cabin—built for $28.12—on the shore of this 100-foot-deep kettle hole formed by the retreat of an ancient glacier. Living alone for the next two years, Thoreau discovered the benefits of solitude and the beauties of nature. *Walden,* published in 1854, is a mixture of philosophy, nature writing, and proto-ecology.

The site of the original house is staked out in stone. A full-size, authentically furnished replica of the cabin stands about a half mile from the original site, near the Walden Pond State Reservation parking lot. During the summer, don't be shocked if you aren't allowed entrance: Walden Pond has a visitor capacity. Get there early or visit later in the day for the best chance of getting in. ⊠ *915 Walden St. (Rte. 126), Concord* ✛ *To get to Walden Pond State Reservation from Concord Center—a trip of only 1½ miles—take Concord's Main St. a block west from Monument Sq., turn left onto Walden St., and head for the intersection of Rtes. 2 and 126. Cross over Rte. 2 onto Hwy. 126, heading south for ½ mile* ☎ *978/369–3254* ⊕ *www.mass.gov/locations/walden-pond-state-reservation* ▧ *Free, but parking is $8 for vehicles with Massachusetts plates, $30 for vehicles with non-Massachusetts plates* ☞ *No dogs allowed.*

The Wayside

HISTORIC HOME | Nathaniel Hawthorne lived at the Old Manse in 1842–45, working on stories and sketches; he then moved to Salem (where he wrote *The Scarlet Letter*) and later to Lenox (*The House of the Seven Gables*). In 1852 he returned to Concord, bought this rambling structure called The Wayside, and lived here until his death in 1864. The

Literary Concord

The first wholly American literary movement was born in Concord, the tiny town west of Boston that, quite coincidentally, also witnessed the beginning of the American Revolution.

Under the influence of essayist and poet Ralph Waldo Emerson, a group eventually known as the Transcendental Club (but called Hedge's Club at the time) assembled regularly in Emerson's Concord home. Henry David Thoreau, a fellow townsman and famous proponent of self-reliance, was an integral club member, along with such others as pioneering feminist Margaret Fuller and poet Ellery Channing, both drawn to Concord simply because of Emerson's presence.

These are the names that have become indelible bylines in high-school anthologies and college syllabi, but Concord also produced beloved authors outside the Transcendentalist movement. These writers include Louisa May Alcott of *Little Women* fame and children's book author Harriet Lothrop, pseudonymously known as Margaret Sydney. Even Nathaniel Hawthorne, whose various temporary homes around Massachusetts constitute a literary trail all their own, resided in Concord during the early and later portions of his career.

The cumulative inkwells of these authors have bestowed upon Concord a literary legacy unique in the United States, both for its influence on literature in general and for the quantity of related sights packed within such a small radius. From Alcott's Orchard House to Hawthorne's Old Manse, nearly all their houses remain standing, well preserved and open for tours.

The Thoreau Institute, within walking distance of a reconstruction of Thoreau's famous cabin in the woods at Walden Pond, is a repository of his papers and original editions. Emerson's study sits in the Concord Museum, across the street from his house. Even their final resting places are here, on Authors Ridge in Sleepy Hollow Cemetery, a few short blocks from the town common.

home certainly appealed to literary types: the subsequent owner of The Wayside, Margaret Sidney, wrote the children's book *Five Little Peppers and How They Grew* (1881), and before Hawthorne moved in, the Alcotts lived here, from 1845 to 1848. Notably, The Wayside is a site on the National Underground Railroad Network to Freedom program, as the Alcotts helped at least one enslaved person on his way to Canada and freedom. An exhibit center, in the former barn, provides information about the Wayside authors and links them to major events in American history. Hawthorne's tower-study, with his stand-up writing desk, is substantially as he left it. ✉ *455 Lexington Rd., Concord* ☎ *978/318–7863* ⊕ *www.nps.gov/mima/learn/historyculture/thewayside.htm* 🎟 *$7* ⏱ *Closed in winter.*

🍴 Restaurants

80 Thoreau

$$$ | **AMERICAN** | This fine-dining restaurant, located in the Concord Depot, offers New American cuisine, with much of the food on the plate coming from nearby local farms. Friendly and knowledgeable servers can help you navigate the menu, which changes with the seasons, along

with what's available at the time. **Known for:** creative cocktails; excellent service; New England ingredients. $ *Average main: $32 ⊠ 80 Thoreau St., Concord ☎ 978/318–0008 ⊕ www.80thoreau.com ◷ Closed Sun. and Mon.*

Main Streets Market & Cafe

$$ | **AMERICAN** | Cyclists, families, and sightseers pack into this brick building, which was used to store munitions during the Revolutionary War. Wood floors and blackboard menus add a touch of nostalgia, but the extensive menu includes many classic dishes, including mac and cheese, fish and chips, and steamed mussels. **Known for:** dog-friendly patio; full bar; open early for breakfast. $ *Average main: $18 ⊠ 42 Main St., Concord ☎ 978/369–9948 ⊕ www.mainstreetsmarketandcafe.com ◷ No dinner Sun.–Wed.*

☕ Coffee and Quick Bites

Bedford Farms Ice Cream

$ | **ICE CREAM** | **FAMILY** | The Concord outpost of the long-running Bedford Farms Ice Cream shop offers just as many tasty, locally made ice creams. "Always Making" flavors include chunky chocolate pudding, green monster, and black raspberry, but there is also a list of "Sometimes Making" flavors, sorbets, and sherbets. You can also order custom ice cream cakes and pies with advance notice. **Known for:** large portions; friendly staff; more than 60 flavors. $ *Average main: $6 ⊠ 68 Thoreau St., Concord ☎ 978/341–0000 ⊕ www.bedfordfarmsicecream.com.*

Haute Coffee

$ | **AMERICAN** | Stop in for freshly brewed coffee and homemade baked goods, like banana bread, granola bars, and cinnamon buns, at this cozy spot. At lunch, enjoy the soup du jour and a selection of sandwiches. **Known for:** coffee ground and brewed to order; gluten-free and vegan options; creative pastries.

$ *Average main: $8 ⊠ 12 Walden St., Concord ☎ 978/369–9900 ⊕ myhautecoffee.com ◷ Closed Mon.*

🏃 Activities

South Bridge Boat House

BOATING | You can reach the North Bridge section of Minute Man National Historical Park by water if you rent a canoe or kayak at the South Bridge Boat House and paddle along the Sudbury and Concord Rivers. You can even paddle all the way to Sudbury or up to Billerica. ⊠ *496 Main St., Concord ☎ 978/369–9438 ⊕ www.southbridgeboathouse.com ⊉ Canoes from $16/hr; kayaks from $16/hr ◷ Closed Nov. 1–Apr. 1.*

Gloucester

37 miles northeast of Boston, 8 miles northeast of Manchester-by-the-Sea.

On Gloucester's fine seaside promenade is a famous statue of a fisherman steering a ship's wheel, his eyes searching the horizon. The statue, which honors fishermen lost at sea, was commissioned by the town citizens in celebration of Gloucester's 300th anniversary in 1923. The oldest seaport in the nation (with some of the North Shore's best beaches) is still a major fishing port. Gloucester has a wonderful downtown filled with boutiques, vintage shops, and independently owned restaurants.

ESSENTIALS

VISITOR INFORMATION Cape Ann Chamber of Commerce. ⊠ *33 Commercial St., Gloucester ☎ 978/283–1601 ⊕ www.capeannchamber.com.* **Cape Ann Chamber of Commerce, Rockport Visitor Center.** ⊠ *170 Main St., (Rte. 127), Rockport ☎ 978/546–9372 ⊕ www.rockportusa.com.*

Sights

Cape Ann Museum

HISTORY MUSEUM | The Cape Ann Museum celebrates the art, history, and culture of Cape Ann. The museum's collection includes fine art from the 19th century to the present alongside artifacts from the fishing, maritime, and granite-quarrying industries, as well as textiles, furniture, a library-archives, and three historic houses. ⊠ *27 Pleasant St., Gloucester* ☎ *978/283–0455* ⊕ *www.capeannmuseum.org* ☒ *$14* ⊘ *Closed Mon.*

Hammond Castle Museum

CASTLE/PALACE | Inventor John Hays Hammond Jr., credited with more than 500 patents, including remote control via radio waves, built this structure in 1926 to resemble a "medieval" stone castle. The museum contains medieval-style furnishings and paintings, and the Great Hall houses an impressive 8,200-pipe organ. From the castle you can see Norman's Woe, the rock made famous by Longfellow in his poem "The Wreck of the Hesperus." In July and August, unique "Spiritualism Tours" are an additional option on Thursday night (for an extra fee), with discussion of topics like the Ouija board, spirit photography, séances, and the science behind Spiritualism. Note: the museum is not wheelchair accessible. Parts of the grounds are free to visit. ⊠ *80 Hesperus Ave., south side of Gloucester off Rte. 127, Gloucester* ☎ *978/283–2080* ⊕ *www.hammondcastle.org* ☒ *$20* ⊘ *Closed Jan. and Mon.–Thurs. in April, Nov., and Dec.*

Rocky Neck

NEIGHBORHOOD | On a peninsula within Gloucester's working harbor, the town's creative side thrives in this neighborhood, one of the oldest continuously working artists' colonies in the United States. Its alumni include Winslow Homer, Maurice Prendergast, Jane Peterson, and Cecilia Beaux. While some venues stay open year-round, expect many to be closed in winter. ⊠ *6 Wonson St., Gloucester* ☎ *978/515–7004* ⊕ *www.rockyneckartcolony.org*.

Thomas E. Lannon

OTHER ATTRACTION | Consider a sail along the harbor and coast aboard the meticulously maintained 65-foot schooner *Thomas E. Lannon,* crafted in Essex in 1997 and modeled after the great vessels built a century before. From mid-May through mid-October the Ellis family offers two-hour sails, including trips that let you enjoy the sunset or music. ⊠ *63 Rogers St., next to Gloucester House restaurant, Gloucester* ☎ *978/281–6634* ⊕ *www.schooner.org* ☒ *$45.*

Beaches

Gloucester has the best beaches on the North Shore. From Memorial Day through mid-September parking costs $20–$30 on weekdays and $25–$35 on weekends. Reservations must be made online in advance for most of the beaches.

Good Harbor Beach

BEACH | FAMILY | This beach has calm, waveless waters and soft sand, and is surrounded by grassy dunes, making it perfect any time of year. In summer (June, July, and August), it is lifeguard patrolled and wheelchair accessible, and there is a snack bar if you don't feel like packing in food. The restrooms and showers are also accessible, and you can pick up beach toys at the concessions. On weekdays parking is plentiful, but the lot fills by 10 am on weekends. In June, green flies can be bothersome. **Amenities:** food and drink; lifeguards; parking (fee); showers; toilets. **Best for:** swimming; walking. ⊠ *Gloucester* ⊹ *Clearly signposted from Rte. 127A* ⊕ *gloucester-ma.gov* ☒ *Parking $20–$35 per car; reserve online at gloucesterweb.yodelpass.com/beaches.*

Long Beach

BEACH | Just as its name implies, this soft-sand beach that is half in Rockport,

half in Gloucester is long, and it's also broad. It draws crowds from the houses that border it, particularly on weekends. Pay attention to the tide schedule, or you may find there's no beach to sit on. Cape Ann Motor Inn is nearby. Parking is very limited. Don't even think of parking on neighborhood streets if you don't have a town parking sticker—you will be towed. However, there is a lot on the Gloucester side. **Amenities:** none. **Best for:** swimming; walking. ✉ Off Rte. 127A on Gloucester-Rockport town line, Off Rockport Rd., Gloucester.

★ Wingaersheek Beach

BEACH | With white sand and dunes, Wingaersheek Beach is a well-protected cove with both a beach side and a boat side. The white Annisquam lighthouse is in the bay. The beach is known for its miles of white sand and calm waters. Make a required parking reservation online after Memorial Day through summer. The parking lot is accessible and beach wheelchairs are available on request. **Amenities:** food and drink; parking (fee); toilets. **Best for:** swimming; walking. ✉ 232 Atlantic St., Gloucester ✛ Take Rte. 128 N to Exit 13 ⊕ gloucester-ma.gov 🅿 Limited parking, from $30 per car; reserve online at gloucesterweb.yodelpass.com/beaches.

🍴 Restaurants

The Franklin Cape Ann

$$$ | **AMERICAN** | This contemporary restaurant offers bistro-style chicken, roast cod, and steak frites, perfect for the late-night crowd (it's open until midnight during the summer). There is usually live music on Thursday evening. **Known for:** friendly vibe; good service; sushi available Tuesday through Saturday. ⑤ Average main: $28 ✉ 118 Main St., Gloucester ☎ 978/283-7888 ⊕ www.franklincapeann.com ☺ No lunch.

Passports

$$$ | **ECLECTIC** | **FAMILY** | In the heart of downtown Gloucester, Passports serves a modern take on classic New England seafood. Whether you sit at the bar or a table, you'll be served delicious complimentary popovers to start. **Known for:** house haddock; great, central location; lively atmosphere. ⑤ Average main: $25 ✉ 110 Main St., Gloucester ☎ 978/281-3680 ⊕ passportsrestaurant.com.

★ Woodman's of Essex

$$ | **SEAFOOD** | **FAMILY** | According to local legend, this is where Lawrence "Chubby" Woodman invented the first fried clam back in 1916. Today this sprawling wooden shack with indoor booths and outdoor picnic tables is *the* place for seafood in the rough. **Known for:** fried clams; open year-round; the popular "downriver" lobster combo plate. ⑤ Average main: $22 ✉ 121 Main St. (Rte. 133), Essex ☎ 978/768-2559, 800/649-1773 ⊕ www.woodmans.com.

☕ Coffee and Quick Bites

Virgilio's Italian Bakery

$ | **ITALIAN** | Since 1961, this bustling Italian bakery and deli has been making fresh breads and rolls, serving some of the tastiest sandwiches around. One of the shop's claims to fame is the now-famous Saint Joseph Sandwich, made with their Italian rolls stuffed with Italian deli meats, olive oil, and oregano. **Known for:** tasty prepared foods; busy in summer; family-owned. ⑤ Average main: $9 ✉ 29 Main St., Gloucester ☎ 978/283-5295 ⊕ www.virgiliosbakery.com ☺ Closed Sun.

🛏 Hotels

Cape Ann Motor Inn

$$$ | **HOTEL** | **FAMILY** | On the sands of Long Beach, this three-story, shingled motel, open year-round, has no-frills rooms except for the balconies and ocean views. **Pros:** exceptional view from every room; kids under age 12 stay free; free Wi-Fi. **Cons:** motel quality; no air-conditioning; thin walls. ⑤ Rooms from: $229 ✉ 33

Rockport Rd., Gloucester ☎ *978/281–2900, 800/464–8439* ⊕ *www.capeannmotorinn.com* ⮑ *31 rooms* ⦿❘ *Free Breakfast.*

Cape Ann's Marina Resort

$$$ | RESORT | FAMILY | This year-round hotel less than a mile from downtown Gloucester comes alive in summer with an on-site restaurant and deep-sea fishing excursions. **Pros:** free Wi-Fi; full marina; indoor pool and Jacuzzi with poolside bar. **Cons:** price hike during summer; bar area can be loud in summer; hotel surrounded by parking lots. ⑤ *Rooms from: $250* ✉ *75 Essex Ave., Gloucester* ☎ *978/283–2116, 800/626–7660* ⊕ *www.capeannmarina.com* ⮑ *30 rooms* ⦿❘ *No Meals.*

★ Castle Manor Inn

$ | B&B/INN | With original woodwork and cozy fireplaces, this restored 1900 Victorian inn perfectly captures the Cape Ann aesthetic. **Pros:** discount parking passes to the local beaches; historic; close to Gloucester's beaches. **Cons:** roads in the area can be winding and confusing; may be too intimate for some travelers; closes for the winter. ⑤ *Rooms from: $175* ✉ *141 Essex Ave., Gloucester* ☎ *978/515–7386* ⊕ *www.castlemanorinn.com* ⮑ *10 rooms* ⦿❘ *No Meals.*

Salem

16 miles northeast of Boston, 4 miles west of Marblehead.

Known widely as the Witch City, with numerous witch-related attractions and shops that draw tourists, Salem is so much more than that. But first, a bit on its infamous past…

The witchcraft hysteria emerged from the trials of 1692, when several Salem-area girls fell ill and accused some of the townspeople of casting spells on them. More than 150 men and women were charged with practicing witchcraft, a crime punishable by death. After the trials later that year, 19 people were hanged and one man was crushed to death.

Though the witch trials might have built Salem's infamy, it'd be a mistake to ignore the town's rich maritime and creative traditions, which played integral roles in the country's evolution. Frigates out of Salem opened the Far East trade routes and generated the wealth that created America's first millionaires. Among its native talents are writer Nathaniel Hawthorne, the intellectual Peabody sisters, navigator Nathaniel Bowditch, and architect Samuel McIntire. This creative spirit is today celebrated in Salem's internationally recognized museums, waterfront shops and restaurants, galleries, and wide common.

To learn more on the area, stop by the **Regional Visitor's Center.** Innovatively designed in the Old Salem Armory, the center has exhibits, a 27-minute film, maps, and a gift shop.

ESSENTIALS

VISITOR INFORMATION Destination Salem. ✉ *81 Washington St., Suite 204, Salem* ☎ *978/741–3252, 877/725–3662* ⊕ *www.salem.org.* **Salem Armory Visitor Center.** ✉ *2 New Liberty St., Salem* ☎ *978/740–1650* ⊕ *www.nps.gov/ner/sama.*

◉ Sights

The House of the Seven Gables

HISTORIC HOME | Immortalized in Nathaniel Hawthorne's classic novel, this site is itself a historic treasure. Built in 1668 and also known as the Turner-Ingersoll Mansion, the house includes the famous secret staircase, a re-creation of Hepzibah's scent shop from *The House of the Seven Gables*, and some of the finest Georgian interiors in the country. Also on the property is the small house where Hawthorne was born in 1804; built in 1750, it was moved from its original location a few blocks away. To visit the house, you must join a guided tour. ✉ *115*

Derby St., Salem ☏ *978/744–0991*
⊕ *www.7gables.org* ✉ *$20 for house
tour and grounds; $10 for grounds only.*

★ **Peabody Essex Museum**

ART MUSEUM | Salem's world-class museum celebrates superlative works from around the globe and across time, including American art and architecture, Asian export art, photography, and maritime art and history, as well as Native American, Oceanic, and African art. With a collection of 1.8 million works, housed in a contemplative blend of modern design, the museum represents a diverse range of styles; exhibits include pieces ranging from American decorative and seamen's art to an interactive Art & Nature Center and photography. While there, be sure to tour the Yin Yu Tang house. This fabulous 200-year-old house dates to the Qing Dynasty (1644–1911) of China.

The museum brought it over from China in sections and reassembled it here. ✉ *East India Sq., Salem* ☏ *978/745–9500, 866/745–1876* ⊕ *www.pem.org* ✉ *$20* ⊙ *Closed Tues. and Wed.*

Salem Maritime National Historic Site

HISTORIC SIGHT | Near Derby Wharf, this 9¼-acre site focuses on Salem's heritage as a major seaport with a thriving overseas trade. It includes the 1762 home of Elias Derby, America's first millionaire; the 1819 Custom House, made famous in Nathaniel Hawthorne's *The Scarlet Letter*; and a replica of the *Friendship*, a 171-foot, three-masted 1797 merchant vessel. There's also an active lighthouse dating from 1871, as well as the nation's last surviving 18th-century wharves. There is also the 1770 Pedrick Store House, moved from nearby Marblehead and reassembled right on Derby Wharf;

Landlubbers can go to sea at Salem's Peabody Essex Museum.

the two-story structure once played a vital role in the lucrative merchant seaside trade. The grounds are open 24/7, but buildings open on a seasonal schedule. ⊠ *193 Derby St., Salem* ☎ *978/740–1650 visitor center* ⊕ *www. nps.gov/sama/index.htm.*

Salem Witch Museum

HISTORY MUSEUM | An informative and fascinating introduction to Salem's witchcraft hysteria, this museum offers a look at 1692 with 13 life-size stage sets featuring narration of what life was like at that time, plus a 15-minute guided tour through the exhibit *Witches: Evolving Perceptions*, which describes witch hunts through the years. Tickets are sold online exclusively. In winter, the museum might not open in bad weather. Call ahead. ⊠ *19½ Washington Sq. N, Salem* ☎ *978/744–1692* ⊕ *www.salemwitchmuseum.com* ⊠ *$16.50.*

Salem Witch Trials Memorial

MONUMENT | Dedicated by Nobel Laureate Elie Wiesel in 1992, this quiet, contemplative space—an antidote to the relentless marketing of the merry-witches motif—honors those who died because they refused to confess that they were witches. A stone wall is studded with 20 stone benches, each inscribed with a victim's name, and sits next to Salem's oldest burying ground. Many people leave small tokens on the sites to commemorate the victims to this day. ⊠ *Liberty St., Salem* ✛ *Between Charter and Derby Sts.* ⊕ *salem.org/ listing/witch-trials-memorial.*

🍴 Restaurants

Finz Seafood & Grill

$$$ | **SEAFOOD** | This contemporary seafood restaurant on Salem Harbor treats patrons to prime canal views. There is an extensive sushi and sashimi menu, plus lots of other seafood favorites, including sesame-crusted tuna and steamed lobster. **Known for:** classic New England seafood; large sushi menu; outdoor seating. ⑤ *Average main: $30* ⊠ *76 Wharf St., Salem* ☎ *978/744–8485* ⊕ *www. hipfinz.com.*

The First Witch Trial

It was in Danvers, not Salem, that the first witch trial was held, originating with the family of Samuel Parris, a minister who moved to the area in 1680 from Barbados, bringing with him two enslaved people, including a woman named Tituba. In 1691 Samuel's daughter, Betty, and his niece, Abigail, began having fits. Tituba, who had told Betty and Abigail stories of magic and witchcraft from her homeland, baked a witch cake to identify the witches who were harming the girls. The girls in turn accused Tituba of witchcraft.

After three days of questioning, which included beatings from Samuel and a promise from him to free her if she cooperated, Tituba confessed to meeting the devil (in the form of a black hog or dog). She also claimed there were other witches in the village, confirming the girls' accusations against Sarah Good and Sarah Osborne, but she refused to name any others. Tituba's trial prompted the frenzy that led to the deaths of 20 accused witches.

Ledger Restaurant & Bar

$$$ | AMERICAN | Housed in a 200-year-old building that was once a bank—Ledger takes its name from the massive amount of banking ledgers found in the building—today diners enjoy a modern-day spin on traditional 19th-century dishes, especially live-fire cooking. Grab a cocktail while checking out the multitude of original features incorporated into the restaurant, including deposit boxes and a huge safe that serves as the restaurant's walk-in refrigerator. **Known for:** New England cuisine; live music once a month; historic digs. $ *Average main: $30* ⊠ *125 Washington St., Salem* ☎ *978/594–1908* ⊕ *www.ledgersalem.com* ☉ *Closed Mon. and Tues.*

🛏 Hotels

★ Amelia Payson House

$$$ | B&B/INN | Built in 1845, this Greek Revival house is a comfortable bed-and-breakfast near all the historic attractions. **Pros:** fireplaces in each room; outdoor lounge with a fire pit; on-site parking. **Cons:** hard to get reservations; might be too quaint for some; no children under 12. $ *Rooms from: $250* ⊠ *16 Winter St., Salem* ☎ *978/744–8304*

⊕ *www.ameliapaysonhouse.com* ⇋ *3 rooms* ⦿ *Free Breakfast.*

The Hawthorne Hotel

$$ | HOTEL | Elegantly restored, this full-service historic hotel celebrates the town's most famous writer and is within walking distance of the town common, museums, and waterfront. **Pros:** lovely, historic lobby; free parking available behind hotel; free Wi-Fi. **Cons:** two-night minimum June through October; pricey pet policy; many rooms are small. $ *Rooms from: $199* ⊠ *18 Washington Sq. W, Salem* ☎ *978/744–4080, 800/729–7829* ⊕ *www.hawthornehotel.com* ⇋ *93 rooms* ⦿ *No Meals* ⇋ *$50 charge per room per night for pets.*

The Merchant

$$$$ | HOTEL | The 11-room Merchant is an intimate, design-forward Lark Hotel property in the heart of Salem's historic district. **Pros:** off-site parking at Riley Plaza is $5; free Wi-Fi; downstairs lounge with fully stocked "BYOB Mixer Bar". **Cons:** no in-room fridge; books up quickly; no elevator. $ *Rooms from: $350* ⊠ *148 Washington St., Salem* ☎ *978/745–8100* ⊕ *www.themerchantsalem.com* ⇋ *11 rooms* ⦿ *Free Breakfast.*

▼ Nightlife

Bit Bar

THEMED ENTERTAINMENT | Old-school arcade fans, and even those brought up exclusively with computer games, love playing on the more than 30 classic games at Bit Bar, where you can play *Pac-Man,* pinball, or air hockey until you drop. A full bar and a menu featuring everything from tater tots to pizza keeps you fueled up. Kids can play until 8 pm; after that, it's 21-plus only. ⊠ *278 Derby St., Salem* ☎ *978/594–4838* ⊕ *bit.bar.*

Notch Salem

BREWPUBS | This outpost of Notch Brewing (there's one in Boston, too) sits on the South River Basin in Salem with plenty of space indoors and out. Open year-round, Notch promises at least 10 to 14 brews on tap, along with snacks such as a cheese plate, pretzels, pickled eggs, and other bar food. Communal tables, Skee-Ball, cornhole, and special events such as artisan fairs, make this a lively place to gather with friends. ⊠ *283R Derby St., Salem* ☎ *978/412–7674* ⊕ *notch-brewing.com.*

⚫ Performing Arts

THEATER

Cry Innocent: The People Versus Bridget Bishop

THEATER | This show, the longest continuously running play north of Boston, transports audience members to Bridget Bishop's witchcraft hearing of 1692. After hearing historical testimonies, the audience cross-examines the witnesses and decides whether to send Bridget to trial or not. Actors respond in character, revealing much about the Puritan frame of mind. Each show is different and allows audience members to play their "part" in history. ⊠ *Old Town Hall, 32 Derby Sq., Salem* ☎ *978/810–2588* ⊕ *www.historyalivesalem.com* 🎫 *$25.*

Rockport

41 miles northeast of Boston, 4 miles northeast of Gloucester on Rte. 127.

Rockport, at the very tip of Cape Ann, derives its name from the local granite formations. Many Boston-area structures are made of stone cut from these long-gone quarries. Today the town is a tourist center with a well-marked, centralized downtown that is easy to navigate and access on foot. Unlike typical tourist-trap landmarks, Rockport's shops sell quality arts, clothing, and gifts, and its restaurants serve seafood or home-baked cookies rather than fast food. Walk past shops and colorful clapboard houses to the end of Bearskin Neck for an impressive view of the Atlantic Ocean and the old, weather-beaten lobster shack known as Motif No. 1, a popular subject for amateur painters and photographers.

ESSENTIALS

VISITOR INFORMATION Rockport Visitor Center. ⊠ *Upper Main St. (Rte. 127), Rockport* ☎ *978/546–9372* ⊕ *www. rockportusa.com.*

🍴 Restaurants

Brackett's Oceanview Restaurant

$$ | SEAFOOD | Enormous windows in this quiet, homey restaurant offer excellent views across Sandy Bay, along with plenty of chowder, fish cakes, lobster, and other seafood dishes. While the restaurant is only open seasonally, next door is Brackett's café, Brother's Brew Coffee Shop, which is open year-round and serves breakfast. **Known for:** every table has a waterfront view; great downtown location; local seafood. ⑤ *Average main: $24* ⊠ *25 Main St., Rockport* ☎ *978/546–2797* ⊕ *www.bracketts.com* ⊗ *Closed Columbus Day–mid-Apr.*

🏨 Hotels

Addison Choate

$$$ | B&B/INN | Just a minute's walk from both the center of Rockport and the train station, this 1851 inn sits in a prime location. **Pros:** free parking; comfortable, spacious porch for relaxing; free Wi-Fi. **Cons:** most rooms require taking the stairs; may be too intimate a setting for some; only one bedroom on the first floor. $ *Rooms from: $299* ⊠ *49 Broadway, Rockport* ☎ *978/546–7543, 800/245–7543* ⊕ *addisonchoate.com* ⟲ *7 rooms* ⏹ *Free Breakfast.*

Bearskin Neck Motor Lodge

$$$ | HOTEL | FAMILY | Near the end of Bearskin Neck, this small brick-and-shingle motel offers guests the best of both worlds: beautiful, oceanfront rooms, as well as easy access to shopping and restaurants. **Pros:** all rooms have balconies and unobstructed ocean views; central location; mini-refrigerators in rooms. **Cons:** heavy "classic motel" vibe; no pets allowed; lots of summertime tourists. $ *Rooms from: $250* ⊠ *64 Bearskin Neck, Rockport* ☎ *978/546–6677, 877/507–6272* ⊕ *www.bearskinneckmotorlodge.com* ☾ *Closed Dec.–Mar.* ⟲ *8 rooms* ⏹ *No Meals.*

The Emerson Inn

$$$ | B&B/INN | An elegant retreat overlooking the ocean, this beautifully restored historic property where, yes, Ralph Waldo Emerson once stayed, dates back 150 years. **Pros:** historic charm; amazing location; heated outdoor pool. **Cons:** steep stairs; not all rooms have ocean views; parking can be tight. $ *Rooms from: $250* ⊠ *1 Cathedral Ave., Salem* ☎ *978/546–6321* ⊕ *theemerson-inn.com* ☾ *Closed in winter* ⟲ *36 rooms* ⏹ *Free Breakfast.*

★ The Sally Webster Collection

$$$$ | B&B/INN | Within walking range of shops, restaurants, and beaches, this historic inn, sister property of Addison Choate, was named for a member of the

Hannah Jumper's "Hatchet Gang," teetotalers who smashed up the town's liquor stores in 1856 and turned Rockport into the dry town it remained until as recently as 2008. **Pros:** full buffet breakfast; free Wi-Fi; free parking. **Cons:** small bathrooms; might be too quaint for some; some rooms accessed via second-floor stairs. $ *Rooms from: $500* ⊠ *34 Mt. Pleasant St., Rockport* ☎ *978/309–8159* ⊕ *www.sallywebster.com* ⟲ *5 rooms* ⏹ *Free Breakfast.*

Plymouth

40 miles south of Boston.

On December 26, 1620, 102 weary men, women, and children disembarked from the *Mayflower* to found the first permanent European settlement north of Virginia (they had found their earlier landing in Provincetown to be unsuitable). Today Plymouth is characterized by narrow streets, clapboard mansions, shops, antiques stores, and a scenic waterfront. To mark Thanksgiving, the town holds activities, including historic-house tours and a parade. Historic statues dot the town, including depictions of William Bradford, Pilgrim leader and governor of Plymouth Colony for more than 30 years, on Water Street; a Pilgrim maiden in Brewster Gardens; and Massasoit, the Wampanoag chief who helped the Pilgrims survive, on Carver Street.

ESSENTIALS

VISITOR INFORMATION Plymouth Visitor Information Center. ⊠ *130 Water St., at Rte. 44, Plymouth* ☎ *508/747–7525* ⊕ *www.seeplymouth.com.*

👁 Sights

Mayflower II

HISTORIC SIGHT | FAMILY | This seaworthy replica of the 1620 *Mayflower* was built in England through research and a bit of guesswork, then sailed across the

South of Boston

Rockport
Gloucester
Manchester-by-the-Sea
Peabody Beverly
Salem
Wakefield Marblehead
Lynn
Nahant

Massachusetts Bay

BOSTON
Hull
Milton
Cohasset
Quincy
Braintree Scituate
Randolph
Norwell
Rockland
Brockton Marshfield
Bridgewater
Duxbury
Kingston
Plympton
Plymouth
Middleboro Plimoth Plantation
Carver
Lakeville Myles Standish State Forest
Assawompset Pond
Long Pond Snipatuit Pond
Wareham
New Bedford
Marion
Fort Phoenix State Beach Reservation
Dartmouth
West Island Buzzards Bay
Woods Hole
Falmouth
Naushon Island
Nashawena Island Vineyard Sound
Tisbury
Oak Bluffs
Martha's Vineyard
Edgartown
Aquinnah

Rhode Island Sound

ATLANTIC OCEAN

Race Point Beach
Provincetown
Herring Cove Beach North Truro
Truro
Cape Cod Nauset Light Beach
Wellfleet
Nauset Light
Cape Cod Bay Eastham
First Encounter Beach
Coast Guard Beach
Sagamore Brewster Orleans
Sandwich Dennis
Barnstable Yarmouth Chatham
Mashpee Harwich
Hyannis

Monomoy I.

Nantucket Sound

Nantucket Town Nantucket Island

KEY
Ferry Lines

0   10 mi
0   10 km

Atlantic in 1957. As you explore the interior and exterior of the ship, which was extensively refurbished in time for Plymouth's 400th anniversary in 2020, sailors in modern dress answer your questions about both the reproduction and the original ship, while costumed guides provide a 17th-century perspective. This attraction is part of the Plimoth Patuxet Museums system. Plymouth Rock is also nearby. ⊠ *State Pier, Plymouth* ☎ *508/746–1622* ⊕ *www.plimoth.org* ⊠ *$15; combination tickets for other sites available* ⊗ *Closed late-Nov.–late-Mar.*

National Monument to the Forefathers

MONUMENT | Said to be the largest freestanding granite statue in the United States, this allegorical monument stands high on an 11-acre hilltop site. Designed by Hammatt Billings of Boston in 1854 and dedicated in 1889, it depicts Faith, surrounded by Liberty, Morality, Justice, Law, and Education, and includes scenes from the Pilgrims' early days in Plymouth. ⊠ *72 Allerton St., Plymouth* ⊕ *www.seeplymouth.com/things-to-do/national-monument-forefathers.*

Pilgrim Hall Museum

HISTORY MUSEUM | **FAMILY** | From the waterfront sights, it's a short walk to one of the country's oldest public museums. Established in 1824, Pilgrim Hall Museum transports you back to the time of the Pilgrims' landing with objects carried by those weary travelers to the New World. Historic items on display include a carved chest, a remarkably well-preserved wicker cradle, Myles Standish's sword, and John Alden's Bible. In addition, the museum presents the story of the Wampanoag, the native people who lived here 10,000 years before the arrival of the Pilgrims, and who still live here today. ⊠ *75 Court St. (Rte. 3A), Plymouth* ☎ *508/746–1620* ⊕ *www.pilgrimhall.org* ⊠ *$15* ⊗ *Closed Mon. and Tues. and Jan.–Mar.*

★ Plimoth Patuxet Museums

MUSEUM VILLAGE | **FAMILY** | Against the backdrop of the Atlantic Ocean, and 3 miles south of downtown Plymouth, this living museum shares the rich, interwoven story of the Plymouth Colony and the Wampanoag homeland through engaging daily programs and special events. A 1620s Pilgrim village has been carefully re-created, from the thatch roofs, cramped quarters, and open fireplaces to the long-horned livestock. Throw away your preconception of white collars and funny hats; through ongoing research, the Plimoth staff has developed a portrait of the Pilgrims that's more complex than the dour folk in school textbooks. Listen to the accents of the "residents," who never break out of character. Feel free to engage them in conversation about their life. Don't worry, 21st-century museum educators are on hand to help answer any questions you have as well. On the Wampanoag homesite, meet native people speaking from a modern perspective on the traditions, lifeways, and culture of Eastern Woodlands Indigenous people. Note that there's not a lot of shade here in summer. ⊠ *137 Warren Ave. (Rte. 3A), Plymouth* ☎ *508/746–1622* ⊕ *www.plimoth.org* ⊠ *$32; combination tickets available for other sites* ⊗ *Closed late Nov.–late Mar.*

Plymouth Rock

HISTORIC SIGHT | This landmark rock, just a few dozen yards from the *Mayflower II,* is popularly believed to have been the Pilgrims' stepping-stone when they left the ship. Given the stone's unimpressive appearance—it's little more than a boulder—and dubious authenticity (as explained on a nearby plaque), the grand canopy overhead seems a trifle ostentatious. Still, more than a million people a year come to visit this world-famous symbol of courage and faith. ■ **TIP→ The views of Plymouth Harbor alone are worth the visit.** ⊠ *Water St., Plymouth* ☎ *508/747–5360* ⊕ *www.mass.gov/locations/pilgrim-memorial-state-park.*

🍴 Restaurants

The Blue-Eyed Crab

$$$ | CARIBBEAN | FAMILY | Grab a seat on the outside deck overlooking the water at this friendly, somewhat funky (plastic fish dangling from the ceiling), Caribbean-inspired eatery. Enjoy fruity cocktails on the patio, or hang out in the colorful dining room. **Known for:** funky decor; tropical cocktails; views of the water. $ *Average main: $27 ⊠ 170 Water St., Plymouth* ☎ *508/747–6776* ⊕ *www.blue-eyedcrab. com.*

Provincetown

115 miles southeast of Boston (2½ hours by car), 90 minutes by ferry.

This outermost Cape resort town known for its beautiful beaches and vibrant summer culture has long been home to tourists, artists, and a dynamic LGBTQ+ community. In summer, a fast ferry whisks you from Boston to Provincetown in about 90 minutes, allowing you to skip all the notorious Cape traffic on the roads and enjoy a relaxing boat ride. It's possible to even make it a day trip, though it's more fun to spend a weekend there.

GETTING HERE AND AROUND

Cape Air offers year-round service from Boston's Logan Airport to Provincetown, and Bay Stay Cruise Company offers daily, summer-season high-speed ferry service from the World Trade Center pier in Boston directly to Provincetown Terminal in 90 minutes.

CONTACTS Bay State Cruise Company.

⊠ *Commonwealth Pier, 200 Seaport Blvd., Boston* ☎ *617/748–1428, 877/783–3779* ⊕ *baystatecruisecompany.com.* **Cape Air.** ⊠ *660 Barnstable Rd., Hyannis* ☎ *800/227–3247, 508/771–6944 outside U.S.* ⊕ *www.capeair.com.* **JetBlue.** ☎ *800/538–2583* ⊕ *www.jetblue.com.*

ESSENTIALS

VISITOR INFORMATION

Provincetown Chamber of Commerce.

⊠ *307 Commerce St., Provincetown* ☎ *508/487–3424* ⊕ *ptownchamber.com.*

👁 Sights

★ Commercial Street

STREET | Take a casual stroll by the many architectural styles—Greek Revival, Victorian, Second Empire, and Gothic, to name a few—used in the design of the impressive houses for wealthy sea captains and merchants. The center of town is where you'll find the crowds and the best people-watching, especially if you try to find an empty spot on the benches in front of the exquisitely renovated Town Hall. The East End has a number of nationally renowned galleries; the West End has a number of small inns with neat lawns and elaborate gardens. There is one-way vehicle traffic on this street, though pedestrians dominate the pavement, particularly in July and August. Commercial Street runs parallel to the water, so there is always a patch of sand close at hand, should you need a break. ⊠ *Provincetown* ⊕ *ptowntourism.com.*

Pilgrim Monument and Provincetown Museum

MONUMENT | The first thing you'll see in Provincetown is this grandiose edifice, somewhat out of proportion to the rest of the low-rise town. The monument commemorates the Pilgrims' first landing in the New World and their signing of the Mayflower Compact (the first colonial rules of self-governance in what would become the United States) before they set off to explore the mainland. Climb the 116 steps and 60 short ramps of the 252-foot-high tower for a panoramic view—dunes on one side, harbor on the other, and the entire bay side of Cape Cod beyond. At the tower's base is a museum of Lower Cape and Provincetown history, with exhibits on whaling, shipwrecks, and scrimshaw. There are

Part of the Cape Cod National Seashore, the beaches of Provincetown stretch more than 30 miles.

also arrowheads, tools, and images of the local Native American Wampanoag tribe, the town's first fire engine, a recreation of a 19th-century sea captain's parlor, a diorama of the Mayflower Compact being signed, and more. Admission includes both the museum and monument. ⊠ *1 High Pole Hill Rd., Downtown Center* ☎ *508/487–1310* ⊕ *www.pilgrim-monument.org* 🖼 *$20.94* ⊗ *Closed Tues. and Wed.*

★ Province Lands Visitor Center

VISITOR CENTER | Part of the Cape Cod National Seashore, the Province Lands stretch from High Head in Truro to the tip of Provincetown and are scattered with ponds, cranberry bogs, and scrub. More than 7 miles of bike and walking trails lace through forests of stunted pines, beech, and oak and across desert-like expanses of rolling dunes. At the visitor center you'll find short films on local geology and exhibits on the life of the dunes and the shore. You can also pick up information on guided walks, birding trips, lectures, and other programs, as

well as on the Province Lands' pristine beaches, Race Point and Herring Cove, and walking, biking, and horse trails. Don't miss the awe-inspiring panoramic view of the dunes and the surrounding ocean from the observation deck. This terrain provides optimal conditions for the deer tick, which can cause Lyme disease, so use extra caution. ⊠ *171 Race Point Rd., east of U.S. 6, Greater Provincetown* ☎ *508/487–1256* ⊕ *www. nps.gov/caco* 🖼 *Free* ⊗ *Visitor center closed Nov.–Apr.*

★ Provincetown Art Association and Museum

ART MUSEUM | Founded in 1914 to collect and exhibit the works of artists with Provincetown connections, this facility has a 1,650-piece permanent collection, displayed in changing exhibitions that mix up-and-comers with established 20th-century figures like Milton Avery, Philip Evergood, William Gropper, Charles Hawthorne, Robert Motherwell, Claes Oldenburg, Man Ray, John Singer Sargent, Andy Warhol, and Agnes

Cape Cod National Seashore

The Cape Cod National Seashore, established in 1961 by President John F. Kennedy, is an expansive 27,000-acre park, extending from Chatham to Provincetown, with 30 miles of superb beaches; great rolling dunes; swamps, marshes, and wetlands; and pitch-pine and scrub-oak forest. Self-guided nature trails, as well as excellent cycling and horse trails, lace through these landscapes. The Cape was a refuge and haven for JFK and we can thank him for saving this part of the region for us for the foreseeable future. A good place to get an overview of the area is at the Salt Pond Visitor Center, at the southern end of the Cape, which offers guided walks, boat tours, demonstrations, and lectures from mid-April through Thanksgiving, as well as evening beach walks, campfire talks, and other programs (many are free) in summer.

Highlights of the National Seashore include **Coast Guard Beach**, a long beach backed by low grass and heathland. A handsome former Coast Guard station is also here, though it's not open to the public. The beach has a very small parking lot that fills up early, but in season visitors can park at the Salt Pond Visitor Center or at the lot up Doane Road from the center and take a free shuttle to the beach. **Nauset Light Beach**, located adjacent to Coast Guard Beach, is a long, sandy beach backed by tall dunes, frilly grasses, and heathland. You'll find **Nauset Light** here, too, a much-photographed red-and-white lighthouse. Another popular beach is **First Encounter Beach**, ideal for watching sunsets over Cape Cod Bay. Pick up maps and more information at the Salt Pond Visitor Center ($\boxtimes$ 50 Doane Rd. ☎ 508/255–3421 ⊕ www.nps. gov/caco).

Weinrich. A stunning contemporary wing has greatly expanded the exhibit space. The museum store carries books of local interest, including works by or about area artists and authors, as well as posters, crafts, cards, and gift items. Art classes (single day and longer) offer the opportunity to study under such talents as Hilda Neily, Selina Trieff, and Doug Ritter. $\boxtimes$ 460 Commercial St., East End ☎ 508/487–1750 ⊕ www.paam.org 🖾 $15 ⊗ Closed Tues. Nov.–April.

🏖 Beaches

Herring Cove Beach

BEACH | FAMILY | Herring Cove Beach is relatively calm and warm for a National Seashore beach, but it's not as pretty as some because its parking lot isn't hidden behind dunes. It's close to town, so in warm weather it's always crowded. The lot to the right of the bathhouse is a great place to watch the sunset. ■ TIP→ **Daily parking is $25; the annual seashore pass grants access to all six national park beaches and costs $60. Amenities:** food and drink; lifeguards; parking (fee); toilets; showers. **Best for:** sunset; swimming; walking. $\boxtimes$ Provincetown ⊕ www.nps. gov/caco 🖾 From late June–Labor Day and weekends and holidays from Memorial Day to mid-Sept. $25 per vehicle, $15 per person.

★ Race Point Beach

BEACH | FAMILY | Race Point Beach, one of the Cape Cod National Seashore beaches in Provincetown, has a wide swath of sand stretching far off into the distance around the point and Coast Guard station. Because of its position facing north, the beach gets sun all day long. Keep an eye out for whales offshore; it's also a popular fishing spot. ■ **TIP→ Daily parking is $25; the annual seashore pass grants access to all six national park beaches for $60. Amenities:** lifeguards; parking (fee); showers; toilets. **Best for:** sunrise; sunset; surfing; swimming; walking. ⊠ *Race Point Rd., east of U.S. 6, Provincetown* ☎ *508/487–1256* ⊕ *www.nps.gov/ caco* ⊠ *From late June–Labor Day and weekends and holidays from Memorial Day to mid-Sept. $25 per vehicle, $15 per person.*

🍴 Restaurants

★ The Canteen

$ | **AMERICAN** | This casual spot specializes in classics like grilled cheese sandwiches, hand-cut fries, and local seafood in a lively spot. Order at the counter, then grab a seat inside or at one of the several outdoor seating options; there's also a large beer menu with New England offerings, a good selection of wines, and fun cocktails. **Known for:** raw bar; great atmosphere out back; hot or cold lobster rolls. ⑤ *Average main: $13* ⊠ *225 Commercial St., Downtown Center* ☎ *508/487–3800* ⊕ *www.thecanteenptown.com.*

★ The Lobster Pot

$$$$ | **SEAFOOD** | Provincetown's Lobster Pot, a mainstay for more than 40 years, is fit to do battle with all the lobster shanties anywhere (and everywhere) else on the Cape; although it's often jammed with tourists, the crowds reflect the generally high quality, and the water views can't be beat. The hardworking kitchen turns out classic New England cooking: lobsters, generous and filling seafood platters, and some of the best chowder around. **Known for:** local icon; extensive menu; award-winning clam chowder.

⑤ *Average main: $35* ⊠ *321 Commercial St., Downtown Center* ☎ *508/487–0842* ⊕ *www.ptownlobsterpot.com* ⊘ *Closed in winter.*

★ The Mews Restaurant & Cafe

$$$$ | **AMERICAN** | This perennial favorite with magnificent harbor views focuses on local seafood and organic meat and produce with a cross-cultural flair (there's also a lighter bistro menu for smaller appetites). The view of the bay from the bar is nearly perfect, and the gentle lighting makes this a romantic spot to have a drink. **Known for:** ambience; two levels of dining; waterfront setting. ⑤ *Average main: $35* ⊠ *429 Commercial St., East End* ☎ *508/487–1500* ⊕ *mewsptown. com* ⊘ *Closed Sun. and Mon.*

★ The Pointe

$$$ | **AMERICAN** | Inside the snazzy Crowne Pointe Inn, this intimate, casually handsome restaurant occupies the parlor and sunroom of a grand sea captain's mansion and serves finely crafted, healthful, modern American food with daily specials focused on local ingredients. There's a substantial wine list, with more than a 125 selections to choose from, as well as a large martini menu. **Known for:** cocktails in the lounge; truffle popcorn; superb service. ⑤ *Average main: $30* ⊠ *Crowne Pointe Inn, 82 Bradford St., Downtown Center* ☎ *508/487–2365* ⊕ *www. provincetown-restaurant.com* ⊘ *Closed Mon.–Wed. No lunch.*

Provincetown Brewing Co.

$$ | **AMERICAN** | This fun and funky establishment offers a range of craft beers and bar food in a convivial space. Relax with a Double Rainbow IPA or nonalcoholic kombucha on a comfy couch inside, or bring Fido and sit on the pet-friendly patio. **Known for:** great brews; great sandwiches; friendly service. ⑤ *Average main: $16* ⊠ *141 Bradford St., Downtown Center* ☎ *508/413–9076* ⊕ *www. provincetownbrewingco.com.*

🛏 Hotels

★ The Brass Key Guesthouse

$$$$ | B&B/INN | One of the Cape's most luxurious small resorts, this meticulously kept year-round getaway comprises a beautifully restored main house—originally a sea captain's home built in 1828—and several other carefully groomed buildings and cottages all centered on a beautifully landscaped pool area. **Pros:** ultraposh rooms; beautiful and secluded grounds; pool on-site. **Cons:** not for those with children; significant minimum-stay requirements in summer; among the highest rates in town. ⑤ *Rooms from: $400* ⊠ *67 Bradford St., Downtown Center* ☎ *508/487–9005, 800/842–9858* ⊕ *www.brasskey.com* ⇆ *43 rooms* ⑩ *Free Breakfast* ☞ *Pets allowed in certain rooms.*

★ Crowne Pointe Historic Inn and Spa

$$$$ | B&B/INN | Created meticulously from six different buildings, this inn hasn't a single detail left unattended—period furniture and antiques fill common areas and guest rooms; a queen-size bed is the smallest you'll find, dressed in 300-thread-count linens; treats are left on the pillow for nightly turndown service; and there's complimentary wine and cheese in the afternoon. **Pros:** great on-site amenities like the full-service Shui Spa; posh and luxurious room decor; professional and well-trained staff. **Cons:** significant minimum-stay requirements in summer; no children allowed; among the highest rates in town in season. ⑤ *Rooms from: $340* ⊠ *82 Bradford St., Downtown Center* ☎ *508/413–2213, 877/276–9631* ⊕ *www.crownepointe. com* ⇆ *40 rooms* ⑩ *Free Breakfast.*

★ White Porch Inn

$$$ | B&B/INN | This sterling, light-filled B&B offers a soothing respite from the bustle of town; opt for one of the carriage-house rooms for even more seclusion. **Pros:** wine hour on summer weekends; open year-round; enthusiastic

and friendly staff. **Cons:** not for those with children; limited parking; somewhat long walk to West End shopping and businesses. ⑤ *Rooms from: $299* ⊠ *7 Johnson St., Downtown Center* ☎ *508/364–2549, 508/487–0592* ⊕ *www.whiteporchinn. com* ⇆ *10 rooms* ⑩ *Free Breakfast.*

🏃 Activities

★ Art's Dune Tours

FOUR-WHEELING | Art's Dune Tours has been taking eager passengers into the dunes of the Province Lands since 1946. A bumpy but controlled ride (about one hour) transports you through sometimes surreal sandy vistas peppered with beach grass, along a shoreline patrolled by seagulls and sandpipers. Head out at sunset for a stunning ride, available with or without a provided dinner and bonfire. Dune and water tours are further options. ⊠ *4 Standish St., Downtown Center* ☎ *508/487–1950, 800/894–1951* ⊕ *www. artsdunetours.com* ⛵ *From $37; must call to reserve* ☉ *Closed Nov.–Apr.*

★ Dolphin Fleet

WILDLIFE-WATCHING | FAMILY | Tours are led by scientists from the Center for Coastal Studies in Provincetown, who provide commentary while collecting data on the whales they've been monitoring for years. They know many of them by name and will tell you about their habits and histories. These trips are most often exciting and incredibly thrilling, with close-up encounters. ■TIP➔ **Look for discount coupons in local free brochures and publications, as well as online.** ⊠ *Chamber of Commerce Bldg., MacMillan Wharf, Downtown Center* ☎ *508/240–3636, 800/826–9300* ⊕ *www.whalewatch.com* ⛵ *$70.*

Index

Photo Credits

Front Cover: Laura Zeid/eStock Photo [Description: Massachusetts, Boston, Public Garden, statue of George Washington, USA.]. **Back cover, from left to right:** SeanPavonePhoto/iStockPhoto. Coleong/Dreamstime. Sepavo/Dreamstime. **Spine:** Lunamarina/Dreamstime. **Interior, from left to right:** Chrisc2000/Dreamstime (1). Chee-Onn Leong/Shutterstock (2-3). Jim Reynolds/Wikimedia Commons/USS *Constitution* (5). **Chapter 1: Experience Boston:** Sean Pavone/Dreamstime (6-7). Luckydoor/Dreamstime (8-9). Marcos Souza/Dreamstime (9). Cpenler/Dreamstime (9). Kwanbenz/Shutterstock (10). Nic Lehoux/Isabella Stewart Gardner Museum (10). Suse Schulz/Dreamstime (10). Photopro123/Dreamstime (10). Wenling01/Dreamstime (11). Christian Delbert(Babar760)/Dreamstime (11). Marcos Souza/Dreamstime (11). Jiawangkun/Dreamstime (12). Appalachianviews/Dreamstime (12). F11photo/Dreamstime (12). Kimberly Vardeman/Flickr (12). Indigochyld/Dreamstime (13). Mikey Colon/Shutterstock (14). Martin Thomas Photography/Alamy (14). Smart Destinations/Flickr (14). DMS Foto/Shutterstock (14). DenisTangneyJr/iStockphoto (15). Jiawangkun/Dreamstime (15). Jay Yuan/Shutterstock (22). Marcio Jose Bastos Silva/Shutterstock (22). James Kirkikis/Shutterstock (22). Museum of African American History/Flickr, [CC BY 2.0] (22). LnP images/Shutterstock (23). Martin Nola/Shutterstock (24). Photopro123/Dreamstime (24). Brent Hofacker/Shutterstock (24). Brent Hofacker/Shutterstock (24). Alessio Orru/Shutterstock (25). Laura Sageata/Shutterstock (25). Max Moraga/Shutterstock (25). RJ Lerich/Shutterstock (25). Elovkoff/Dreamstime (26). Dbvirago/Dreamstime (26). Spencerprice/Dreamstime (26). Jon Bilous (27). Michael Blanchard Photography/Boston Tea Party Ships & Museum (27). **Chapter 3: Beacon Hill, Boston Common, and the West End:** Kindra Clineff/George Washington Statue (63). M_Sovinskii/Shutterstock (70). **Chapter 4: Government Center and the North End:** Marcio Jose Bastos Silva/Shutterstock (85). Jorge Salcedo/Dreamstime (90). M_Sovinskii/Shutterstock (92). Jorge Salcedo/Dreamstime (98). **Chapter 5: Charlestown:** Maxim Gorishniak/Shutterstock (107). Page Light Studios/Shutterstock (113). **Chapter 6: Downtown and the Waterfront:** Jon Bilous/Shutterstock (117). F11photo/Dreamstime (124). Shananies/iStockphoto (137). **Chapter 7: The Back Bay and South End:** Jiawangkun/Dreamstime (143). Mbastos/Dreamstime (146). Lcypop/Dreamstime (148). COLeong/Dreamstime (158). **Chapter 8: Fenway and Kenmore Square:** Israel Pabon/Shutterstock (181) ChrisDag/Flickr (182). Kindra Clineff/The Fenway (183). Kindra Clineff/Fenway Park (183). **Chapter 9: Brookline and Jamaica Plain:** Alyssa Tortora/iStockphoto (193). Wangkun Jia/Shutterstock (196). Micha Weber/Shutterstock (201). **Chapter 10: The Seaport, South Boston, and East Boston:** Marcio Jose Bastos Silva/Shutterstock (205). Danita Delimont/Alamy (211). Darryl Brooks/Shutterstock (217). Miguel Rincon/Shutterstock (222). **Chapter 11: Cambridge and Somerville:** Jorge Salcedo/Shutterstock (229). Audrey I Anderson/Harvard Crimson (237). Janniswerner/iStockphoto (246). Jorge Salcedo/Shutterstock (251). **Chapter 12: Side Trips from Boston:** Denis TangneyJr/iStockphoto (265). Ken Sawyer/Peabody Essex Museum (284). Lunamarina/Shutterstock (291). **About Our Writers:** All photos are courtesy of the writers except for the following: Cheryl Fenton, courtesy of Claire van der Lee.

*Every effort has been made to trace the copyright holders, and we apologize in advance for any accidental errors. We would be happy to apply the corrections in the following edition of this publication.

Fodor's BOSTON

Publisher: Stephen Horowitz, *General Manager*

Editorial: Douglas Stallings, *Editorial Director;* Jill Fergus, Amanda Sadlowski, *Senior Editors;* Kayla Becker, Brian Eschrich, Alexis Kelly, *Editors;* Angelique Kennedy-Chavannes, *Assistant Editor*

Design: Tina Malaney, *Director of Design and Production;* Jessica Gonzalez, *Senior Designer;* Erin Caceres, *Graphic Design Associate*

Production: Jennifer DePrima, *Editorial Production Manager;* Elyse Rozelle, *Senior Production Editor;* Monica White, *Production Editor*

Maps: Rebecca Baer, *Senior Map Editor;* Mark Stroud and Harry Colomb (Moon Street Cartography), David Lindroth, *Cartographers*

Photography: Viviane Teles, *Senior Photo Editor;* Namrata Aggarwal, Neha Gupta, Payal Gupta, Ashok Kumar, *Photo Editors;* Eddie Aldrete, *Photo Production Intern;* Kadeem McPherson, *Photo Production Associate Intern*

Business and Operations: Chuck Hoover, *Chief Marketing Officer;* Robert Ames, *Group General Manager*

Public Relations and Marketing: Joe Ewaskiw, *Senior Director of Communications and Public Relations*

Fodors.com: Jeremy Tarr, *Editorial Director;* Rachael Levitt, *Managing Editor*

Technology: Jon Atkinson, *Director of Technology;* Rudresh Teotia, *Associate Director of Technology;* Alison Lieu, *Project Manager*

Writers: Cheryl Fenton, Leigh Harrington, Kim Foley MacKinnon

Editors: Kayla Becker, Brian Eschrich

Production Editor: Monica White

32nd Edition

ISBN 978-1-64097-553-8

ISSN 0882-0074

SPECIAL SALES

This book is available at special discounts for bulk purchases for sales promotions or premiums. For more information, e-mail SpecialMarkets@fodors.com.

PRINTED IN CANADA

10 9 8 7 6 5 4 3 2 1

About Our Writers

Cheryl Fenton is a Boston-based freelance writer who specializes in all things lifestyle, with bylines in such publications and online outlets as the *Boston Globe, Cooking Light,* USAToday.com, Boston.com, *Women's Health and Fitness,* and USAirways. Her career has spanned decades of reporting on the next best thing in dining, travel, interior design, fashion, beauty, and more. To see her work, visit ⊕ *www.cherylfenton.com* and follow her on Instagram @cherylfenton. For this guide, Cheryl updated the Travel Smart; Government Center and the North End; Charlestown; The Back Bay and South End; and Cambridge and Somerville chapters.

Kim Foley MacKinnon, a Boston-based, award-winning journalist and author, contributes to *Forbes Travel,* the Food Network, *U.S. News & World Report,* and the *Boston Globe,* among others. Her latest book, *Secret Boston: A Guide to the Weird, Wonderful, and Obscure,* came out in April 2020. She is a member of SATW. Visit her website ⊕ *www.escapewithkim.com,* or follow her on Instagram and Twitter @escapewithkim. Kim updated the Fenway and Kenmore Square, Brookline and Jamaica Plain, and Side Trips from Boston chapters for this guide.

Leigh Harrington has been a writer and editor for 20 years, curating content for a variety of different titles, travel-oriented and otherwise. She squeezes in freelance projects around her two full-time jobs: as Senior Editor at Reviewed.com and as wife-mom to her husband and one very curious kid. When there's free time, she likes to hike and work on DIY projects. Follow her adventures at ⊕ *www.lahlah-land.com.* For this edition of *Fodor's Boston,* she updated the Experience Boston; Beacon Hill, Boston Common, and the West End; Downtown and the Waterfront; and The Seaport, South Boston, and East Boston chapters.